ENLIGHTENED AID

ENLIGHTENED AID

U.S. Development as Foreign Policy in Ethiopia

Amanda Kay McVety

UNIVERSITY PRESS

Oxford University Press is a department of the University of Oxford.
It furthers the University's objective of excellence in research, scholarship,
and education by publishing worldwide.

Oxford   New York
Auckland   Cape Town   Dar es Salaam   Hong Kong   Karachi
Kuala Lumpur   Madrid   Melbourne   Mexico City   Nairobi
New Delhi   Shanghai   Taipei   Toronto

With offices in
Argentina   Austria   Brazil   Chile   Czech Republic   France   Greece
Guatemala   Hungary   Italy   Japan   Poland   Portugal   Singapore
South Korea   Switzerland   Thailand   Turkey   Ukraine   Vietnam

Oxford is a registered trade mark of Oxford University Press
in the UK and certain other countries.

Published in the United States of America by
Oxford University Press
198 Madison Avenue, New York, NY 10016

© Oxford University Press 2012

First issued as an Oxford University Press paperback, 2015.

All rights reserved. No part of this publication may be reproduced, stored in a
retrieval system, or transmitted, in any form or by any means, without the prior
permission in writing of Oxford University Press, or as expressly permitted by law,
by license, or under terms agreed with the appropriate reproduction rights organization.
Inquiries concerning reproduction outside the scope of the above should be sent to the
Rights Department, Oxford University Press, at the address above.

You must not circulate this work in any other form
and you must impose this same condition on any acquirer.

Library of Congress Cataloging-in-Publication Data
McVety, Amanda Kay.
Enlightened aid : U.S. development as foreign aid policy in Ethiopia / Amanda Kay McVety.
    p. cm.
Includes bibliographical references and index.
ISBN 978-0-19-979691-5 (hardcover : alk. paper); 978-0-19-025778-1 (paperback : alk. paper)
1. Economic assistance, American—Ethiopia—History. 2. Economic development—Finance—
Ethiopia—History. 3. Ethiopia—Economic conditions. I. Title.
HC845.M38   2012
338.91'73063—dc23   2011031591

To my parents,
Bruce and Elaine McVety

CONTENTS

Acknowledgments	ix
Introduction: The American Answer	1
1. Improving Nations	5
2. A Global Economy	38
3. Strategic Ethiopia	62
4. Truman's Fourth Point	83
5. The Ethiopian Experiment	121
6. The Development Decade	161
7. Rethinking the "American Answer"	195
Notes	223
Selected Bibliography	265
Index	287

ACKNOWLEDGMENTS

Many people helped to make this book possible. Theodora Ayot of North Park University told a much younger me that she was going to send me to Africa. She did, and my life was never quite the same. When this project began taking shape as my dissertation at UCLA, Jessica Wang challenged me to connect intellectual and diplomatic history in more sophisticated ways, and Christopher Ehret urged me to think more broadly about Ethiopia's place in world history. After graduation, I put the dissertation aside for two years to focus on my teaching. The time apart proved critical as I was able to restructure the boundaries of the work, stretching it backward to the Scottish Enlightenment and forward to Ethiopia's present. During my third year of teaching, I picked it up again and rewrote it. Many of my colleagues in the Miami University History Department read and commented on chapter 4 at a department workshop. Allan Winkler, Erik Jensen, Judith Zinsser, Jeff Kimball, and Carla Pestana read additional chapters at various stages of development and provided helpful feedback. I am fortunate to work among such talented and generous historians. Special thanks must go to Drew Cayton, who not only offered insightful comments on chapters, but also helped me to rethink the intellectual framework of the entire project. I could not have done it without him. Elizabeth Vitanza graciously provided some valuable translating. John Lauritz Larsen and Walter Lafeber read sections of the work and offered useful criticisms. My anonymous readers at *Diplomatic History* helped me to refine the arguments presented in chapter 4, and my anonymous readers at Oxford University Press did the same for all of the chapters. Nancy Toff and Sonia Tycko at Oxford University Press helped me turn the manuscript into a book. I am very grateful for all of the assistance. Any errors are my own.

Additional thanks must go to the efficient and knowledgeable archivists at the numerous museums and libraries that opened their doors to me for research. The talented folks at the Truman, Eisenhower, Kennedy, and Johnson Presidential Libraries; the National Archives in College Park; special collections at Oklahoma State University; and the Institute for Ethiopian Studies in Addis Ababa provided brilliant service with a smile. These visits were partially funded by the generosity of the Truman and Eisenhower Library Foundations, the Department of Education's Jacob Javits Fellowship Program, the Dolibois Fund, and Miami University.

My final acknowledgements are for my family. My sister, Christina Rowe, offered loving encouragement. My cousin, Jessica Seifert, took care of Dante when I was traveling. My grandparents, Harvey and Bonnie Vernell Franks, allowed me to live with them when I was writing the dissertation, and I will always be thankful for that time we had together. My parents, Bruce and Elaine McVety, read drafts of each chapter, traveled with me to Ethiopia, and endlessly discussed the stories and ideas contained within these pages. This book is dedicated to them.

INTRODUCTION

THE AMERICAN ANSWER

Harry S. Truman first introduced the concept of a global assistance program in his 1949 inaugural address, proclaiming that America's future security demanded a strong United Nations, a flourishing European economy, a mutual security alliance, and the development of the underdeveloped world. This last point—the fourth point—he later insisted, "is in the long run the most important of all."[1] The idea resonated with the press and with the public, who immediately dubbed it "Point IV." Truman told them, "We must embark on a bold new program for making the benefits of our scientific advances and our industrial progress available for the improvement and growth of underdeveloped areas" in order to make the world a better, safer place. For the most part, the American public agreed and widely celebrated this new vision.[2] Such popularity stemmed from the program's perceived multiple purposes and benefits. "Politically, economically, social or humanitarian, from any of these points of view, this is a good program," explained the assistant secretary of state for economic affairs. "Whatever emphasis the individual puts on it he can find it met."[3] Point Four promised to do almost everything, for almost nothing. Although some were skeptical about the "almost nothing" part, they believed its central tenet of progress via economic growth.

The International Technical Cooperation Act of 1949 turned the fourth point of Truman's speech into policy. It picked up where Truman had left off, declaring that "the United States and other nations of the world have a common interest in the material progress of all peoples, both as an end in itself and because such progress will further the advance of human freedom, the secure growth of democratic ways of life, the expansion of mutually beneficial commerce, and the development of international understanding and good will." They believed that material progress held the key to all of the other kinds of "progress." Underdevelopment was an economic problem, but development was an economic, political, and social solution. The roots of such confidence stretched back over two hundred years, drawing on the intellectual traditions of both Great Britain and the United States. If material progress had wrought such marvelous changes within the world's developed nations, why would it not do the same in its underdeveloped ones? Thoughtful, "modern" men of the mid-twentieth century refused to doubt that it would. They declared it "the policy of the United States" to "promote the development of economically underdeveloped areas."[4] Development was now foreign policy.

Defenders were charmed by its promised transformational powers. "I would like to say that I consider this program to be a product of topflight American foreign-policy thinking," announced Representative Jacob K. Javits of New York. "First, because you cannot fight communism only with words; you can only fight it with bread, and you can only fight it with better opportunities for bread than the other side offers." Second, because "here is a situation where we are trying to devote America's best commodity, brains, for the purpose of enabling the free people's [sic] of the world to help themselves. I say more power to it. That is the way to do it. This is a real American answer to communism." We, Javits concluded, are trying "to make the world a better place in which to live, instead of trying to make a living off of it" as the imperial nations did in the past. The United States, he implied, was nothing like France or Britain in its approach to non-European peoples. "Our belief is that, if we make it better for the other fellow, we will make it better for ourselves. . . . I think fundamentally this is the American answer. It is the first basically new idea that has come along in our foreign policy."[5]

An ocean and a continent away, an emperor in Ethiopia seized the enthusiasm. Eight years younger than the U.S. president, Haile Selassie had ruled his nation for more than thirty years, with the exception of a few years of Italian occupation, and he had tried mightily to develop his nation for just as long. It had been a difficult battle, and he was eager for some outside assistance. The first Point Four technicians arrived in Ethiopia in 1952, dedicated to the proposition that progress was a transformative process open to all, not just the historic explanation of the rise of the West. Yet it was impossible to separate the two, for the notion of progress that drove Point Four was intimately connected to the specific experiences of the United States over time. Indeed, many Americans viewed their nation's entire history as one grand narrative of improvement with leading roles appointed to democracy, capitalism, and that famous entrepreneurial spirit. Haile Selassie was skeptical, but too practical not to see the potential benefits of this new American dedication to international development. There was a chance it might produce what it promised, or, more specifically, what he wanted of what it promised.

Haile Selassie believed that his nation was special: God had chosen to bless Ethiopia in return for its long centuries of faithfulness, for its constancy in the face of Islamic and Italian invaders. Even while he celebrated its unique history, however, the emperor struggled to import the trappings of Western modernity. He liked luxurious cars, advanced hospitals, and top-of-the-line fighter jets—such things were required of a relevant nation in the contemporary international order. The emperor looked to the United States for inspiration and for assistance. Godless communism held little appeal. Neither did kingless democracy, which, he insisted, would never work in Ethiopia. But the American experiment with development was otherwise appealing, just as Truman boasted it was. Foreign aid was a useful diplomatic tool because leaders all over the world wanted what it promised: development. They were not always certain that they wanted the specific version of development that Washington was selling: born in the coffee houses of London, baptized in the steam engines of Lancashire, rejuvenated in the iron furnaces of Pittsburgh, and glorified in the offices lining Wall Street. But they wanted something like it. Many still do, which begs the question why development remains elusive for so many despite the hundreds of billions of dollars that the U.S. government alone has spent on foreign assistance.

Aid's ability to promote change is not a solely academic question. Ideas gain power over people's lives when they are transformed into policies. The move from imagination to implementation has consequences, and this book's diplomatic history grounds its intellectual history in a case study of U.S. relations with Ethiopia. Although it travels across time and space, the story always returns to two places: Washington, D.C., and Addis Ababa. There were many options; over the past six decades, the U.S. government has given foreign aid to many countries. But Ethiopia was on the list in the beginning, and it is on the list today. In between, it became the world's most infamously underdeveloped nation. The Ethiopian people's continuing struggles with poverty, illiteracy, disease, and hunger offer a particularly troubling example of aid's failure to fulfill its promises. Foreign aid was supposed to make itself unnecessary. The story of the U.S. relationship with Ethiopia explains why it did not.

There was no room for doubt in the beginning. At the moment of its creation, Point Four made sense economically, politically, strategically, and morally. "Our belief is that, if we make it better for the other fellow, we will make it better for ourselves," Javits cheerfully explained.⁶ Such confidence had a long history. Two centuries earlier, Adam Smith had chided his readers for envying "the internal happiness and prosperity" of a neighboring nation, "the cultivation of its lands, the advancement of its manufactures, the increase of its commerce, the security and number of its ports and habours [sic], its proficiency in all the liberal arts and sciences." Doing so is a mistake, Smith announced, because "these are all real improvements in the world we live in. Mankind are benefited, human nature is ennobled by them. In such improvements each nation ought, not only to endeavor to excel, but from the love of mankind, to promote, instead of obstructing the excellence of its neighbors."⁷ Point Four was a product of just such enlightened self-interest, as were the other global aid programs that followed in its footsteps. In its most optimistic moments, the U.S. government truly believed that by doing good it could indeed do well. The problem is that foreign aid seems to have done more harm than it has good, which means that the United States has not done nearly as well as it hoped.

1 IMPROVING NATIONS

In the winter of 1903–1904, Robert P. Skinner, the American consul at Marseille, represented the United States on its first diplomatic mission to Ethiopia. He had been thinking about the trip for years, watching from the French Riviera as the European powers expanded their presence across Africa. Excepting only Liberia, Ethiopia—or, Abyssinia, as Europeans and Americans liked to call it—remained the sole independent nation on the continent, and Skinner wanted the United States to form an official relationship with this holdout to European imperialism. When Skinner set out for Ethiopia, he was one of a long line of foreign travelers who had ventured into its highlands in search of souls, slaves, gold, ivory, and knowledge.[1] More recently, they had come for land. His quest was different, he proudly boasted, because "America was the first country to establish diplomatic relations for the avowed purpose of protecting and extending commerce, and without a political issue of any character to discuss."[2] We wanted, he insisted, only the freedom to sell our goods—most importantly cotton sheeting—and buy theirs—most importantly coffee. The United States went to Ethiopia in search of a treaty of amity and commerce with its emperor, Menelik II. It was a particularly benevolent manifestation of America's growing power.

By the time Theodore Roosevelt became president in 1901, the interventionist ideology crystallized in Henry Cabot Lodge's 1895 boast that "We have a record of conquest, colonization and expansion unequalled by any people in the Nineteenth Century.... We are not to be curbed now" had left the United States with a continuing war in the Philippines, troops in Cuba and Puerto Rico, and a domestic argument about how far the Constitution would follow the flag.[3] William McKinley viewed his 1896 victory as a mandate from the people to expand the nation's economic opportunities, and he had done so through treaties and, albeit perhaps a bit reluctantly, through a war that raised troublesome questions about the limitations of American expansion. Roosevelt learned from his predecessor's misadventures in the tropics to pursue open doors without annexation.[4] The opening of his second annual message to Congress read, "the events of the last four years have definitely decided that, for woe or for weal, our place must be great among the nations." The United States can no longer "play a small part" in world affairs, he asserted, both because of its enlarged empire and because its economic might depended on market expansion, but such expansion would come through reciprocity treaties instead of territories. "They can be used to widen our markets and to give a greater field for the activities of our producers on the one hand," he insisted, "and on the other hand to secure in practical shape the lowering of duties when they are no longer needed for protection among our own people." Promoting American business would promote America's future—not only by securing continued economic growth, but also by encouraging more nations to become "civilized," and, as such, friends. "As civilization grows," he concluded, "warfare becomes less and less the normal condition of foreign relations." Future peace depended on future prosperity.[5]

Roosevelt's words and subsequent actions convinced Skinner that now was the time to pursue funding for his long-imagined trip to Ethiopia. Commerce there, he wrote to the assistant aecretary of state, "has created itself in spite of American indifference to the desirability of having direct contact with consuming markets, and is susceptible of being greatly increased."[6] It was a message that the White House was ready to hear.

Skinner went to Ethiopia in 1903 confident that its emperor, Menelik II, would be interested in everything America was selling. "He wishes to lift his people up to the point of being able to comprehend and utilize these modern improvements and inventions, and to turn them to their own advantage, for the defense of their country and their national liberty," the American diplomat wrote in his 1906 account of his journey.[7] Although Skinner jumped back and forth in his account between naively describing Ethiopia as "in all essential respects identical with that which prevailed in Bethlehem 2,000 years ago" and highlighting Menelik's "modern" rule, he clearly believed that Ethiopia had the capacity to absorb the American products he understood as the markers of "civilization."[8] He envisioned a future where Menelik's empire more closely resembled the United States. Indeed, he viewed that as the likely fate of the entire world. For what leader would choose to deny a progress that would help him consolidate his own power while raising his nation's presence in the international arena?

Skinner's confidence in the inherent desirability of the civilization that he represented came from two hundred years of Anglo-American economic growth and imperial expansion. Ideas born in the excitement of emerging eighteenth-century prosperity had blossomed in the heady decades of nineteenth-century power. When Skinner went to Ethiopia promising development through trade, he was engaging in a two-hundred-year-old conversation about individual improvement and national progress. That conversation framed the way that, first, Great Britain, and second, the United States, visualized their places in the world and their relationships to other nations. Understanding America's twentieth-century drive to spread its way of life requires at least a brief introduction to Great Britain's eighteenth-century quest to explain its sudden, dramatic prosperity. As John Maynard Keynes wryly noted in 1936, "The ideas of economists and political philosophers, both when they are right and when they are wrong, are more powerful than is commonly understood. Indeed, the world is ruled by little else. Practical men, who believe themselves to be quite exempt from any intellectual influences, are usually the slaves of some defunct economist."[9] This chapter examines the lasting intellectual influence of two defunct economists in particular: David Hume and Adam Smith, who together convinced the world to believe in progress.

It began with ego. Life in Great Britain—the fresh creation of the 1707 union of England and Scotland—in the early eighteenth century was fundamentally different, and seemingly better, than it had been the previous century and as it still was for most people in other parts of the globe.[10] The world seemed changed. They called it "progress," and they believed that its presence on their island made them special. The word came from the Latin *prōgressus*, which meant forward movement or advance. The Anglo-Norman *progress* continued the idea of physical movement forward. By the early modern period in England, it was both a noun and a verb.[11] Daniel Defoe—journalist, author, sometime government spy, and sometime government prisoner—echoed the sentiments of his brethren when he declared his nation "the most flourishing and opulent country in the world," for "where-ever we come, and which way soever we look, we see something new."[12]

The key, Defoe knew, was trade. Ships "from all parts of the world" sail up and down the Thames, bringing goods to "the greatest city in the world," whose recent progress was evident in "the opulence of its merchants," he boasted.[13] Protected by the royal navy, "the sinews of our strength," the tradesmen of Great Britain sent out wool cloth, miscellaneous manufactured goods, and numerous reexported colonial products, while bringing wine, spices, china, brandy, tea and more into British homes.[14] "The citizen's and tradesmen's tables are now the emblems, not of plenty, but of luxury, not of good house-keeping, but of profusion, and that of the highest kind of extravagance," he wrote in 1726.[15] Some worried about the change, but Defoe's nationalism trumped his fear of luxury's corrosive effects, an arrangement that signaled the victory of economics over religion and the state over God.[16] Many people, though certainly not all, decided to stop striving for piety and start striving for things. They became unabashedly acquisitive.

The international trade that defined the commercial revolution then changing Britain gained momentum in the late seventeenth century in response to a demographic surge in China and a new thrust in European colonial expansion. World trade increased throughout the early eighteenth century, giving rise to Defoe's "increasing" England, which quickly became famous (along with its Dutch neighbors) for its all-consuming dedication to the pursuit of the buying and selling of goods.[17] Defoe concluded that this passion brought prosperity to all, for "as frugality is not the national virtue of England, so the people that get much spend much," and their consumption increases "the rent and value of the land," which consequently "increases the employment of people" and raises their wages. The expanded income went to buying products in a neat, reinforcing system. The working people of Britain, he satisfactorily concluded, thus "eat the fat, and drink the sweet" and just generally "live better" than their counterparts in any other European nations.[18] The truth was a little more complicated. Defoe correctly located the households of working peoples as the central players in Britain's commercial revolution, but modern analysis of eighteenth-century prices reveals that real wages did not rise during the period.[19] There is no denying that households were purchasing more goods, but they were doing it by sacrificing leisure for work. This "industrious revolution" did help drive the commercial revolution, but it demanded more sacrifices than Defoe was willing to admit.[20] Nevertheless, he correctly perceived that the average Briton's desire for newer and better products helped fuel national prosperity. The people were notable for their wanting.

Even when moderated by the wisdom of recent historical research, Defoe's descriptions *of* and explanations *for* the wealth of his nation are striking. He clearly identified the ways in which trade was transforming Britain into a global power—distancing the nation from its own past and the rest of the world at the same time. In his 1719 bestseller, *Robinson Crusoe*, Defoe delighted his audience with the tale of Englishman overcoming the forced savagery of being shipwrecked on a deserted island by virtue of his intellect, his faith in God, and the few articles of English manufacturing that he was able to harvest from his ship. Crusoe saves himself from becoming like the other men who live on islands in the Caribbean by effectively using what remains to him of civilization. He meets "savages," but he is never in real danger of becoming one, because he carries too much cultural baggage, even when holding nothing in his hands. The popularity of Crusoe's adventures speaks to the British fascination with their nation's place in the world. Fully aware that their prosperity depended on relationships with other peoples in other lands who controlled the luxuries that they wanted and could potentially buy the goods that they wanted to sell, many Britons longed to know more about them.[21]

Early eighteenth-century citizens of Great Britain consumed travel books with great enthusiasm, as had their parents and grandparents before them.[22] Indeed, the most popular of them, *Gulliver's Travels*, was actually written in part to mock the craze (and to criticize the imperialism that helped their popularity). By this time, the educated few had lost some of their tolerance for the public's fascination with incredible accounts that required the suspension of more disbelief than a thoughtful man could allow. When Samuel Johnson was asked in 1735 to translate Father Jerónimo Lobo's seventeenth-century travels in Ethiopia, *A Voyage to Abyssinia*, from French into English, he justified his labor by defending the original author's credibility. In the introduction to the translation, Johnson noted that Lobo "has amused his readers with no romantick absurdities or incredible fictions," such as those found in *The Travels of Sir John Mandeville*, which entertained readers with stories of one-eyed Ethiopians who ate only raw meat through mouths in the middle of their chests. "The reader will here find no Hottentots without religion, polity, or articulate language, no Chinese perfectly polite, and completely skill'd in all sciences," Johnson continued. Instead, "he will discover, what will always be discover'd by a diligent and impartial enquirer, that wherever human nature is to be found, there is a mixture of vice and virtue, a contest of passion and reason, and that the Creator doth not appear partial in his distributions, but has balanced in most countries their particular inconveniences by particular favors."[23] Humans, Johnson fervently believed, are everywhere the same, and Lobo helped to prove it. This conviction, so clearly expressed in the prologue to his 1735 translation, stayed with him throughout his life. When his mother's death in 1759 left him with her unpaid debts and funeral expenses, Johnson seized his pen and in one week wrote what would become one of his most famous works: *The History of Rasselas, Prince of Abyssinia*.[24]

Although dotted with geographic truths, *Rasselas* is a fictional account of events that occur in a romanticized Ethiopia and Egypt. Johnson's story begins in the Happy Valley, a beautiful Eden where the princes and princesses of Abyssinia are locked up to ensure that they do not foment rebellion against the king. Feeling stifled by his overwhelming abundance, Prince Rasselas longs to leave the perfection of the valley for the world beyond, which he knows only through his tutor. In pursuit of his goal to experience more and, thus, to know more, Rasselas and his tutor escape in the company of a similarly determined princess. They journey to Cairo. Along the way, they learn that greater happiness comes from greater learning on a path open to all men and women, regardless of their place of birth.[25] When Rasselas asks his tutor why the Europeans are so powerful that they can "easily visit Asia or Africa for trade or conquest," Imlac tells him, "They are more powerful, Sir, than we, because they are wiser; knowledge will always predominate over ignorance." As the conversation continues, Imlac notes that the Europeans have "many advantages," including "engines," better communication, more secure possessions, and "roads cut through their mountains." They have such things because they have spent more time cultivating knowledge, he assures the prince, not because they are inherently superior.[26] Do not be too haughty, Johnson wryly instructed his readers, because the only thing distinguishing you from the Ethiopian you may think "savage" is your society's ability to profit off its past. It was not a question of the ability to learn, but of what is already known. Progress was possible to all.

Johnson was not alone in his sentiments. Indeed, he shared them with the only European known to have visited Ethiopia during the eighteenth century. On September 19, 1769, James Bruce of Kinnaird landed in Massawa, a loosely controlled Ottoman port that offered the best point of entry into the Ethiopian empire. Bruce came with books, telescopes, and a movable quadrant that the famous French scientist, the Comte de Buffon, had requested Louis XV send to him in the spirit of international scientific cooperation. Bruce had been in North Africa since an ill-advised 1763 appointment as the British consulate-general in Algiers. He did not stay long at the post, but he was too intrigued by the possibility of adventure to head back to Scotland. So, he stayed on, arriving in Egypt in 1768 to explore the pyramids and study the transit of Venus. Afterward, he planned to pack up his observations and head home, but pleas from friends, as he described it, steeled his resolve to continue his explorations into new lands. Buffon got Bruce his quadrant because the latter promised to journey into Abyssinia to find the source of the Nile—a quest dear to the heart of many scientifically minded Europeans.[27]

Bruce remained in Ethiopia until 1771, when he finally returned to Egypt via the land route through Sudan. He did indeed reach the source of the Blue Nile, but, despite his claims to the contrary, he was not the first European to do so. That honor actually belonged to Johnson's Portuguese Jesuit, Jerónimo Lobo, who had visited in the 1620s. In addition to his rather dubious "discovery," Bruce engaged in numerous scientific pursuits while in Ethiopia, filling journals with drawings of plants and animals and detailed descriptions of the climate and culture.[28] The massive Scotsman (he was six feet four and by all accounts brash and intimidating) ingratiated himself with members of the royal family by treating smallpox victims and quickly found himself caught up with them in a civil war. He diligently recorded all of his experiences, to the point of hinting rather indelicately at a romantic relationship with Princess Esther, the wife of the powerful *Ras* Michael, whom Bruce described as "in face and person . . . more like my learned and worthy friend, the Comte de Buffon, than any other man I ever saw."[29] The comment is revealing, for although Bruce spiced his narrative of his travels with accounts of raw-meat-eating and banquet orgies certain to shock his readers (and keep them reading), he did not present the Ethiopians as inherently different from Europeans. Their society was wild, exotic, and sometimes even "barbarous," but the individuals within it were utterly familiar.

When writing about the Shangalla people, Bruce noted that "it has been the custom to describe these people as vicious and immoral in the highest degree" and "I do not scruple to assert, that great injustice has been done them in these accounts." To describe them fairly, he argued, we would have to see them in "their native purity of manners, among their native woods, living on the produce of their daily labours," but that is not an option, because their Abyssinian rulers have turned them into savages. Plied with alcohol, "torn from their own country," and "forced to labour for a being they never before knew," the Shangalla have been "reduced to the condition of brutes." Clearly seeing the connections between his fellow Europeans' imperialism and that practiced by the Abyssinians, Bruce concludes with disgust that "after we have made them monsters, we describe them as such," conveniently forgetting "that we ourselves have wrought the change."[30] It is a telling moment of the book. Slaves on West Indian sugar plantations could sympathize with Shangallas hunted by Abyssinians for sport and their owners with the nobles on horseback. Remarking on intrigues in the capital city of Gondar, he later wrote, "Man is the same creature everywhere although different in color. The court in London and that in Abyssiania are in their principles the same."[31]

The message that Ethiopians were different in circumstance, but not substance, struck a particularly strong cord in Bruce's Scottish homeland, which suffered from an inferiority complex that the English loved to exploit. The Scots were reading all of the same books as their countrymen to the south and running better schools and universities, yet they remained the poorer half of Great Britain.³² Speaking of the Scots in *Travels*, Defoe wrote that "they are where we were, I mean as the improvement of their country and commerce; and they may be where we are."³³ Scotland spent the eighteenth century trying to catch up with England, and, to some degree, it succeeded. When Samuel Johnson journeyed there with James Boswell in 1773, he went hoping to see "an antiquated life" in the Highlands. He was disappointed to discover that "we came thither too late." By then, economic and political ties with Britain, and reform efforts at home, had already significantly "improved" the countryside from the older society that Johnson had hoped to see. That transformation, which happened much more quickly than it had in England, offered those watching a unique opportunity to study progress. In Scotland, a select group of men developed a revolutionary discourse that centered economic change in social transformation. That discourse did not, as a recent book title claims, invent the modern world, but it certainly played a pivotal role in shaping it.³⁴

By the second half of the eighteenth century, Edinburgh was behind only Paris and London in the quality of its intellectual output—a particularly astounding feat considering that it had a population of around only 50,000 people. In his 1785 *View of the British Empire*, author John Knox reported, "This city is considered as the modern Athens, in politeness, science, and literature. The writings of its professors, divines, and lawyers are read everywhere and admired."³⁵ Scotland had by far the best universities in Great Britain and men (alas, women were not welcome) came from all over Europe and North America to study natural and moral philosophy in its lecture halls. Anyone truly interested in medicine could go nowhere else. Although tainted by the events surrounding Bonnie Prince Charlie's 1745 rebellion and the theological struggles behind the 1697 hanging of a university student for publically admitting atheism, post-1750 Edinburgh loudly embraced stronger economic ties to England and weaker allegiances to the Presbyterian Church. Improvements in communication assisted both tasks. Between 1700 and 1786, the time it took to travel in a carriage between London and the Scottish capital gradually dropped from 256 to 60 hours. It became far easier for people and their ideas to move in and out of Scotland, freeing the country from its historic geographic isolation. Building off its equally historic education system, a group of middle-class professionals took advantage of the new opportunities to transform Scotland's international reputation. They did it by writing and publishing books, which spread previously private club and coffeehouse conversations around the Atlantic world.³⁶

The Scottish Enlightenment became an enlightenment because it was a community of thinkers united by common ideals and interests; it became famous because those ideals and interests spoke to the wider concerns of imperializing Europe. They took Isaac Newton's faith in universal order, John Locke's empiricism, and the Baron de Montesquieu's theories on social change and blended them to explain how Defoe's England was different from its own past and from Lobo's Ethiopia. They created a science of man as a social being who gained understanding (and progressed as an individual) through his relationship with the people around him. The history of humanity was a history of society, they insisted, particularly the development of its laws and institutions. This was the Scottish Enlightenment's most important contribution to the Atlantic world and it made its largest impact through the dissemination of the ideas of its two most important philosophers: David Hume and Adam Smith.

It all began with history. "I believe this is the historical Age and this the historical Nation," Hume wrote to his publisher, William Strahan, in 1770.[37] Although labeled a philosopher today, Hume was originally far more famous as a historian, but he, notably, did not see a need to make the distinction, for philosophy and history were intimately connected. He looked to the past to find explanations of the present. He was most particularly interested in explaining where virtue came from, because he did not believe that God had anything to do with it. And if it was not from God, then it had to be from man—more specifically, his relationships with other humans.

In *A Treatise of Human Nature*, Hume argued that our moral sense did not come from a shared understanding of justice (as fellow Scottish philosopher Francis Hutchinson had argued) but developed as society developed, because the needs of society meant that its members had to learn to be virtuous—had to learn to appreciate justice—in order to survive.[38] As society advanced, so too did virtue, with the natural virtues, which would have been sufficient for kin groups, replaced by artificial virtues that taught people to respect the property that dominated social relations in larger settings.[39] People accepted these changes because they wanted the things—most importantly the ownership of property—and the security that went along with the development of society. They recognized that they could have better lives in social organizations and they were willing to give up some freedom to get it.

Hume explicitly rejected the popular theory of a "state of nature," where "the oaks yielded honey; and nature spontaneously produc'd her greatest delicacies," and "the distinction of *mine* and *thine* was banis'd from that happy race of mortals." If nature had supplied all of man's needs, he pointed out, then there would never have been scarcity and mankind would never have developed a sense of ownership and a sense of justice. "Tis only from the selfishness and confin'd generosity of man, along with the scantity provision nature has made for his wants, that justice derives its origin." Justice was a product of group-sanctioned self-interest.[40] As society developed, so too did morality, because humans were willing to restrain their actions to satisfy their wants. Though the *Treatise* never became popular outside of a select scholarly circle, it became the foundation of all of Hume's later work. In his 1752 *Political Discourses,* he added to his explanation of the allure of society by explaining how it gave people more than security: it gave them sociability. "They flock into cities; love to receive and communicate knowledge; to show their wit or their breeding; their taste in conversation or living, in clothes or furniture." They become refined, and their society improves because of it. "Thus *industry, knowledge,* and *humanity,* are linked together by an indissoluble chain, and are found, from experience as well as reason, to be peculiar to the more polished, and, what are commonly denominated, the more luxurious ages."[41] Such writings proved essential to the philosophical musings of Hume's friend and fellow philosopher Adam Smith, who by the late 1740s had become "a committed Humean."[42]

Smith was born in 1723, in Kirkcaldy, to a solidly middle-class, though well-connected, family. His father trained as a lawyer and worked in a variety of professional capacities before becoming the comptroller of customs in Kirkcaldy, a position that both he and his son held at the times of their respective deaths. In 1737, Smith set off for Glasgow University, where he studied under Francis Hutcheson and experienced the commercial trade boom that was making Glasgow's merchants rich. Both proved critical to his later theories on societal development. In 1740, he left for Oxford, which was depressingly behind the Scottish universities. He spent six years in Oxford before returning to Scotland to offer public lectures at Edinburgh from 1748 to 1751, at the behest of Henry Homes, Lord Kames, Hume's cousin and a famous scholar in his own right. Hume and Smith met at this time, beginning a friendship based on a mutual recognition of shared intellectual talent. The lectures catapulted Smith to a professorship at Glasgow, where he began shaping a new generation of minds with his highly influential lectures on moral philosophy. This he divided into four parts: natural theology (his least favorite), ethics, jurisprudence, and politics. The last three, he insisted, were connected by the history of society.[43]

The same year that Smith began lecturing in Edinburgh, the Baron de Montesquieu published *De l'Esprit des Lois,* which transformed traditional thinking about politics and society.⁴⁴ It particularly appealed to British readers, who shared the French philosopher's dedication to conservative radicalism, just as they shared his appreciation for their own political system. Montesquieu looked to the past for explanations of present social differences. "Many things govern men: climate, religion, laws, the maxims of the government, examples of past things, mores, and manners; a general spirit is formed as a result," he argued.⁴⁵ Political systems were products of nations' complex pasts. He was not ambivalent about the results, insisting that the system that secures the greatest liberty for its subjects is best. He found it in Britain's constitutional monarchy, because its balance guaranteed stability, which, in turn, guaranteed a better life for its citizens. Montesquieu had lived in England from 1729 to 1731 and had developed a great fondness for its politics and its philosophy. At the time, many of his countrymen had shared his love, but they had since lost it. The 1748 publication of *De l'Esprit des Lois* marked a transformational moment in eighteenth-century thought, with the French decisively moving to embrace radicalism and the British continuing along a more conservative road.⁴⁶ Montesquieu proved more influential in Edinburgh than in Paris. Hume read the book in 1749 and corresponded with its author, agreeing with him that history is a continual process, but he hesitated to accept the Frenchman's climatic determinism. Smith also read it and integrated it into his investigations of the history of mankind.⁴⁷

In his capacity as the chair of moral philosophy at Glasgow, Smith used his lectures throughout the 1750s to further work out his ideas on society. He followed Hume's (and Hutchinson's) examples by first examining the root of morality in the individual. He published his findings in 1759 in the well-received *Theory of Moral Sentiments*. Like Hume, Smith believed that morality was intimately tied to society. "Every faculty in one man is the measure by which he judges of the like faculty in another," he wrote, because we have no "immediate experience of what other men feel," and can only rely on our own experiences. We use sympathy, our "fellow-feeling with any passion whatever," to make virtuous decisions, which we inherently know are good for their own sake, but also have the beneficial role of tending to promote greater social harmony and justice.⁴⁸ People are born experiencing feelings, but they only learn how to judge those feelings through their relationship to other people. "Were it possible that a human creature could grow up to manhood in some solitary place, without any communication with his own species, he could no more think of his own character, of the propriety or demerit of his own sentiments and conduct . . . than of the beauty or deformity of his own face." We learn to be good by considering what others might think of us,

Smith argued, and, because man "has a natural love for society," we are generally in agreement that that which best promotes social harmony is virtuous and that which does not is evil. As time passes, both individuals and the societies in which they live become better, because virtue keeps improving.[49]

The Theory of Moral Sentiments presented Smith's defense for the centrality of society to mankind's moral progress. It proved highly influential, but the Scotsman had larger plans. He wanted to show how history offered scientific evidence of the theory in action. In the final sentence of the book, Smith promised that "in another discourse," he would "give an account of the general principles of law and government, and of the different revolutions they have undergone in the different ages and periods of society." He was unable to publish such a work, but he transformed the Scottish discourse on the subject through his public lectures at Glasgow University, where he presented audiences with a structured theory of the development of society. His most famous pupil, John Millar, later described: "Upon this subject he followed the plan that seems to be suggested by Montesquieu; endeavoring to trace the gradual progress of jurisprudence, both public and private, from the rudest to the most refined ages, and to point out the effects of those arts which contribute to subsistence, and to the accumulation of property, in producing correspondent improvements or alterations in law and government."[50] Changes in possession inspired changes in law, which created progress. In Smith's framework, highland Scots were not inherently different from Londoners, or, indeed, Ethiopians, they were just living in a different level of improvement. In its most essential form, human history was the story of that improvement.

Smith knew where the story ended: the superior laws and lifestyles of contemporary Great Britain, but the trick was explaining how mankind had gotten there. He went back to *Robinson Crusoe* to do it. "If we should suppose 10 or 12 persons of different sexes settled in an uninhabited island," he instructed his audience, "the first method they would fall upon for their sustenance would be to support themselves by the wild fruits of wild animals which the country afforded." The race or origins of the settlers does not matter: Because they are human they will act a certain way in the conditions afforded them. "Their sole business would be hunting the wild beasts or catching the fishes." This is the age of hunters. "In process of time, as their numbers multiplied, they would find the chase too precarious for their support," and "would be necessitated to contrive some other method whereby to support themselves." Like Crusoe and his goats, they "would tame some of those wild animals they caught, and by affording them better food than what they could get elsewhere they would enduce them to continue about their land themselves and multiply their kind." Such is the age of shepherds. Here, Smith interjected facts into the theory, noting that "the Tartars and Arabians subsist almost entirely by their flocks and herds." American Indians were the exception to the rule, Smith explained, because they have agriculture, but no domesticated herds. In general, however, as the numbers increased, societies keep their herds and then gradually add agriculture as they discovered how plants grow from seeds. "As society was farther improved, the several arts, which at first would be exercised by each individual as far as was necessary for his welfare, would be separated; some persons would cultivate one and others others." They would then exchange commodities first between "the individuals of the same society" and gradually between "those of different nations" (one apparently must assume that the islanders have neighbors reachable by boat). "Thus at last the age of commerce arises," he concluded with finality, which eventually brings a nation to the state of having "done all in its power towards its ease and convenience." In the end, Robinson Crusoe gets back to London, and so does Smith's audience.[51]

Smith shared Hume's conviction that "there is a great uniformity among the actions of men, in all nations and ages," and he agreed that this meant that "the same events follow from the same causes." History and travel narratives were thus valued as the tools of the scientist of human nature, allowing him to use "records of wars, intrigues, factions, and revolutions" as "so many collections of experiments."[52] They were not alone in this confidence. The Scottish historian William Robertson wrote, "our human mind, wherever it is placed in the same situation, will, in ages the most distant, and in countries the most remote, assume the same form, and be distinguished by the same manners." Similarly, Dugald Stewart explained that "it has long been received as an incontrovertible logical maxim that the capacities of the human mind have been in all ages the same, and that the diversity of phenomena exhibited by our species is the result merely of the different circumstances in which men are placed."[53] This confidence allowed the Scottish philosophers to create *stadial theory* (evidenced in Smith's Glasgow lecture) using *conjectural history*, which Stewart described as a comparison between "our intellectual acquirements, our opinions, manners and institutions, [and] those which prevail among rude tribes" of the past or present. Because the historical record on earlier/ruder peoples is necessarily limited, "we are under the necessity of supplying the place of fact by conjecture" about "how men are likely to have proceeded" from a savage to a civilized state. The quest to understand difference led the Scots to search out unity, because they believed in universality.[54]

Although a cursory analysis of history did appear to enforce the basic premises of stadial theory, the evidence was by no means conclusive that movement was always linear. Reflections on the fall of Rome and the so-called Dark Ages of Europe made Smith, and many of his Scottish counterparts, wary of positing that societies always moved forward.[55] Hume argued that slavery corrupts the moral sense of the slave owner to such a degree that it might actually decay their human nature and push society backward.[56] Smith was quick to point out that the age of commerce is the most socially unequal age, as the poor laborer "bears the burden of society" and has "the fewest advantages," but he still had more possessions than his counterpart in the age of agriculture and those possessions were more secure. Such "exceptions" to the story of human progress encouraged Smith to think more specifically about the age of commerce, which by its very definition was the most complicated of all of the ages and the least understood. His ponderings resulted in one of the most influential books every published.

In *An Inquiry into the Nature and Causes of the Wealth of Nations*, Smith tried to apply the rules of social development that he had seen in ancient history (and current barbarous societies) to recent European—most particularly British—history, which offered the fullest expression of the age of commerce. In his previous lectures, Smith had argued that population growth and consequent food shortages were initially responsible for pushing societies into new modes of production. Hunters became shepherds because they wanted a more stable food supply. Shepherds became farmers for the same reason. In the process, they became willing to believe in the morality of more socially beneficial virtues and to adopt new ownership laws and accept more "government." Their understanding of justice changed. Meanwhile, the society of farmers began dividing up tasks, which proved a more efficient use of the group's combined time and resulted in surpluses that inspired even more property laws and encouraged even more specialization, which eventually transformed the age of agriculture into the age of commerce. Economic growth had been a primarily unintended consequence of the earlier stages, but it was the intended consequence of the last. This necessarily changed the rules and Smith wanted to know how.[57]

The answer seemed to be (although Smith never stated this explicitly) a switch in the primary force of change. Population growth, which had initially been most important, was exchanged for the division of labor, which had initially not even existed. Because the division of labor was more efficient, it amplified the speed of growth and, consequently, the speed of the linked transformations in virtue and law. The division of labor, which increases the productive power of society by increasing "the dexterity of every particular workman," saving "the time which is commonly lost in passing from one species of work to another," and facilitating "the invention of a great number of machines" that "enable one man to do the work of many."[58] As this change results in a more stable food supply and secure property system, people begin looking for new things to buy with their expanding incomes. Once they are able to move past necessity, their hunger to expand their property and convenience "seems to have no limit or certain boundary," which, in turn, feeds the division of labor and creates more growth. Society gradually turns acquisitiveness into a virtue, because it supports this process. Society also becomes more generous in its definition of property and more vigorous in its defense of it, until, one day, it looks exactly like eighteenth-century Great Britain, where a man who did not own land was nevertheless able to own himself and the profits of his specialized labor.

Smith's focus on the division of labor distanced him from Hume, who had focused on foreign trade as the essential force behind economic growth.[59] Both believed that growth came from the insertion of capital back into the market, but Smith had a much firmer grasp of the ability of the domestic market to expand through the efficient plowback of the profits born in the greater productive powers of labor, which were, in turn, the product of greater specialization.[60] The "natural progress of England toward wealth," he insisted, stemmed from "private frugality," the "good conduct of individuals" who sought efficiency and expansion in the course of their "uninterrupted effort to better their own condition." In helping themselves, they helped the nation as a whole.[61] Their efforts both increased scarce capital and expanded the market, which is why it was neither necessary nor good for the state to try to direct capital. "No regulation of commerce can increase the quantity of industry in any society beyond what its capital can maintain," Smith insisted. "It can only divert a part of it into a direction into which it might not otherwise have gone; and it is by no means certain that this artificial direction is likely to be more advantageous to the society." Individual statesmen do not have the ability to see where capital needs to go, so they should simply provide greater liberty to the individual citizen to make such determinations for his or her self. And so was born Smith's famous, and sometimes infamous, doctrine of *laissez-faire*.[62]

Economic growth began with greater individual liberty and ended with greater social progress. A man in pursuit of his own individual wealth was the best weapon in the state's quest for national wealth. "The capital of all the individuals of a nation is increased in the same manner as that of a single individual, by their continually accumulating and adding to it whatever they save out of their revenue."[63] Growth came from wisely using and improving land and labor. Foreign trade could certainly help, but it was not required, because the market could be widened from within by expanding the populace's ability to purchase goods.

Smith's modern reader is instantly struck by what is largely missing from the story: technology, but the movement that would be labeled Britain's Industrial Revolution was only just beginning. Smith was aware of what the historian Joel Mokyr has labeled *microinventions*, the "small, incremental steps that improve, adapt, and streamline existing techniques already in use, reducing costs, improving form and function, increasing durability, and reducing energy and raw material requirements."[64] Smith argued that the division of labor encouraged such inventions by having the laborer focus on one particular aspect of production. He recognized the valuable role ingenuity could play in increasing the efficiency of labor, but he did not recognize that ingenuity could transform an entire economy with one invention.[65] Because he did not see the possibilities inherent within technology for revolutionizing production, Smith envisioned economic growth as a gradual process that had natural limits.

Smith did not believe that economic growth would continue indefinitely. There were limits to his faith in specialization. Success would eventually be halted by the system itself: "In a country which had acquired that full complement of riches which the nature of its soil and climate, and its situation with respect to other countries allowed it to acquire; which could, therefore, advance no further, and which was not going backwards, both the wages of labour and the profits of stock would probably be very low." Capital would become scarce and the system stagnant. Perhaps "no country has ever yet arrived at this degree of opulence," Smith admitted. China offered a potential example, because it "seems to have been long stationary," but its progress was halted by "the nature of its laws and institutions," not the limits of its market.[66] In contrast, England had been blessed in recent centuries with the most advantageous laws in the world, combined with a fortunate geography, and its commerce and manufactures had "been continually advancing during all this period." Smith feared that it might all end soon. "It is now more than two hundred years since the beginning of the reign of Elizabeth, a period as long as the course of human prosperity usually endures."[67] It is a startling statement and one that Smith seems to have included just for that purpose. Other statements in the book demonstrate that he did not believe that Britain's growth would soon end, most particularly because "the discovery of

America" had opened "a new and inexhaustible market to all the commodities of Europe."[68] With improved institutions, it seemed unlikely that Britain would not continue its reign as the world's leading economic power. But, and this was an important *but*, eventually the market would reach full capacity. At some point, economic growth had to end. Nature demanded it. Systems, Smith believed, cannot expand indefinitely.

Smith's prophecies that economic growth had natural limits did not discourage him from viewing it as a positive good that deserved greater political attention. Eventually things would stagnate, but they would necessarily stagnate at a point higher than where they had been at the beginning. British acquisitiveness had moved it further into the age of commerce than any nation before, and, in consequence, the people had greater liberty, more convenience, and the ability to participate in public conversations about virtue, government, culture, and more. Smith found evidence of economic improvement not only in luxurious clothing on a common laborer, but in that laborer's ability to watch and understand a scientific demonstration on air pumps. All parts of society were connected, so improvement in one area naturally spurred on improvement in another. There was only one catch in the system and it was one Smith himself readily recognized: The division of labor threatened the intellectual well-being of the poorest of its participants.

In the lowest stages of societal development, "every man does, or is capable of doing, almost every thing which any other man does, or is capable of doing." The divisions between men are not very great, because everyone is working to acquire the basic necessities of life and no one owns more property than what is in his possession at a given moment. Everyone is equal in their lacking. "In a civilized state, on the contrary, though there is little variety in the occupations of the greater part of individuals, there is an almost infinite variety in those of the whole society. These varied occupations present an almost infinite variety of objects to the contemplation of those few, who . . . have leisure and inclination to examine the occupations of other people." Specialization results in inequality, because some people wind up with more property than others and those people have more time to devote themselves to thinking as opposed to working. This divide requires government intervention on behalf of the poor in the form of public education. Teaching young laborers "to read, write and account," Smith insisted, will enable them to overcome the inherent disadvantages of the limited imagination required to labor within a greatly specialized economy. "A man, without the proper use of the intellectual facilities of a man . . . seems to be mutilated and deformed" in an essential way that the state can easily prevent.[69] The

Scotsman famous today for advocating less government intervention was famous in his time for demanding the state take responsibility for the education of its poorest citizens.

The difference between life in eighteenth-century Britain and fifteenth-century Britain convinced Smith that, on the whole, economic growth brought social improvement. "No society can surely be flourishing and happy, of which the far greater part of the members are poor and miserable," he famously argued, and many more people were poor and miserable in the earlier ages than they were in the later ages.[70] The age of commerce opened the door to magnificent social change, highlighted by widespread literacy, freedom from famine, and the flourishing of coffee houses in the new public sphere. The key was that commerce and manufacturing enabled those who did not have land to participate in the economy in a meaningful way. The division of labor created wealth and everyone benefited. Smith and Hume both believed that the age of commerce was more *just* than any other age because it widened the definition of property and increased everyone's ability to acquire it. There were definable limits to land, but the limits to wealth itself were much less clear. Certainly the expansion of the definition of property meant that some men would own much more than others, but it also meant that those who would have been relegated to complete dependence in a previous age were now able by virtue of their ability to participate in the expanding economy as the owners of their own labor.[71]

Toward the end of the century, Thomas Malthus accused Smith of mixing the question of "the wealth of nations" with that of "the happiness and comfort of the lower orders of society."[72] Had he been alive, Smith undoubtedly would have viewed the criticism as a compliment. He believed society to be an interdependent system where the good of one was intimately connected to the good of the whole. Economic growth was a valuable because it improved the lives of all—not just in terms of the things that they could own, but because it also meant expanded liberty and a greater flourishing of ideas. Life got better as societies moved through the prescribed ages, because individuals gained increasing access to expanded opportunities. Instead of being weighed down by the monotonous quest to fulfill their needs, they were freed (in various degrees) to pursue their wants. As Emma Rothschild has noted, "the liberty and security of individuals is for Smith the condition for the growth of commerce, and its most important consequence as well."[73] Economic growth increased and expanded justice.

Through their combined intellectual efforts, Smith and Hume created a system of social change focused on the development of laws and institutions that furthered human progress. This creation reflected the peculiar circumstances of their time and place. Their fascination with man's inner "moral sense," insistence on using historical "facts," and preoccupation with society came from their participation in a grand conversation that we now call the Enlightenment. Because they regarded the British political and commercial system as the pinnacle of human achievement, they created a system of history that explained its creation and offered solutions to push it further along a path it had already chosen. Their evident satisfaction with their nation, which they shared with most of the members of the Scottish Enlightenment, prevented them from embracing the increasingly radical ideas of their French counterparts and meant that this particular strand of the larger Enlightenment would be the most conservative one. They rejected revolution in favor of gradual progress.

Both men believed that humans were born with the "desire of bettering our condition" that "never leaves us till we go into the grave," but there were limits to their own vision of social improvement.[74] Neither spent much time worrying about women, who, in being barred from the Scottish universities, seemed also to have been barred from both attendance and even mention in most of the "enlightened" conversations in that took place in that nation.[75] In the same way, neither spent much time worrying about racial barriers within their own society. Although both disagreed with slavery, they did not emerge as champions of racial equality. Indeed, Hume admitted in an infamous footnote to his essay "On National Character," that he "was apt to suspect the negroes to be naturally inferior to the whites," because "there scarcely ever was a civilized nation of that complexion."[76] Such a statement clearly does not fit with claims of the universality of human character and it is difficult to know what to make of it. These Scottish philosophers seem to have been bested by their acceptance of British tradition and their belief in the origins of morality. If a person's moral sense develops along with his society, then there are no true moral absolutes—there is only a recognition that certain laws and institutions are of greater benefit to social progress. Their system made it difficult to fight accepted social mores in the country that they necessarily defined as the most improved on earth. Those looking for equality had to go to Paris to find "sympathetic" philosophers. There, general dissatisfaction with the entire religious, political, and commercial system led to the adoption of truly radical thought.[77]

The conservatism at the heart of Scottish philosophy left it open for digressions as well as progressions. In his 1774 work, *Sketches of the History of Man*, Hume's cousin and Smith's early champion, Henry Home, Lord

Kames, took deliberate aim at the French naturalist Buffon's claim that man is one species. "Is he seriously of the opinion, that any operation of climate, or of other accidental cause, can account for the copper color and smooth chin universal among the Americans, the prominence of the *pudenda* universal among Hottentot women, or the black nipple no less universal among female Samoides?" He dismissed the idea that climate could have created so much variation. "The black color of negroes, thick lips, flat nose, crisped woolly hair, and rank smell, distinguish them from every other race of men," he wrote in obvious disdain. "The Abyssinians, on the contrary, are tall and well made, their complexion a brown olive, features well proportioned, eyes large, and of a sparkling black, lips thin, a nose rather high than flat" and "there is no difference of climate between Abyssinian and Negroland as to produce these striking differences." Even the people who live in the desert of Zaara, Kames continued, "commonly termed as Lower Ethiopia, though exposed to the vertical rays of the sun in a burning sand . . . are of a tawny color, far from being jet-black," like their neighbors in similar climates. Europeans who move to such places have children who look the same as their parents did at birth—the climate changes nothing.[78]

Had he met *Ras* Michael, Kames may well have agreed with James Bruce's belief that he looked like Buffon, but he would not have agreed that they were of the same race. Kames insisted that Ethiopians were better looking than the other "negroes" of Africa and that their Christianity saved them from being savages, but they were still different. Climate had not altered men, Kames concluded; God had made men different to fit their climates in the scattering that had followed Babel. Had mankind not been so bold as to try to build a tower to the heavens, "all men would not only have the same language, but would have made the same progress towards maturity of knowledge and civilization."[79] But, mankind had been proud and had suffered the consequences. Progress would not be so easy for everyone after all. Kames was not alone in his pessimism.

In 1798, a thirty-two-year-old British parson, Thomas Malthus, anonymously published *An Essay on the Principle of Population as It Affects the Future Improvement of Society*. The book offered a depressing conclusion to a century of optimism, taking issue with the great question of the time: "Whether man shall henceforth start forwards with accelerated velocity towards illimitable, and hitherto unconceived improvement; or be condemned to a perpetual oscillation between happiness and misery."[80] The answer, he concluded, was the latter, for "the power of population is indefinitely greater than the power in the earth to provide subsistence for man."

Population increases in a geometric ratio and "subsistence" in an arithmetical ratio, Malthus argued, and "a slight acquaintance with numbers will show the immensity of the first power in comparison of the second."[81] Passion drives population, but food production is limited by the land, so mankind will ultimately be trapped by famine. Life can improve for the wealthiest members of society, the parson acknowledged, but the masses will eventually be done in by malnutrition and disease. Such has it ever been and such will it ever be. Where Smith had seen population growth as a positive good that helped push societies through the early stages of development, Malthus saw it as a hindrance to social welfare.

The irony of Malthus is that he was right at the wrong time. Economic historians now argue that everything pre-1800 can be labeled the Malthusian era, a time when "the scourges of failed modern states—war, violence, disorder, harvest failures, collapsed public infrastructures, bad sanitation—were the friends of mankind," because they reduced population pressures and allowed the survivors to maintain a higher standard of living.[82] Malthus wrote his famous little book in the middle of Britain's great transformation, but he did not fully realize its potential, distracted as he was by the negative economic ramifications of the current war with France. By the late 1790s, Britain was forced to buy grain from abroad to feed its growing population and much of that population was living in squalor. Things looked dire for the island. The progress Defoe and Smith had celebrated seemed hollow in the face of the social realities of the era. Yet the change was happening. Between 1740 and 1820, Great Britain's birth rate soared and its death rate declined, but its standard of living continued to rise.[83] The Industrial Revolution was revolutionizing everything, but those living within it did not yet know how it would alter their society.

Malthus proved incredibly influential, but not in the way that he anticipated. His message provoked a great deal of conversation, but it did not fundamentally alter economic policy. Even though he argued the limitations of economic growth, British businessmen and politicians kept pushing for the progress Smith had promised them. Smith himself was transformed in those years into the hero of laissez-faire—something that would undoubtedly have made him uncomfortable had he been alive to see it. Smithian concerns for social welfare were replaced by an intense individualism that ignored his arguments in support of proper government intervention in society and celebrated his calls to end mercantilist government controls. Smith had actually had greater faith in sympathy than in selfishness, but his nineteenth-century devotees, on the whole, did not.[84] They placed their faith in something else:

technology. Economic growth convinced Western Europeans and Americans that they had indeed found the true path to progress, because they no longer lived in a society governed by Malthusian rules of cyclical prosperity and decline. Their egos expanded accordingly.

Europeans had long believed themselves special, but such assumptions had been primarily based on Christianity and largely unsupportable in any tangible way. That changed during the early nineteenth century as the technological innovations of the eighteenth began bearing obvious fruits. European peoples became more centrally focused on science, technology, and economics, and, when they did not find new insights in those particular areas in foreign places, they dismissed the people of those places as inherently inferior.[85] As they grew wealthier and commanded control over more space, Europeans grew increasingly convinced that they were both special and *right*. They adopted the term *civilization* to explain it and they always used it in the singular when talking about the present, making it clear that the term could not be divorced from Europe. The French historian François Guizot provided a foundation for the new ideas in his 1828 work, *Histoire générale de la civilization en Europe*. The "first fact comprised in the word civilization," Guizot insisted, "is the fact of progress, of development; it presents at once the idea of a people marching onward, not to change its place, but to change its condition; of a people whose culture is conditioning itself, and ameliorating itself."[86] Long-standing egoism blended with awe at the mighty power inherent in the products of industry to solidify European faith in its "civilization," and its practitioners went out into the world to prove its superiority.

When Major W. Cornwallis Harris journeyed to Ethiopia in 1841, he eyed the other nation with smug confidence. Sent by the British government to initiate relations with Sáhela Selássie, the king of Shoa, Harris traveled not from Europe as others had in the past, but from India, which was already perceived to the be the star jewel in Victoria's imperial crown. The mission was, Harris wrote in his account of his journey, to establish "a more intimate connection with a Christian people, who know even less about the world than the world knows of them." Like travelers in the past, the English desired to extend "the bounds of geographical and scientific knowledge," but they were particularly interested in "the advancement of the best interests of commerce, and the melioration of the lot of some of the less favored portions of the human race."[87] Harris delighted in the technology that was making British global power possible. "Immortal Watt!" He extolled when describing the steam frigate that transported them out of Bombay. He celebrated the dramatic scene that accompanied the presentation of the gifts: Dehli scarves, "ornamented clocks," music boxes that played "God Save the Queen," some "rich manufactures of the loom," and three hundred muskets. All delighted the king and court, "but astonishment and admiration knew no bounds, as the populace next spread over the face of the hills to witness the artillery practice, which formed the sequel to the presentation of these princely gifts." The "dwarf father confessor" announced in response, "no such miracles as these have been wrought in Ethiopia," which are the fulfillment of a dream the king's grandfather had forty years ago where "red men were bringing into his kingdom curious and beautiful commodities, from countries beyond the great sea."[88] Such, at least, is the story as Harris tells it.

The British journeyed to Ethiopia for trade, not for land, but they justified the mission with the same certainty of white supremacy that inspired their domination of India. Harris explained the desirability of securing trade with Ethiopia by insisting how, "compared with other nations of Africa, she unquestionably holds a high station. She is superior in arts and in agriculture, in laws, religion, and social condition, to all the benighted children of the sun." Her Christianity is weak and damaged by the influence of local gods, but "there is, perhaps, no portion of the whole continent to which European civilization might be applied with better ultimate results." It will come, Harris firmly insisted, in the form of British commerce, whose "operation promises to open the only means of improvement of civilization." Trade with Britain offered the "half-civilized Abyssinians" the only path out of their darkness. Luckily for them, they differed enough from their less-fortunate (darker-skinned and pagan) neighbors that they had a chance of making it.[89] To ensure that his English readers left his account with renewed confidence in their society and its global mission, Harris ended the book with Sáhela Selássie's message to Victoria that "although far behind the nations of the white men, from whom Ethiopia first received her religion, there yet remains a spark of Christian love in the breast of the kind of Shoa."[90] They were clever words for a man who had just been introduced to the stunning power of the latest in European firearms. There would be more where those came from and Sáhela Selássie's son would eventually use imported guns not only to make a king of Shoa into the emperor of Ethiopia, but also to keep Italy from conquering his nation. All that, however lay fifty years in the future. In 1841, Europeans viewed Ethiopia as simply a technologically deprived nation of inherently inferior people for whom trade with Britain offered the "only means of improvement."

This certainty that the Ethiopians could never progress on their own, and that their neighbors could never do it all, stemmed from European (and

American) awe at what its "civilization" was accomplishing at home and abroad. The steam frigate that carried Harris out of India was part of an Industrial Revolution that powered nineteenth-century imperialism. Anxious to explain the secret of their success, Europeans and Americans seized on a new vision of history that celebrated the rise of the West as "progress." They turned the fact that they often did succeed into the belief that they *should* succeed. They even created a science to prove it.

It began with skulls. In the early 1820s, Edinburgh resident George Combe popularized a continental theory called phrenology, which held that the brain was divided into separate organs (Combe believed there to be thirty-five) which determined the workings of the mind and which could be deciphered by "reading" the skull. A subject's nature could be discovered, phrenologists insisted, through consideration of the size of the head and the peculiar distinctions of its bones. Combe also recommended an interview, but others were not so picky. For them, the skull revealed everything important.[91] Although originally focused on individuals, the reality that classes, nations, and races are merely collections of individuals quickly led to conversations about phrenology's larger implications. Investigations of hatter-supplied national skull-size statistics and of skulls mailed from Bengal by the British East India Company turned phrenology into a science of the biological reasons for social difference.[92] Combe embraced the implications of his theory, cheerfully boasting that phrenological determinism "holds good in the case of nations as well as of individuals."[93] His 1828 celebration of phrenology became one of the highest-selling "science" books of the nineteenth century. The English-speaking world adored descriptions of its superiority.

In the United States, phrenology—popularized by Combe's 1839–1840 visit—supported slavery and the expansion of white farmers across the continent. "The existing races of native American Indians," Combe argued, "show skulls inferior in their moral and intellectual development to those of the Anglo-Saxon race, and that, morally and intellectually, these Indians are inferior to their Anglo-Saxon invaders, and have receded before them."[94] The progress of the English-speaking peoples in particular was now understood to be natural. In 1839, Philadelphia physician Samuel George Morton published *Crania Americana,* using his investigation of American Indian skulls to defend his claim that "the intellectual faculties of this great family appear to be of a decidedly inferior cast when compared with those of the Caucasian or Mongolian races."[95] Josiah Nott and George Gliddon followed with *Types of Mankind* in 1854, a massive compilation of pseudoscience dedicated to a hierarchy of race. Though expensive, the book went through ten editions by

1871, which speaks to the popular hunger for descriptions of white superiority. The "Caucasian races," the author's argued, "were fulfilling the law of nature" by expanding around the globe. "Some are born to rule, and others be ruled," they concluded in words that undoubtedly delighted their slave-owner readers.[96] Adherents of this new ethnology understood "improvement" to be the triumph of the white race (subdefined as Caucasian, Teutonic, and Anglo-Saxon) over nonwhite or not-as-white peoples.

The fascination with difference pushed attention back to the origins of humankind. By the mid-nineteenth century, *polygenism*—the belief in separate creations for separate races—had become the dominant scientific view in the English-speaking world. Polygenists used skeletal and cranial evidence to assert black inferiority and Egyptian hieroglyphs to argue that inferiority's long history. High rates of white mortality in the tropics were employed to support their view that the races had been separately created to live in separate climates. Tossing in bogus figures about the infertility of interrace offspring, they concluded it foolish to imagine that mankind was one species.[97] Not everyone agreed.

In 1859, Charles Darwin shocked the world with *On the Origin of the Species,* in which he introduced the principle of natural selection as the driving force of biological history. The idea, he admitted, came to him on September 28, 1838, when he read *An Essay on the Principle of Population* for the first time. Malthusian economics became the foundation of biological evolution.[98] "Thus," Darwin concluded at the end of the book, "from the war of nature, from famine and death, the most exalted object which we are capable of conceiving, namely, the production of the higher animals, directly follows." Creatures develop in their niches in response to the forces of the environment around them, gradually changing over time into separate species. Mankind is no different, Darwin hinted, although did not state. Instead, he left his readers contemplating the "grandeaur" in this view of biological history as the transformation of one or "a few forms" into "endless forms most beautiful and most wonderful."[99]

When Darwin addressed the question of human evolution directly in his 1871 work, *Descent of Man,* he admitted, "At the present day civilized nations are everywhere supplanting barbarous nations, excepting where the climate opposes a deadly barrier; and they succeed mainly, though not exclusively, through their arts, which are the products of the intellect." It seems "highly probable," he continued, that mankind's "intellectual faculties have been mainly and gradually perfected through natural selection."[100] Darwin did not want to put forth a biological argument in defense of British imperialism. He was just admitting what the science seemed to have proven, but defenders of Anglo-Saxon superiority on both sides of the Atlantic found much to love in the new doctrine of natural selection. "We must remember that progress is no invariable rule," he wrote. "It is very difficult to say why one civilized nation rises, becomes more powerful, and spreads more widely, than another; or why the same nation progresses more quickly at one time than at another." He postulated it must depend "on an increase in the actual number of the population, on the number of the men endowed with high intellectual and moral faculties, as well as on their standard of excellence."[101] For Darwin, civilization appeared to come from the gradual supplanting of nonmoral, less-intelligent members of a group with moral, intelligent ones. We all share the same ancient ancestors, he insisted, but nature had worked on different groups of peoples to different results. Imperialists in Britain and America rejoiced. They had lost their separate creations, but gained a more definitive scientific explanation of human progress that permitted a racial hierarchy.

Darwin considered himself a scientist, not a social theorist, but people reading his work seized its potential social applications with eagerness. Darwin was careful to argue that evolution does not lead to perfection but to creatures that are better adapted to their particular circumstances, which could change, thereby making previous adaptations a liability. Evolution was not the goal of natural selection, just the by-product.[102] Many of his contemporaries disagreed. Most notable among them was fellow Englishman, Herbert Spencer, who had been thinking and writing about the social consequences of evolution during the decades that Darwin was researching *On the Origin of the Species*.

Spencer had been introduced to the idea of evolution through the work of Jean Baptiste Pierre Antoine de Monet, chevalier de Lamarck, who published the first comprehensive theory of organic evolution in 1802. Lamarck promoted the "transmutation hypothesis," which argued that all organisms were gradually progressing to greater complexity through ongoing spontaneous generation. Most important for nineteenth-century social thought, he believed in the transmission of acquired characteristics.[103] Born in 1820 into a middle-class family decidedly involved in England's Industrial Revolution, Spencer trained as a civil engineer. He was always interested in progress, philosophy, economics, and science. Like Darwin, reading Malthus in the fall of 1838 convinced him of man's struggle with nature; unlike Darwin, he dedicated himself to working out its social ramifications.[104] Both Darwin and Spencer shared a fascination with the question of how population drove progress and, in that, they were merely picking up where Malthus had left off Smith. Where Smith had viewed population growth as a positive good that encouraged societies to develop more complex property laws and an increasing division of labor, and Malthus had viewed it as a natural check to unlimited progress, Spencer saw it as driving evolutionary force. For him, population growth created progress by weeding out the weakest members of society, encouraging only the strongest to stay alive and bear children. It was Spencer, not Darwin, who coined the phrase, "survival of the fittest." Blending his economics with his Lamarckian evolutionary bias, Spencer argued that both mental and physical characteristics could be inherited, which meant that evolution was progressing toward perfection.[105] "The grand and irresistible law of human existence," he posited, "is progressive improvement."[106]

Spencer's philosophy, popularly labeled *Social Darwinism* (even though it preceded Darwin's publications on evolution and displayed a decided adherence to Lamarckian views of transmission), took early nineteenth-century views of progress to their "natural" conclusion. Evolution offered a means of justifying imperialism as the triumph of the more developed or specialized peoples over those who had not yet reached that "stage of development." It also offered a scientific defense of the English-speaking world's revised understanding of Smith's teachings on laissez-faire capitalism. If the struggle that produced natural selection held the key to progress, then it was dangerous for societies to interfere too much in the process. Spencer fretted about increased state intervention on behalf of society's least powerful members. Poor laws, he insisted, favor "the multiplication of those worst fitted for existence, and, by consequence, hinders the multiplication of those best fitted for existence—leaving, as it does, less room for them."[107] Progress demanded that the government allow nature to take its course.

Social Darwinism reached the peak of its intellectual influence in the United States in the writings of Yale Professor of Political Economy William Graham Sumner, who argued the intimate connections between policy and progress. The "duty of the social scientist," he told his students, "is to teach that moral and social deterioration follows inevitably upon economical mistakes." We have a responsibility to the next generation, he insisted, to exercise a strict adherence to the ideal of free competition.[108] There is no way around the triage of "liberty, inequality, survival of the fittest," Sumner argued, except to choose "not-liberty, equality, survival of the unfittest." Because, in modern times, the market was nature, to "denounce capital," Sumner insisted, was "to undermine civilization." "The truth is that the social order is fixed by laws of nature precisely analogous to those of the physical order," he wrote. "The most that man can do is by ignorance and self-conceit to mar the operation of social laws."[109] Sumner did not idolize the capitalists making money off the laboring poor; he simply accepted present suffering in the pursuit of future glory. Nature had to take its course. His work was very popular in the 1870s and 1880s, but gradually fell out of a favor with a public increasingly worried about where semi-unbridled capitalism was headed. Americans believed in progress, but in the middle of their own industrial revolution, they feared a progress that they could not control. By the 1890s, the vast majority wanted action, not passivity, and their vision of how progress happened changed once again.[110]

It began with ego. "A world is sad today for the death of the great white rose which filled with its fragrance a summer," began the *Chicago Daily Tribune*'s article about the closing of the 1893 Columbian Exposition. "More than one century of the world's progress blossomed in the white witchery that has away before the advent of winter's snow." It began with steel, which men harnessed to construct architectural wonders that stirred the minds of observers. They then covered the structures with electric lights that, at night, stirred the souls. They filled the buildings with exhibits of the latest technologies, displays of historic memorabilia, and shows that contrasted American "civilization" with foreign "barbarism." Anyone who doubted what America had accomplished needed only to head over the ethnology exhibits, where "the civilization of the East, decrepit, stunted, here gazed at the civilization of the West, aspiring, triumphing." "What an opportunity was here afforded to the scientific mind," the article continued, "to descend the spiral of evolution, tracing humanity to its highest phases down almost to its animalistic origin." Just look, it taunted visitors, at who we are and what we have done.[111]

The Chicago World's Fair spoke to the desires of the American people to throw off the shackles of nineteenth-century determinism. It started with the buildings. "We are the priests of material development, of the work which enables other men to enjoy the fruits of the great sources of power in Nature," the president of the American Society of Civil Engineers insisted in 1895. Engineers made human ability visible in remarkable new ways and people loved them for it. Successes in engineering encouraged academically inclined men and women to take control over human progress back from nature.[112] Mechanical and materialist determinism had previously governed existence; now man was fighting back and demanding that he rule himself, albeit under the conditions demanded by scientific laws. In a wave of sociological and psychological discourse, mankind declared its independence from nature.[113]

Although this new vision of human ability found its greatest popularity in the pragmatism of William James and John Dewey, it had its greatest impact on the social sciences in the writings of Lester Frank Ward. Born in Illinois in 1847, Ward grew up in a world dominated by Spencerian thought. After the war, he got a job as a clerk in the Treasury Department and earned a college degree through five years of night classes. In 1883, he gained the title of chief paleontologist in the U.S. Geological Survey and published *Dynamic Sociology*, a book he had been working on for the previous fourteen years.[114] His varied scientific interests tied him to current ideals of scholarship, but his focus on the emerging discipline of sociology emphasized his link to late-nineteenth-century specialization. American social science "professionalized" during this period, as did all the academic disciplines, bequeathing to the new century hierarchically organized, community-oriented, and training-specific fields of study. New ideas about the interdependence of society and human freedom supported the shift. What famed sociologist Talcott Parsons later called the "voluntaristic theory of action" encouraged people to focus their academic efforts in order to better determine how human action in that particular field could improve.[115] Ward's work helped convince people that they could make their own progress by utilizing social science theories in the construction of public policy. "Nature's ways," Ward insisted, should not be "man's ways." He called for "the scientific control of the social forces by the collective mind of society for its own advantage."[116]

In 1893, when more than twenty million people journeyed to Chicago to experience the fair's delights, Ward published *The Psychic Factors of Civilization*, a definitive explanation of the mind's ability to shape the world through the power of choice. All humans have desires, Ward wrote, and these desires inspire them to act and to change their environments in ways impossible for the rest of the animal kingdom. "The fundamental principle of biology is natural selection, that of sociology is artificial selection." The point turned Social Darwinism on its head. Nature, Ward wrote, "progresses through the destruction of the weak," but "man progresses through the protection of the weak."[117] The science had clear policy implications: "*individual freedom can only come through social regulation.*" Ward believed that the state had to intervene to narrow the gap between the powerful and the weak. This meant reducing economic protections on corporations, offering better public education to all, and increasing the bargaining power of labor.[118] "Is not civilization itself with all that it has accomplished the result of man's not letting things alone," he asked, "and of his not letting nature take its course?"[119] Ward resuscitated human agency.

With his scientific critique of laissez-faire capitalism, his calls for increased regulation and expanded public education, and his skillful blending of evolution with human ability, Ward introduced a radical new vision of human possibility and purpose. In the past, the majority of the American public had tended to see government as a necessary evil. Ward encouraged them to see it as a positive good—a potential force for change. He did not call for the artificial equalities of socialism, but for the removal of the artificial inequalities of capitalism.[120] Although he rarely got the credit he deserved outside of the academy, in his writings lay a great deal of the foundations of twentieth-century American liberalism. Ward helped to create a United States where most people saw minimum wage laws, the Sherman Antitrust Act, and the New Deal as progress.

There was, however, a troubling side to this renewed confidence in mankind. With its emphasis on expertise and academic specialization, it necessarily privileged the thoughts and sentiments of a select few. The education requirements alone meant that most people in the United States—let alone those in Ethiopia or the Philippines—could not participate in the intellectual effort promising to move humankind into progress. Although the goal was democratic in its claims of social beneficence, the process was not. Development demanded the combined intellectual and physical efforts of engineers, economists, sociologists, and doctors, and only a select group of nations possessed the institutional facilities to create them. Those that could not appeared to be at a terrible disadvantage. But knowledge can easily spread across borders.

When Robert P. Skinner went to Ethiopia in 1903, he met a man who was developing his country. Menelik II, Skinner wrote in admiration, "has created the United States of Abyssinia, a work for which he was endowed by Nature with the constructive intelligence of a Bismarck, and the faculty for handling men of a McKinley."[121] Born Sahle Maryam in 1844 to a family that had ruled the province of Shoa for nine generations, the future Menelik II was raised to be a king and skillfully became an emperor.[122] Moving southward down out of the highlands and across the plains, Menelik turned an empire of competing ethnic groups, religions, and classes into a nation strong enough to stand against the Europeans who wanted to possess it.

Menelik claimed the throne of Ethiopia in 1888, during one of the most calamitous moments in that nation's history. European ingenuity and expertise had finally created the tools—repeating rifles and quinine in particular—necessary for conquering the unconquerable continent. Faced with internal divisions at home and an Italian army advancing from the

FIGURE 1.1 Emperor Menelik II poses with members of his court in Addis Ababa for a photographer from the 1903–1904 U.S. diplomatic mission. The talented ruler managed to maintain his country's independence in the face of relentless European expansion across the continent and became a legend in the colonized world. *Massillon Museum, Massillon, Ohio*

coast, Menelik had to act quickly and decisively to secure his throne. Desperate not to lose everything, he decided he had to give up something. In 1889, he reluctantly acknowledged Italian authority over the land its army had already claimed. The Treaty of Wuchalé ceded Eritrea (Ethiopia's Red Sea territory) in return for Italian recognition of Ethiopian independence, a loan, and weapons. Hungry for more land and disdainful of Africans, Rome altered the Italian-language version of the treaty, deliberately changing a passage from the Amharic stating that Menelik "may, if he so desires, avail himself of the Italian government for any negations he may enter into with other Powers and Governments" to he "consents to avail himself."[123] Boasting of their falsely claimed authority around Europe, the Italians tried to sever Menelik's relations with Britain, Germany, Russia, and France. Furious at the deception, Menelik paid back the loan, declared the treaty null and void, and sent a letter to the European powers explaining, "My country is strong enough to maintain its independence, and it does not care for any protectorate." He then reminded his readers of Psalm 68:31: "Ethiopia stretches her hands to God." The Italian prime minister shot back, "Ethiopia stretches her hands to us!" and continued plans to steal Menelik's nation.[124] Wisely, Menelik decided to keep the guns that the Italians had given him, for Rome's machinations against him culminated in the Battle of Adwa in 1896, where a united Ethiopian force soundly trounced the invading Italians, driving them back to Eritrea. "I have no intention of being an indifferent spectator while far distant powers make their appearance with the intention of carving out their respective empires in Africa," Menelik had written in 1891. "As the Almighty has protected Ethiopia to this day, I am confident that he will protect and increase her in the future."[125] Adwa seemed to justify his faith.

Europeans were shocked. "No one here—with the sole possible exception of one or two dimwitted persons or a few habitually malevolent minds—wishes for the success of the Abyssianians at the price of the discomfiture of a civilized nation," explained an 1895 *Paris Temps* article. After the results of the battle arrived on the continent, the *Times of London* lamented, "The fact must be faced, although it is nowhere more sincerely deplored than in England, that events in Abyssinia constitute a grave embarrassment for Italy." Trying to make sense of the African victory, the *Times* promptly declared Ethiopia "a civilized power both in the way they made war and in the way they conducted their diplomacy."[126] It was a strategic reversal from early descriptions, providing literary evidence of an intellectual scramble to make sense of the unthinkable: The largest European force ever to set foot in Africa had just been defeated. Even admitting, as Theodore Roosevelt did in an 1899 letter to an English friend, that the Abyssinians had been victorious at Adwa because they were fighting Italians instead of members of the superior northern Teutonic race, left the primary question unanswered.[127] How had Ethiopia changed the rules of European expansion? Menelik's ability to make his nation a "problem" for the Europeans stemmed from a variety of sources, but it was largely due to his determination to embrace the very thing that had turned eighteenth-century universalism into nineteenth-century racism: technology.

Menelik's fascination with innovation began long before he became emperor and lasted until his death in 1913. He introduced telephones and telegraphs and modern public administration to Ethiopia. He set up a printing press to publish regular periodicals, a mint to produce coins to facilitate more complicated exchanges, and modern flourmills to grind grain. He sent government representatives to European capitals and received foreign visitors in his own new capital city of Addis Ababa in return, which opened the door to commercial relationships that resulted in an ever-expanding stockpile of imported weapons.[128] Menelik consolidated his hold over Ethiopia, won the Battle of Adwa, and secured his nation's independence by utilizing many of the same tools and techniques of his would-be oppressors. By showing that black men could wield the tools of empire as effectively as white men, Adwa challenged "scientific" racism, but it did not challenge the link between technology and power. "All European countries will be obliged to make a place for this new brother who steps forth to play in the Dark Continent the role of Japan in the Far East," exclaimed the French newspaper *La Liberté*.[129] Like the Meiji before him, Menelik proved that Europeans were not inherently better adept at using technology.

Bitter, virulent racism remained rampant in the "civilized" West in the opening of the twentieth century, but the science of racial difference began losing credibility and ideas about development changed in turn. The anthropologist Franz Boas's efforts to remove race as a source of human difference proved critical. With his assault on the cephalic index, Boas destroyed almost one hundred years of scientific efforts to establish racial hierarchies through measurements of the head and brain. With his emphasis on culture—understood to be "a system of ideas and values spread by language and other forms of social behavior"—over heredity, he (and, more vehemently, his followers) drove biology out of anthropology.[130]

The social sciences were still exclusive, but they were gradually becoming less racist, which opened the door to a return to the universality that had dominated the intellectual realm a hundred years earlier. The key was no longer deterministic biology, but access to the techniques and technologies that the experts were using to guide development. Economic growth was the still the goal and people were more confident than ever before that they knew how to achieve it. It had been all about the wanting; now, it was all about the knowing.

2 A GLOBAL ECONOMY

In 1927, the American adventurer Gordon MacCreagh and his wife set off for Ethiopia. Along the way, he sent back regular triumphal accounts of their year-long journey for publication in *Adventure Magazine*. The following year, he published the entirety as *The Last of Free Africa*, announcing in his introduction that indigent Liberians need only to think about the control the big rubber and oil companies wielded over their nation's politics to silence their protests about his choice of title. "This is a book about Abyssinia," he boomed. "The Unconquered. Free since before the beginning of history."[1] He dedicated it to "His Imperial Majesty Haile Selassie in recognition of His Great Achievements for the Progress of the Ancient Kingdom of Ethiopia" and filled it with amusing tales of his group's adventures. In the midst of the cavorting, however, MacCreagh included serious critiques of European behavior toward the nation, which displayed a manifest lack of respect and no recognition of universal equality. "The European finds it difficult to the point of impossibility to lay aside his inborn conviction that he is the dominant white man and to accept the absurd grotesquerie that in Ethiopia he is not the superior of the free and independent Ethiopian."[2] MacCreagh disdained such attitudes. Ethiopia "should be given not only a chance but a helping hand to climb into an assured position of independent progress," he insisted and America was the ideal nation to do so. "Abyssinia is enormously rich in potentialities, needing only development. She offers the opportunity to American business to help in that development," he concluded at the end of the book.[3]

MacCreagh's "development" revolved around industrialization, transportation, and education. It represented the triumph of universalism over European particularism. It was open to all and useful to all. "To-day," read the editor's introduction to MacCreagh's book, "the more progressive and far-sighted Ethiopians led by His Highness Tafari Makonnen realize the necessity of modernizing their ancient kingdom. They realize that the resources of the country must be developed if Ethiopia is to take her place with the nations of the world." They know that the "masses must be educated to understand modern political concepts and the machine age." And they know that it will not be easy, for "what development we have attained to by natural growth during a thousand years they must miraculously accomplish immediately."[4] It is a revealing statement. The editor's insistence on the West's "natural growth" over centuries directly referenced Smith's history of the gradual social progress that turned hunters into merchants. But ideas about economic growth were changing in the early twentieth century and the experts—the practitioners of the science of economics—were less convinced of the applicability of Smith's theories to postindustrial societies. What Smith had left out suddenly seemed a great deal more interesting than what he had put in.

"Political Economy or Economics is a study of mankind in the ordinary business of life; it examines that part of individual and social action which is most closely connected with the attainment and with the use of the material requisites of wellbeing."[5] So began the most influential economic text of the early twentieth century: Cambridge professor Alfred Marshall's *Principles of Economics*. First published in 1890, Marshall's work helped to establish what became known as the neoclassical school, most notable for present purposes for its role in rescuing Smithian economics from its nineteenth-century distortions and opening the door to the Keynesian revolution of the 1930s. Marshall placed the focus on the individual as a member of "the social organism" and encouraged fellow economists to study micro exchanges in search of macroeconomic laws.[6] Lester Ward called for academic specialization in pursuit of the social laws that would allow humans to organize society to the greatest advantage of all. Marshall shared his passion to use science for the benefit of mankind. As economics was a "science ... still almost in its infancy," there was a lot of work to be done.[7]

Even a cursory reading of *Principles* reveals its Smithian roots, though Marshall himself was not quick to see the connections. Like his Scottish predecessor (and his Progressive contemporaries), Marshall was primarily concerned with the well-being of the laboring classes and defended the virtue of the age of commerce for its ability to distribute wealth to all. Adam Smith's belief that the last stage of social progress was the most just had been proven correct by "the steady progress of the working classes" over the past century. "The steam-engine has relieved them of much exhausting and degrading toil; wages have risen; education has been improved and become more general" and increased demand "for intelligent work" has caused the skilled labor to come to outnumber unskilled, Marshall explained. Technology had made Smith's fear that mindless work might produce mindless laborers a moot point. Like Hume and Smith, Marshall rejected out of hand the old romantic nostalgia for life before commerce. "In every stage of civilization, in which the power of money has been prominent, poets in verse and prose have delighted to depict a past truly 'Golden Age,'" he wrote. "Their idyllic pictures have been beautiful . . . but they have had very little historical truth." The *truth* is that "we never find a more widely diffused comfort alloyed by less suffering than exists in the western world today."[8] Capitalism works, Marshall concluded, because it enhances the ability of every member of society to attain greater material well-being. History proved it.

As Marshall shared Smith's faith in the transformational power of secure private property and open economic competition, he also shared his insistence on limited government intervention for the good of society as a whole. "Excesses" must be curtailed in order to "diminish [free enterprise's] power or doing evil and increase its power of doing good." He had no doubt that it did both, but time seemed to bear out the greater influence of the latter over the former. One side effect of one hundred years (or so) of free enterprise in the West was increased altruism. "The growing earnestness of the age, the growing intelligence of the mass of the people, and the growing power of the telegraph, the press, and other means of communication," he wrote, "are ever widening the scope of collective action for the public good." In a decisive strike at turn-of-the-century reformers shouting the evils of free enterprise, Marshall urged people to remember that it had created a world where they could unite across a large field in pursuit of a more altruistic society.[9] Marshall did not specifically explain technology's relation to free enterprise, but the tone of his assault on those preaching against it implies that he believed them to be inherently connected. That absence places his work definitively within its time—the second period of great economic thought, which lasted from the 1870s into the 1930s and dominated the opening decades of *professional* economics.

New economics arose in the early 1870s, a product of the efforts of several key figures—Stanley Jevons, Leon Walras, and Karl Menger—to untie wealth from land. Smith and Hume had both found progress in population growth, which prompted the creation of more elaborate property rights and an increased division of labor. Ricardo used their ideas to create nineteenth-century economics with its focus on rent, production, and labor as the roots of wealth. John Stuart Mill and Karl Marx used Ricardo's principles as the foundation of their separate investigations of the distribution of money, resources, and power within the social classes. All were united by their passionate interest in the development of wealth and its movement through society and all lived and worked in an industrializing Europe. The effects of that revolution changed the way that economists understood their discipline.

Between 1868 and 1878, Britain went from producing four-fifths of its basic food and fiber to producing scarcely one-half.[10] Europe and America were globalizing, companies were specializing, and the world was changing in ways that made the idea of wealth tied to a specific geographic space increasingly obsolete. To cope with the change, professional economists shifted from a macro to a micro focus, using mathematical equations to explain individual economic behavior. Recognizing that their new, more "scientific" approach worked better in stable systems, and swayed by a general acceptance of Jean Baptiste Say's theory that full employment and full utilization of resources were the natural endpoints of free competitive market exchange, economists stopped talking about "growth" and started talking about "equilibrium." They created artificially perfect systems to do it. Instead of studying the world as it was, they studied it as they thought it should be, creating theories about individual behavior within static systems. The science of "economics" replaced the philosophy of "political economy."[11]

But Marshall was not a perfect follower of the new economic theories. Unlike many of his colleagues, he remained committed to using his discipline for the betterment of society. Although a brilliant mathematician, he eschewed elaborate formulas, which partially explains why his book dominated the teaching of economics for so long. Marshall did, however, share his colleagues' fascination with "marginal utility," which identified consumer desire as the source of an object's or a service's value. It was "marginal" because, as Marshall wrote, "the additional benefit which a person derives from a given increase of his stock of a thing, diminishes with every increase in the stock that he already has."[12] Because we know what people want, he insisted, we can figure out how they will tend to act in most situations. Unlike other economists of the day who were content to work with an idealized "economic man," Marshall warned in the introduction to the first edition of his book that Say's law would never be realized because people are ruled by many passions and cannot be trusted to be always selfish or always wise.[13] He believed that economics was controlled by fundamental laws, but when you are dealing with people, the results cannot be perfect. Marshall shared the general belief that equilibrium was the natural result of a competitive free economy, but outside influences dictated its realization in reality. He located those influences in changes in supply and demand over time.[14] Marshall thereby brought questions of growth and development back into economics by asking people to think about the linear impact of time on the expression of economic laws. With his focus on the role of "individual" individuals and the influence of time, Marshall helped lay the groundwork for a new, more radical understanding of economics that emphasized change over stasis. Younger economists picked up where he left off.

In a 1934 letter to his publisher, Joseph A. Schumpeter wrote of his 1911 masterpiece, *Theorie der wirtschaftlichen Entwicklung* (The Theory of Economic Development), "Fundamentally it is an attempt at framing a purely theoretical description of the nature and mechanism of economic change, its motive power and the phenomena incident to it."[15] Schumpeter broke out of the stationary mold, which was viewed as the only "scientific" way to study economics and insisted that the discipline could find and study change. We all know that "economic life changes," Schumpeter wrote. Some of those changes are small and can be understood in the old system of inputs and outputs, but some are much larger and cannot be located in the traditional explanations. "What we are about to consider," he explained in a tantalizing footnote, "is that kind of change arising from within the system *which so displaces its equilibrium point that the new one cannot be reached from the old one by infinitesimal steps.* Add successively as many mail coaches as you please, you will never get a railway thereby."[16] The wealthiest nations in the world did not become so through long-term, small-scale growth, Schumpeter insisted, but through moments of radical change when new ideas transformed their economic systems.

Schumpeter's economic development was an historic phenomenon found in the capitalist systems of the past one hundred years. Such systems were *dynamic*, because they contained within themselves the force for their own change. "Development in our sense," he wrote, "is then defined by the carrying out of new combinations," actualized by the ingenuity of the entrepreneur, who employs "existing resources in a different way."[17] The key is *innovation* (defined as "doing things differently"), which alters the paradigm of equilibrium and introduces growth that is oft times rapid, uncomfortable, and revolutionary. Changes in production spark changes in wants and the entire economic system is forced to adapt. Such economic development is cyclical, Schumpeter insisted, for just as the young entrepreneur eventually becomes the settled, stable capitalist, so too will the economic system. But the changes that it sparked remain. And new ones will always come, because innovation often results in greater profits, and the desire for wealth drives the humans who drive the capitalist system.

Like Marshall, Schumpeter believed capitalism to be ideally designed to produce economic growth and, in consequence, further the material well-being of the many. In emphasizing its dynamic capacity for development, he revitalized the eighteenth-century struggle to explain how certain nations became and remained wealthy by adapting nineteenth-century theories of evolution for economics. Crucially, he found a place for technological innovation within the economic system at a time when everyone else saw technology as an external factor for growth.[18] People largely overlooked the profundity of his accomplishment, however, because Schumpeter possessed academically unfashionable concerns.[19] His work was known, but few economists were eager to share his fascination with development in capitalist systems. In addition, Schumpeter was not a skilled mathematician and *Theorie* contained no mathematical "proofs" of its ideas, which consequently discredited it for many in the field. During the following decades, most economists who talked about Schumpeter's work talked about its application for understanding business cycles and ignored his wider vision of economic development. In 1928, however, another economist put growth back on the table.

Allyn A. Young titled his presidential address before the British Association for the Advancement of Science "Increasing Returns and Economic Progress." The old economists, he began, naturally assumed that there would be diminishing returns in agriculture and increasing returns in industry, which was more naturally inclined toward "improvements." "They were living in an age when men had turned their faces in a new direction and when economic progress was not only consciously sought but seemed in some way to grow out of the nature of things," Young explained. "Improvements, then, were not something to be explained. They were natural phenomena." When they tried to explain them, they returned to Smith's point that the division of labor reduced complex processes into simpler processes that encouraged the adoption of technology at various stages of production.[20] But Young wanted his audience to think about improvements in a new light. When we add Marshall's insight of the distinction between an individual firm and an individual industry, he told them, we can see the various ways that capitalism encourages economic growth.

It all begins with the market, Young insisted, which should be defined as "an aggregate of productive activities, tied together by trade." We cannot think about the market as simply "an outlet for the products of a particular industry ... but as the outlet for goods in general," which means that it is the center of both consumption and production. The market itself is the counter-force to equilibrium, Young continued with rising enthusiasm, because "every important advance in the organization of production," be it an "invention" or "a fresh application of the fruits of scientific progress to industry, alters the condition of industrial activity and initiates responses elsewhere in the industrial structure which in turn have a further unsettling effect. Thus change becomes progressive and propagates itself in a cumulative way."[21] The point is that all industries are tied together in a meaningful way and the growth that happens in one sector flows through the market to influence another—some firms and/or industries move ahead of others, then lag behind while others advance—creating a "*moving* equilibrium." This is what makes the persistent search for markets the most important factor in "that continuing economic revolution which has taken the modern world so far away from the world of a few hundred years ago." The market links everything together and makes continued growth possible. "The division of labour depends upon the extent of the market, but the extent of the market also depends upon the division of the labour," Young concluded, modestly describing his insights as simply "variations on a theme from Adam Smith."[22]

From the perspective of ninety years of economic history, it is difficult to overstate the revolutionary nature of Young's ideas. Though he clearly built off of Smith's understanding of long-term growth through the division of labor, Marshall's insight about internal and external economies, and Schumpeter's insistence on technology as a force for endogenous growth, Young went further than any of his predecessors in seeing "the market" as the center of economic development. In doing so, he helped to transform the discipline's focus on "economic systems" into a focus on "the economy." Until the 1930s, economists did not talk about an object called *the economy*. The term was an adjective, not a noun.[23]

This transformative change in vocabulary stemmed from both dynamic economics and a new interest in statistics that enabled the creation of *macro*economics. Intrigued, Young had written in 1925, "The growing use of quantitative methods is the most promising development in contemporary economics. But it will prove relatively sterile if it does not lead to a renaissance of theory."[24] It did lead to just such a renaissance; although Young would not be alive to see it, his work encouraged people to think about progress—and thereby development—in exciting new ways.

Young's insights went beyond identifying the chief characteristic of "an economy"; he also inferred the potential political ramifications of a new understanding of a centralized, all-connected market that is open, therefore, to manipulation from the top down. Progress "takes time," Young insisted. "An industrial dictator, with foresight and knowledge, could hasten the pace somewhat, but he could not achieve an Aladdin-like transformation of a country's industry, so as to reap the fruits of a half-century's ordinary progress in a few years." Such a person would face two primary challenges: "the human material which has to be used is resistant to change" and "the accumulation of the necessary capital takes time." Neither would be easily tackled.[25]

It seems certain Young was thinking about the Union of Soviet Socialist Republics (USSR). Although Tsar Nicholas II began Russia's industrialization officially in the 1890s, heavy mobilization toward industrialization did not occur until the years of Soviet control. The motivation came from Lenin himself and his reaction to the Treaty of Versailles. "The war taught us much," he said, "not only that people suffered but especially the fact that those who have the best technology, organization, discipline and the best machines emerge on top; it is this the war has taught us. It is essential to learn that without machines, without discipline, it is impossible to live in modern society. It is necessary to master the highest technology or be crushed."[26] The Soviet Union, he insisted, would never again be lacking in either technology or discipline. At this point, Lenin looked primarily to the United States for directional assistance, having decided that its superior technology made it the best model for development. Focusing on mining, metallurgy, and machine building through a series of five-year development plans (which started in 1928—the same year as Young's speech), the Soviet Union vastly expanded its industrial capabilities. Success, its leaders claimed, came from tightly controlled top-down development focused on heavy industry from the very beginning. The Soviets would not move first through light industry as the Western nations had done in the nineteenth century.[27] "We are advancing full steam ahead along the path of industrialization—to socialism, leaving behind the age-old 'Russian' backwardness," Stalin boasted in 1929. "And when we have put the USSR on an automobile, and the muzhik on tractor, let the worthy capitalists, who boast so much of their-civilization, try to overtake us! We shall yet see which countries may then be 'classified' as backward and which as advanced."[28]

Americans watched, fascinated by what George Kennan called "the romance of economic development" that was unfolding in the USSR. Thousands of Westerners visited each year to see how the Soviets were balancing industrial advance with cultural advance, which, particularly in the aftermath of World War I, they believed lagged in the West. Its intense program seemed to offer an ideal opportunity for studying the pressures of modernizing upon a society. Most ignored what Young had labeled "costs" of trying to achieve a half-century's worth of progress in a few years, dismissing the very real sufferings of the Soviet citizens as a by-product not of rapid development, but of the Russian way of doing things.[29] Less confident than their parents had been about the glories of capitalism, a new generation of American intellectuals looked to the USSR for new ideas. Most were not communists, but neither did most *fear* communism—particularly after 1929, which ushered in a revolution in Western economic thought. Early twentieth-century growth theory focused on the capitalist system's inherent ability to create growth; post-1930 growth theory focused on human manipulation of the market to create growth. It was the "natural" outcome of faith in specialization and expertise. Economists first set themselves to understanding the economy, and then to controlling it.

In his 1944 classic work, *The Great Transformation*, Karl Polanyi described the nineteenth century as having been held together by four institutions: the balance-of-power political system, the international gold standard, the liberal state, and the self-regulating market. Based primarily on the concept of gain in what Polanyi dubbed the "utopian" dream of a self-regulating market system, this structure, he maintained, was bound to fail. And it did, finally, in the international breakdown of World War I and the long periods of economic depression that followed on its heels, first in Europe and then in America.[30] In the midst of this alleged collapse of the old order, many economists found themselves almost entirely focused on scarcity and security. No longer believing that the market could function successfully on its own, most Western economists began looking for ways in which governments could regulate the market into stability, thereby guaranteeing growth and full employment. *The Great Transformation* is particularly informative regarding this shift in economic paradigms, because it was really a critical history of the old system from the viewpoint of the then-present one and openly reflected the new Keynesian mistrust of the "free" market.[31]

Notably, the same year that Polyani's book came out, the Austrian American economist F. A. Hayek published *The Road to Serfdom*, a sweeping critique of the dangers central planning posed to individual liberty. "There has never been a worse and more cruel exploitation of one class by another," he wrote, "than that of the weaker or less fortunate members of a group of producers by the well-established which has been made possible by the 'regulation' of competition."[32] The more the government tried to make the market stable, Hayek concluded, the more it robbed people of their freedom to choose their own ends and means.[33] For Hayek, the central point was not which type of economic system produced the most efficient economic growth, but which best preserved individual liberty. His concern was largely dismissed.

By 1944, another economist's work had created a world where government-sustained economic security seemed more essential than market-supported economic freedom. John Maynard Keynes changed everything.

The prominent economic historian Mark Blaug described the advance of this Keynesian system as "a genuine revolution in economic thought: a sudden and amazingly rapid transformation in a whole body of theoretical ideas, including the metaphysical 'vision' of the economic process from which all theorizing begins."[34] Keynesianism offered a new paradigm—a different way of thinking about economics and the relationship between markets and society. People latched onto it because it offered hope, which the Great Depression had taken away from them. This abrupt, devastating halt to a century of almost continual economic expansion left people fearful on the now presumed inevitability of growth.

Keynesian economics demanded the rejection of the classical economic paradigm. "Let us clear from the ground," he asked his audience in a 1924 lecture, "the metaphysical or general principles upon which, from time to time, laissez-faire has been founded." Private and social interest, he continued, do not always match up. "Nor is it true that self-interest generally *is* enlightened; more often individuals acting separately to promote their own ends are too ignorant or too weak to attain even these." Smith had claimed too much. While insisting that he did not reject the "essential characteristic" of capitalism, which he defined as "the dependence upon an intense appeal to the money-making and money-loving instincts of individuals as the main motive force of the economic machine," Keynes called for greater collective action in the market system. History had proven some of Smith's argument wrong. The issue, he explained, is not capitalism's effectiveness as an economic system, but its ability, in its traditional form, to provide "a satisfactory way of life," which meant that it needed to be open to increased government regulation, although not complete central planning as the Soviets were doing.[35] Capitalism must not be allowed to fail; therefore, it had to become less "capitalistic."

As the depression deepened, Keynes became more committed to the idea of government intervention. The market, he argued in the 1936 book, *The General Theory of Employment, Interest, and Money*, cannot always fix itself, and sometimes it needs government involvement to force it to stabilize. In such efforts, investment would be more crucial than savings, for governments can step in with investments in a way that they cannot with savings. The investment of capital was the key to a healthy economy.[36] Keynes's major breakthrough was the observation that an economy might not always recuperate automatically in a depression because people are not going to invest money back into business when they have less of it and people are buying less. The economy thus becomes paralyzed and the government has to step in and fix the problem by investing where business will not.[37] "The enlargement of the functions of government . . . would seem to a nineteenth-century publicist or to a contemporary American financier to be a terrific encroachment on individualism," Keynes admitted at the end of *The General Theory*, but he maintained his position that it was "the only practicable means of avoiding the destruction of existing economic forms in their entirety and as the condition of the successful functioning of individual initiative."[38] Saving capitalism meant relying on human ingenuity to do what the market alone could not.

By the time the book came out, governments were ready. They had already begun involving themselves in *the economy*, before the term even existed, not because they believed the system inherently flawed, but because they were so confident in human ability. They were products of turn-of-the-century faith in mankind's ability to promote positive change by taking control of nature. A highly successful mining engineer, Herbert Hoover initiated an enhanced role for social scientists within the government when he became president. He and his academic allies shared a desire "to combine progressive humanitarianism, statistical data, and scientific management to insure that socio-economic and political institutions did not fall too far behind technological developmentalism."[39] Human manipulation, he argued, "could triumph over any alleged 'laws' of economics."[40] Hayek would later famously dub such confidence in humankind's abilities "the fatal conceit," but, in the 1920s, the technological world that capitalism had helped build in America only seemed to reinforce men's and women's ability to construct their own economic destiny.[41]

Hoover's diligent efforts toward government regulation in the name of a better economic society opened the door for the Keynesian economic policies of his successor.[42] Although it is dangerous to try to summarize New Deal ideology, for it changed over time and was never as cohesive as history would make it out to be, it is not, for present purposes, unfair to argue that it revolved around a macroeconomic vision of the economy. As such, it required governments to adopt macroeconomic approaches—most readily visible in large planning projects—to economic problems.[43] The government's role was to promote growth—something it had done under the classical paradigm primarily via free trade and secure patent rights—by creating "full employment" via government stimulation. The idea was pure Keynesianism and came at a time when the Englishman was reveling in his status as the most famous economist of his generation.[44] In the final expression of New Deal ideology,

American public policy met back up with economic theory, leading Keynes to remark after a 1934 visit that it was the United States and not the USSR that was "the economic laboratory of the world."[45]

By the middle of the 1930s, studying economics meant studying technology and change. In his 1934 book, *Dynamic Economics*, Charles Frederick Roos, the director of research for the National Recovery Administration, explained how new technologies forced the discipline to offer new theories. "Instead of an economy of basic scarcity," he wrote of the United States, "there is now present an economy of basic surpluses and clogged distributive mechanism." We can produce the goods, we just need to figure out how to distribute them throughout the economy most efficiently. The "new era ushered in by James Watt and his steam power" has gradually become an era defined by growth and, "therefore, it is essential to revise the old static theories of economics and to construct a more adequate theory based upon dynamic conceptions."[46] "An accurate dynamic conception should consider economic phenomena and functions in the process of change and the interrelation of these changes in the course of time," Roos explained. Bringing time back in the equation makes it clear that the so-called laws of economics exist at the mercy of innovation, changes "in social taste," and a host of "unexpected phenomena."[47] There can be overall equilibrium, he concluded, but it can never be static.

Roos's portrayal of dynamic economics offered his readers an introduction to the manifold ways in which the discipline was changing before their eyes. Cementing a rejection of static, idealized theory, the new practitioners confronted the practical economic reality of change. In addition, Roos's use of the term *economy* as a noun signaled the dramatic shift currently occurring in academic thought. Building off of Allyn Young's concept of the interconnectedness of "the market," Roos urged his readers to visualize the economy as the locus of "economic phenomena and functions in the process of change." Reflecting his own work in the National Recovery Administration, he warned that such changes were never fully predictable, because the economy could be manipulated by human behavior—be it the ideas of Schumpeter's entrepreneurs or the policies of Roosevelt's New Deal. The key to dynamic economics was the recognition that individual behavior played a fundamental role in economic change, but then to move beyond that role in pursuit of a grand theory of economic growth. Static focus on the individual (idealized) economic actor had hidden the presence of the economy itself. Dynamic theory proposed an explanation of the latter at the sake of the former. To many, it seemed the only possible way of truly understanding the wealth of nations.

The difficulty of the shift began with the question of how to understand "an economy." American economist Simon S. Kuznets wrote in 1930 that the search begins in the history of nations. "If we take the world from the end of the eighteenth century, there unrolls before us a process of uninterrupted and seemingly unslackened growth.... But if we single out the various nations or the separate branches of industry, the picture becomes less uniform. Some nations seem to have led the world at one time, others at another." This makes it clear that development does not just happen—it is a response to specific changes. "It seems advisable," Kuznets concluded, "to resolve the general problem of economic growth into the narrower question as to the long-time changes which can be observed in various national branches of production and trade."[48] Although he did not yet use the term, he clearly meant the economies of individual nations, and studying national economies depended on national statistics.

Although statistical thinking dates back to John Graunt's 1662 *Natural and Political Observations Made upon the Bills of Mortality*, the discipline did not come into its own until the twentieth century. Initially connected with the idea of the state—hence the *stat*—statistics offered economists the data that they needed to turn from microeconomics to macroeconomics. Indeed, there was no other way to get to "know" an economy and economists began encouraging countries to fund statistical research centers for first time.[49] Kuznets's 1930 book marked the opening of one of the most fruitful decades of economic thought and the most harrowing of economic reality. Necessity bred invention. The Great Depression made previously "academic" questions of economic growth practical and governments joined the quest—happily seizing on the concept of "an economy" that could be studied and manipulated. The work began with economic history, but it ended in economic policy.

In search of "broad characteristics of the process of development," Kuznets himself used national statistics (to give just a few examples) on the output of pig iron production in the United States between 1854 and 1924, imports of raw cotton to the United Kingdom from 1781 to 1914, the price of zinc in Belgium from 1845 to 1914, and the tonnage of freight moved on the Erie Canal between 1837 and 1922. He charted, graphed, and analyzed the numerical data from "the five most important industrial countries" and found that the numbers "fulfilled the expectation that the statistical data would show a rough similarity in the course of development."[50] Like Schumpeter before him, Kuznets viewed innovation as the key to understanding growth. Unlike Schumpeter, he analyzed it on the ground through historical statistics, which led Kuznets to a much less triumphalist vision of the history of economic growth. Industries, he concluded, always pass through periods of growth and retardation in response to competition from the same industry in a different country, a dependence on the slower-growing raw materials sector, a relative decline in funds available for investment in innovation, and a gradual slowdown of technological change.[51] Kuznets's work focused on the stories of specific industries, and he admitted that "the question of what happens to the interrelations of certain parts of the system is not thereby solved.... It will require a vast amount of additional statistical investigation as well as a deeper study of the history of every industry to be able to develop this first and feeble attempt at a general description into a complete theory of economic development."[52] He clearly believed that such a theory would revolve around industrialization. Less certain was what would be the ultimate result of the modern world's pattern of growth and retardation. Technology had limits.

During the 1930s, economists around the world used the ideas of Schumpeter, Young, Kuznets, Keynes, and others to construct the foundation of a discourse on development. Economics moved in a variety of directions, but "dynamic theory" occupied a place of great importance, tied as it was to both exciting new avenues of academic thought and practical real-world applications. Economists were confident in their work's importance. "One visualizes the dynamic theory of economics arising from the long vision of a statistician and the penetration of a theoretical analyst, framing a complete account of economic reality as it presents itself to our eye," Kuznets boasted. "It will give us a complete account of why and how economic phenomena are as they are, and what brought them to the form in which we conceive them."[53] Although many economists continued working in the more traditional microeconomic field, macroeconomics grew increasingly fashionable and increasingly influential. In search of "a complete account of why and how economic phenomena are as they are," economists dove headfirst into statistics and quantitative analysis. Convinced that "knowing" economies gave them the power to change them, they worked diligently to create "a complete theory of economic development." Such efforts began at the level of the nation state, but had international repercussions, for, as Kuznets had found in his statistics, one nation's industry's growth was another's retardation. National economies were part of a global economy.

In 1940, Colin Clark, an economist at Cambridge, made visualizing the global economy possible with his book, *The Conditions of Economic Progress*. "Very little attention has been devoted to ascertaining the causes of the tremendous differences in real income which prevail between different parts of the world," he explained. His book filled the lacuna in the literature.[54] The first ever major quantitative comparative study of international incomes, *Conditions* changed the way that people saw the world. The League of Nations and the International Labor Office had done similar investigatory work in the 1920s and 1930s, but they had focused on nutritional standards in the case of the league, and on general health, medical, and educational standards in the case of the ILO, not on income per se.[55] In contrast, Clark combined piles of statistics on wages, employment, exports, acreage, animal herds, population, savings, and investments, to name just a few, to create the most informative presentation of international incomes ever seen. Though most of his data came from wealthier (noncolonized) nations, Clark also used his general findings to say something definitive about countries whose governments did not have the funds to support large-scale recordkeeping. His examination of real incomes around the world led Clark to conclude, "more than half of the world's population must immediately be placed in the poorest category of all, with real income insufficient to provide a subsistence."[56] With those words, half of the globe suddenly became "poor," because their real income per head was less than two hundred international units, with a unit defined as the "amount of good and services which one dollar would purchase in the U.S.A. over the average of the period 1925–1934."[57] Economic expertise suddenly changed the way that people understood development. It was no longer primarily a question of race, religion, or culture; it was a question of income.

Like Adam Smith and Alfred Marshall, Clark concerned himself with the social ramifications of economic growth. "The economist," he insisted, "must discover methods which will advance, and counsel the rejection of proposals which will hinder" three specific objectives: increasing "the average national dividend," regularizing "its flow through time," and equalizing "its distribution between persons."[58] His emphasis on the economist as a political actor openly reflected the work of Arthur C. Pigou, whose 1920 book, *The Economics of Welfare*, established a definitive link between social welfare and national income. A former student of Marshall's, Pigou had replaced his mentor (at Marshall's design) in 1908 as the chair of political economy at Cambridge in honor of his interest in the social responsibilities of the new profession. "What we wish to learn," he told readers, "is not how large welfare is, or has been, but how its magnitude would be affected by the introduction of causes which it is in the power of statesmen or private persons to call into being."[59] Another important addition to the idea of "an economy," Pigou's research helped to convince fellow economists of their discipline's practical importance. "There is some purpose in discovering and in saying that the national income has increased," Clark insisted at the beginning of his 1936 work, *National Income and Outlay*, because it allows us to examine the distribution of funds throughout the nation as a whole.[60] Clark researched national income because he believed "knowing" the economy was the first step toward shaping it for the greater benefit of all. He took it to a global level, because he knew that national economies did not exist in isolation from one another. Or, at least, they could not do so if they wanted to grow.

Although *The Conditions of Economic Progress* was not published until 1940, its statistical information was already circulating in 1939, the same year that Professor Eugene Staley of the Fletcher School of Law and Diplomacy produced a report, published by the Council on Foreign Relations, on the current state of the global market, titled *World Economy in Transition* with the subheading "Technology vs. Politics, Laissez Faire vs. Planning, and Power vs. Welfare." He noted the importance of having, for the "first time," pictures of "actual levels of consumption" in countries around the globe.[61] These statistical accounts of living standards led Staley to the conclusion that "certainly human needs are not being adequately met in any country today."[62] For Staley, this observation meant that economics had failed people everywhere, because "the primary object" of a government's economic policy "should be to meet human needs and desires more effectively." All other economic policy questions, he continued, are secondary and important only insofar as they help achieve that end.[63]

Staley insisted that an international policy of welfare economics—guided by the idea that there must be transfers of people, capital, and knowledge between different areas to allow for a more even distribution of resources around the globe—offered the only possible solution to the problem of uneven consumption. Such a policy could not be undertaken without government involvement for economic change. The "enormous increase in the economic role of the state over the last few years," he observed, "has the greatest possible importance for the future of international economic relations."[64] His main point was to encourage international aid, carried out by governments for other governments. In his conclusion, he even called for the launching of a "development program designed to carry modern capital equipment and technical knowledge into parts of Asia, South America and Africa."[65] It would take a few more years, and a world war, however, before other economists began publicly lining up on the side of international development.

Paul N. Rosenstein-Rodan, a Polish-born economist who moved to Britain in 1930, was the first one. He became secretary to a committee on postwar reconstruction during World War II and met frequently with

Eastern European economists to discuss the problems facing the area.[66] These discussions led him, in the summer of 1943, to publish one of the most influential articles in the history of developmental economics. He opened, "it is generally agreed that industrialization of 'internationally depressed areas' like Eastern and South-Eastern Europe (or the Far East) is in the general interest not only of those countries, but of the world as a whole."[67] Focused primarily on finding employment for the growing number of displaced agricultural workers and, somewhat more generally, on reducing the income gap that Clark had pointed out, Rosenstein-Rodan argued for industrialization funded by international investment in these "internationally depressed areas." He emphasized the necessity of foreign involvement. If they chose the "'Russian model' (by which we do *not* mean communism), aiming at self-sufficiency, without international investment," he warned, then "that would imply the construction of all stages of industry . . . with the final result of a national economy built like a vertical industrial concern." That path would lead to industrialization, but it "can proceed only slowly" and demands internal capital "at the expense of a standard of life and consumption . . . already at a very low level." In addition, such a path would lead to "an independent unit in the world economy" where unnecessary heavy industry was sustained at great cost to all. "The alternative way of industrialization," Rosenstein-Rodan continued, "would fit Eastern and South-Eastern Europe into the world economy, which would preserve the advantages of an international division of labour, and would therefore in the end produce more wealth for everybody."[68] We cannot draw a clear line between national economies and the world economy, he insisted, and investments one place aid growth in another and so forth.

Rosenstein-Rodan's argument marked the culmination of the previous decade's efforts to establish the idea of "an economy" and to emphasize human ability to manipulate it toward growth. He firmly believed that investment for industrialization involved more than individual investors putting money into specific businesses. In the case of countries on the verge of industrialization, governments were primarily responsible, because all the external economies had to be viewed as internal and growth had to be balanced among them. The key was to see the economy as a single entity and to recognize that if many sectors expand at once, then they will be self-supporting, even if by itself no sector could break even. This argument stemmed directly from Allyn Young's 1928 address to the British Association for the Advancement of Science in which he analyzed the role of increasing returns in expanding an economy. A growing market, he had insisted, with synchronized expansion, continues to grow at a continually faster rate. "What is required is that industrial operations be seen as an interrelated whole." Essentially, investments have to be made in the economy itself, not in specific businesses, in order to stimulate major economic growth.[69] Because the inducement to invest was limited by the size of the market, it would be necessary to force investment through the use of government funds, both domestic and foreign, in the early stages of growth. "Industrialization of internationally depressed areas," Rosenstein-Rodan concluded, "may create an equilibrium, from which onwards normal private incentives may operate successfully. But it seems hopeless to rely on them before that point is reached."[70] In the meantime, however, governments in the nondepressed areas of the world should feel compelled to share money and expertise.

In his 1943 article, Rosenstein-Rodan spoke only of industrialization for raising income, not of "development," and his argument revolved around raising income levels in order to expand world trade, not to better living conditions as such. He gave welfare economics explicit attention in a 1944 article titled, "The International Development of Economically Backward Areas," which initiated a significant change in the discourse. "If we want to ensure a stable and prosperous peace," he insisted, "we have to provide for some international action to improve living conditions of those peoples who missed the industrialization 'bus' in the nineteenth century."[71] Such people, he continued, came from "five vast international depressed areas," namely, the Far East, Africa, the Caribbean area, the Middle East, and Eastern and Southeastern Europe. In expanding his argument to include those areas of the world that Clark had previously shown to suffer from "poverty," Rosenstein-Rodan did not change his focus on investment for industrialization as the key to economic growth.[72] "The movement of machinery and capital towards labour," he concluded, "instead of moving labour towards capital, is the process of industrialization, which, together with agrarian improvement, is the most important aspect of the economic development of the depressed areas."[73] As had almost every twentieth-century economist before him, Rosenstein-Rodan linked progress with industrialization—the mechanization of a society made visual in dramatic technologies of production—but he did so not because technology was good in its own sake, but because it enabled more people to work efficiently and, therefore, to create wealth that spread (however unevenly) throughout the global economy. Economic development made everyone wealthier in the long run.

Rosenstein-Rodan laid out the principle, but the idea initially lacked hard economic theoretical proof. That came in 1946 when Massachusetts Institute of Technology economist Evsey Domar revisited Roy Harrod's efforts to apply his friend Keynes's work on capital investment within a static economy to an expanding one, thereby "dynamizing" Keynes.[74] His "fundamental equation" demonstrated that "a higher propensity to save does, in fact, *warrant* a higher rate of growth" [his emphasis].[75] In order to have an expanding economy, individuals and companies must have high amounts of savings that they can use to invest in necessary capital goods. Domar expanded on this idea in the postwar period, offering the government a way of staving off another depression through preemptive, strategic investments in the economy, which would both increase productive capacity and generate income.[76] The essence of the argument was that growth will be proportional to the share of investment put back into the economy. Because the rate of growth is determined by the rate of capital formation (particularly in the creation of new machines), it only makes sense to argue that a state with insufficient capital could not experience significant economic growth. The international application, though Domar did not say it, appeared obvious: international investment of capital to overcome the "savings gap." The problem of poverty, it seemed, had been at least partially solved. It meant thinking globally about national economies.

Between Alfred Marshall's 1890 description of economics as a "science... still almost in its infancy" and Evsey Domar's 1946 argument that the government could promote growth through the strategic "movement of machinery and capital towards labor," the discipline of economics revolutionized itself and dramatically altered the way the people and governments understood the world.[77] The most important change was clearly the creation of the idea of an economy—an entity "knowable" through statistics, which could be manipulated and managed by the professional economist. Although readily shedding its old "political economy" label, economics became more overtly political in the first half of the twentieth century with great numbers of its practitioners moving easily between universities and government offices. Economists made themselves indispensable by proving that their theories and ideas had the practical effect of stimulating growth to create wealth throughout, first, the nation and, second, the world. Initially introducing the economy as a national concept, they quickly began talking about the economy of the world itself, which could ideally be manipulated in similar ways. Colin Clark's statistical introduction to the global economy emphasized its great discrepancies, confronting readers with a world sharply divided between "rich" and "poor" nations. This statistical reality encouraged the ideals of welfare economics and greater international cooperation. If everyone in a national economy profited from growth, then so too, it seemed clear, did everyone integrated into the world economy. "Poverty" became opportunity, because economic growth could be created through the proper stimulations.

As the Great Depression politicized economics on a national scale, World War II did so on a global one. In the United States, policymakers seized the idea of a single world economy, viewing control over it a necessary foundation of postwar American foreign policy.[78]

As Dean Acheson later recalled, we envisioned a "brave new world of expanding trade and employment."[79] In July 1944, while Allied troops began liberating France, members of the forty-four Allied and Associated powers met in Bretton Woods, New Hampshire, to begin planning the world's postwar recovery. The United States and Great Britain led the way, referencing their 1936 Tripartite Declaration with France to consult together on ways to expand trade and encourage growth through joint policy decisions. By the time that they arrived in New Hampshire, key figures at the conference—John Maynard Keynes, U.S. Secretary of the Treasury Henry Morgenthau, U.S. Treasury Undersecretary Harry White, and Assistant Secretary of State Dean Acheson—believed that they needed not just organized action, but an internationalized financial institution. Many of the same concerns that had led Alexander Hamilton to call for a national bank long before anyone used the noun *national economy* led the representatives at Bretton Woods to call for a world bank to be the stabilizing force of the "world economy." The bank, Keynes explained during a British Broadcasting Corporation broadcast, would pick up where the United Nations Relief and Rehabilitation Administration would leave off, providing the funds necessary to support "more permanent reconstruction and the restoration of industry and agriculture." It will also assist in "the development of the less developed areas of the world in the general interests of the standard of life, of conditions of labour, and the expanse of trade everywhere."[80] Morgenthau worked hard to ensure that the Soviet delegation agreed to cooperate, fearful of the potential ramifications of its permanent exclusion from the world economy. The conference ended with high hopes and an international agreement to create the World Bank and the International Monetary Fund.[81]

Much of the initial optimism had diminished by the time of the first World Bank meeting in Savannah, Georgia, in March 1946. The Soviets had not ratified the agreements and Allied wartime collaboration had turned into postwar tension. Keynes, the British governor of both the bank and the fund, stopped in Washington on his way to Savannah to consult with U.S.

Treasury Secretary Judge Frederick Moore Vinson. There he learned that the United States had decided to situate the headquarters not in New York, as expected, but in Washington. Vinson defended the decision by explaining that these were public institutions that would "come under the taint of 'international finance,'" if placed in New York. Keynes's response that they would certainly now be viewed "as an appanage of the American Administration" proved unmoving.[82] The Americans, he wrote in a letter to a friend, "plainly intend to force their own conceptions through regardless of the rest of us... since they are the biggest partners, they think they have the right to call the tune on practically every point." Vinson, he telegrammed the permanent secretary to the treasury, "has enough stooges, more particularly China and Mexico, with a scattering of smaller powers, such as Ethiopia, Egypt, Honduras and Guatemala who have been prominent, to feel able to act independently of the views of the rest of us."[83] The problem of running the global economy was that it was composed of so many national economies and the most powerful of them were certain to dominate. Despite the tensions, the meeting went generally well and the staff of the new organizations soon set about their work of managing postwar recovery.[84] Keynes's letters reflect a general lament for the passing of the era where Great Britain had made the most important decisions. The world had changed and Washington and Moscow, not London, were the new strategic centers of power.

While the Truman administration struggled to implement American authority on a global scale, it also had to confront postwar issues at home. In the spring of 1946, many more Americans feared depression than the USSR and demanded appropriate government action. Declaring it the federal government's responsibility to create and maintain a healthy economy, Congress passed the Employment Act of 1946. Based on policy initiatives put forward in Britain by William Beveridge, the act called for the creation of the Council of Economic Advisors to the President (or CEA) to advise the White House to make sound economic decisions and to monitor the economic activities of other federal agencies.[85] The CEA is the key to understanding economists' political influence in the postwar world, because the council, one senior official later wrote, had a "monopoly" on economists in Washington.[86]

Truman himself had not been particularly taken with the idea of an economic council of advisors, but he found it politically useful once established. He nominated Edwin G. Nourse to be chairman, with Leon H. Keyserling and John Davidson Clark to be the other two principal economists. Nourse studied economics at Cornell and Chicago and subsequently headed several economics departments in the Midwest in the opening decades of the century.

He was particularly interested in agricultural economics and had spent several years teaching on that subject in the Middle East before moving on to the Brookings Institute, then known as the Institute of Economics, in 1923.[87] A Harvard lawyer who had done graduate work in economics at Cambridge, Keyserling arrived in Washington in 1933 to join the New Deal as an aide to Senator Robert F. Wagner. He helped draft the Wagner Act of 1935, the U.S. Housing Act of 1937, and the Employment Act of 1946, which soon led to his CEA appointment. Clark came out of the University of Nebraska as a lawyer, but had spent most of his life as a businessman, becoming a millionaire as a vice president of Standard Oil of Indiana. In his forties, resting secure with his fortune, he had decided to go to Johns Hopkins and get a Ph.D. in economics. This council was supported by a staff of professional economists, including the aforementioned Walter S. Salant. A Cambridge-trained economist who had been working in Washington since the mid-1930s (and had helped Keyserling draft the Wagner Act), Salant was the youngest senior staff member at the CEA and the only international economic advisor. As the Cold War heated up, Salant's role became increasingly important as it gradually grew impossible to consider America's domestic economic security without giving due attention to the global market.[88]

Although Truman appointed Nourse as the chief economist, Keyserling and Clark ended up being much more influential. Nourse believed in controlling government spending and in not allowing policy concerns to dictate economic choices—neither of which meshed well with the administration's fears of a postwar depression and the growing Soviet "problem."[89] Keyserling and Clark stood in direct contrast to Nourse's views, with Keyserling quickly moving to become the most powerful member of the CEA, and its chair after Nourse's resignation in 1949. Keyserling defined the administration's "economic philosophy," because Truman, as Keyserling himself later purported, "was guided very considerably by our policies."[90]

Keyserling firmly grounded the administration's philosophy in the economic growth theories coming out of Harrod's and Domar's dynamic expansion of Keynesian principles. Salant later wrote that the Truman Council, under Keyserling's direction, "pioneered" the move from a cyclical model of the economy to a growth-oriented one dedicated not only to forestalling depression, but also to maintaining continual economic expansion.[91] Keyserling argued that such expansion would occur if consumption, investment, and government involvement all grew in proportion to each other, an idea that embraced the principles of Harrod's fundamental equation.[92] Salant became fascinated with growth theory during his time at Cambridge, when Keynes had been tossing around the ideas he later published in *The General Theory*. He engaged in a brief correspondence with Keynes during the early 1940s on the role of government in economic growth, and he always respected the older man's economic theories.[93]

Despite the popularity of Keynesian ideas in the CEA, Keyserling hesitated to "claim too much for it" and continued to recognize the importance of the market itself for producing growth. "I had always pointed out that the behavior of investments, profits, prices, and wages in the private economy had an even larger quantitative influence," he later explained, and "unlike many later CEA Keynesians, he insisted upon integration of needs from the public and private sectors.[94] The Americans were less willing than their European counterparts to reject Smith's writings on the "natural" sources of the wealth of nations, but they were no less dedicated to the pursuit of economic growth. "Economic stability," Keyserling wrote to Truman in 1949, "requires economic growth, and the maximum employment and production objectives of the Employment Act require an expanding economy from year to year." "We cannot stand still," he further insisted during an address in Ohio on America's economic future; "either we forge ahead or we fall behind."[95] With Keyserling at the helm, the CEA made economic growth Washington's economic philosophy.

Even though the CEA remained primarily focused on establishing and maintaining full employment within the United States, its members were well aware that national economic concerns could not be separated from global ones, and neither could national *security* concerns. "The period," Acheson wrote of 1941 to 1952, "was marked by the disappearance of world powers and empires, or their reduction to medium-sized states, and from this wreckage emerged a multiplicity of states, most of them new, all of them largely underdeveloped politically and economically. Overshadowing all loomed two dangers to all—the Soviet Union's new-found power and expansive imperialism, and the development of nuclear weapons."[96] In the immediate postwar period, American officials did not concern themselves overly much with such "underdeveloped" states, focusing instead on reconstructing Western Europe, the principle non–Western Hemisphere location of American prewar investments. With the increase of tensions with the Soviet Union, however, Washington's area of concern spread beyond its traditional borders to embrace new regions of the world. The American attitude toward the World Bank and the International Monetary Fund changed between July 1944 and March 1946 because the world had changed. Treasury Secretary Vinson lined up his "stooges," as Keynes dubbed them, because the Truman administration keenly felt the need for allies outside of London and Paris. American policymakers were concerned about a recent broadcast in Moscow.

In his February 9, 1946, speech promoting the new five-year development plan, Stalin described the war that had so devastated his nation as the "inevitable result of the development of the world economic and political forces on the basis of monopoly capitalism." He went on to talk about how the "uneven development" between capitalist countries leads to sharp distinctions in wealth and eventually divides the capitalist world into "two hostile camps." Capitalist development, Stalin maintained, is slow and cannot compete with the rapid results born of state-enforced heavy industrialization and agricultural collectivization.[97] His words, though not dissimilar to previous Soviet boasting, rang loudly in a sensitive Washington. Feeling vulnerable in their new role of world power (despite their monopoly on nuclear technology), the Americans fretted over the potential international implications of Stalin's rhetoric. The USSR refused to participate in the global economy in the way that the United States desired and boasted of the benefits of its nationalist development. Effective Soviet industrialization posed two major problems for Washington. Its strong technological/military industrial machine could produce vast amounts of weaponry. Its successful communist "development" into a major industrial nation could seduce underdeveloped countries, aligning them with the Soviet agenda. This would not only reduce American influence, it would limit the size of the global economy, thereby limiting its capacity for growth. Equally threatened by the military and economic problems of Soviet industrialization, the United States searched for ways to restrict Moscow's influence around the globe.[98]

As the Cold War divide widened, American reactions to Soviet development moved from fascination to fear, and growth theory moved from the periphery to the center of economics. In the mid-twentieth century, as had been the case two hundred years earlier, it became impossible to tell where economics ended and politics began.

3 STRATEGIC ETHIOPIA

Like Menelik before him, Haile Selassie had been born to rule a province, but made himself an emperor. *Lij* Tafari Makonnen was born in 1892 in the village of Ejersa Goro in Harar, where his father was governor.[1] His primary identity came from his noble parentage. His mother, *Woizero* Yeshimebet Ali, was the daughter of a prominent Oromo ruler in Wollo province. His father, *Ras* Makonnen Welde Michael, claimed a link to the Amhara royal line through his paternal grandmother. The child Tafari could claim to be a member of the Oromo, Amhara, and Gurage ethic groups. Although fluid, ethnic identity based primarily on language and cultural practices mattered a great deal in late nineteenth-century Ethiopia. Tafari primarily identified himself with his father's Amhara roots because it was politically expedient to do so. Makonnen shared his grandmother's heritage with his cousin, Sahle Maryam, the king of Shawa, who had declared himself Emperor Menelik II only three years before Tafari's birth. Makonnen's valiant service in the struggles leading up to the coronation won him the trust of his imperial sovereign and an important place in the bureaucracy of the new Ethiopia, which was more of an idea than a geographic reality at that point.[2]

Menelik found it convenient to portray his rule as a restoration of the natural royal line that had been disrupted by Oromo might and Tigrayan machinations—ending the exile of the legitimate heirs to the throne of a nation that had existed for over three thousand years. Many disagreed, pointing out the rather inconvenient truth that Ethiopia had always been more of a concept than a geographic or political fact. Its borders were fluid, its peoples diverse (to the point of not considering themselves "a people" at all), its historic identification with the ancient city of Axum shaky, and its claimed royal bloodline from the mating of Solomon and Sheba a blatant (though romantic) falsehood. When Menelik granted Italy territory along the Red Sea in 1889 in return for promises that his authority over the rest of "Ethiopia" would remain unmolested, he turned over Tigraya-speaking peoples who did not consider themselves linked in any political way with the new emperor. They maintained their own claims to be the heirs of Axumite civilization. Situated on the coast, these future Eritreans spoke different dialects and did not consider themselves a nation. They eventually found unity in their colonial experience and overcame their own religious divisions, but their initial discord reflected the situation in Ethiopia as a whole.

Identity was a complicated issue in Menelik's Ethiopia. But it bears noting that when the emperor faced the Italians again, at Adwa in 1896, men and women from every ethnic group stood with him and some Eritreans joined in the struggle from behind enemy lines. More than anything else, the battle galvanized the people into a nation. Menelik placed his capital city in the middle of the highlands of Shawa Province, but it also happened to be the middle of "Greater Ethiopia"—the nation as it would be once Eritrea was reclaimed from the Italians.[3]

Tafari was not quite four years old at the time of the battle that defined what he never doubted was the *nation* of Ethiopia. He identified himself as an Amhara, in part because his future depended upon the government in Addis Ababa, which spoke and wrote Amharic. With his mother dying in his infancy, Tafari grew close to his father, whose service as Menelik's foreign minister convinced him of the importance of providing his son with a modern education. His early mastery of French delighted the emperor, leading him to award the rank of *Dejazmach* and the governorship of a district in Harar. When *Ras* Makonnen died in 1906, depriving Menelik of his most influential friend and suspected heir, the emperor brought *Dejazmach* Tafari to Addis and enrolled him in the Menelik II School to continue his education in English. There, he found himself in regular competition with *Lij* Iyassu, the son of the Menelik's daughter and the Oromo ruler of Wollo Province and, as of 1908, the designated heir. Menelik's declining health gave the young men's horse races and taunting an underlying tension. Iyassu perceived his aunt Zawditu and Empress Taitu to be his main opposition, but he kept a close eye on Tafari as the latter rose in power and status. Following Menelik's death in 1913, the tensions of boyhood erupted into high stakes politics. Tafari soon found himself under house arrest in Addis Ababa, deprived of his governorship of Harar, and separated from his wife (Iyassu's niece *Woizero* Menen) and young children. Furious at his treatment, and troubled by Iyassu's flirtation with the Central Powers and disdain for the Shawan nobility, Tafari helped to lead a 1917 coup that ended with Zawditu as empress and himself regent and heir to the throne. The empress held the title, but Tafari (now *Ras*) ran the country.⁴

Although younger than the empress by twenty years, Tafari had served as governor of a number of provinces and was skilled at both domestic and international politics. Both served him well in his struggle to continue reform efforts begun under Menelik. In 1918, he announced the abolition of slavery and the regularization of weapons sales. Such changes benefitted both Ethiopia's international prestige and Addis Ababa's domestic authority. Similar motivations guided Tafari's decision to centralize the customs administration, noting that "customs constitute the main source for the prosperity of a state" and, thus, should be directed at the national, rather than regional, level. Taking advantage of the newly completed railway to Addis Ababa, Tafari encouraged landholders to switch from subsistence to commercial agriculture—primarily coffee—to raise customs revenues by increasing international trade. The change encouraged the transformation of slaves into sharecroppers, thereby freeing the government from forcing uneconomical changes on a resistant nobility, while still impressing foreign observers.⁵ Such things mattered as they were crucial to Tafari's efforts to secure Ethiopian membership in the League of Nations, which promised, he wrote the league in 1923, to allow "this Christian Government . . . to govern its people in peace and tranquility, and to develop its country under prosperous conditions."⁶ If you fear that you cannot forever beat them, then join them. He traveled to Europe, read French books voraciously, filled his electrified home with European furniture, built a hospital, made plans for an Ethiopian air force, and committed himself to modernizing his nation. "We need European progress because we are surrounded by it," a British traveler reported him as saying. "That is at once a benefit and a misfortune. It will expedite our development, but we are afraid of being swamped by it."⁷

Tafari's power grew throughout the 1920s and after a failed attempt to oust him in 1928, Zawditu was forced to crown him *negus* (king), though she retained her status as empress. Upon her death from paratyphoid fever two years later, *Ras* Tafari became Haile Selassie I, "Emperor of Ethiopia, King of Kings, Lord of Lords, Conquering Lion of the Tribe of Judah, Elect of God, Light of the World," and 225th descendant of Sheba and Solomon. The *Negusa Negast* ordered Ethiopia's first asphalt road be laid down in the capital in preparation for the ostentatious coronation attended by dignitaries from around the world. Haile Selassie's first major act was the presentation in 1931 of Ethiopia's first constitution, meant to symbolize the emperor's commitment to social, economic, and political progress. Its fifty-five articles instituted the rule of law, created the Senate and the Chamber of Deputies, and vested "supreme power" in the emperor. The document centered on the relationship between the emperor and the *masafent* (hereditary nobility) and the *makwanent* (nobility whose rank is earned by service), although it made some "provisions... to guarantee the rights and benefits of the people due to them as Ethiopians." The *gabbar* or *balanger* (peasants) gained recognition, but little else, though it is important to note that the *makwanent* had long been fluid and open to people of talent regardless of birth. Intent on centralizing authority, Haile Selassie worked to reign in the potentially dangerous nobility. The constitution enshrined his lineage, which "continues unbroken from the dynasty of Menelik I, son of King Solomon... and the Queen of Sheba." The emperor was "sacred" and "His power incontestable." The 1931 constitution seems today a strange blend of imperial pomp, feudalism, and progressive reform. To the man who titled his autobiography, *My Life and Ethiopia's Progress*, it was a logical expression of the distribution of power necessary for maintaining national unity and directing positive change.[8]

Haile Selassie desperately wanted to modernize his nation's economy and improve its international standing, and those were not easy tasks. Between 1932 and 1934, the emperor directed the building of roads, hospitals, schools, and administrative buildings. He introduced a national currency through the new Bank of Ethiopia and sent students to study abroad. He hired Belgian military officers to train soldiers and spent millions on arms and ammunitions. The last was done with a keen eye toward neighboring Eritrea, where the Italians sat watching his modernization efforts with concern. The emperor's plans, they noted, "demonstrate [that there] exists a will to lead Ethiopia through a phase of rapid evolution, to form a country different from the traditional Abyssinia." Rome was concerned about what an Ethiopia "civilized, armed, and united through the exceptional ability of the present emperor" would mean for its East African colonies.[9] Hoping to forestall Italian action, Haile Selassie had gotten Mussolini's government to sign the Treaty of Peace and Friendship in 1928 that was meant to be in effect for twenty years. It did not last ten.

In August 1934, the U.S. military attaché in Rome reported home that "the Italian Army have drawn up plans for the military conquest and occupation of Abyssinia [and] the contemplated operation will be undertaken whenever Abyssinia commits an 'overt act.'" That November, Washington recalled Resident Minister Addison Southard, who had represented America in Addis Ababa since 1928, replacing him with an interim charge d'affaires.[10] As the United States retreated, Mussolini, with the tacit acceptance of the other European powers in Africa, readied his assault. By the end of 1936, the Unconquerable Nation had been conquered. Haile Selassie asked the League of Nations to fulfill its promises of mutual defense. "It is international morality that is at stake," he told fellow member nations in an eloquent and emotional call for assistance.[11] They refused. Mexico, New Zealand, China, the Soviet Union, and the United States alone denied Italian sovereignty.[12] Even though Britain remained satisfied with the current status quo in Addis Ababa, it did open its doors to the exiled emperor in its tradition of royal sanctuary. In London, Haile Selassie strove to keep Ethiopia's misfortunes on the international radar and sent words of support to the tireless freedom fighters back home, choking on the poison gas used by the "civilized" Italians. When the Allies finally got involved in the liberation, it was not because they had a change of heart about imperialism, but because Mussolini had made unwise choices in his international friendships. In addition, they had their own plans for northeastern Africa, which they considered the western boundary of the newly reimagined "Middle East." A change in Western perspective dramatically altered Haile Selassie's probable future.

"The Second World War," E. A. Speiser told members of the American Oriental Society on April 24, 1946, "may be said to have brought about the rediscovery of the Orient by the western world." Speiser, a professor of Hebrew and Jewish Studies in the Department of Oriental Studies at the University of Pennsylvania and the society's current president, told his audience (and readers of the American Oriental Society's journal that summer) that this was due to the fact that "of the two war theatres, one engulfed in the main the Far and Middle East while the other extended to the Near East for the major part of the conflict. East and West," he concluded, "met thus along the line. Now the post-war world is finding out that the twain cannot be separated."[13] The postwar world is also finding out, Speiser continued, that the Near East "has resumed its former role as the key to world power," for it now "commands all-important air communications and boasts fabulous underground treasures—quite apart from those which beckon the archaeologist." The changing fate of the Middle East would, in turn, change the fates of Ethiopia and its emperor.

Throughout most of its history, the United States showed little interest in what is now known as the Middle East beyond appreciating its culture, or, more accurately, the Western perception of its culture. Some missionaries went abroad in the late nineteenth and early twentieth centuries, but the region was generally believed to be a territory of European—primarily British—concern, and the U.S. government, tending toward isolationism anyway, was generally content to ignore it.¹⁴ The credit for this isolationist tendency usually went to Washington and his famous Farewell Address. American conditions of the time, the great naval historian Alfred Thayer Mahan wrote in 1902, gave Washington good reason to warn against "foreign influence," but the world, and America's position within it, had changed. "As the phrase 'world politics' more and more expresses a reality of these latter days," Mahan wrote in typical convoluted fashion, "the more necessary does it become to consider each of the several [centers] of interest as not separate, but having relations to the whole; as contributory to a general balance of constitution, to the health of which it is essential to work according to nature, not contrary to it."¹⁵ The world today, Mahan insisted, is much more interconnected than in Washington's time, and although the United States still rested geographically, politically, and economically outside of much of it, such would not long be the case. "Whatever the merits of Free Trade as a system suited to these or those national circumstances," he argued, "it probably carries with it a defect of its qualities in inducing too great an antipathy towards the exertion of Governmental action in trade matters."¹⁶ Trade and government, Mahan firmly believed, were mutually dependent. It was an idea that most Europeans firmly adhered to, even if most Americans were not yet ready to live by it.

European faith in the connection between trade and government stemmed, in large part, from the legacy of imperialistic enterprises around the globe. Such enterprises had been taking Europeans eastward and southward for decades, creating what Mahan had labeled "centers of interest" around the globe. For Britain, the most important of these was India, which while blessed with resources that added to London's coffers, had the geographic misfortune, in British eyes, of residing far from Europe. Government efforts to maintain secure and steady access to Indian trade dominated British foreign policy, driving it into the region that Mahan dubbed the "Middle East," a term, he noted, that he had "not seen" before, in his 1902 article.¹⁷ The term, alas, did not become popular, despite the fact that British journalist Valentine Chirol, after properly giving Mahan credit, used it in the title of a book he published the following year. Chirol's Middle East encompassed a larger territory than Mahan's, including everything between the Persian Gulf and India.¹⁸ Although the name did not stick, both men's emphasis on the strategic value of the region in the hazy borderlands of the "Near East" (a term invented by the French in the late 1700s to refer to the Ottoman Empire) and the "Far East" (India and beyond) proved more prophetic than they could have imagined.¹⁹ A few years later visitors from abroad discovered a resource buried beneath the sands that permanently altered the area's international status.

In 1911, Winston Churchill, famous for his enthusiasm and his tenacity, became the first lord of the admiralty. Convinced that Germany was preparing to go to war with the British fleet, Churchill began looking for ways to improve Britain's chances of victory and soon found his primary weapon in oil. At the time, all of the navy's ships ran on coal, but the new internal combustion engines promised to take up less room, provide faster speed, and require less man power.[20] Churchill was hooked and persuaded the British government to order the switching of all Royal Navy ships to burn oil. Now that he had the ships, however, he had to find the oil, and his eyes naturally turned east toward the newly discovered riches in Persia. In 1914, Anglo-Persian, which had developed around the 1908 discovery of the first sustainable oil well in the region, signed a contract with the British government to supply Churchill's ships, with the caveat that the British government would hold the major share in the company, to best ensure that the promised oil was always delivered.[21] Oil was now firmly moving to a place of prominence in both global economics and global politics; it carried the Middle East along with it. Confronted with the pieces of the broken Ottoman Empire in the aftermath of World War I, France and Britain divvied up the region to maintain access to its most desired commodity. "I do not care under what system we keep the oil," British Foreign Secretary Arthur Balfour wrote to a colleague in 1918, "but I am quite clear it is all-important for us that this oil should be available."[22]

Those Americans who did venture into the region, following in the footsteps of missionaries, though with a very different purpose, were businessmen attracted by the same oil discoveries that had brought in their European counterparts. Leading the way were men from Standard Oil, whose forced breakup by the Supreme Court in 1911 and consequent stripping of domestic reserves drove the new companies abroad in search of new sources. The importance of petroleum had now permanently shifted from kerosene to gasoline, because both the navy and the growing automobile industry depended on combustion engines. As a result, the world's major oil companies—Shell, Royal Dutch, Anglo-Persian Oil Company, and all of the former Standard Oil companies—engaged in an international struggle to secure control over the increasingly valuable resource. By 1941, American companies Jersey Standard, Socony, Socal, Texaco, and Gulf were all drilling wells in the Middle East and had given almost a billion dollars in petroleum concessions in Iraq, Saudi Arabia, and Kuwait. United States oil executives, as a general rule, wielded more influence in the region than U.S. diplomats, because oil remained, for Americans, primarily an economic, not a political concern.[23] The U.S. government, although occasionally assisting its companies abroad, largely left things to the capitalists, preferring to yield to British dominance in the area, which suited Britain just fine. The outbreak of another world war, changed Washington's perception of the strategic importance of the Middle East and its oil reserves.

Popular use of the term *Middle East* arose largely as a product of World War II military efficiency. In 1932, the Royal Air Force merged its Middle East Command in Iraq with its Near East Command in Cairo to save money, and it decided to retain the former name for the new headquarters. When the war started, the army decided to follow the air force's lead and created the British General Headquarters Middle East Force in Cairo to command all of the operations, from 1940 to 1943, in northern Africa, Ethiopia, Somaliland, Egypt, Eritrea, Syria, Iraq, Iran, Greece, and the eastern Mediterranean.[24] When it became clear that the British needed to take control of the shipment of goods in and out of the region to ensure that needed military supplies got through, they created a new organization with the same name to keep things organized. The United States soon joined this Middle East Supply Centre (MESC) operation in Cairo to help funnel lend-lease supplies to the Soviets through Iran. In the midst of all the military operations and the MESC, the *Middle East* gradually became the standard term of reference for the region among the Allies.[25] The exact geographic boundaries of the newly designated region remained fluid, with countries moving in and out according to the particular interests of the moment.

By the time the Allies had won the war in North Africa, the British government had solidified its position as the leading force in the region, having retained control of the ostensibly independent Egypt and Iraq, while establishing a military presence in the "newly liberated" former Italian colonies. Peace brought new economic challenges as the British worked to strengthen their economic supremacy in an area that they recognized had become of central importance to world affairs. While Washington publicly supported London's influence in the region, tensions gradually arose between the Allies about the extent of British economic dominance in the region to the exclusion of American dollars.

Roosevelt sent out a special economic mission to the region in the fall of 1944 to get a better sense of its potential for trade relations with the United States. The mission reported back that such relations would remain unimportant unless the countries in the area began successfully developing their oil resources. For the time being, American involvement remained economically motivated, principally interested in maintaining U.S. oil and airfield interests in Saudi Arabia and working to promote free trade policies, much to the consternation of the British.²⁶ "In the Middle East, as elsewhere," Roosevelt wrote to the American director of economic operations in the Middle East, "the objective of the United States is to make certain that all nations are accorded equality of opportunity. Special privileges," he continued, undoubtedly referring to Britain, "should not be afforded to any country."²⁷ Changes on both the domestic and international fronts, however, soon revolutionized the way Washington viewed the Middle East. Growing tensions with the formerly allied Soviets and a sudden rise in domestic oil consumption forced the Truman administration to reconsider the Middle East's role in the postwar world and, consequently, Britain's role in the Middle East.

"The United States," Loy Henderson, the director of Near Eastern and African Affairs, wrote to Truman in 1945, "looks with sympathy upon the efforts of certain countries in the Near East to extricate themselves from commitments . . . to various great powers giving those powers special privileges and positions which detract from the full independence of these countries." The United States could not, he continued, stand "idly by" as it did after World War I when it allowed the British and French to carve up spheres of influence in the Near East, but should, instead, pursue a type of "open door" economic and political policy to prevent Soviet influence from making progress into the Arab states. "Moscow," he asserted, "seems determined to break down the structure which Great Britain has maintained so that Russian power and influence can sweep unimpeded across Turkey and through the Dardanelles into the Mediterranean, and across Iran and through the Persian Gulf into the Indian Ocean." It must not be allowed to do so, Henderson argued, and the best way to make sure that the Soviets did not get power was to reduce the British influence by promoting political independence and self-rule.²⁸ Haile Selassie wholeheartedly seconded the notion.

When Ethiopian Vice Minister of Finance Yilma Deressa set out for Washington, D.C., in the summer of 1943, he carried with him the weight of a nation in turmoil and the aspirations of a monarch on a hobbled throne. Italy's decision to ally with the Axis powers in 1940 turned London's former friend into an enemy and an unwanted interloper in northeastern Africa, so British troops joined the long-fighting Ethiopian resistance. The joint forces quickly overwhelmed the Italians, but when a thrilled Haile Selassie returned from exile in February 1941, British troops prohibited him for entering the capital. The question of exactly whom Ethiopia was going to be independent became a source of great debate in Addis Ababa, London, and Washington.

Having played such a vital role in reclaiming Ethiopia from the Italians, the British remained hesitant to exit and maintained military occupation through the British Military Mission to Ethiopia. Haile Selassie struggled to regain the authority he had lost in 1935 and ostensibly got it with the 1942 Anglo-Ethiopian Agreement, which recognized his nation as "a free and independent state," but all was not as it seemed. In return for a loan, the emperor was forced to grant the British minister "precedence over any other foreign representative" and to allow British advisors a dominant role in the nation's finances—there was a war on, after all. In addition, London maintained full control over Eritrea and the Ogaden (an area about one-third of the country, which Britain wanted to annex into British Somaliland). Anthony Eden announced in February 1941, "His Majesty's Government would welcome the reappearance of an independent Ethiopian State" and has "no territorial ambitions in Abyssinia," but Haile Selassie's nation sat on the borders of the Middle East and was simply too valuable to set free.[29] So, Britain allowed it semi-independence, nodding to the emperor's authority while monopolizing the country's railroads, air service, and economy. They also, although they would deny it for decades, stripped the nation of 80 percent of all of the industries built by the Italians during their long occupation of Eritrea and brief occupation of Ethiopia. British troops dismantled factories, packed up the parts, and shipped them to India and Kenya.[30]

In July 1942, Haile Selassie sent a letter to the White House, announcing Ethiopia's eagerness to contribute to the war effort. "We the first nation to regain its freedom and independence wish to place the military and economic resources of our country at the disposal of those nations who gladly sacrifice all for liberty and justice." Roosevelt responded with a promise of the "steadfast friendship" and "sympathy" of "the American people" in this time of laborious reconstruction. Haile Selassie wanted more, but he could wait.[31] Things were changing in the Middle East. Unable to continue supplying needed goods to the region, London reopened the Red Sea to American merchant ships at the end of the year and U.S. exports boomed. The following year, a U.S. official visiting Egypt observed that "Great Britain no longer possesses within herself the essentials of power needed to maintain her traditional role as the dominant influence in the Middle East area."[32] The Americans were coming; thousands arrived in Eritrea in 1942, which had been fitted as a distribution center for the war effort. Their presence altered the rules of the game.

E. Talbot Smith, the American consul to Ethiopia, sent letters to Washington protesting British behavior. "Happily the Axis propaganda experts do

FIGURE 3.1 A 1943 U.S. Office of War Information cartoon of Haile Selassie by the African American artist Charles H. Alston celebrates Ethiopia's liberation and its membership in the new United Nations. While working for the Office of War Information, Alston produced more than 100 war effort illustrations for publication in black newspapers across the county. *Still Picture Records Section, National Archives, College Park, Maryland*

not know" what is happening here, he wrote to Secretary of State Cordell Hull, "for if they did, they would be shouting it to the heavens, and could make out a fine case proving that Allied promises to rehabilitate countries the subject of aggression was pure [hypocrisy]." All they would have to say is "Look at Ethiopia and be warned! When the British got through with it, what was left?" Instead of letting the British strip Ethiopia of the industrial remnants of its colonization, Smith continued, we should use Ethiopia as an "experimental field" to help us determine "what the best form of organization will be for [the U.N. to use] in the conquered countries of Europe when they are freed." Send a committee of "agronomists, timber experts," and "agricultural experts in general" to "study first hand what the nation needs to put it on its feet."³³ His argument struck a chord in a Washington determined, at least outwardly, to maintain the principles enshrined in the Atlantic Charter. The point was to build up the free world, not to tear it down, and, if Britain was not willing to do that in Ethiopia, then the United States needed to get involved. Haile Selassie could not have agreed more.

Ethiopia's emperor wisely perceived friendship with the United States to be his nation's best hope. In a February meeting in Addis Ababa, he told representatives of the U.S. government that "there should be more effective relations" between the two peoples and said that "nothing would please him more" than a meeting with President Roosevelt. American efforts "to help backward peoples will achieve its purpose and lead to satisfactory results," the emperor insisted, so please send aid.³⁴ Haile Selassie soon petitioned Washington to reopen its legation in Addis Ababa and sent Yilma Deressa off to the United States to represent Ethiopia at the United Nations Food Conference and to secure American military and economic assistance. Yilma met with members of the State Department that June and asked for rehabilitation assistance in accordance with "the declared policy of the United Nations." In an interview with reporters, he highlighted his nation's potential value to the world market, noting that Ethiopia would be able to "offer wheat, barley and coffee to the Near East after the war, provided transportation was available." He stressed Haile Selassie's reform and modernization efforts and hinted that they could only continue if the country felt secure. He was more frank with policymakers, asking for weapons, control of the nation's transportation facilities, and economic assistance. He urged the State Department to send a technical mission to figure out how to make the most of the nation's vast resources. Then, he went to the White House.³⁵

In a July meeting with Roosevelt, Yilma handed the president an aide-mémoire full of frustration with the continued British presence and fear that London was planning to annex strategically vital sections into British East Africa. The "Ethiopian people are simply striving toward self-determination, the right of every free people, and look to America, the arsenal of democracy, for aid in the complete realization of this desire." We urgently need a loan, Yilma told Roosevelt, and added that "His Imperial Majesty will be glad to have American citizens to advise him" in affairs of state and "will welcome the cooperation of American capital and technical skills to help him develop the natural resources of his country"—resources that had the potential to make Ethiopia a key provider of "foodstuffs" to hungry Europeans in the postwar period. Roosevelt told Secretary of State Cordell Hull the next day he found Yilma's note "extremely interesting" and asked to hear more about Ethiopia. Hull confirmed the truth behind most of Yilma's complaints about the British and reported that the State Department looked favorably on extending financial aid and supporting Ethiopia's request for at least part of Eritrea in order to gain an outlet to the sea. The United States was not insensitive to the difficult situation facing the emperor back in Addis Ababa.[36]

To Haile Selassie's delight, Yilma's efforts paid off in the "Mutual Aid Agreement," where the United States promised "to supply such articles, services, and information as we may be in a position to furnish for the defense of Ethiopia, and, through other means as may be possible, to render all practical assistance in the rehabilitation of your country." Lend-lease aid eventually totaled $5,152,000, along with arms and ammunition. In addition, the United States agreed to help Ethiopia negotiate a more favorable treaty with Great Britain when the initial Anglo-Ethiopian Treaty expired the following year and began preparations for sending the requested technical mission.[37] For the emperor, it marked the beginning of a fruitful, if not always beautiful, friendship, that provided badly needed security to a man desperate not to simply regain what had been lost in 1936, but to create something better. Haile Selassie had grand plans and he needed the United States to realize them.

At 5 a.m. on February 12, 1945, a U.S. Air Force DC-13 took off from Addis Ababa carrying the emperor and his entourage to Cairo in preparation for a meeting planned with President Roosevelt the following afternoon. The group spent the evening watching recent Hollywood films, to the emperor's delight. When he boarded the U.S.S. Quincy in the Great Bitter Lack the following afternoon, Haile Selassie carried with him a four-inch globe made of 24-karat Ethiopian gold and a list of requests that included terminating British authority over Eritrea and the Ogaden, securing Ethiopian control over the Djibouti–Addis Ababa railroad, obtaining reparations from Italy, and increasing U.S. financial and military assistance. The meeting, conducted variously in French, Amharic, and English, with Yilma Deressa serving as interpreter, was described by a viewer as "an exceptionally cordial and agreeable meeting."[38] Haile Selassie's requests, which were answered over following years, represented the emperor's vision of integration, centralization, and modernization for his country. He demanded the establishment of "Greater Ethiopia," ruled by its God-appointed monarch through a tightly controlled government apparatus dedicated to improving the nation's economy and international status.[39] That was his "progress" and his obsession.

As evidenced in his conversation with Roosevelt, Haile Selassie attacked all of his goals at once, largely because he did not see how they could be separated

FIGURE 3.2 Haile Selassie and Franklin D. Roosevelt talk on the U.S.S. *Quincy* in Egypt's Bitter Lake in March 1945. In addition to requesting financial assistance, the emperor asked the president to support his efforts to make Eritrea and the Ogaden part of Ethiopia. *Franklin D. Roosevelt Presidential Library, Hyde Park, New York*

from each other. Like the American president, the emperor was an astute politician. "He is clever and tactful and is not assuming his new power by leaps and bounds," an observer had noted during the 1920s. "He tries first one apparently audacious step in administration and waits for the effect. If satisfied ... he tries something more important next time. Such is his present progress."[40] By the 1940s, reticence had given way to boldness as the emperor wisely perceived that his claims to divinity were best served by a sincere lack of humility. Desperate to ensure that British liberation did not result in either a London-based mandate or a new domestic Ethiopian government, the emperor pursued power with vicious determination masked by outward regal mystery and aloofness.

Centralization began at home with an assault on the regional powers of the nobility. The attacks took various forms. Power in Tigre Province was divided between two direct descendants of Emperor Yohannes; Haile Selassie arranged to have one marry his daughter and the other's daughter to marry his eldest son, thereby ensuring that the feuding parties would remain divided. He reorganized the provinces, redrawing boundaries to create thirteen large provinces (Eritrea would later make fourteen). Shawa and Wollo, which was made a fief of the crown prince, emerged larger than before and Tigre smaller, giving geographic evidence of the movement of power southward into the highlands. A 1941 decree announced that provincial officials were to be salaried and would no longer reap their rewards in the right of collecting tribute from peasants under their control. Forbidden to collect taxes, their authority diminished to that of judicial and police control over their people.[41] Thus, the provincial nobility found themselves tied more firmly than ever before to the emperor and his ministers, most of whom were not of noble birth and owed all of their loyalty to the man who had brought them into power.

In addition, Haile Selassie accelerated the process of government land grants begun by Menelik, awarding vast swaths of property to political favorites. Almost all such property was in the south—land conquered by Menelik's forces and given away to northern soldiers and ministers in lieu of salary. The process expanded Amhara wealth and authority, promoted commercial agriculture, raised the state's tax base, and increased the spread of tenancy where there had once been communal farming. The new private property marked an important shift from traditional northern land practices that had passed on rights *to* property instead of the property itself. Even though adopting the Western understanding of private property was celebrated as progress, it actually served to make Ethiopia more "feudal-like" by expanding the divide between the propertied and the propertiless.[42] Farmers who used to eke out an independent subsistence on shared lands found themselves tenants on giant estates where they had to grow both the (often absentee) landlord's coffee and their own food. Haile Selassie's efforts to rein in his northern nobles helped to impoverish his southern peasantry who saw their own opportunities diminished by the state's promotion of commercial, modern agriculture.[43]

The emperor pursued integration concomitantly with centralization, understanding them to be two sides of the same coin: his own power. "The statement made by Theodore Roosevelt that Ethiopia is an Empire and must remain so is not forgotten by President Roosevelt," he had insisted in a 1943 conversation.[44] In a world of slowly crumbling empires, Haile Selassie was determined to build a stronger one, and he needed help to do it. He centered his vision on Eritrea. Ethiopia's claim, he explained in a memorandum to Roosevelt, was not "based solely upon the ground of necessity for economic reasons or for the equally pressing and vital need for access to the sea," but on history and tradition. "Eritrea and its inhabitants have been an integral part of Ethiopia" since before recorded time, he insisted, and cession recognizes "the existing historical, racial, cultural, economic and geographic ties which bind Eritrea integrally to Ethiopia and redress in part the injustices visited upon Ethiopia by the Fascist regime."[45] He also reaffirmed his intention of reclaiming control over the Ogaden back from the British who wanted to annex it, along with Italian Somaliland, into British Somaliland. Haile Selassie knew the correct buttons to push. Franklin Roosevelt viewed European imperialism as a threat to the international prestige of the Allied powers and was not inclined to add to Britain's power by giving it new African territories, but little could be decided before the war was over.

The question of what to do with the former Italian possessions in Africa (including Libya, Eritrea, and Italian Somaliland) went to the council at the 1945 London Conference and continued, with much debate between the Four Powers, into the Paris Peace Conference in the summer and fall of 1946. All generally agreed that Italy would be forced to renounce its titles, but remained divided as to what should then be done with them.[46] At the 1947 Pentagon Talks, British delegates offered a comprise: "Eritrea should be ceded in full sovereignty to Ethiopia, except for the area in the northwestern part of Eritrea inhabited by Moslem-Sudanese, which should be incorporated into the Anglo-Egyptian Sudan."[47] American policymakers remained uncommitted, but certain that whatever its boundaries, Ethiopia needed to be strong and stable. Its "geographical location vis-à-vis Aden, the strategically important Red Sea area and contiguous British territories," State Department employees wrote of Ethiopia, ensure that "it is in the interest of both the British and American Governments that the Government of Ethiopia should be sufficiently strong to enable it to maintain internal law and order." The two countries should also, they continued, "be prepared to render all appropriate assistance to the Emperor in his efforts to centralize the administration of the country [referring to his desire to annex Eritrea] and to institute programs of reform and development which would have the effect of increasing the prestige and authority of the Crown."[48] The Sinclair Oil Company, the State Department noted, has a "concession for the development of Ethiopia's oil resources," which gave further weight to the argument of the nation's importance to the West, particularly because of the "problem presented by Russian penetration in Ethiopia," which, though "not currently serious," still merited "continued attention."[49]

For Britain and the United States, the question of Ethiopia's future represented one small part of the larger question of the future of the Middle East as a whole. The previous spring, Britain's request for U.S. assistance with

Greece and Turkey had resulted in the Truman Doctrine, and the White House and the Pentagon had been busy ever since trying to figure out the most appropriate policy regarding neighboring countries potentially facing the same dangers. March 12, 1947, when Truman gave his famous speech, was a transformative moment, its importance was unappreciated only by a Britain still stubbornly proclaiming its power. The Truman Doctrine marked a turning point in Middle Eastern history, because it meant that the defense of the area against Russia was now a shared task.[50] The new dimensions of power became clear in October of that year at the Pentagon talks, when the State Department invited key British policymakers to Washington for a top secret planning meeting to formulate a general policy for maintaining Western influence in the Middle East.

In preparation for the talks, the State Department produced a long memorandum elucidating both sides' general positions. Traditional British policy in the region, the memo read, "has centered around the hard core of Empire defense, with emphasis upon communications. Subsequently, oil became an additional and related vital interest. Commercial advantage was not overlooked, but defense was the prime factor in basic policy decisions." British policy changed during World War II with the establishment of the MESC, which started dealing with the region as an entirety instead of on a country-by-country level and which substituted economic cooperation for the older policy of forced coercion. Whitehall had even begun offering the use of their technicians to encourage local development and promote goodwill between the British and the local states, many of which Colin Clark had labeled "poor" in *The Conditions of Economic Progress*.[51] This assistance refined work that London had begun undertaking in their official colonies in 1940, with the passage of the Colonial Development and Welfare Act. This interest in technical development in the colonies sprang from a combination of guilt and a growing awareness of the need to develop agricultural resources, for both export and domestic consumption, in the shadow of war.[52] It also seemed useful to make better provisions for the economic status of its colonial dependents to help ensure that they would not collude with the enemy against their imperial governments. In the postwar climate, Whitehall continued to value economic aid as a means of suppressing the rise of anti-British nationalism and, correspondingly, the rise of pro-Soviet feelings.[53]

Washington shared Britain's concern, a point made clear in the State Department's opening summary of the U.S. position for the Pentagon Talks. In contrast to the past, "we now take full cognizance of the tremendous value of this area as a highway by sea, land and air between the East and the West; of its possession of great mineral wealth; of its potentially rich agricultural resources." Apprehensions about rising nationalism led the Americans to share the British interest in economic development as a tool to secure loyalty to the West, thereby stymieing the "clearly demonstrated Soviet expansionist aspirations in the Middle East." In the end, the memo concluded, it was in America's advantage to give Great Britain primary responsibility for the area with promises to aid them in their work of securing allegiances through economic development via the assistance of Western technical advisors.[54]

Accompanying the first State Department memo came another, entitled "Specific Current Questions," dealing with military, political, and "politico-economic" issues in each of the "Middle Eastern" countries/regions, which here included Egypt, Cyrenaica, Transjordan, Kuwait, Iraq, Palestine, Cyprus, Syria, Saudi Arabia, Iran, Turkey, Greece, Ethiopia, Eritrea, Libya, Italian and British Somaliland, Afghanistan, French North Africa, and the Arabian Peninsula States of Bahrain, Yemen, and Qatar. In the breakdown of subjects and countries, State Department writers addressed a number of issues not limited to the British presence, internal political struggles, military bases, economic development, petroleum, the "Palestine problem," and the "Communist problem."[55] Acknowledging that the "major American economic interest in the Middle East relates to the development and exploitation of petroleum resources," the memo reflected U.S. policymakers' primary concerns of maintaining regional stability and securing Western influence. The report listed the "major petroleum developments" as being in Iran, Saudi Arabia, Iraq, and the other Arab States in the Peninsula, but also made a point of noting that active exploration had begun in "other Middle Eastern areas, including Egypt, Palestine and Ethiopia, and to a moderate extent in Libya, Turkey and Afghanistan."[56] Many of these same countries also housed military bases left over from the war, which were suddenly vital again in the fight against a new enemy.

During the war, the Allies had relied extensively on a series of military supply centers, air fields, and radio bases throughout the Middle East to enable them to defeat the German and Italian forces. In the face of peace, military leaders remained reluctant to let such strategic facilities go and political leaders tended to agree with them that the wisest course would be to ensure continued access, if not continued control. By the fall of 1947, a large number of British troops remained stationed in Egypt, securing access to the Suez Canal and using their base there as the main supply center for activities in Greece and Turkey. The British were also in the process of establishing new bases in Transjordan and Kuwait. American military interests centered not only on military installations surrounding the Dhahran airfield in Saudi Arabia, but also on the U.S. Air Force facility at Wheelus Field near Tripoli and a radio communication base in Asmara, Eritrea, that they had inherited from retreating Italians. Although viewed as a lucky "find" during the war, the importance of the Asmara base grew exponentially in the postwar period as the American military recognized the strategic importance of its surveillance capabilities. Blessed by an ideal location, it would prove one of the most important monitoring stations in the world. The United States and Great Britain also maintained a military presence in those countries where they did not have permanent bases—training local military forces in Iran, Turkey, and Greece as well as in Ethiopia and Saudi Arabia, and selling them arms and munitions.[57]

In each of these countries, with their oil and their military bases, it seemed clear that the United States and Great Britain needed to do all that they could to ensure the presence of stable governments favorable to the West. Both governments agreed that the best way to do so was to encourage economic development. "A general increase in the economic prosperity of the peoples of the Middle East, as broadly distributed as possible through the masses of the population, is most desirable, if not essential," State Department policymakers concluded. "It is needed as a basis for internal stability and security of the area, and to reduce the danger of revolutionary developments and communist penetration."[58] Such an increase in economic prosperity could result from an expansion of present British technical advisory programs, but London was still worried about feeding its own people and did not have funds to spare. As the United States had no legislation enabling it to supply technical and economic aid in the region (with the exception of Greece and Turkey), as it could in the "American Republics" under the Interdepartmental Committee on Scientific and Cultural Cooperation, it seemed that little would come of that line of thinking. It appeared more practical to examine other ways of promoting economic development in the region, including fixing the "Dollar–Sterling Problem," increasing the flow of international private capital by stabilizing local governments, and encouraging outside petroleum exploration.[59] Such efforts would, U.S. officials believed, promote American economic interests in the region as well as strengthen the Middle East against communist penetration. Allowing for some minor adjustments for America's economic advantage, continuing established British policy appeared to U.S. policymakers to be the best path for their initial inroad into the Middle East. They soon changed their minds.[60]

In the summer of 1949, Gordon P. Merriam of the Policy Planning Staff in the State Department noted in an official memo that while "the primary security interests of the United States outside of the Western Hemisphere lie in the North Atlantic area... nevertheless, the political and territorial integrity of the Middle East area as a whole... are of such importance to U.S. security as to justify strenuous efforts in the political field," and, as circumstances permit, "non-provocative" efforts "in the economic and military fields."[61] He deemed the region's integrity important not only because of oil, but also for access to important military facilities in Dhahran, Tripolitania, Cyrenaica, and Eritrea, with the "long-term" availability of facilities in the latter three dependent upon the "ultimate disposition" of those territories. He noted that U.S. action in the region also needed to assist the British in safeguarding their own facilities in Egypt and Iraq, because such bases could "probably be used by the U.S." in the event of "serious trouble with the U.S.S.R."[62]

Merriam's memo shows the evolution of U.S. policy toward the region, partially shifting from relying on the British to handle all the countries (as seen in 1947 and 1948), to a recognition that the United States needed to make "strenuous efforts" in the political, economic, and military fields. The previous year, as Merriam noted in his memo, the new National Security Council had insisted, "the security of the Eastern Mediterranean and of the Middle East is vital to the security of the United States," and Soviet encroachment must be prevented at all costs.[63] The Joint Chiefs of Staff took up the issue in 1948 and set forth five primary strategic requirements for U.S. security interests in the region: denying any "potentially hostile power" any "foothold" in the area; maintaining "friendly relationships" through social, economic, and limited military assistance to "ensure collaboration by the indigenous peoples in the common defense"; developing oil resources by the United States and "such other countries as have and can be expected to have a friendly attitude towards the United States"; ensuring access of the U.S. military to enter "militarily essential areas upon threat of war," and, correspondingly, ensuring "the right to develop and maintain" facilities required to implement the former.[64] By 1949, U.S. policymakers believed that they needed to adopt a much stronger role in the Middle East. The later events of that year, including the Soviet test of the atomic bomb and China's "fall" to communism, further solidified such conviction.

Washington no longer faced the question of the Middle East along the lines of what it could do to support the British goals in the region, but along the lines of what it must itself do to prevent the Middle East, with all of its oil and facilities, from falling to the Soviets. The danger, Merriam noted, could come from outside or inside the region, and demanded U.S. action to confront the possibility on both fronts. "So long as a precarious security situation exists, or is felt to exist by the countries in the area, economic and social progress will be slow and uncertain and they will be promising subjects for revolution and for communist domination from within," he wrote.[65]

The Middle East needed to be defended from Soviet incursion both on the edges of its borders and in the middle of its cities. Various options were considered. In his memo, Merriam asked the question of whether or not Middle Eastern countries should be eligible to join the newly established North Atlantic Treaty Organization as a means of securing their allegiance through military cooperation. The idea never became reality. Washington policymakers remained unsold on the idea, particularly because they already had a new, nonmilitary policy idea in play to combat communism's temptations in exactly the sort of situations facing Middle Eastern countries. America's future involvement in the Middle East, they decided, would use "economic warfare," fighting the Soviets off from within the countries themselves through foreign aid for development.[66]

Seven thousand miles away, in a marble palace eight-thousand feet above sea level, a diminutive man in a military uniform watched the shift in power with delight. The year 1948 had been intense for him. In March, he had received notice from Prime Minister Clement Atlee that British troops would begin withdrawing from "the Ethiopian territories now under British Military Administration," meaning the Ogaden. The Sinclair Oil Company resumed explorations in the area that had recently been halted in response to militant protests by the Somali Youth League. The Somali Youth League moved on, knowing that Addis Ababa was not going to passively tolerate its agitations for "Greater Somaliland" from within "Greater Ethiopia."[67] Unable to resolve the Eritrean question, the Four Powers passed it on to the United Nations and a five-man commission with representatives from Norway, Pakistan, Burma, Guatemala, and South Africa was now investigating the wishes of the Eritrean people.[68] He worried about what they would find. That summer, he circumvented U.S. and U.K. refusals to sell him desperately needed weapons by reaching an agreement with Czechoslovakia.[69] This had the benefit of not only getting him arms and ammunition, but also Washington's attention. He had informed the United States in January that he would be asking for a loan of $130,088,870 to carry out "projects necessary to the rehabilitation and the economic development of Ethiopia." They had countered with a loan of five million.[70] He was confident his new arrangement with Czechoslovakia would alter the stakes of the political game, but by how much he did not yet know. He could afford to wait. The Lord had restored his throne for a reason. Ethiopia was on its way up.

4 TRUMAN'S FOURTH POINT

On June 24, 1949, Harry S. Truman sent a special message to Congress recommending "the enactment of legislation to authorize an expanded program of technical assistance" and "an experimental program for encouraging the outflow of private investment" to enable the United States to "assist the peoples of economically under-developed areas to raise their standards of living." The "grinding poverty and the lack of economic opportunity for many millions of people in the economically under-developed parts of Africa, the Near and Far East, and certain regions of Central and South America, constitute one of the greatest challenges of the world today," the message read, because the peoples in these areas have seen what we have, know what we can do, and want it for themselves. This is not a threat, the president continued, but an opportunity. "For the United States the great awakening of these peoples holds tremendous promise. It is not only a promise that new and stronger nations will be associated with us in the cause of human freedom, it is also a promise of new economic strength and growth for ourselves."[1]

This confidence in the utility of other peoples' desires had intellectual roots that stretched from early twentieth-century economics back to its eighteenth-century predecessor. If, as growth theorists insisted, the world economy grew stronger as all integrated national economies grew stronger, then promoting development abroad was a long-term investment in the U.S. economy. "Assistance in the development of the economically under-developed areas has become one of the major elements of our foreign policy," Truman's message continued, because studies have shown that we trade more with developed than with underdeveloped nations and that the latter are not producing at their full capacity, thereby wasting man power and resources. "As the economies of the under-developed areas expand, they will provide needed products for Europe and will offer a better market for European goods," which will assist in Europe's recovery.[2] Such confidence in the benefits of trade predated the modern sense of "an economy." Hume had argued in a 1752 collection of essays, "the "encrease of riches and commerce in any one nation, instead of hurting, commonly promotes the riches and commerce of its neighbors," because "the Author of the world" gave every nation different "soils" and "climates" in order to produce different commodities. As people's wants knew no boundaries, it was foolish to try to limit their consumption only to commodities produced at home and wise to encourage a healthy trade relationship with one's neighbors. As a "British subject," he concluded, "I pray for the flourishing commerce of Germany, Spain, Italy, and even France itself."[3] Truman prayed for the same, but his circle of desired trading partners was a great deal larger than Hume's.

Two hundred years of development had broadened the scope of international trade and had moved its locus from Britain to the United States. A few years of rising tensions with the Soviet Union had altered the stakes of that trade's success. Our recovery programs in Europe, Truman warned, will not succeed if the world economy is limited to a few nations, which will leave those citizens open to the nefarious influence of local communist parties. The danger was starker in the world's poorest nations: "They may turn to false doctrines which hold that the way of progress lies through tyranny," instead of freedom, and that, we cannot allow. "Under Article 56 of the [United Nations] Charter, we have promised to take separate action and to act jointly with other nations 'to promote higher standards of living, full employment, and conditions of economic and social progress and development.'" Let us fulfill the underdeveloped world's wants and ease its burdens and thereby pave the way to a truly global economy, immune to the temptations of communism. Let us transform Point Four from a promise into a program.[4] It was a radical foreign policy tactic by an unradical man. He embraced it because, once considered, it seemed only common sense.

A humble man of humble beginnings, Harry Truman was born in Missouri in 1884. A bright boy, he read "everything I could get my hands on—histories and encyclopedias and everything else." A cousin later recalled, "I don't know anybody in the world that ever read as much or as constantly as he did. He was what you call a 'book worm.'" That same cousin also observed that Truman was at heart a nineteenth-century man.[5] When he unexpectedly found himself president in April 1945, he set about the job with the same determined practicality he had demonstrated his entire life. He relied on his knowledge of American history for guidance, insisting that if there ever was "a clean break from all that had gone before, the result would be chaos." He never embraced progress for the sake of progress, but insisted on a reason for change. "I don't want experiments," he announced. "The American people have been through a lot of experiments and they want a rest from experiments."[6] When his staff had good ideas, however, he listened—unlike his predecessor, who had encouraged infighting and confided in no one. "I may not have much in the way of brains," Truman told one cabinet member in 1945, "but I do have enough brains to get hold of people who are able and give them a chance to carry out responsibility."[7]

He knew that he was making history and he wanted to make sure that the decisions coming out of the White House were based on a solid knowledge of the past, the latest information about the present, and a sense of responsibility to the future. He loved Point Four because it demonstrated all three. He saw it as part of a long tradition of American humanitarianism—an urge to share the experiment with others. It responded to specific needs—demonstrable by statistics and by images of malnourished, naked children.[8] It promised to help the United States by helping others. It offered a Cold War weapon that was not a weapon and promised peace through peaceful means. It announced that the (white) West had done "progress" correctly and was now going to share the hitherto secret formula with those (nonwhite peoples) who had not "progressed" at all. Leaving out the paternalism would perhaps have been too much of a "clean break" from America's past. Harry Truman was a compassionate man, but he was a nineteenth-century man.

Most American Cold War policies started in the center and then moved into the periphery; Point Four was no different. Fighting hunger in the underdeveloped world began in the fight against hunger in Europe. World War II weakened Europe in every way, but strengthened the United States. Most of the housing in major cities across Europe was destroyed. Bridges were gone; railroad lines torn up; and fields ripped open by bombs and trenches. "Nations," Truman later wrote, "had to be raised from the wreckage."[9] On February 1, 1946, a few days before Stalin gave his infamous speech, the departments of agriculture, commerce, and state produced a joint statement warning, "For the world as a whole, the next six months will bring a food crisis which may well be the worst in modern times." There is simply not enough food available and not sufficient means of transporting what exists, they admitted, so "more people seem likely to die from starvation or the effects of lack of adequate food in the first year of liberation than in any war year and possibly all war years combined," unless "heroic measures are taken by countries with relatively favorable food supply situations, particularly the United States."[10] Fearful of the outcome of the rapidly deteriorating situation, Truman instructed the American people to grow more, eat less, and allow the government to send the surplus abroad. He called Herbert Hoover to the White House—the former president's first time back since 1932—and asked him to work with the new United Nations Relief and Rehabilitation Administration to conduct a survey on the world food situation. Hoover reported back that spring after a 35,000 mile trip across Europe, the Middle East, and Asia with the grim news that "Famine, Pestilence, and Death are still charging over the earth" and "hunger hangs over the homes of more than 800,000,000 people." We must act and act quickly, he warned. By July, Truman was able to announce that the United States had exported more than six million tons of grain that was subsequently given out around the world. A desperate British government asked for additional funds to replace money that ended with ending of lend-lease. Truman sent $3.75 billion.[11]

Despite American generosity, conditions in Europe continued to decline, leading up to the horrific winter of 1946/47, which was the coldest in living memory. Snow piled up across Europe (falling even in St. Tropez), shutting down those factories and trains that had managed to survive the war and escalating an already desperate situation. "We have dedicated ourselves to the task of securing a just and lasting peace," Truman announced in a radio address that October. "We cannot turn aside from that goal." The countries of Western Europe, he continued, must be maintained as "free self-supporting democracies" and "they cannot do it if thousands of their people starve." Our "friendly aid" will mean "the difference between success and failure." There is no other option. "If the peace should be lost because Americans failed to share their food with hungry people there would be no more tragic example in all history of a peace needlessly lost." Mrs. Truman has directed the White House kitchen not to serve meat on Tuesdays, or use poultry or eggs on Thursdays, he announced, and everyone in America should do the same to show our commitment to small sacrifices at home in order to help our friends.[12] There was an undercurrent of fear. "There is no choice between becoming a Communist on 1,500 calories a day and a believer in democracy on 1,000," U.S. military commander Lucius Clay reported from Germany.[13]

The European food crisis went hand-in-hand with the production crisis. Between 1938 and 1947, the U.S. share of world trade rose from one-seventh to one-third, while Europe's share dropped from one-half to one-third. The Western European nations suffered a five billion dollar trade deficit with the United States in 1947 alone as they imported desperately needed items they could not afford. The collapse of Britain's financial system and Germany's industry had left European nations barely able to trade with each other, let alone with anywhere else. Hungry to protect what little they had, they began entering into bilateral trade and payment agreements that directly contradicted the spirit of what the Allies had tried to create at Bretton Woods.[14] Washington was sympathetic, but unwilling to allow concern for national economies to trump the creation of strong, stable world economy. Meanwhile, the Truman administration watched the rising influence of communist parties in Paris and Rome with increasing alarm—not to mention the fighting in Greece and the Soviet troops along the border of Turkey. "Peace" in Europe was proving almost as tricky as war had been.

Maintaining a strong military presence in Europe was something Truman neither wanted nor could have done. "No people in history," he wrote of his countrymen in his memoirs, "have been known to disengage themselves so quickly from the ways of war."[15] The only weapons available to him in the immediate postwar years were economic ones and he wielded them fiercely, determined to make the European nations work together and work with the United States. In April 1947, Secretary of State General George C. Marshall returned from a meeting of foreign ministers in Moscow convinced that the Soviets were determined to use the crisis in Europe to further the spread of communism. His report, Truman later remembered, "confirmed my conviction that there was no more time to lose in finding a method for the revival of Europe." The month before, he had announced the Truman Doctrine of aid to counter the emergency situations in Greece and Turkey; now, it was time to take that same approach toward all of Europe. The Truman administration focused on two separate, but intimately connected issues: trade and recovery. Both met fierce resistance from a Congress weary of spending and leery of international commitments.[16]

Exasperated by a protectionist Congress that seemed as determined as their counterparts in Europe to stymie his hope for a unified world economy, Truman managed to push through the General Agreement on Tariffs and Trade, which provided a starting point for negotiating the gradual lowering of barriers to trade with participating countries. This had the unfortunate immediate effect of actually increasing the balance-of-payments problem as the lowered European barriers encouraged a larger inflow of American products. Current levels of American aid could not bridge the gap, and the World Bank did not possess anywhere near the funds deemed necessary by State Department economists. Under Secretary of State Dean Acheson addressed the recovery side of the situation in a May 8th speech that emphasized the intimate relationship between food and freedom and warned that the United States would actually have to increase its aid to Europe, instead of backing off as Congress hoped. Marshall elaborated on the point in his now famous commencement address at Harvard that June. We must do more, he told the audience of Harvard graduates. Our "purpose should be the revival of a working economy in the world so as to permit the emergence of political and social conditions in which free institutions can exist. Such assistance must not be on a piecemeal bases as various crisis develop," he continued, but must be organized into a single program funded by the United States, but directed by Europe.

The Truman administration remained emphatic about the last point, committed to the idea that the recovery of the world economics demanded the creation of an identifiable European economy. "The response to Marshall's speech was immediate," Truman recalled in his memoirs, "electrifying the free world." Representatives of the United States and the Organization for European Economic Cooperation worked together throughout the summer and fall to come up with a plan for the recovery of what was referred to as "the European economy." Truman presented it to Congress in a December 1947 message. Congress responded three months later with the passage of the European Recovery Act, popularly known as the Marshall Plan. There had been initial hope that the Soviet Union would get involved, opening the door to the creation of a true "world economy," but Stalin would not allow the Marshall Plan to pass through the iron curtain. The Cold War got a little colder.[17]

"Like the Marshall Plan," Truman wrote in his memoirs, "the Greek-Turkish program accomplished its purpose magnificently. But—like the Marshall Plan—it was an emergency aid program only," whose life was determined by the specific Congressional appropriation. "These two programs, however, gave notice to the world of America's purpose to lead the free nations in building the strength to preserve their freedoms. They hinted at a new concept which was to be enunciated two years later," he continued, "the idea of a continuing and self-perpetuating program of technical assistance to the underdeveloped nations of the world which would enable them to help themselves to become growing, strong allies of freedom."[18] The Marshall Plan and the aid flowing from the Truman Doctrine were based on the idea of the distribution of emergency funds to "recover" nations from the devastations and upheavals of the war. In contrast, the Truman administration based Point Four on the concept of long-term aid to "develop" nations who had never been industrialized or connected to the global economy in a meaningful way. When asked by reporters for background on the fourth point of his 1949 inaugural address, Truman responded that it "has been in my mind and in the minds of the government, for the past two or three years, ever since the Marshall Plan was inaugurated. . . . Been studying it ever since."[19] He had certainly at least been considering it, thinking about the additional ways that economic weapons could wage political war. He explicitly looked to America's past for answers to the world's future.

"I knew from my study of American history," Truman later wrote, "that this country was developed by the investment of foreign capital by the British, the Dutch, the Germans, and the French," in American railroads, industry, mines, and more. If it worked here, he intoned, then it should work everywhere else. Truman believed that the key was to develop underdeveloped nations through public loans to the level where they became attractive to private investors, at which point the market could largely take over to push them further down the path of progress.[20] Along the way, such nations would naturally become more democratic. The idea made sense to him, because it reflected his reading of nineteenth-century American history and his understanding of twentieth-century economics.

In Charles and Mary Beard's 1930 classic book, *The Rise of American Civilization*, the famous historians noted, "It is one of the significant phases of history that the development of political democracy during three revolutionary centuries was accompanied by the rise and growth of science and invention. Students," they admitted, "have been baffled in their efforts to establish causal relations. . . . Yet the fact remains that political democracy and natural science rose and flourished together." The Beards offered no explanation for why science and technology prospered best in those nations with the "freest" political systems, but they observed that a flourishing scientific community "pointed the way to progressive democracy in its warfare against starvation, poverty, disease and ignorance." We do not know "why Rousseau was working on his Social Contract at the very time that Watt was bringing the steam engine to an operating basis," they admitted, but we know that that steam engine's technological descendants helped to inspire "the practical methods by which democracy could raise the standard of living for the great masses of the people."[21] Democracy and modern technology arrived around the same time and had ever since assisted each other along the path of progress. Science and freedom seemed to be mutually reinforcing, opening the door to new questions about the old debate on the origins of progress.

The search to understand American development was taken up with renewed energy in the 1940s, in a discourse that hearkened back to the Scottish Enlightenment. Even though the Beards proved unable to explain the connection between technology and political philosophy that had given birth to the modern world, they knew it had to exist. It was now widely believed in the United States that the American experiment had been successful precisely because it had benefited from the eighteenth century's burst of ideas about government and science and history. American advancement had stemmed not from the identity of its citizens, but from their notions of the value of freedom, education, creativity, and, above all, progress. They trained themselves to want the things most essential to success in the modern world and made their nation the wealthiest and most powerful in the world in the process. In this version of the story, the American people were the most obvious connection between technology and democracy.

The historian Louis M. Hacker concluded his 1947 account of the "unique" American experience, *The Shaping of the American Tradition*, with a selection from former Republican presidential candidate Wendell Willkie's 1943 account of his trip around the war-plagued world. Wilkie emphasized that the great truth of the "American Tradition" was nationalism founded on loyalty to an idea, which transcended everything else. "Our nation is composed of no one race, faith, or cultural heritage. It is a grouping of some thirty peoples possessing varying religious concepts, philosophies, and historical backgrounds. They are linked together by their confidence in our democratic institutions." Democracy knows no natural bounds, he insisted, so there is no reason to think that other nations will not be able to share our faith in political freedom. They could also benefit from the central lesson of our economic successes. "Many reasons may be assigned for the amazing economic development of the United States," Wilkie acknowledged. "The abundance of our natural resources, the freedom of our political institutions, and the character of our population have all undoubtedly contributed. But, in my judgment the greatest factor has been . . . there was created here . . . the largest area in the world in which there were no barriers to the exchange of goods and ideas." Hacker ended his edited collection of American history with Wilkie's voice emphasizing the universality of those principles he believed central to its successful development. Democracy and free trade were open to all and presumably desired by all, and it was time for Americans to help them get them. "Other peoples . . . are waiting . . . for us to accept the most challenging opportunity of all history," Wilkie concluded, "the charge to help create a new society in which men and women the world around can live and grow invigorated by independence and freedom."[22] The starting point appeared obvious: share American success by sharing the American attitude and the American political and economic system.

Even though various members of the administration contemplated the idea of expanding foreign aid from the center to the periphery, the impetus for turning ponderings into policy came from the determination of one man: Benjamin Hardy, an ex-newspaperman from Georgia working in the State Department. He began thinking about development while working in Brazil as a press officer for Nelson Rockefeller, the coordinator of the Office of Inter-American Affairs during the mid-1940s.[23] His experiences stuck with him, and when he returned to Washington to work as a speech writer on foreign affairs issues, he decided to pursue his vision of a global technical assistance program. Hardy presented his idea to his superiors in the State Department in November 1948, but they did not greet it with enthusiasm, on the premise that Congress would never agree to the cost. He subsequently reworked his proposal, making it more anticommunist by stressing the point that the government needed to do something "on the positive side to eliminate the social and economic conditions on which Communism thrives."[24] Bypassing continued State Department dismissal of the idea, Hardy took it straight to White House, arranging a meeting with Truman's aide George Elsey, who then took it to Clark Clifford. Both agreed that Truman should see it. Having recently won an unexpected victory over Dewey in the November elections, Truman and his devoted staff wanted to find a concept that would make his upcoming inaugural address "unique and outstanding." Hardy's idea of technological assistance, which meshed well with loosely structured plans already floating around the White House, seemed perfect.[25]

Meanwhile, that December, Walter Salant, in his role as the international expert at the Council of Economic Advisors, continued worrying about the balance-of-trade issues. Over lunch one afternoon with White House aide David Lloyd, Salant observed that the Marshall Plan was going to end before European countries had built up their economies enough to be able to pay for U.S. imports. The best way to fix the problem, Salant casually informed his friend, would be to extend capital to the underdeveloped world, thereby increasing poorer economies to the point that they could begin purchasing goods from Europe. Aid would naturally create trade, he concluded. Lloyd, thinking of Hardy's memo about technical assistance, shocked Salant by being urgently interested in the idea, asking him if he could prepare a memo on the subject that afternoon. Lloyd promptly shared Salant's trade concepts with Clifford, who decided that the two ideas of technical assistance and capital export should be combined into one general vision of foreign assistance that Truman could present to the public in his inaugural address.[26] Truman liked the notion immediately because it gave substance to ideas he had been considering the past few years, his daughter Margaret recalled, but was initially indecisive about including it in his address due to a desire to stick to domestic issues. Elsey convinced him otherwise, urging him to view the inaugural as an address to the world. As an added bonus, Margaret noted, the White House "took special pleasure in finding so much genuine merit in an idea that the striped pants boys [the State Department] had pooh-poohed."[27] The originally domestic-oriented inaugural address became almost entirely international. It announced a new vision of foreign policy to the world, and the world listened.

January 20, 1949, proved to be a glorious day in Washington: The weather was exemplary for winter—chilly, but not a cloud in the sky—and the inaugural festivities were the grandest in history. The Depression and the war had put such things on hiatus for years, but the year before, confident of getting the presidency back, the Republican-dominated Congress had voted to budget an amazing $80,000 for inaugural festivities. As it turned out, they did not get the presidency, but they did get a party, along with the more than a million people who had poured into Washington to experience this historic day. The crowd included many African Americans, because Truman had announced that for the first time in history, they were as welcome as everyone else at the main events. Another historic first came in the coaxial cable that made it the first inaugural to be broadcast on TV. More people saw Truman sworn in as president that day than had witnessed all previous presidential inaugurations combined, and more than one hundred million listened in on their radios. The crowd in the Capitol's rotunda, Truman recalled in his memoirs, was so great that the chief and associate justices had difficulty making it out to the inaugural stand, and the ceremony ended up starting fourteen minutes late. The president did not mind; it was one of the happiest days of his life.[28]

FIGURE 4.1 In his 1949 inaugural address, Harry S. Truman urged fellow Americans to support the administration's international efforts for peace and prosperity. The United States must, he told them, create "a bold new program for making the benefits of our scientific advances and industrial progress available for the improvement and growth of underdeveloped areas." *Harry S. Truman Presidential Library, Independence, Missouri*

After being sworn in, he stepped to the rostrum and addressed the world. "Today marks the beginning not only of a new Administration, but of a period that will be eventful, perhaps decisive, for us and for the world." The wars of the first half of the century have taught us, he continued, that what the world really needs, is peace. "The peoples of earth face the future with grave uncertainty," and "they look to the United States as never before for good will, strength, and wise leadership." At this moment, we must act to ensure that free nations everywhere possess the means to maintain their freedom and the knowledge that the United States would not back down and allow the "false philosophy" of communism to dominate the globe. We will do this, he assured his listeners, by supporting the United Nations, continuing our global economic recovery plans, providing support to "freedom-loving nations" against the dangers of aggression, and, most notably, by embarking upon "a bold new program for making the benefits of our scientific advances and industrial progress available for the improvement and growth of underdeveloped areas." We need to share our technological bounty and our excess capital with those less fortunate in order to keep communism at bay. "Greater production is the key to prosperity and peace. And the key to greater production is a wider and more vigorous application of modern scientific and technological knowledge." The entire world, Truman announced, will benefit from our endeavor. "With God's help, the future of mankind will be assured in a world of justice, harmony, and peace."[29] The speech lasted only eighteen minutes, but it was long enough to proclaim a new vision of America's place in the world and the role her foreign policy would play within it.

The radical promise of his fourth point caught the attention of everyone listening, creating a surge of interest in the idea of a technical assistance program for the underdeveloped countries as the new weapon against communism. It was, a reporter noted the next day, "generally interpreted in the capital as one of the most ambitious pronouncements on foreign affairs ever made by an American President."[30] Truman's public audience members had announced their approval throughout the speech, at first by clapping, but then quickly shifting to stomping their feet on the planks, because their gloved hands produced little effect.[31] His Congressional observers, however, had to reserve their own judgments until after the speech, because their prime seating behind the president had left them able to catch "only snatches" of what Truman was saying at the time. The next day, the *Times* announced mixed reviews from representatives of both parties. As quickly as they had gotten copies of what they had not heard, they had offered official statements. Republican Jacob K. Javits told reporters he considered the proposal to extend technological aid abroad "one of the most fruitful concepts for the future development of the world and for resisting communistic influences." Democrat Harry F. Byrd stated that he did not believe it to be either "wise or practical." Most viewed the idea positively, telling reporters that they only needed the details "spelled out" in order to give their full approval.[32]

The press shared their interest in getting things "spelled out," and at his first press conference following the inaugural address, they bombarded Truman with questions about the newly dubbed Point Four and its implementation. "I can't tell you just what is going to take place," he told reporters, "where it is going to take place, or how it is going to take place. I know what I want to do," and that, it seemed, was all.[33] The State Department, having recovered quickly from its rejection of Hardy's idea only two months before, immediately began producing a variety of interdepartmental and public documents placing Point Four in the larger context of U.S. foreign policy.[34] The program proved a source of conflict in Washington as the various parties involved tried to wrap their brains around this new idea. Truman had given them a vision, but he had not told them how they were going to be able to implement it, leaving that up to the State Department, though some of his advisors, particularly Clifford, had wanted the program to be separate from existing government bodies. "I thought that in order to maintain the concept that this program was bold and new," Clifford later reported, "we should bring in new people with new ideas." Salant seems to have shared this opinion, noting that the State Department appeared to have been "caught quite flatfooted by the Point 4 proposal," and it spent the rest of the winter and much of the spring scrambling to "catch up," as it were, with the White House's new vision for American foreign policy.[35]

By March 1949, Secretary of State Dean Acheson had had enough time to compile a seven-page memorandum for Truman describing the State Department's idea of the program's substance and objectives, as well as its place in the larger framework of international relations. Presumably written for the president to have a clearer idea of what he should be sending to Congress, the memo emphasized that Point Four could help the United States achieve existing policy objectives, including national economic productivity, a more balanced world economic structure, a stronger United Nations, peace, and the wider spread of democracy abroad.[36] Point Four, Acheson wrote, "does not imply a re-definition of United States policy objectives," but, rather, "that cooperation in economic development is now raised to a major role among the instruments" designed to secure those objectives.[37] While Acheson correctly noted that the United States had been actively working both during and after the war to stabilize the international economy and strengthen the international system under the United Nations, he "forgot" to mention one key policy objective in his memo: stopping Soviet expansion.

By the time Acheson's memo became "Building the Peace," an official State Department publication that spring, the "mistake" had been corrected. "In evaluating the significance of Point Four," it read, "particular emphasis must be given to its relation to the present-day struggle for the hearts and minds of men being waged by profoundly conflicting philosophies." One "promises man material security only at the cost of unconditional surrender of his human dignity and personal freedom," whereas the other, "exemplified by Point Four," seeks "material security" as "a means to the greater nonmaterial end of personal fulfillment."[38] Point Four, with its dedication to "expanding employment of productive resources, whether these be natural, human, or capital," by introducing "the evolutionary element of modern technological knowledge," promised freedom from poverty as the beginning of freedom *period*. The program, the State Department author's wrote, "reflects a belief that visible progress toward the elimination of poverty can alone sustain the hope necessary to keep alive faith in political democracy."[39] To save people from communism, it seemed, America had to offer tangible economic incentives, centered around a rise in living standards, so that people could see a path out of poverty. Point Four was intent on fostering "a continuing effort on the part of all free nations to relieve the poverty and misery afflicting more than half the earth's peoples—a condition which not only handicaps them and denies the world society the fruit of their productive talents but also provides a vulnerable point for attack by malign forces upon the security of free people."[40] It was the perfect foreign policy program: morally good, economically feasible, and, most importantly, diplomatically strategic, all of which made it palatable to the American public.

The White House sold the program to Congress and to the American people as an instrument necessary for stabilizing both the economic and political troubles of the shaky postwar global system. It was always a two-part battle and no one more keenly recognized this than Truman himself. Tension had increased between Washington and Moscow since the Berlin crisis of the previous summer, giving rise to the belief that military conflict between the two entities was a distinct possibility in the near future.[41] "The world was undergoing a major readjustment," Truman recalled in his memoirs about late 1948, "with revolution stalking most of the 'have-not' nations." The Soviets were "making the most of this opportunity," challenging the "course of freedom," and the United States and its allies had to "lead from strength" in order to show the Russians that they were not afraid of a military confrontation.[42] Leading from strength, it seemed to the administration, necessarily required strong unity between allies, particularly those in Europe, residing along the Iron Curtain's border. As Clifford had noted back in 1947, when discussing the Marshall Plan, the United States was not "insensitive" to the desires of other areas of the world for "improvement of the standard of living beyond the pre-war," or even of their importance for the "interest of the world at large," but Europe took precedence.[43]

Truman touched on the issue in his inaugural address. Work on a joint agreement to "strengthen the security of the North Atlantic area" had actually been his "third point." The State Department had been working on creating a formal agreement with "freedom-loving" European nations (a designation apparently fitting for only twelve of them) throughout the fall. That effort resulted in the successful creation and implementation of the North Atlantic Treaty in April 1949.[44] Now that all the ducks were in a row in Europe, the United States had to do something about all those "have-not" nations that were seemingly also "freedom-loving" and in imminent peril of being seduced by the communists. Moscow had announced a new "Economic Council for Mutual Aid" on the heels of Truman's inaugural address. It "seems to mean in effect," Benjamin Hardy asserted at the time, "that the USSR has taken the President's pronouncement as a challenge to prove whether communism or democracy can actually provide the greatest benefits for the people."[45] The race was on.

Despite Truman's firm conviction that Point Four was the answer to the underdevelopment problem, debates on the program's merits continued in Washington throughout the spring, thereby preventing the scheduling of House and Senate hearings on the issue.[46] While Washington stalled, Truman took the debate to the American public, assuming if he garnered support there, Congress would follow. On June 10, he spoke at the dedication of the World War Memorial Park in Little Rock, reassuring his audience that the United States would not fail to fulfill its international duty as it had after the First World War. Because "our economy is the center of world economy," he announced, we must act decisively, for "we know that despair over economic conditions will turn men away from freedom and into the hands of dictators." The prospect for a peaceful future "will be immeasurably brighter if we can offer a future of hope and a better life" to people living in the world's underdeveloped regions.[47] International security could not be separated from international economic prosperity.

Tired of waiting, Truman sent a special message to Congress on June 24 asking for legislation for technical assistance and encouraging private investment in underdeveloped countries. It will help us to help them, he announced, because "if they are frustrated and disappointed" in their "democratic aspirations," they "may turn to false doctrines which hold that the way of progress lies through tyranny."[48] Truman highlighted the issue most likely to get Congress to grant the $35 million that he wanted for the program. He additionally argued that although technical assistance was essential, it was really just the first step and needed to be followed by capital investment, as Walter Salant had argued. Democratic Representative John Kee of West Virginia, chairman of the Committee on Foreign Affairs, got the ball moving officially a few weeks later, introducing H.R. 5615, a bill titled the "International Technical Cooperation Act of 1949," on July 12. It proposed "to promote the foreign policy of the United States and to authorize participation in a cooperative endeavor for assisting in the development of economically underdeveloped areas of the world." It was not a long bill. It centered on giving the president permission "to participate in programs . . . for the interchange of technical knowledge and skills which contribute to the balanced and integrated development of the economic resources and productive capacities" of poor nations. It loudly encouraged the government to seek assistance from the United Nations and private agencies in the name of efficiency. It authorized the creation of "an Institute of Technical Cooperation within the Department of State" to coordinate activities. All in all, it was a very modest bill proposing a modest initiative: it revolved around supporting aid in action, not creating a permanent foreign aid bureaucracy.[49]

Having sponsored the bill, the White House spent the rest of the summer working on a public relations campaign to get America firmly behind it before Congressional hearings began that fall. David Lloyd sent a message to Walter Salant on July 22 asking if he could get together to chat about "the broader implications of Point IV—and what can be done in the public relations field to gather up some support for it."[50] Salant responded five days later with a five-page memo titled "The United States Economic Interest in Point Four," continuing his insistence that "economic affects arise mainly from foreign investment, not technical assistance."[51] After all, American development had been funded by British investments, though it had been inspired by British innovation. That being said, Salant prepared a basic economic argument supporting the Point Four program in terms that noneconomists could understand. The economics were the central issue, he implied, but they were central only because they laid the groundwork for confronting the larger matter of securing America's place in the international arena:

> The most far-reaching domestic influence to be hoped for from Point IV is its effect upon international tensions, which condition the whole environment in which our economy operates and which makes it necessary for us to devote billions worth of resources to defense that we would prefer to devote to meeting better our current and future wants. The Point IV Program may reasonably be expected to contribute to the easing of these tensions. It will show the under-developed countries that instead of disregarding or positively exploiting them, we mean to use our great ability to help them in pursuit of their economic aspirations, thereby removing the attraction of the Soviet Union's only basic appeal to them.[52]

There were also clear economic benefits to the program. Exporting capital to these countries would not only remove the threat of communism, but would also help out the American economy by allowing these countries to purchase goods from both the United States and Western Europe, which would allow the latter to pay back their war loans and continue importing American goods. This argument fit well with the administration's general philosophy and became the standard presentation in White House and State Department stumps for Point Four.[53]

Hearings on Kee's bill finally began at the end of September 1949, in a Washington still recovering from Truman's announcement that the Soviet Union had detonated an atomic bomb. The bill's supporters emphasized its modest structure and noble purpose. "The idea of exchanging knowledge and skills is not new," James E. Webb, the acting secretary of state, explained on the opening day of the hearings. The United States government and private organizations (e.g., missionaries, foundations) had engaged in such activities in the past. "The new and essential factor in the present proposal is its emphasis on the great importance of economic development in underdeveloped areas and on the concept of an expanded and coordinated approach to the stimulating of technological exchange and capital investment."[54] Point Four was not an effort to "civilize" nations via schools and soap; it was an organized assault on "economic underdevelopment" that fought poverty with technology and technological know-how. The bill's supporters turned back to the 1939 national income statistics that Colin Clark had helped assemble, holding up maps of the world with countries shaded from white to gray to black in recognition of their annual national incomes. "This is not just an economic program," Willard Thorp, assistant secretary of state for economic affairs, explained, "because by placing Americans in other countries the program has a general education value and is of importance both in bringing about political democracy and improving our relations with other countries. But I also want to point out the fact which is perfectly obvious to the committee that you do not sell as much in underdeveloped areas as you sell in well-to-do areas." In the years leading up to the war, Thorp explained, we averaged sales of only 70 cents per capita to poor nations, but $5.80 per capita to rich ones. Technical assistance would make the world better by making it wealthier. American aid would prove that "our system of organization, of economic operation, is a superior system" that "can bring about results that most everyone wants, in contrast to other systems." Progress was a capitalist product.[55]

Congress continued hearings on Kee's bill into October when Republican Representative Christian Herter (Mass.) introduced H.R. 6026, "a bill to establish a program of foreign economic development." Herter's bill was longer and more complex than Kee's, reflecting Republican concern that a new American aid program could be hijacked by the international community unless it were more firmly constructed and controlled within Washington. The H.R. 6026 bill declared Congress's commitment to encouraging "the flow of investment of capital and technical knowledge and skill to those foreign countries expressing a desire and a willingness to cooperate with the United States in a joint endeavor of economic development." The new bill prioritized encouraging private investment and highlighted the goal of "strengthening" countries "in their struggle against communism." It also insisted that the United States needed "a well-integrated program for foreign economic development" and called for the creation of a "Foreign Economic Development Administration," housed within the Department of State. This "administration" would have more power than the "institute" described in Kee's bill and it would be run by an advisory board and a deputy administer for foreign economic development appointed by the president and approved by the senate. In addition to distancing the foreign aid program from the White House, Herter's bill set up clear steps for establishing aid relationships with partner countries: bilateral agreements, joint commissions, and obligatory treaties of friendship, commerce, and navigation. Getting aid from the United States meant promising to protect the lives and assets of American investors. Herter's bill allowed for cooperation with all U.N. agencies, but its tone differed from Kee's, which had declared that U.N. participation "shall be sought wherever practicable." American aid needed to be firmly tied to the pursuit of America's best interest.[56]

The hearings reveal strong support for the basic idea of Point Four, but dissent over its structure and the scope of its international mission. After listening to dozens of testimonies, the committee decided to postpone further action until January in the hope that Point Four's promoters would be able to reach some agreement on its desired shape. Meanwhile, the White House kept up its public relations campaign throughout the winter and spring, working to bring in support from business groups and academics.

At the 1949 meeting of the Academy of Political Science, Paul G. Hoffman, the director of the Economic Cooperation Administration, reported that although great progress had been made, European productivity remained 50 percent of that of Canada and the United States. The struggle for a truly integrated European market continued apace. George Kennan, the director of the policy planning staff at the State Department, also attended to encourage support for the Truman administration's programs. "The problems of this world are deeper, more involved, and more stubborn than many of us realize," he grimly warned his audience. We cannot step out of leadership, so we must use new strategies for peace. "It is clear from the nature of the world situation we see before us that foreign aid is a valuable and indispensable instrument of our foreign policy at this stage in our national development." Foreign aid, Kennan pointed out, helps us to project "our strength and our spirit beyond our borders" in new and exciting ways. He was a realist, and he warned his audience not too expect too much from foreign aid. It was only "one instrument of our foreign policy," but he left them with no doubt that it was an important one.[57]

While Hoffman and Kennan tried to persuade political scientists, Salant worked to garner support from American economists. He presented "The Domestic Effects of Capital Export Under the Point Four Program" on the panel "U.S. Foreign Investment in Underdeveloped Areas" at the December 1949 Annual Meeting of the American Economic Society. He went straight to the heart of the issue, arguing that foreign assistance provided the only reliable means of ensuring full employment and, consequently, American economic stability. Foreign investment in both Europe and the "underdeveloped areas of the world," he insisted, will have an "expansive effect upon the economy," by giving them the opportunity to buy American products and pay off war debts.[58] This focus on capital export stemmed from Evsey Domar's argument, which Salant directly quoted, of investment for growth, with American investment helping underdeveloped countries overcome their "savings gap" in order to achieve sustained economic growth to the point that they would become meaningful partners in the global economy.[59] Salant perceived there to be an intimate connection between funding growth in the underdeveloped world, restoring the European economy, and securing American full employment. All were separate parts of one global capitalist economy. The point took Allyn Young's and Paul Rosenstein-Rodan's arguments that the domestic economy be understood as a whole—with growth in one industry affecting growth in another—to an international level.[60]

It is in America's best interest, Salant told his fellow economists, to support capital expansion under Point Four, because even if such investment did not reap an equal amount of monetary return through exports, it would undoubtedly reduce the "domestic and foreign expenditures arising from the cold war." Foreign aid made economic as well as strategic sense. If we failed to support Point Four, then not only would Europe fall victim to its "deep-rooted political and social cleavages," but problems would arise around the world. The "aspiration" of "new sovereign nations . . . to develop their economic resources and improve their present desperate living standards is one of the most basic drives of the postwar world. If these aspirations are frustrated, the political orientation of these countries appears likely to develop unfavorably for us," Salant warned. "Thus the success of the Point Four program may be a major factor in determining whether or not we have to live in a garrison state."[61] He insisted that they understand foreign aid to be an offensive weapon in the fight against the spread of Soviet power. When Rosenstein-Rodan warned fellow economists in 1943 that underdeveloped nations could choose from one of two paths, he spoke of national versus international development, not communism. Six years later, Salant replaced nationalism with communism, but the argument was the same. When telling his audience that "foreign investment to develop resources can yield a future income to the American economy," he was also making it clear that it would yield a better future to America itself—one not encircled by a garrison.

Whereas Salant emphasized Point Four's strategic necessity, fellow panelist H. W. Singer, of the United Nations, directed his attention to the welfare of the world's underdeveloped peoples. Industrialization has a purpose beyond increasing the productivity of the world market, he insisted. "The most important contribution of an industry is not in its immediate product . . . and not even its effects on other industries and immediate social benefits (thus far economists have been led by Marshall and Pigou to go) but perhaps even further its effect on the general level of education, skill, way of life, inventiveness, habits, store of technology, creation of new demand, etc." As we help to enhance the underdeveloped world's contribution to the world economy, Singer argued, let us make sure that we move beyond old colonial investment practices that emphasized the exportation of natural resources and truly invest in the future productivity of these countries. He supported Point Four because Truman's program recognized the importance of human capital, using knowledge and technology to alter the makeup of the economy. "The emphasis on technical assistance may be interpreted as a recognition that the present structure of comparative advantage and endowment is not such that it should be considered as a permanent basis for a future international division of labor." Just as national economies changed over time, with various areas dominating at various times, so too would a strong, vibrant world economy. It was to be expected that Singer, as a representative of the United Nations rather than the United States, would emphasis the global rather than national ramifications of foreign aid, and his argument demonstrates the evolving complexity of the academic argument about development. The Marshall Plan, Point Four, the World Bank, and a series of United Nations programs offered economists the chance to see their ideas in action. It was exciting and stimulating, and it encouraged vigorous debate about the West's path to progress and its global applicability.[62]

The seriousness of the situation encouraged retrospection. Chairman Louis M. Hacker opened the meeting with some reflections on the point. "There may be generally accepted measures of economic progress; but, clearly, noneconomic values are once more asserting themselves. Are we happier, freer, more secure?" he asked the audience. "Public policy flows from our efforts to answer these questions rather than our estimation of our successes in economic terms."[63] The statistics and data spreadsheets that provided the tangible knowledge of national economies that preoccupied most growth theory economists were not, Hacker implied, the most important indicators of economic improvement. Strengthening an economy was simply the best way to achieve the real goals of a "happier, freer, more secure" society. A historian, Hacker was likely well aware of the deep roots of his argument. Were he still alive, Thomas Malthus could have accused Hacker, as he did Adam Smith of mixing the question of "the wealth of nations" with that of "the happiness and comfort of the lower orders of society."[64] Despite the centuries that separated them, Smith and Hacker (and many others like them) shared a conviction that economic growth mattered because of its impact on people, not spreadsheets. They defended the fundamental morality of economic progress.

When Hacker asked his audience, "Are we happier, freer, more secure?," he got to the heart of the debate about Point Four, for although most would likely have insisted that the American people were indeed happier and freer than they had been one hundred years ago, they would have been less certain that they were more secure. The Soviet Union—now a member of the atomic club—seemed a greater, more menacing enemy than any the United States had ever known. And now China had gone communist as well. Securing the growth of the American economy depended upon securing the growth of the global economy, and that required foreign aid.

While the White House proselytized, Congress debated. On January 18, 1950, Kee and Herter "introduced identical bills in Congress," explained a July 1950 State Department report. "Further hearings were held by the House Foreign Affairs Committee on this 'compromise' bill and after some additional modifications the bill was favorably recommended as part of the Foreign Economic Assistance Act of 1950." It passed in the House with an allocation of $25,000,000 and all eyes turned toward the Senate.[65]

The Senate Foreign Relations Committee took up the issue in March with hearings on S. 3304, an "amendment... to the Economic Cooperation Act of 1948." Acheson spoke on the first day of the hearings, telling the committee that "the bill now before you establishes economic development of underdeveloped areas for the first time as a national policy." Acheson insisted that Point Four would encourage private investments and support the United Nations, while never becoming "a big-money enterprise." Senator Alexander Wiley, a Republican from Wisconsin, was particularly struck by the last point. "You know we are the great Santa Claus of the world and everybody thinks that there is no bottom to our barrel," he grumbled, but still vocalized support for the larger goal of expanding the global economy.[66] S. 3304 recommended $45,000,000 for Point Four and barely passed in the senate with a vote of 37 to 36. House and Senate supporters moved quickly to try to come to some agreement. In the end, the Senate voted on the House bill "substantially unchanged" (agreeing to a compromised allocation of $35,000,000 that was added to the omnibus appropriation bill later that year). There was a vigorous debate, with the Republic opposition led by conservatives Robert Taft of Ohio and Eugene Millikin of Colorado, but enough Republicans supported the bill to get it passed that May as Title IV of the Foreign Economic Assistance Act of 1950. The Russians had the bomb and the Chinese had Mao; for many, it seemed a foolish time to grumble about not wanting to be Santa Claus to the world, and Point Four moved from a promise to a policy.[67]

Truman signed his "Act for International Development" into law on June 5, 1950. "The peoples of the United States and other nations have a common interest in the freedom and in the economic and social progress of all peoples," the bill read. "Such progress can further the secure growth of democratic ways of life, the expansion of mutually beneficial commerce, the development of international understanding and good will, and the maintenance of world peace."[68] The language recalled two-hundred-year-old ideas about the multiple blessings associated with trade. David Hume had cheerily insisted, "nothing is more favourable to the rise of politeness and learning, than a number of neighboring and independent states, connected by commerce and policy." China's lack of progress, he continued, proved the point. It was hampered by being "one vast empire, speaking one language, governed by one law, and sympathizing in the same manner."[69] Nations needed competition to improve. Frequent positive relations between foreign peoples boosts growth, Hume insisted, by increasing wants, opportunities, and knowledge. Nations that trade together, prosper together.

The White House's argument for Point Four was persuasive because it drew on long-accepted ideas about the value of economic improvement and newly endorsed ideas about the manipulation of an economy through technology and investment. The American public was, on the whole, thrilled with new program, which they found both intellectually and emotionally satisfying. They could do well by doing good. Few actions by an American president, Harvard economist John Kenneth Galbraith wrote in September 1950, "ever produced a more whole-souled response" than Truman's fourth point in his inaugural address, and now the point was officially a program.[70] A few months later, officials established the Technical Cooperation Administration (TCA)—the official organization of Point Four—within the State Department, and Truman appointed Henry Garland Bennett, the president of Oklahoma A&M, as its administrator.[71] Along the way of its passage from an idea to a program, Point Four had become slightly more openly anticommunist, more supportive of America's economic self-interest, and more devoted to strengthening world trade. The Truman administration secured the program's passage by touting its economic and strategic benefits; Congress, and the American people, waited hungrily for proof.

Getting the program was the first step. Implementing it successfully was the second. Initial decisions revolved around what Point Four assistance would look like and where it would be headed—issues that proved trickier than they initially appeared. The United States already had some experience with administering assistance in Latin America and with capital aid to Europe, but Point Four was a different animal. Indeed, its closest model appeared to be Britain's Colonial Development and Welfare Program, which it had established in 1940, and which France and Belgium had copied in 1946 and 1947, respectively. There were two perplexing obstacles to following these models, however. They quite obviously stank of imperialism, and they not so obviously had limited development objectives. These were so limited, in fact, that it led American policymakers to question whether or not their unwilling colonies should be able to apply for Point Four assistance, which, in turn, raised the question of how to keep Point Four from looking like just old imperialism in a new guise.

Dependent areas, a confidential, 1949 Advisory Committee on Technical Assistance report noted, are, "in most instances, the most underdeveloped parts of the world," because they are "too poor to finance extensive development and welfare programs," and because, "until recent times, it has not been the practice of metropolitan powers to place at their disposal special grants for these purposes." Because our objectives are ostensibly the same for dependent and independent areas, "where colonial powers have formulated and are carrying out programs which are consistent with the broad objectives of the Point IV," we should provide any additional assistance necessary for "accelerating and expanding existing programs." Concerns that this might lead to the United States being painted by the Soviets and by the colonial peoples as an imperial power led the Advisory Committee to recommend that "maximum publicity should be given to specific steps taken to associate colonial people in the program and to appointments of colonials to posts of some significance and responsibility . . . [and] the extent to which the Point IV Program is related to political and strategic objectives of the United States should be played down, as well as the extent to which the program may further indirectly [help] the economic recovery of Western Europe."[72]

Not everyone agreed. David Lloyd wrote to Walter Salant that summer that "I think that the way the State Department has handled the Point Four Program has obscured the essential differences between the colonial and other areas as well as between under-developed areas, and European countries, in the field of foreign economic policy. . . . Everybody, I think, is groping in the muddle created by this failure to talk and think in terms of areas—and put the emphasis on the functional aspects of the program."[73] Although seemingly a politically acceptable, though morally distasteful, approach to the "imperialism problem," the Advisory Committee's recommendation to "play down" the program's economic benefits was impossible. While many policymakers recognized the intrinsic humanitarianism of promoting economic development for its own sake, the realities of international relations and domestic politics dictated that self-interest—enlightened though it certainly could be—had to be the foundation of U.S. foreign policy. No one in Washington wanted colonial peoples to remain poor and hungry, but, as Lloyd implied in his letter to Salant, their misery was not the point, because they were not vulnerable to communism in the same way that *independent* nations were.

By the time Point Four had become a political reality, the debate about its possible extension to colonial regions had been conclusively decided in the negative. There was only so much money to go around, so it was going to go where it was the most useful for U.S. national security.[74] The number of potential national partners instantly got a great deal smaller. In Africa, it left only Liberia, Ethiopia (which U.S. policymakers believed included Eritrea), Egypt, and Libya, and all but the first were primarily viewed not as African, but as Middle Eastern. They were both underdeveloped and strategic, which was a valuable combination.

In his 1939 submission to the International Studies Conference, Eugene Staley had argued that the most "constructive move" that the world could make toward "economic welfare and peace" would be to create "a great international development program for the improvement of equipment and knowledge in regions most lacking these things." Such a program would not only help people meet their needs, but even the "very existence" of plans for such a program would promote peace by "offering a concrete and attractive alternative to armament races and to the risky gains of aggression."[75] Correspondingly, he warned, not doing something to assist countries to improve their economic realities threatened world peace, and nowhere was the situation more volatile than in the countries of the "Far East and Middle East."

> Economic development is bound to come somehow to the countries of the Orient, as to other areas of the world. If left to unguided "natural forces" and to the play of nationalistic imperialisms this development will be accompanied by a long series of wars and revolutions and by repeated sudden upsets imposed upon economic life elsewhere. Here is the challenge for an international program of positive cooperation to bring the Orient *into the world economy* in a manner that benefits all people, making the development a promise rather than a menace to the prosperity of the rest of the world [emphasis added].[76]

Closing the "economic gap" between the East and the West, he concluded, is "one of the greatest problems of the present time" and the United States in particular, as the world's leading economic power, needed to work actively to create a peaceful system dedicated to securing the economic well-being of all the world's peoples. It made sense to start in the middle.[77]

FIGURE 4.2 Haile Selassie tours Hyde Park with Eleanor Roosevelt during his 1954 visit to the United States. *Franklin D. Roosevelt Presidential Library, Hyde Park, New York*

In June 1950, George McGhee, the assistant secretary of state for Near Eastern, South Asian, and African affairs, sent Acheson a memo, urging him, in light of Truman's having just signed Point Four into law, to consider the dire need for "a more positive policy of economic development assistance" to countries in South Asia and the Near East. "Most of these states have newly achieved their independence, have non-Communist governments, and face grave internal political and administrative problems," he warned. "They are weak financially and are underdeveloped. All are exposed to Communist pressures. Experience has shown that countries in such close proximity to the USSR orbit need the stiffening and confidence provided by the United States economic assistance." They need tangible evidence of our friendship. McGhee actually did not think that the money allocated for Point Four would be enough to stabilize the situation, but at least it was a start. "I hope," he wrote Acheson, "that Point Four operations can be conducted with our political ends in mind."[78] He need not have worried.

Even though the center of the debate over how much Point Four aid would go to whom remained in Washington, the international community was quick to get involved. Many Middle Eastern leaders responded favorably to Truman's inaugural promise of international assistance out of their eagerness to gain support from a non-European source to fund their efforts to bring their countries into the international marketplace.[79] Many freshly independent, such countries recognized the need for outside aid, but feared any hint of another round of colonialism. Point Four's emphasis on empowering local peoples to engage in their own development soothed fears and raised hopes. In her biography of her father, Margaret Truman recalled that "excited farmers in the Middle East sent letters to the local American embassy, addressed to 'The Master of the Fourth Spot.'" They were not alone.[80]

The Egyptian ambassador to the United States called on Willard Thorp, assistant secretary of state for economic affairs, to discuss the possibility of Point Four aid to his country in July 1949 and was encouraged to get his government to submit a survey of its development needs.[81] The Ethiopian government shared Egypt's enthusiasm and actively worked to ensure its participation in the program as it watched the congressional debate unfold. In March 1950, Haile Selassie held a meeting with George Merrell, the American ambassador to Ethiopia, thanking the United States for its support on the Eritrean issue and asking for a guarantee of Point Four assistance once the program officially began. Ethiopia was ready for development, the emperor insisted, but required outside expertise and capital. He ended the meeting assuring Merrell that he was "confident that, with the cooperation of the United States, Ethiopia will enter upon a period of great economic development."[82] Other world leaders acted as quickly, for Point Four appeared to represent the Western world's first significant attempt to fulfill the United Nations' charter's promise to "promote social progress and betters standards of life" through "international machinery for the promotion of the economic and social advancement of all peoples."[83] Viewed in light of the Marshall Plan that had preceded it, Point Four was generally identified as one of the most internationally beneficial ideas ever to enter diplomatic discourse. There was little to fear and much to desire in a program that promised technological aid and capital investment and asked (often indirectly) only for "good" relations.

Washington was quick to use this foreign enthusiasm for promoting "economic and social advancement" to assist in its international diplomacy. In this sense, Point Four became a foreign policy tool long before it became an actual program. A clear example of this practice can be seen in U.S. correspondence with Saudi Arabia in the months following Truman's inaugural address. In the spring of 1949, Washington found itself in a diplomatic struggle with Saudi Arabia to maintain access to the Dhahran airfield based on a 1945 agreement that the Saudis wanted to renegotiate. On May 23, Truman sent King Ibn Saud a letter assuring him that the United States was looking into the matter and reminding him that "the program being developed under Point Four" could "bring to complete fruition the mutual economic interests" of their two countries, so Truman looked forward to further cooperation with the kingdom. When George McGhee went to Saudi Arabia a year later, he reiterated America's commitment to bringing Point Four aid to the country; in the event, he qualified, that Congress actually approved the program.[84]

Congress finally approved Point Four appropriations in September, allotting the promised $35 million for fiscal year 1951.[85] Diplomats could now use the more persuasive tactic of offering official "Point Four General Agreements" and corresponding program activities to secure their goals. The first such agreement (in any region) was signed with Iran on October 19, 1950, with an initial allotment of $500,000 to improve living conditions in rural villages that was eventually raised to $1,500,000 for fiscal year 1951.[86] Libya, still under British occupation, got its first program that November via Anglican pressure, but did not officially get its Point Four General Agreement until June 15, 1951, after most of the rest of the "essential" countries in the region had signed their agreements.[87] Saudi Arabia signed its Point Four General Agreement in January of 1951, followed by Israel in February, Jordan in March, Iraq in April, Lebanon and Egypt in May, and Libya and Ethiopia in June.[88] Additional Point Four agreements were signed by Liberia, Bolivia, Brazil, Chile, Colombia, Costa Rica, Cuba, Dominican Republic, Ecuador, El Salvador, Guatemala, Haiti, Honduras, Mexico, Nicaragua, Panama, Paraguay, Peru, Uruguay, Venezuela, Afghanistan, Burma, India, Indonesia, Nepal, and Pakistan.[89] The "underdeveloped world" was hungry for development.

"The Government of the United States of America and the Imperial Ethiopian Government," Ethiopia's Point Four agreement began, "undertake to cooperate with each other in the interchange of technical knowledge and skills and in related activities designed to contribute to the balanced and integrated development of the economic resources and productive capacities of Ethiopia."[90] The wording was typical of all of the previous Point Four agreements. In each case, the parties involved, ostensibly "moved by the desire of cooperation in the exchange of technical knowledge and experience aiming to reach a higher standard of economic development, social welfare and the diffusion of good understanding and predisposition among states," saw Point Four as a way to establish a mutually beneficial, long-term diplomatic relationship, often where few relations had previously existed.[91] Development via technical assistance had become foreign policy.

These initial Point Four agreements did not set out specifics, but provided for the "services" of U.S. technical advisors, the technical training of a select number of a country's workers in the United States, and the equipment and materials necessary for recommended technical projects, with the understanding that the partner government would bear an "equitable" or "fair" share of the burden by granting free facilities, paying local technicians to work on projects, and generally finding funds to help pay for various projects.[92] "Particular technical cooperation programs and projects," as noted in Iraq's Point Four agreement, were then carried out "pursuant to the provisions of such separate written agreements or understandings concerning them as may later be reached by the duly designated representatives of Iraq and the Technical Cooperation Administration."[93] These first agreements were followed by a number of specific agreements that dealt with the particulars of defined cooperative programs generally focused on public health, education, industry, agriculture, living standards, and water.

These secondary agreements were critical to the establishment of the various programs that represented the heart of Point Four. The Technical Cooperation Administration's initial fiscal year (FY) 1951 budget was rather modest, with a little more than $2.3 million allocated to the Middle East division, so the earliest Point Four country programs in the region had correspondingly limited goals that tended to emphasize agricultural and water resource development. Iran, viewed as critical to America's Middle East security mission, received by far the largest portion of the allocated Point Four funds (more than a million dollars) for antilocust and antimalaria campaigns and for a more general rural development program.[94] In the spring and summer of 1951, Iraq, Lebanon, and Jordan began water development projects addressing the issues of sanitation, irrigation, and hydroelectric power with Point Four assistance, whereas Libya, Syria, and Ethiopia focused on agricultural education programs.[95]

Additionally, the TCA began working to encourage private capital investment by U.S. companies into Point Four countries. Such initiatives rested on the belief that capital and human investment in agriculture and infrastructure through technology would effectively challenge the problem of "economic backwardness."

Much of the world clearly supported the idea of development, but the motivations for the *developers* were not the same as those driving the *developees* to ask for assistance. Point Four was "enlightened self-interest," but it was still self-interest—both economic and strategic.[96] The anticommunist rhetoric that had surrounded Point Four's creation had moved from theoretical to practical the previous summer with the outbreak of the Korean War at the end of June 1950. The war, Acheson later wrote, proved that "the U.S.S.R. was willing to use forces in battle to achieve objectives."[97] It also proved that the United States was willing to go up against them, and it reinforced opinion at home that the Cold War needed to be fought with all possible weapons, save atomic ones, making Point Four's technology for democracy and capitalism even more appealing.

Walter Salant, always on the forefront of international economics, had recognized the importance of identifying the intellectual link between economic aid and military aid before the rest of Washington. The present situation, he wrote to Clark Clifford's assistant Charles Murphy in December 1950, does not call for us to drop our aid plans, but necessitates that we recognize that the "common danger calls for cutting out, for the time being, elements of such plans which do not contribute to the common strength in its military and non-military aspects." Long-range plans needed to take a back seat to short-term ones whose results would secure Europe and the underdeveloped world against "Soviet-dominated aggression." Our foreign aid plans must serve "high priority purposes," Salant continued, one of the most important of those being the continued control of major raw materials.[98] Salant's voice was quickly joined by many others in Washington. An emphasis on promoting growth for the sake of the global economy gave way to promoting growth in order to quell communist voices in underdeveloped nations. The difference was subtle, but it was there, and it had ramifications on the ground.

"Our own national security," Truman announced during his 1951 State of the Union address, "is deeply involved with that of the other free nations. While they need our support, we equally need theirs. Our national security would be gravely prejudiced if the Soviet Union were to succeed in harnessing to its war machine the resources and the manpower of the free nations on the borders of its empire." In the coming months, he continued, the government "must give priority to activities that are urgent."[99] Point Four made the list.

The program had already proven itself wildly popular, and it seemed to hold an almost limitless ability to maintain friendly relationships according to the amount of money the United States was willing to put into it. In FY 1951 that was not very much; FY 1952 would be a different story.

Policymakers were not the only ones worried. In published proceedings from the early 1951 meeting of the American Economic Association, economists led by Evsey Domar discussed the potential strengths and weaknesses of the Soviet Union in comparison with the United States. Although all agreed that the United States stood out as the stronger nation, they urged caution rather than optimism. "United States military-economic potential is greater than that of the U.S.S.R. if the comparison is limited to those two countries," one acknowledged. "But what if the Soviet Union controlled and exploited the rich resources of Western Europe?" And, although he did not specifically mention it, he likely was also thinking about the Middle East, whose vast oil reserves were already of key interest to the U.S. government. "I suggest," another gloomily predicted, "that then the balance of power would indeed have swung against us catastrophically—perhaps for all time."[100] Keyserling, now the chairman of the Council of Economic Advisors, shared this sentiment. In a letter to Truman later that year he noted that his voluntary attendance at National Security Council meetings had brought home to him the reality that "the Communist danger is the central, overwhelming danger which our economy faces. If that danger is not met, our economy and our way of life may be destroyed."[101]

Whereas it now seemed clear to almost everyone in Washington that economic aid could be a key weapon against the Soviets, the issue of how to most effectively wield it took on new dimensions in the Korean War era. Special Assistant to the President Gordon Gray had turned in a report, which Salant helped write, the previous November, which called for the consolidation of all of its economic programs, be they military, technological, or monetary, under one agency.[102] By the spring of 1951, Truman was convinced that such a move would be a wise step toward ensuring that the "people armed with weapons" would be on America's side, and he sent a message to Congress in May suggesting the idea. The new Mutual Security Program would take over the Mutual Defense Assistance Act of 1949, the Economic Cooperation Act of 1948, the Far Eastern Economic Assistance Act of 1950, the China Area Aid Act of 1950, and the Act for International Development.[103] The idea became a bill that summer and a reality that fall.

Truman signed the Mutual Security Act of 1951 on October 10, proclaiming, "we are joining with other peoples to prove by deeds that the way to freedom is the way of peace and human progress."[104] The "way to freedom," however, now only stood open to countries that met the new security-benefit requirements. Congress amended the "Act for International Development" to include the proviso that Point Four "military, economic and technical assistance to friendly countries" should primarily be undertaken to "develop their resources in the interest of the security and independence of the national interests of the United States."[105] The following year, it pushed the issue even further, stipulating that "no country shall receive any assistance hereunder unless it takes decisive action to marshal its resources collectively and participate in programs which promote collective security in the appropriate areas."[106] Countries that could not offer strategic assistance could not get aid. Luckily for them, most could.

The Mutual Security Act of 1951 forced the State Department to make immediate structural changes to the TCA. A State Department memo dated November 24, 1951, declared that the act "has considerably expanded the size, content, and geographical scope of the program, particularly in the critical areas of the world."[107] That proved to be the case with the budget, but not the geographic scope. By the fall of 1951, Point Four agreements had already been signed with almost all the countries that would get them. The political shift to foreign aid for military purposes, made official policy in the Mutual Security Act, had been floating around the State Department all year and had already largely determined which countries were going to be able to get funds. The key change for Point Four was not in the countries, but in the cash: budget appropriations shot up to $211 million—in contrast to the original allotment of $35 million. Thirty-five countries in Central and South America, South Asia, and "the Near East and Independent Africa" were going to be the direct beneficiaries of the ever-rising Point Four budget.[108]

Along with the expanded funds and publicity came an expanded responsibility for efficiency and effectiveness. The TCA had originally been organized along three functional lines: food, health and education, and industry and government, respectively. Following the Mutual Security Act of 1951, however, the State Department reorganized the program along geographic lines: the Near East Development Service, the African and Asian Development Service, and the Inter-American Development Service. The countries receiving Point Four aid did not change, but the bureaucracy enabling them to receive that aid did, reinforcing the idea that specific areas deserved greater attention.[109] The most attention and the most money consequently went to the Near East and the African and Asian Development Services, with the drive for security against the Soviets outweighing the historic ties of assistance to Latin and South America. The TCA budget proposal for

1952 devoted about 80 percent of its bilateral aid to Asia, the Near East, and Africa.[110] Washington's strategic interest had moved east; so too its foreign policy program. Point Four remained a humanitarian endeavor, but its humanitarianism would be limited to those countries that could and would be useful allies in the fight against the Soviets.

Assistant Secretary of State George McGhee was quite blunt about the change, telling a British advisor in Libya who was arguing that the Point Four program should not be used as a *quid pro quo* for base rights because it was supposed to be altruistic that the "old Point Four concept must be forgotten in connection with [the] mutual security program." McGhee emphasized that the "mutual security program is not, in its application to Libya, to be considered [the] price for bases," for, the two matters "need not necessarily be tied together, but," he noted, "Libyans should be able to see that if they denied the U.S. bases, [the] application of [the] mutual security program to Libya might be affected."[111] After the conversation, the Libyans, under the direction of their British occupiers, who would not be leaving until December, decided to continue to allow the U.S. military to land its planes at Wheelus Field. Plans to bring Libya into the international economy in order to create a market for European and American imports—and even those to find oil reserves—were subsumed by the overwhelming concern to secure rights to an airfield outside of Tripoli.

Such changes were not limited to Libya. The Mutual Security Act of 1951 included a provision to create a new post of special representative of the secretary of state to coordinator for economic and technical assistance programs in the Near East. It also officially raised the level of funds available for regional assistance to $160 million.[112] Additionally, it unofficially gave TCA officials more freedom in choosing the types of programs to which Point Four funds could be applied. McGhee acknowledged this freedom in his conversation on Libya, telling the British advisor that the Mutual Security Program's "greater flexibility should make it possible" to use at least part of the allotted funds to help relieve the country's budget deficit by earmarking funds for projects that might fall "within the scope of the Libyan budget."[113] In order to achieve its strategic plans, the U.S. government was more willing than before to give national leaders more influence in decisions about what its foreign aid would be used for. It knew that they wanted what it was offering—that they believed its underlying premise.

Point Four became a useful instrument of U.S. foreign policy because both sides benefited. If foreign leaders had not thought that investment for growth would work, then it would have faded from the international scene.

The "underdeveloped world" had, in a sense, accepted its underdevelopment back in 1947, when the United Nations Committee of Trade declared the "industrial and economic development, particularly of underdeveloped countries," to be one of its primary objectives.[114] What the security shift of 1951 really signaled, then, was a greater awareness of the power of the development idea abroad. Economic aid was the ultimate weapon for securing policy goals without direct military involvement. Abroad, it was sold as all carrot, no stick, and leaders around the world were willing to stand in line to get a piece. At home, it was sold as the last best hope for the future.

"We know that the men now in the Kremlin are the center of a vast conspiracy whose inexorable purpose is to blot out human freedoms throughout the world," Truman asserted in a letter preceding the "Third Report to Congress on the Mutual Security Program" in January 1953.[115] Point Four, now under the Mutual Security Program, was a force for freedom. "When we strike against the enemies of mankind—poverty, illiteracy, hunger, and disease—we work for freedom," Truman promised, and "when we build the conditions in which freedom can flourish we destroy the conditions under which totalitarianism can grow," which benefited, he emphasized, the entire free world.[116] The security of the United States depended upon "strong military defenses beyond our shores," which, in turn, meant that foreign assistance, which had "to be tied to achievement of stated foreign policy objectives," needed to be directed to countries in possession of the bases and the resources necessary to the "requirements" of the U.S. armed forces.[117] Truman had not forsaken Point Four's initial humanitarian agenda; he had simply come to believe that the international situation demanded that American time and resources go where they could be of greatest use in the Cold War struggle. Middle Eastern nations made it to the top of the list. In FY 1951, the United States sent around $2.5 million in Point Four assistance to the Middle East; in FY 1952, the amount jumped to around $55 million.[118]

In Iran, Point Four held classes on job instruction, leadership, safety, and improvement for local textile, chemical, and tobacco industries. Iranian doctors were sent to the United States with Point Four funds for more training and seven hundred rural teachers took a summer course on how to teach. English medical books were translated into Persian and plans for starting midwifery and nursing schools got underway. In addition to training, Point Four technicians brought new technologies—such as an X-ray machine, medications, and tractors—and introduced new breeds of livestock, including ten "brown Swiss bulls" and thousands of chickens.[119] In Israel, U.S. technicians and their local trainees established industrial training centers, built sewage facilities, introduced chemical fertilizers to increase yields, and set up programs to clean and store water and milk supplies.[120] In Ethiopia, as will be discussed in detail in chapter 5, they created agricultural improvement centers, subsidized the vaccination of thousands of cattle against rinderpest, dug wells, and helped fund a public health training center. A similar story played out across the Middle East as a whole. Countries dubbed "underdeveloped" could look forward to increasing amounts of aid. Whether they could also look forward to development remained to be seen.

Fighting underdevelopment was largely an academic and political issue for Americans, but it was a daily struggle for leaders around the world. They looked to the wealthier nations for money, technology, and, with more skepticism, leadership. For them, the question of following the Soviet or the American example was not one of ideology, but of practicality. They knew that the United States encouraged participation in one grand world economy, which would benefit the United States and Western Europe, but how much it would benefit newly integrated underdeveloped nations remained open to debate. The

FIGURE 4.3 Dwight and Mamie Eisenhower welcome Haile Selassie, his granddaughter Sebla Desta, and his son Sahle Selassie to the White House in 1954. The state visit was the most important stop on the emperor's two-month tour of the United States. *Dwight D. Eisenhower Presidential Library, Abilene, Kansas*

question of urban versus rural development also remained open, with economists of all types weighing in on the alleged virtues of initially plunging into heavy industry or pushing time and funds into agricultural modernization. Allyn Young and Paul Rosenstein-Rodan had theorized that the modernization of one area of the economy would promote modernization in all areas, but the idea had not been proven and the results on the ground seemed likely to differ from country to country.[121] The Marshall Plan had emphasized both, but that had been about recovery, not development, so the uncertainty continued.

In the spring of 1951, the United Nations weighed in on the debate, publishing a report to the General Assembly titled, *Measures for the Economic Development of Under-Developed Countries*, with "under-developed countries" defined as "countries in which per capita real income is low when compared with the per capita real incomes of the United States of America, Canada, Australasia and Western Europe. In this sense, an adequate synonym would be 'poor countries.'" The definition emphasized the influence of Colin Clark's national income statistics. People might always have known poverty when they saw it, but now they had an "objective" way of measuring it that could be plugged into equations and pasted on graphs. Nations could be ranked according to their incomes—displayed next to one another on charts that depicted a gradual incline from "poverty" toward "wealth." Poverty was now understood to be a problem for everyone and development the necessary solution. What seemed in some ways to be a step backward, however, was really a step forward, because the "modernization of poverty," as the anthropologist Arturo Escobar labeled this process, showed that the international conversation about progress no longer excluded nonwhite peoples and opened the door to new possibilities within the international community. Racism had certainly not disappeared, but it had been discredited and international conversations about the "fitness" of a people for development seemed highly distasteful in a post-Auschwitz world. Despite where a nation might be ranked at the moment, the U.N. report read, "we believe that . . . all countries are currently in a position where their national incomes could be greatly increased by better utilization of what they have." The United Nations was clearly selling a particular path to progress— the one endorsed by the United States—which was a marked departure from earlier conversations about progress that had essentially limited hope to those with fair skin in colder climates. Biology and geography no longer mattered.[122]

"Progress occurs only where people believe that man can, by conscious effort, master nature," the U.N. report's authors insisted. "This is a lesson which the human mind has been a long time learning," but, "where it has been learnt, human beings are experimental in their attitude to material techniques, to social institutions, and so on." This "scientific attitude," they concluded, "is one of the preconditions of progress." People first have to believe that they have the power to change almost everything about the old system, and then they have to have the ability to effect change, so progress begins with education and gains ground with freedom. Such freedom is defined by secure property rights and social mobility, which give people motivation to seek out new ways of doing things. If people are encouraged by their government to pursue progress on an individual level, then the nation will follow suit.[123] Once "the enthusiasm of the masses for improvement" has begun, then the door is open for the successful adaptation of new technologies, which people have motivation to learn how to use. This is the most important step, the report's authors insisted, because "the gap in technology between the developed and under-developed countries has grown wider and wider." Although the United Nations technically defined poverty by national income statistics, it manifested itself on the ground most obviously in missing technology. "The gap is even more impressive than is the great inequality in wealth which separates them; the two are not unrelated. On the basis of a long cumulative scientific tradition, the advanced countries of Europe and America have made great strides in technological development which have led to remarkable increases in productivity." Technology is a cumulative process, they continued, echoing Joseph Schumpeter, always building on itself and pushing the economy forward, and sustained progress is impossible without it.[124] Like TCA administrators, they emphasized starting with technological investments in education, agriculture, and infrastructure, but insisted that "progress must be made on all fronts simultaneously" and industry cannot be ignored "in the initial stages of the development programme."[125]

Although progress had to begin at home, the U.N. report concluded, domestic development programs would fail without an international component. This took two main forms: participation in the global market and infusions of capital from abroad. "As Adam Smith pointed out, the division of labour is limited by the extent of the market," so countries needed to look beyond their borders for trading partners who would help stimulate the domestic economy. Trade should start on a regional level, from which it would then naturally progress to the global level, and it should be as free as possible to encourage economic efficiency. Questions about the rules governing trade, however, meant little to nations not equipped with domestic economies strong enough to participate in any meaningful way. They needed development before they could benefit from trade. Because many underdeveloped nations did not have the finances necessary to engage in "rapid economic progress," the report's authors "urge[d] most strongly that some mechanism be created for transferring from the developed to the under-developed countries, by way of grants-in-aid, a sum of money which should increase rapidly." Low domestic savings rates in underdeveloped nations prohibited them from investing necessary capital into the economy, but money moves even more easily than technology, so the world's wealthy nations could do it for them. Presumably, they would be suitably grateful for the economic intervention.[126]

The 1951 report encouraged capitalism, free trade, public education, and, less emphatically, democracy. Above all, it emphasized mankind's ability to conquer nature via the application of new technologies and new ideas. Noting that "in recent years" some governments "have adopted the practice" of drawing up "five-year plans" of public expenditures for development, the report's authors "highly recommended" that underdeveloped countries do the same, because such plans force the government to rank priorities and encourage cooperation within the national bureaucracy and with private citizens. Comprehensive planning was both possible and productive in the current era, they concluded, and made development easier to manage.[127] For U.S. policymakers, the term "five-year plan" inspired images of the Soviet development model and raised hackles, although it was simply one manifestation of twentieth-century confidence in the state's ability to effect positive change and, as such, displayed the critical similarities between the seemingly opposite Soviet and American development models. Though their differences were obvious in the center, they were harder to see from the periphery. There, national leaders were often open to trying various combinations of urban and rural modernization, global and national integration, and capitalist and communist economic systems in pursuit of progress. They knew that neither the Soviet Union nor the United States had developed via theoretically pure systems, so why should they? Anyway, progress was fundamentally about wealth and power at the international level, and ideology could not be allowed to stand in its way. They had plans.

In a 1952 article in the journal *L'Observatuer*, the French demographer Alfred Sauvy likened the underdeveloped world to the Third Estate in pre-Revolutionary France. This "Third World," as Sauvy dubbed it, looks at the two other worlds and considers, "Should we follow one of them or try another way?" Meanwhile, Western capitalists and Eastern communists watch hungrily, longing to conquer the third world "or at least to have it on their side." It had created a tragic situation. "There is a mathematical fatalism in this adventure that only a giant brain could understand," Sauvy wrote. "Preparation for war being the number one concern, secondary ones like world hunger must not garner any more attention than is necessary to avoid explosions or trouble that could compromise the primary goal." Yet, he concluded, perhaps he was too harsh. "And perhaps, the bright, gleaming first world could not, beyond all human solidarity, remain insensitive to the slow, irresistibly humble and ferocious, movement toward life. Because an ignored, exploited and scorned Third World wants, like the Third Estate, to be something."[128] The desire for change had inspired a revolution in 1789, and it would do so again. The West needed to be prepared to ensure that the coming revolutions would end up transforming the world into its own image, rather than the Soviet's. Danger lurked in desire.

5 THE ETHIOPIAN EXPERIMENT

In a 1951 article, Technical Cooperation Administration (TCA) Director Dr. Henry Garland Bennett wrote of Point Four that "some Americans are attracted by the humanitarian element" whereas others see in it "a unique opportunity to expand international trade," thereby missing the program's most innovative and critical point: creating national security through international progress. The "progress" began at home, with a new type of diplomacy that emphasized democracy from the bottom up. Point Four focused on one-on-one relationships, on "people working with people." This is "diplomacy in a new dimension," Bennett explained, a dimension in which American doctors and engineers "ply their trades" alongside the economists and professional diplomats traditionally responsible for building and maintaining foreign relationships. "If Point Four continues to develop and expand in the direction it has taken in its first year," he ended, "it may create better patterns of co-operation and, in time, a new art of human relations in the service of economic and social progress."[1] He believed that democratic systems of development would inspire local people to want democratic systems of government. He was right, but wanting and achieving were two different things, and, sometimes, the very aid programs that encouraged people to want political reform helped keep them from getting it.

Such things were not publically discussed, but American policymakers were aware from the very beginning that their plans to enhance standards of living, halt the spread of communism, expand the global economy, and encourage the spread of democracy were often not compatible. In such cases, it was the democracy that was the most easily forgotten and the people on the ground the most easily forsaken. In the Horn of Africa, it started with Eritrea.

The State Department's spring of 1951 policy statement on Ethiopia revealed the administration's willingness to give up part of its development plans to secure others. The report opened with an acknowledgment that the 1950 U.N. resolution providing that "Eritrea shall constitute an autonomous unit federated with Ethiopia under the sovereignty of the Ethiopian Crown," should make it "considerably easier in the future to reach amicable understandings with Ethiopia in regard to other matters." Denying Eritrean independence seemed a small price to pay for securing the emperor's beneficence. Sending him weapons did as well. Ethiopia "has strongly supported the United Nations war in Korea," with contributions of money for medical supplies and a contingent of more than 1,000 officers for service, the State Department reported, and its use "is highly desirable politically." Participation in the U.N. struggle would "help the Ethiopians to obtain United States arms and military equipment which, by mitigating their previous disappointments, should assist the United States in negotiations with Ethiopia for the continued use of certain military facilities in Eritrea." In addition, "including among the UN armed forces a contingent of troops from an independent, colored nation in Africa" would be of "great propaganda value" and "help to offset the Soviet claim that the Korean war is white imperialist aggression against the colored races of the world."[2] The same could be said of economic development, if the United States could manage do it.

The State Department insisted that it was in America's best interest "to encourage and assist Ethiopia to achieve a sound, balanced and orderly development of its economic potentialities through development of its natural resources, improvement of the methods and means of agricultural and industrial production, and expansion of multilateral trade." Options already existed. The 1944 Fellows Mission had created a ten-year plan for development, the report acknowledged, which was "too ambitious for the Ethiopians to undertake in its entirety," but "selected projects in the plan . . . are worthy of consideration by this Government." Addis Ababa "has shown a preference for American advisors" and the groundwork has already been laid for the implementation of a successful assistance program. "The Point IV Program, if adequately administered, should increase the cordiality of the US-Ethiopian friendship." In the end, the report concluded, our policy toward Ethiopia "must reflect the problem which Ethiopia itself presents." It is a weak nation in an internationally critical area, and we cannot afford to allow it to fall to communist pressures—from without or from within.[3]

Largely unbeknownst to policymakers in early 1951, the "problem" of Ethiopia proved to be the question of reconciling economic development with political stagnation. Haile Selassie had not worked his entire life to become the most powerful emperor in Ethiopian history to give it up in return for some American aid. He had bigger plans. Truman's program was created to pursue multiple objectives and Washington was not averse to denying Ethiopians liberty in the name of American safety. The U.S. government had bigger plans as well.

On March 15, 1950, Haile Selassie held an audience with George C. McGhee, the assistant secretary for African affairs, during which the emperor first thanked the United States for its assistance with the "Eritrean question" and then went on to make a case for granting Ethiopia "assistance under Point Four of the Truman Programme." Ethiopia, the Ethiopian minister of foreign affairs reported the emperor as saying, "stands in need of greatly increasing her means of production and of transportation and, certainly, in this respect, the United States is in the best position for aiding in this development, by experts and capital."[4] Haile Selassie insisted that Ethiopia not only required assistance, but that it was in an ideal position to receive aid, because most of its exports went to the United States; it had allowed the Sinclair Petroleum Company "complete freedom and tranquility" to go about its activities in the country; Ethiopian Airlines was under American administration; and, crucially, American experts had already established a systematic plan for Ethiopia's economic development. The American government "has never failed to demonstrate its friendly attitude towards Ethiopia," and Point Four offered the perfect opportunity to do so again.[5]

Opportunity became reality when Truman signed Point Four into existence that June. Before the year was up, the same Perry Fellows who had led the original 1944 American technical mission to Ethiopia submitted to the TCA a forty-page Point Four proposal he had created on behalf of the Imperial Ethiopian Government (IEG), which had appointed him director of planning. After all, it could not hurt to have an American pleading their case to the United States. Fellows structured the proposal as a three-part plan divided into (1) a program for educating Ethiopian students in Near East colleges currently run or assisted by America; (2) a program of "special operations" to be undertaken by U.S. government agencies; and (3) a three-year program of projects to be undertaken by the IEG. The first program was designed for about one hundred students, a number that reflected both the scarcity of qualified students and the additional absorption capabilities of the colleges themselves, and would cost the United States about $150,000 (all sums in U.S. dollars) and Ethiopia about $50,000 for the first year. The second program was to consist of three projects: an agricultural experiment station run by the U.S. Department of Agriculture at a cost of $425,000 over three years; a vaguely titled "Educational Activity" run by the U.S. Office of

Education at a cost of $430,000 over three years; and a hydroelectric power project at Lake Tana run by the U.S. Department of the Interior at a cost of $280,000 over three years. The three programs required a Point Four appropriation of $1,135,000, with the expectation that the IEG would cover "the costs incurred in Ethiopia," including those for land, labor, and housing, which were estimated to total around $210,000 for all three programs for all three years.[6]

Fellows dedicated by far the vast majority of the proposal to the third section where he elucidated projects that would be run by the IEG, but funded by a combination of Point Four and IEG funding, with Point Four support estimated at $3,000,000 and IEG's "slightly higher." These programs would not be allowed to have any foreigner in the "line of command," but would have U.S. technicians employed in an advisory capacity. "In view of the demands of the World situation on American technical personnel," Fellows wrote, "preference will be given projects making minimum demands for such personnel or for strategic materials," additionally bearing in mind that preference also had to go to projects that will "promote Ethiopian health, education, industry and commerce."[7] He broke down projects in this third section according to IEG ministries, with agriculture working on poultry development and "bee culture," education on building libraries and laboratories, public health on establishing a domestic pharmaceutical supply, and interior working on the "standardization of names," to name a few.[8]

With its primary emphasis on education, small-scale agricultural technology, and infrastructure, the IEG proposal demonstrated a keen awareness of the international conversation about development. Fellows described Ethiopian "poverty" in the strict statistical terms now sanctioned by the international community. "The average income per head in the U.S.A. has been estimated at $1,400 by the Statistical Office of the United Nations," he reported, "and the average income in Ethiopia is *much less* [his emphasis] than $100 per head, probably about $30. The objective of the Point Four program is to close this [$1,370] gap." Proposed solutions repeated ideas present in the United Nations's 1951 *Measures for the Economic Development of Under-Developed Countries*, particularly its emphasis on a Western scientific education. Select Ethiopians would travel abroad to study and then return with the knowledge necessary both to implement new technologies and to teach others to do the same. Foreign donations could also fund new laboratories and libraries to further democratize education. "The knowledge the students get" from visiting such institutions, Fellows insisted, "is a development of Ethiopia's greatest resource and this will, in turn, lead to more rapid development of all the others." The authors of the U.N. report had written that a "scientific attitude" is "one of the preconditions of progress" and Fellows knew that U.S. readers of his proposal would be looking for programs that demonstrated an awareness of the value of human capital.[9] Such capital had to be developed into scientific literacy; it also had to been organized by the state in new ways—as demonstrated in the proposed project to work on "the standardization of names."

Twentieth-century nation states were entrusted with the responsibility of enhancing their citizens' well-being, which was difficult to do in a nation full of politically invisible people. Greater knowledge of the populace enabled the state to provide for the people's welfare in a more meaningful way. It also enabled the state to control people in a more dangerous way. Haile Selassie viewed modernization and centralization as intimately connected goals. Although seemingly unnoticed by recipient U.S. officials, and probably Fellows himself, the potential tensions between development and tyranny in Ethiopia lay innocently next to one another in the proposal.

Fellows took great care analyzing the feasibility and potential costs of each proposed project and essentially handed the TCA almost everything it needed for a three-year Point Four program in Ethiopia. The only thing he did not consider was the TCA preference of formulating its own plans. Point Four was certainly a joint effort, but countries, as Ethiopia soon learned, could not simply order money and technicians from America. Getting Point Four assistance meant accepting Point Four personnel in the "line of command" and, usually, at the very top. Additionally, activity had to wait for the creation and acceptance of specific agreements. Point Four came one project at a time.

Although Fellows's proposal on behalf of the IEG received some attention in Washington in the winter of 1950/51, it did not become the foundation of an active Point Four program.[10] Ethiopia had to wait until June to get its initial agreement and until May of 1952 for actual Point Four projects to begin. In the interim, the United States worked to ensure that the IEG received funds from the United Nations, the Import-Export Bank, and the International Bank for Reconstruction and Development to assist in livestock inoculations, road construction, telecommunications development, and the establishment of the Ethiopian Development Bank.[11] Haile Selassie needed the money, because it was virtually impossible to run a development program for a country as large and as populous as Ethiopia on a budget, one U.S. administrator later remarked in a letter to Fellows, "only approximately as large as the school budget for the metropolitan area of Washington, DC."[12] The delay stemmed from bureaucracy, not hesitation. There was no doubt that Ethiopia—"poor," "strategic," and "loyal"—qualified.

Ethiopia, the 1952 TCA's preparatory evaluation of the country noted, "is almost completely underdeveloped. The rate of illiteracy is extremely high and health and sanitation conditions are very primitive." In addition, it "is strategically located . . . on the defense perimeter of the Middle East, and possesses favorable climatic and topographical conditions, for defensive and offensive purposes." Admitting that "Communist activities have made little progress in the country so far," TCA analysts warned that "there are indications it may soon become a prime target of Communist infiltration." Ethiopia was poor, geographically strategic, and potentially vulnerable to communist incursion, which meant that it met all of the basic requirements for Point Four. Once it was clear that Ethiopia was going to get aid, discussion began about how that aid would be distributed. From the perspective of national security, the central point was just to provide enough aid to keep Ethiopia friendly with the United States and distant with the USSR, but aid carried economic expectations as well. The TCA analysts believed that "the fertile lands of Ethiopia probably are potentially the most productive of any presently underdeveloped agricultural areas in the World," and its geographic location means that it could potentially become a major food supplier for the Middle East. Ethiopia's agricultural development will be of great significance to Ethiopia's economy and "to the World food supply."

However much the IEG might desire balanced rural and urban development, U.S. aid was first going to go to the countryside. The chief of the TCA mission to Ethiopia later wrote to Perry Fellows, "the factors which I would take into account establishing priorities for projects . . . would not necessarily be the same factors which the Ethiopian Government would take into account in determining priorities for its total program of economic development. At least the order of importance might change." In 1952, the TCA ranking began with agriculture, and then listed health, education, government administration and service, transportation and communication, and natural resource development (the nation's lack of oil had become apparent), before ending with industry. The plan was to develop Ethiopia into the breadbasket of the Middle East, not into a clone of the industrial West.[13]

The possibility of Ethiopia's successful development depended on the government's support—despite that government's questionable structure. "Ethiopia is nominally a constitutional monarchy," TCA analysts admitted, "although the Emperor continues to exercise virtually absolute powers." He, "however, is progressive and has the social and economic welfare of his people at heart." He is "intensely interested" in improving living standards. Additionally, they continued, the emperor had shown himself to be "strongly oriented toward the United States and the rest of the democratic world" by taking part in the U.N. action in Korea. As Haile Selassie held up the strategic side of the bargain, so the United States needed to do its part to bring technology and capital into his economy. In 1952, Point Four aid to Ethiopia called for a modest $1,000,000 and about fifty American technicians. If it could do what it promised, it was a foreign policy steal.[14] It was not a bad deal for Haile Selassie, either; even though Point Four did not always offer the kinds of development that he wanted when he wanted it, it was a lot more than nothing.

Things got started on May 15, 1952, when the two countries signed an agreement to begin construction on the Imperial Ethiopian College of Agriculture and Mechanical Arts. Oklahoma A&M volunteered to partner with the IEG in formulating plans for classroom learning and countrywide extension services. The project, the TCA reported, "is aimed directly at building up Ethiopia's major potential contribution to the economic strength of the free nations of the world," in the hope that the more than 80 percent of its population engaged in agriculture would be able to vastly improve their production in order to provide "foodstuffs to the food-short countries in the Middle and Near East."[15] The emphasis upon agricultural education combined two essential fields of development and seemed an ideal opening project. The U.S. Government and the IEG both contributed $400,000. In addition, with assistance from Oklahoma A&M, the U.S. provided nine administrators to fill the leadership roles in the college and Ethiopia provided a liaison officer and fifteen "trainees," and, importantly, the land in Harar on which it was to be built. Because starting the nation's agricultural development was too important to be left waiting until the facilities could be built, the next month they signed a new agreement to begin holding classes at a school in Jimma starting that fall. The Jimma Agricultural Technical School demanded additional U.S. technicians to teach classes to about a hundred students, and another $200,000 to fund it for the year. Extension projects also began right away, sending U.S. technicians out into the countryside to demonstrate "modern" farming techniques to a wider audience.[16]

Even though agriculture remained the primary focus of the U.S. mission, education and public health concerns also warranted a great deal of attention. Officials with the TCA estimated that less than 5 percent of the population was literate, which would, they worried, prove "one of the most serious obstacles to the introduction of modern techniques and equipment" in their efforts to improve agricultural productivity and raise living standards.[17] The problem was so vast it was difficult to think of feasible ways to combat it. In June, the United States and the IEG signed an agreement for a Cooperative Education Program for the express purpose of assisting "the Ministry of Education in developing a modern educational program and school system adapted to the needs of Ethiopia." The project agreement was quite distinct from other (both previous and later) agreements, in that it contained within it seventeen different goals/miniprojects, varying from simply increasing the number of teachers to training them in "modern" techniques and providing them with books and equipment. Whereas the plans were large, the input was modest. The United States provided only about $100,000 and seventeen technicians/advisors/teachers. Ethiopia did the same.[18]

Additional projects for 1952 included sending a handicraft specialist and a modest amount of funding to assist in the work of Her Imperial Majesty's Handicraft School, which trained craftsmen in making furniture, clothing, jewelry, and other products; implementing a water resource study; and establishing a Pest Control Unit in the Ministry of Agriculture. The latter involved a U.S. contribution of three American sprayer planes, the necessary chemicals, an entomologist, and three pilots on loan from the regional locust program office. In return, Ethiopia donated the fuel and sent eleven men to be trained in the technology involved in the process. The water resource study included both examining the country's potential for hydroelectric power and researching irrigation feasibility schemes. It required nine U.S. scientists and around $60,000, combined with forty Ethiopian trainees and a matching dollar contribution.[19] All three of these projects, along with the ones discussed previously, continued to be funded (at varying levels) for at least another two years, but in the opening days of 1953, Point Four's future was uncertain.

On January 12, 1953, the *New York Times* ran a lengthy article publishing the very favorable findings of an investigation it had made into Point Four operations in all of the thirty-five countries that had official agreements.[20] Truman had arranged the article as part of a publicity campaign strategy to save Point Four from the new president, Dwight D. Eisenhower, who more than once during the campaign had announced that the United States "cannot go on forever being Santa Claus to the world."[21] Concerned about the program's efficiency, Eisenhower sent Eric Johnston of the International Development Advisory Board overseas that spring to investigate operations in Israel, Jordan, Syria, Lebanon, Saudi Arabia, Egypt, and Ethiopia. He liked what he saw.

In the opening of his report on his trip, Johnston told the president that "the technical cooperation program is well received; a good U.S. investment in friendship and goodwill; effective in helping others acquire knowledge and skills useful in their social and economic development; relatively inexpensive and well worth the time and expense in terms of world peace and development." Writing particularly about Ethiopia, Johnston noted that he had met with many officials, the most important being Haile Selassie and Yilma Deressa, who was now the minister of commerce and industry. Both "seemed pleased with the Point 4 program and its personnel." The British ambassador showed decidedly less enthusiasm, telling Johnston "in the strongest possible terms the danger of proceeding too far and too fast with the Point 4 program." The Ethiopians, he insisted, are "inclined to play one group of foreigners against another to keep them in balance," and the influx of American personnel is making their game easier. When asked, the Ethiopians strongly disagreed, no doubt helpfully pointing out that the British were concerned about their own agenda. Yilma Deressa insisted that his country needed more, not less U.S. involvement. Johnston agreed.[22]

Despite initial misgivings, Eisenhower acknowledged that Point Four seemed to be both popular and effective. Though willing to maintain Truman's program, however, the new president severed the program's overt ties with the previous administration. In July 1953, Point Four and the TCA became the Foreign Operations Administration and then, in 1955, the International Cooperation Administration (ICA), which is the name that will be used henceforth to avoid unnecessary confusion. The changes took Point Four out of the Department of State and into its own agency. The move showed the increasing value that the Eisenhower administration placed on foreign aid, but did little to change the program's essential nature. The term *Point Four* managed to show up frequently in letters and documents throughout the 1950s. People continued to associate foreign aid with Truman, but Eisenhower worked to put his own stamp on it. In 1954, he signed the strategic Food-for-Peace Program (Public Law 480) into creation, which allowed the United States to donate domestic agricultural surpluses to countries that needed food. In 1957, he created the Development Loan Fund within the ICA to support development projects not considered standard technical assistance. Foreign aid funding actually rose a great deal under the man who had once worried about being "Santa Claus to the world."[23]

With the exception of its name, Point Four remained largely unchanged. In 1953, ICA officials listed nine goals for the U.S. mission to Ethiopia: to improve agricultural production by "training in basic agricultural elements" and "raising the level of study to specialized fields of agriculture"; to explore the possibility of increasing coffee and livestock production for export; to cooperate with the international locust control program; to "broaden the educational base by training teachers and educational administrators"; to explore feasible means of increasing water utilization; "to produce a corps of trained personnel to bring health services to the local communities"; to encourage more effective marketing of products; "to develop a body of trained government personnel"; and "to assist in the organization of institutions and government mechanisms through which trained Ethiopians can accomplish the principles outlined above."[24] The ICA attempted to meet these goals by increasing its staff, using more funds, and initiating more projects. By March 1953, Point Four had forty-five staff persons working in Ethiopia with six more on the way.[25] The funding allotment from Washington more than doubled to $2,600,000. New projects, dedicated to cattle vaccination, well drilling, nurse and midwife training, and public health education, were initiated in 1953. These were joined in 1954 by projects focused on further agricultural improvement initiatives, cooperative coffee development-for-exportation schemes, water safety studies, and rural vocational development through the establishment of handicraft centers around the country.

FIGURE 5.1 A pith-helmeted Haile Selassie and other guests view a poultry demonstration during a 1955 Field Day at the Jimma Agricultural Technical School. *Still Picture Records Section, National Archives, College Park, Maryland*

Two additional 1954 projects inspired greater attention, namely, the Commerce and Industry Development Service and the Public Administration projects. Both shared a common goal of working with the Ethiopian government to alter, to varying degrees, its governmental/legal structure. The Commerce and Industry Development Service focused primarily on helping the IEG to create an "attractive investment climate" for both domestic and international businessmen. This was done by persuading the IEG to instigate measures such as tax exemption for five years, import duty exemption, and repatriation of investment and profits. Additional measures, including required participation of Ethiopian private capital jointly with foreign private capital, were also instigated to ensure that investment would be of the greatest benefit to the local market. By April 1954, there were fifty-three active private investments underway in Ethiopia, divided almost equally between foreign and domestic companies.[26] The U.S. efforts to assist the IEG in making this possible were founded on classic development discourse ideology, harkening back to Rosenstein-Rodan's initial call for substantial international investment in "international depressed areas," ideally by states, but supplemented by private capital whenever possible.[27] Point Four staffers knew that the ICA program was "very small in relation to Ethiopia's needs" and could not offer the kinds of capital necessary for sparking natural, continued development. Anyway, the program had always been designed simply to start nations on the road to progress, getting them to the point where they could enter the world economy in a meaningful way and rely on the power of the market for continued development. Technical assistance was the beginning, not the end of development.[28]

Thinking along these lines, U.S. Operations Mission Director Marcus Gordon urged Perry Fellows to divert more IEG funds toward coffee development, which is something that Haile Selassie had been promoting since the 1920s. "I would agree with you that there may be some danger in the long run of spending extensive amounts for the further development of a commodity upon which Ethiopia is already dependent," Gordon admitted, "however, the economic factors seem to indicate clearly that Ethiopia will benefit" from expenditures in this area. You have the best land in the world for coffee, he insisted, and coffee consumption is on the rise in the United States, in Europe, and even in Asia. Brazil dominates the market currently, but you can produce it and sell it for less, changing the stakes of the global market. "With relatively little effort Ethiopia's coffee production can be multiplied by several times" and you will see high returns on your investment right now and probably well into the future. Because the United States consumed roughly half of the world's coffee production, challenging the Brazilian monopoly would also be beneficial at home, Gordon implied, but did not acknowledge directly.[29] Fellows was justly nervous about betting everything on coffee, because commodities are fickle things, but without industry, Ethiopia only had the products of its land and coffee was by far the most valuable of those products. The ICA was working on the ground to enhance the general agricultural yields of small farmers around the country, but coffee—primarily grown in the south on lands controlled by northern nobles, and already a pet project of the emperor—could be expanded more quickly and easily. You need money now, Gordon wrote, so put emergency money into the one crop that already has a presence on the world market. Haile Selassie, as will be demonstrated later in the chapter, could not have agreed more. He had always placed a great deal of hope in coffee.

While the Commerce and Industry Development Service worked on enhancing Ethiopia's attractiveness to private investors, the Public Administration project directed its efforts toward the more general goal of equipping the government bureaucracy to deal with the changing demands of an expanding economy and an expanding social services sector. "Both day to day administration and long range governmental planning in Ethiopia," Point Four officials noted, "are handicapped by the lack of effective and coordinated public administration," so efforts were undertaken to train Ethiopian officials in the effective administration of government.[30] This training included compiling records, archiving data, taking proper accounting of funds and coordinating work between different ministries. The Public Administration project also funded a couple of studies of specific ministries in order to appraise their organization and their administration. The U.S. administrators were, perhaps, anticipating a day when Ethiopia would no longer be run by an emperor with "virtually absolute powers" and trying to assist the country in establishing a bureaucracy that could run on its own. Haile Selassie, however, had no intention of allowing the United States to develop Ethiopia out of his control. Presidents come and go, but an emperor can reign for a century, or at least something close to it.

In June 1954, Haile Selassie visited Oklahoma A&M to thank the college for its assistance in establishing and maintaining Ethiopia's own A&M. At the formal banquet marking the event, the college presented the emperor with a scroll pronouncing "appreciation for his courageous and enlightened leadership of his people" and gratitude for the opportunity to "assist him in some measure in bringing to fruition the humanitarian and progressive dream he holds for his great nation and its people." Haile Selassie graciously thanked the college and expressed his hope that his visit would "stimulate an even greater program of technical assistance and private capital investment" than the one currently in existence. "I have always been mindful of the importance of economic cooperation as one of the parts of understanding between nations," he continued, which is why Ethiopia encourages "persons of good intent to come and participate in the program which we have outlined for the progress and welfare of our people."[31] By referring to the plan Perry Fellows had created during the 1940s, the emperor reminded his listeners that Ethiopia had created its own plan for its development years before Point Four aid first reached the country. Haile Selassie had been trying to modernize his nation since the 1920s and although he gladly welcomed U.S. assistance, he insisted on Ethiopian autonomy as much as possible. "We," he emphasized, "have outlined" a program, and we hope that you will "participate" in it. In his ideal modernization scheme, the money and the technicians came from abroad, but the ideas came from the palace.

Just a few days earlier, Haile Selassie had spoken (partly in English, partly in Amharic) to a joint session of Congress explaining "the circumstances which make Ethiopia a significant factor in world affairs." In the last seven years, he noted, Ethiopia's foreign trade, currency, and foreign exchange had quadrupled, and holdings of American dollars had increased ten times over due to coffee sales. Ethiopia became the only country in the Middle East to have a dollar-based currency, and the assets of its national bank of issue had increased 1,000 percent. Since the end of the war, he continued, picking up on a topic that he knew was dear to American leaders, Ethiopia "has become the granary of the Middle East, as well as the only exporter of meat, cereals and vegetables." The nation was seemingly fulfilling its side of the development bargain. Even though all its educational facilities were destroyed during the war, schools were now "springing up throughout the land." We have, he concluded, "become a land of expanding opportunities where the American pioneering spirit, ingenuity and technical abilities have been, and will continue to be, welcomed."[32] Although he did not say it directly, the message announced that such progress would certainly continue if the aid continued. In less public venues around Washington, he did not display such confidence, expressing worry that Ethiopia's very existence—let alone its modernization—was at risk from threats at home and abroad. He needed more.

Haile Selassie had, one U.S. official at the Ethiopian embassy wrote in 1955, "an inordinate interest in military affairs."[33] While the emperor continued to plow money into economic development, his primary preoccupation proved to be expanding and modernizing his military forces. The United

States helped him do it. By the end of March 1954, Washington had shipped $3.8 million worth of small arms, artillery, and small vehicles to Addis Ababa.[34] It was a start. "Last year by favoring Ethiopia over other countries of the Middle East," the Ethiopian embassy wrote in a 1954 memorandum to Eisenhower, "the United States enabled Ethiopia to lay the basis for a fruitful collaboration on the military plane." His Imperial Majesty believes it "absolutely essential that this program go forward as rapidly as possible," and Ethiopia is "happy" to agree to any desired escalation of the U.S. military presence in return for new equipment.[35] So 1954 became the first, but certainly not the last, year that American military aid to Ethiopia outstripped economic/technical aid. Washington's desire to maintain a strategic presence in the region blended well with the emperor's grand visions of being the leading political figure in both Africa and the Middle East. He possessed something that the United States wanted, and he worked very hard to make sure that it became dependent upon it.

Initial American military interest in Ethiopia centered on the Asmara Barracks radio communication center. Located far from the North and South poles, Asmara was in a tropic zone with very little seasonal variation between the time of sunrise and sunset, which had the beneficial effect of limiting the number of frequency changes necessary for continued radio contact. It was the perfect radio tracking center for monitoring the region, and the United States wanted it. Its location had ensured U.S. support for Ethiopia's petition to the United Nations for federation with Eritrea.[36] The federation became final in September 1952, and the following year, the United States formalized access to the recently dubbed Kagnew Station (in honor of the Ethiopian battalion that had served in Korea), in a twenty-five-year lease agreement at the cost of around $10 million a year. The agreement also granted the United States complete freedom of access to all Ethiopian facilities and freedom of flight over the country. In return, along with continued Point Four assistance, Haile Selassie attained another agreement that required the United States to establish a Military Assistance Advisory Acceptance Group, which would train and equip three Ethiopian divisions of around 6,000 men each and an additional $5,000,000 in military assistance.[37]

By the time Haile Selassie made his first official state visit in May 1954, the agreements of the previous year had convinced him that his future relationship with the United States rested on a combination of economic and military assistance in return for his continued loyalty to the West. Changes in the U.S. perspective of the region in the mid-1950s proved to further strengthen his cause in Washington and resulted in millions more dollars worth of aid and equipment to continue securing this strategic ally resting on the border between the Middle East and Africa. Haile Selassie himself had stressed the point during his speech to Congress. "Situated along the shores of the Red Sea, with the desert area of Africa to the north and west, it is but natural," he explained, "that Ethiopia should be the filter through which the ideas and influences of the Continent of Africa should pass to the East and vice versa."[38] That position had historically belonged to Egypt, but Egypt was proving troublesome to both Haile Selassie and, increasingly, the United States.

While the Eisenhower administration spent most of its time working to stop the spread of communism around the world, members of the IEG in Addis Ababa spent their time worrying about how they would maintain control over a state that contained hundreds of thousands of unwilling subjects. Newly federated Eritreans had hoped that they would get independence after the Italians were forced out, but instead wound up subordinate to Addis Ababa. Domestic resistance to Ethiopian rule led many to turn to Egypt's Gamal Abdel Nasser for support, and he promptly opened his door to Muslim (and also a few Christian) Eritrean expatriates. Nasser, Haile Selassie's premier rival for regional influence, was a source of great distress for the emperor, who feared that the Egyptian would (as, indeed, he did) promote Muslim dissatisfaction with his regime.[39] This posed a problem much greater than Eritrea itself, for the countryside outside of the highlands surrounding Addis Ababa was populated with ethnic and religious groups that felt little loyalty to the ruling Christian Amharas. In order to keep control, the IEG relied increasingly on dictatorial rule in the periphery.[40]

In addition to struggling to keep the empire's unwilling participants *in*, Haile Selassie was also constantly working to keep other empires *out*. Although the British had evacuated most of the country by 1950, they kept troops stationed in a 25,000 square mile territory known as the Haud in the Ogaden, which shared a border with French and British Somaliland. The Haud was primarily populated by ethnic Muslim Somalis, who evidenced little desire to be united with Ethiopia, but Addis Ababa had an official claim to the region dating back to an 1897 treaty with Britain. Haile Selassie demanded that the territory be returned to him and it was in early 1955. The French and the British, however, remained just across the border, engaging in regular conversations about the benefits of an eventual "Greater Somaliland."[41] Clearly the IEG had reason to worry about the stability of its power, particularly as it remained hazy what Washington policymakers, who were trying "to keep both colonizers and colonized together as part of the 'free world,'" would do in the face of a European onslaught against his country.[42] Haile Selassie challenged European authority in neighboring countries. For much of Africa—and, indeed, for the descendents of Africans around the world—Ethiopia and its ruler served as proof that white oppression could be effectively resisted.

A "modernized" Ethiopia would provide even greater legitimacy to Haile Selassie's status as Africa's leading figure and the emperor continued to pursue the economic development of his nation with great zeal in the midst of transforming its military. He decided in 1954, ten years after Perry Fellows's original technical mission, to embrace a new development scheme for Ethiopia. The emperor ordered surveys of the country's economic situation and set up a National Economic Council consisting of Ethiopia's ministers and vice-ministers of commerce and industry, agriculture, finance, defense, and public works, as well as "experts" from the University of Belgrade and various IEG departments. He was the chair. With his "guidance," he announced, the council would develop a new plan to help Ethiopia "achieve a modernization of her economy." Officials spent the next three years working out the details.[43] In the same spirit, he decided in 1955, in honor of the silver jubilee of his coronation, to grant his people a "Revised Constitution consolidating the progress achieved, and preparing the way for future advances." The past twenty-five years, he announced in a speech introducing the constitution, "have been characterized by material, including commercial, industrial and financial progress, a steeply ascending curve of cultural and political development, an expanded population and national territory, and ever-widening national horizons." We have accomplished much, but Ethiopia "under Our guidance, must consolidate this progress. She must do more. She must advance yet further." Progress demands "increasing governmental supervision and control," which the new constitution provides.[44] Although it introduced universal adult suffrage and provisions for a Chamber of Deputies elected by the people, the constitution as a whole did little more than reaffirm the emperor's absolute power. Article 4 announced he was "sacred" and his power "indisputable." It symbolized progress, but codified continued absolutism.[45] What the constitution did on paper, military modernization did in practice. Haile Selassie pursued development projects designed to make him untouchable. He had a lot of enemies. The one in Cairo was still considered a "friend" to the United States, but such things have a way of falling apart. He watched and waited.

The United States had been openly working with Nasser since the 1952 coup that brought his government to power, but the Egyptian leader's increasing resistance to Western intervention in his affairs and public hatred of

Israel was proving troublesome for Washington. By 1954, U.S. policymakers had two major concerns regarding Egypt. The first was to ensure continued Anglo influence over the Suez Canal by helping create an agreement that sanctioned the British presence in the Canal Zone. The second was to determine Egypt's role in future Middle East security. Convinced that they needed to build a northern tier of defense as a buffer against Soviet expansion into the region, U.S. officials began working with Turkey, Iran, Iraq, and Pakistan to establish the Baghdad Pact. In order to further a more positive relationship with the Revolutionary Command Council and its now overt head, Nasser, the Eisenhower administration offered $40 million in economic assistance. British interests once again delayed the delivery of the money until after Egypt had signed an evacuation agreement for the Canal Zone that included the right to reoccupy in the event of an attack by an outside force on any Arab League state or on Turkey, but by the end of summer negotiations ensued between Washington and Cairo.[46] Nasser signed the economic aid agreement in November, but, much to Washington's consternation, he refused any military aid, because he did not want the conditions that came with it. Also, despite the economic aid, he refused to join the Baghdad Pact and even began campaigning to get other Middle Eastern nations to follow his example. In 1955, he solidified his commitment to neutrality by attending the Bandung Conference in Indonesia, which unnerved the Eisenhower administration with its efforts to bring racial and imperial issues to the forefront of international relations, thereby taking the focus off of the East versus West fight. A few months later, he purchased large quantities of arms through Czechoslovakia.[47]

Relations between Washington and Cairo steadily deteriorated throughout 1954 and 1955, even though U.S. policymakers continued sending large amounts of Point Four aid in attempts to keep Nasser friendly to their interests.[48] Between the original agreement in 1951 and July 1954, the United States contributed $16,589,427 to Point Four programs in Egypt. In 1955, the United States distributed an additional $3,444,000 to the U.S. mission to Egypt. Along with this technical assistance, Washington provided a further $40 million in development funding between 1954 and 1955, of which the majority ($27 million) went to improving the nation's transportation system.[49] By the end of fiscal year (FY) 1955, Egypt had received almost $60 million in foreign aid from the United States. The next year, everything changed.

In 1956, frustrated over America's abrupt withdrawal of a loan offer to construct the Aswan Dam in response to his attacks on Israel, Nasser nationalized the Suez Canal, announcing that its revenue would be used to pay for the dam. When Britain, France, and Israel subsequently attacked Egypt, the United States demanded that they cease hostilities, but the United States–Egyptian relationship was seriously damaged by the whole incident. The hostilities, combined with Nasser's continued reluctance to acknowledge U.S. aid publicly, led the Eisenhower administration to call a halt to Point Four activities in the country.[50]

At this critical juncture, Haile Selassie once more displayed a shrewd ability to anticipate Washington's desires by permitting Israel to open a permanent consulate in Addis Ababa. Ethiopia had been a subtle supporter of the Jewish state since its inception, but had resisted a public relationship for fear of damaging its influence over its Middle Eastern neighbors. As America's relationship with Nasser went from bad to nonexistent, Haile Selassie recognized that the moment was ripe for him to secure greater concessions for his own loyalty to Washington's Middle East agenda.[51] His plan worked. In a November 1956 National Security Council (NSC) meeting, Eisenhower "stated very firmly his great anxiety to be assured of the friendship of Ethiopia."[52] An NSC policy paper released a few days later asserted, "Ethiopia's importance to the United States transcends the country's limited power and somewhat isolated position. Current developments in the Near East increase the value to the United States of a friendly, stable government in this region of Africa." Ethiopian support is also ideologically important, for, "from a political point of view, it is of value to maintain close relations with an African state which has become a symbol of resistance to aggression and a champion of collective security."[53] Sending troops to Korea had been one of Haile Selassie's wisest moves. Opening his doors to Israel would prove to be another.

In the midst of consolidating his authority at home, the emperor also validated such consolidation abroad, convincing policymakers in the United States that he was far too loyal a friend to risk damaging in the pursuit of spreading democracy. "The political stability of Ethiopia, its present pro-Western orientation and its still apparent freedom from communist subversion, is at present almost solely dependent upon the prestige and power of His Imperial Majesty, Haile Selassie I," read an Operations Coordinating Board report in December 1956. He is under siege by a number of groups: "dispossessed political leaders," "progressive young army officers," "tribal leaders and provincial lords whose traditional power is threatened by the growing power of the central government," the "Moslems group which constitutes a strong minority of the population," "young intellectuals and middle and upper class civil servants who are dissatisfied with their present status," the "Communist

Bloc," and Egypt. We have "an unquestioned interest" in "offsetting" the "latent threats to Ethiopia's security and independence from communist and Egyptian tactics," maintaining political stability, and "developing" it "along Western standards," the report continued. By the end of 1956, the U.S. government viewed the IEG as a central player in its international security agenda.[54] Increased attention brought increased aid. Through 1956, U.S. military and economic aid to Ethiopia totaled a little more than $24 million, but the budget for 1957 quickly shot up to $13.6 million for one year alone, including a $5 million grant aid to be used at the IEG's discretion.[55] It also brought visible American attention.

"Important steps have been taken to strengthen Ethiopia's alignment with the U.S.," insisted a 1957 progress report on U.S. policy. The nation "was included within the area covered by the American Doctrine, and was recently visited by Vice President Nixon and other high-ranking United States officials."[56] In the now famously dubbed Eisenhower Doctrine, following on the heels of the Suez Crisis, the president proposed legislation to "authorize the United States to cooperate with and assist any nation or group of nations in the general area of the Middle East in the development of economic strength dedicated to the maintenance of national independence" and to "authorize the Executive to undertake in the same region programs of military assistance and cooperation with any nation or group of nations which desires such aid." The United States had already been doing as much through programs associated with the mutual security programs, but Eisenhower informed Congress that he was going to be asking for an additional $200,000,000 for "discretionary use in the area" during both FY 1958 and 1959. Lest there be any doubt about the U.S. commitment to the region, he also asked that the president be given the authority to employ the armed forces in order to protect any state in the region under the threat of "overt armed aggression from any nation controlled by International Communism." Congress granted him the authority by the end of the month.[57] Eisenhower promptly sent Special Ambassador James P. Richards to the Middle East to generate support for the doctrine. Ethiopia and the Sudan were included because, in the words of a 1957 NSC report, "these countries tend in their political, cultural and economic outlooks to be oriented much more towards North Africa and the Middle East . . . than they are towards tropical Africa." They are additionally united by their concerns about "Egypt's ambitions in the area," and "direct their attentions and energies northwards."[58] Haile Selassie certainly would have agreed that he spent a lot of time worrying about Egypt, but his regional interests did not focus on the Middle East alone. He also looked southward toward a changing "tropical Africa."

Haile Selassie saw himself as a model for aspiring African leaders just beginning to push off their colonial overlords and many viewed him—as they had Menelik before him—as a symbol of Black independence. The United States was not so sure. Ethiopia, Richards pointed out in his country report, was not as stable as Haile Selassie made it out to be and his government not as benign. "The predominant prominent personal role played by the Emperor is a source of weakness as well as strength," Richards commented. "He is now 64 years old and it is by no means certain that his succession will be peaceful." Even talking about succession, however, highlighted the question of how very undemocratic was the nation's political system. Though the emperor could be justly congratulated for pursuing development, it was always implemented on his own terms. "Thus far the political passivity of a backward population has enabled the Ethiopian Government to rule the country with inadequate recognition of basic human rights and with little apparent concern for the needs of its people as judged from an occidental standpoint," Richards noted.[59] One wonders if Haile Selassie had yet recognized that the wave of decolonization that was about to sweep over Africa meant that the United States was going to be distributing aid to dozens more nations. Independence from Europe could not be allowed to mean the freedom to align with the USSR.

On March 6, 1957, the British retreated from Ghana, initiating the beginning of the end of the colonial era. Vice President Richard Nixon flew in to Accra to enjoy the celebration, infamously embarrassing himself by enthusiastically asking a man next to him how it felt to be free, only to hear, "I wouldn't know, sir, I'm from Alabama." The incident addressed America's difficulty of trying to capture the loyalties of nonwhite leaders abroad while denying equality to nonwhite citizens at home.[60] Institutionalized racism within the United States did not go unnoticed by rising African leaders such as Ghana's new president Kwame Nkrumah, and it did not hold up favorably in comparison to racially tolerant Soviet system, which made other aspects of that system more appealing. Nkrumah, who became known as "the father of African socialism," was vocal from the start about capitalism's limited ability to bring rapid economic progress *and* social justice to Ghana. Capitalism seemed too closely tied to imperialism to be an acceptable choice.[61] The potential attractiveness of Ghana's initial political/economic structure to other African states on the verge of independence made Washington policymakers even more determined to prop up loyal African allies wherever they could be found—including Ethiopia.[62]

FIGURE 5.2 An American nurse registers future students at the Itegue Menen School of Nursing in Asmara, Eritrea, in February 1955. On the wall above hangs a framed image of Haile Selassie with the Eisenhowers during his 1954 visit to the United States. *Still Picture Records Section, National Archives, College Park, Maryland*

When Nixon left Accra, he flew to Addis Abba, where he met with Foreign Minister Aklilu Habte Wolde on March 12, who began their conversation by saying that "he wished first of all to emphasize the growing importance of Africa." Ethiopia welcomed the birth of new self-governing states, Aklilu told him, and lent its support. "He spoke of Ethiopia as being both a Middle Eastern and African nation, which it enhances its importance to the United States," Nixon reported, and emphasized its years of loyalty. An IEG statement, "Defense Problems of Ethiopia," repeated the message to the vice president with greater vehemence, noting that although Ethiopia "is playing the stooge of the Colonel Powers, in sending her sons to die in Korea and in being the stalking horse for the imperialist designs of those same Powers on freedom of national development," the United States "has never intended seriously to support Ethiopia's defense efforts." The paper went on, not unpredictably, to list all of the military equipment that the IEG believed the United States needed to supply. The emperor continued the attack, albeit with his classic dignity and restraint, emphasizing to Nixon "the need for a re-examination of relations" between the two nations.⁶³ The IEG's combined efforts worked, for Nixon wrote to the secretary of defense a few days after his return, "I believe that Ethiopia will have an increasingly important influence in African affairs, and that our enlightened self-interest requires that we ensure their continued friendship and support of our policies." In addition, he continued, getting to the heart of IEG frustrations, "I further believe that the Armed Forces of Ethiopia could have an important stabilizing role in the Middle East in addition to their primary mission of internal security."⁶⁴ Neither economic nor military assistance, Nixon insisted, would be wasted on Ethiopia. Eisenhower trumped him by insisting that it would not be wasted anywhere.

In February 1958, the president sent Congress a request for $142 million for the ICA for FY 1959, along with an additional $3.9 billion for the other components of the Mutual Security Program. Throughout the decade, his message read, the program had dramatically increased the military power of the free world and "afforded the critical margin of assistance" required by "newly developing" nations "to make the economic progress essential to their survival." Our programs show their more than one billion citizens that "growth can be achieved more readily in conditions of freedom, that it is not necessary to sacrifice liberty for bread." We cannot slowdown our efforts, Eisenhower continued, because in the past three years, the Soviet Union and Communist China "have been offering increasing amounts of economic and technical aid to countries of the free world, often under conditions that, on the surface, are appealing." Free countries would not willingly indebt themselves to Moscow, but if "forced to choose between abandoning development programs demanded by their people, or achieving them through Communist bloc assistance," they would pick the latter. We began providing assistance years before "the Soviet economic offensive began" and "so long as the uncommitted countries know that the rest of the free world shares their aspirations and is prepared to help them achieve economic and social progress in independence and freedom, we can be confident that the cause of the free world will prevail." Eisenhower punctuated his request for continued aid with a dramatic flourish, insisting, "For the safety of our families, the future of our children and our continued existence as a nation, we cannot afford to slacken our support of the mutual security program."⁶⁵

The next month, as Congress debated a new bill based on Eisenhower's request, the Senate Foreign Affairs Committee held hearings on the Mutual Security Act. Stuart H. Van Dyke, the regional director for Africa and Europe in the ICA, reported "until about a year ago, African programs were limited to technical cooperation in Ethiopia, Liberia, Libya, Somalia, and a few projects in the British overseas territories," but we have plans to expand into Ghana, Kenya, Uganda, Nigeria, Morocco, Tunisia, and the Federation of Rhodesia. Our activities revolve around agriculture and education, and "we plan to continue in such fields as building extension systems; crop research, range management, and livestock improvement; development; conservation, and improved use of water supplies; reforestation; fisheries; and development of local institutions for agricultural education, credit, and various cooperative activities." Our "industry effort is still relatively small," he admitted, "because the opportunities for technical assistance in this field are limited at the present stage of development in most of Africa."[66]

Van Dyke cited Ethiopia as an example of the program's success. The Agriculture and Technical School at Jimma, he reported, which had opened in 1952 with 80 students, had since graduated 121, and now had an enrollment of 215 "drawn from most of the provinces of Ethiopia." The Imperial Ethiopia College of Agriculture and Mechanical Arts, he continued, opened in 1956 and estimated a class size of more than three hundred students by 1961. Joint efforts with Oklahoma State University to improve coffee production had created the cultivation of a seed with a 90 percent survival rate, compared to the 30 to 40 percent survival rate of transplanted wild seedlings. Of these improved plants, 298,000 were sold in 1957, and demand continues to rise. In addition, the ICA had introduced a new "wet method" of processing that increased the value of the coffee as much as 25 percent per pound. Three hundred tons were processed that way in 1956 and 1,500 in 1957 as extension workers spread the technology throughout the countryside. Cognizant that illness hindered Ethiopia's national productivity, Point Four spent $949,000 on public health projects between 1952 and 1957, with most of that going to the Gondar training program and the malaria control project that had started in 1956 in conjunction with the World Health Organization. As of 1958, the malaria project had provided protection for about eighty thousand people and made it possible to reclaim about eight hundred square miles of agricultural land previously too dangerous to farm. "Our objective," Van Dyke concluded, "is a stable, prosperous, friendly Africa," and continuing our aid programs will enable us to reach that goal. "The character and degree of United States support to Africa's economic development can mean the difference between an orderly evolution in keeping with democratic ideas and institutions, and violent and authoritarian movements that arise from poverty, disease, and despair."[67]

The rhetoric was moving, but senators have to worry about elections and they had questions. "Are we creating a dependency economically," asked

Alexander Wiley of Wisconsin (who had complained about being Santa Claus to Acheson back in 1950) about Morocco in particular and all aid recipients in general, "or are we improving their own economy so that eventually they may be able to get along without our support?" Van Dike insisted that the ICA was building an "economic base" that would hold self-sustaining economies. Wiley went on to ask how much of the Mutual Security Act money was spent on goods purchased in the United States and was a little disgruntled to learn that it was only as high as 75 percent. He was hoping for ninety. William F. Knowland of California asked about the difficulties surrounding Ethiopia's ability to absorb foreign capital, and Van Dyke responded with a brief explanation of the complications of establishing land ownership throughout the country. The ICA is training people about the benefits of "modern practices," he continued, but it is "going to be a long and difficult process." No one questioned whether or not it was beneficial, they just wondered how long it would take to do so. On that front, Van Dyke stressed the positives: "They can of course leapfrog all the difficulties we faced in developing the legal and procedural institutions which make our modern economy operate." What had worked in the United States presumably worked everywhere. There was one path to progress and American aid funds made sure that more nations could follow it. Heaven help us, Van Dyke gloomily implied, if we fail to do so.[68]

International leaders wisely used the fear to their own advantage. When Washington did not respond quickly enough to his request for a larger amount of assistance, Haile Selassie went on a highly publicized trip to the Soviet Union, which resulted in more than $100 million of economic credits. The United States knew about the trip beforehand and worried about its potential ramifications. Discussing the situation at a 1959 NSC meeting, Director of Central Intelligence Allen Dulles warned that the move might be "the first major attempt of the Communist Bloc to penetrate into the deeper parts of Africa." It might also be possible that the emperor is, "in a quiet way, attempting to blackmail the U.S. Some opposition to his agreements has already made itself apparent in Addis Ababa," he continued, "but the opposition groups, who have approached us with the idea of putting the Crown Prince on the throne, have very little popular backing." We are, Dulles gravely noted, following the situation carefully.[69] "In subsequent months, not entirely coincidently, U.S. assistance increased very substantially," noted a confidential State Department report. We do not "plan to outbid the Soviets," Deputy Director John Root announced in a secret January 1960 meeting, but we will move "to block Soviet dominance over key sectors." Between 1959 and 1962, Ethiopia received $66 million in technical, economic, and military assistance from the United States. It was less than the Soviets had promised, but it was enough to keep the emperor friendly. Haile Selassie promptly sent troops to the Congo to assist U.S. troops in a public gesture of support. He had always been adept at international politics.[70]

On returning to Ethiopia after his 1959 world tour—which included stops in Egypt, the Soviet Union, Czechoslovakia, Belgium, France, Portugal, West Germany, and Yugoslavia—Haile Selassie explained his main objective had been, as it always was, "to find ways and means of raising the standard of living of Our people and the economic development of Our country." He went in search of aid to finance Ethiopia's five year plan, the final result of the National Economic Council he had created back in 1954. He had formally presented the plan to the people in 1957, promising that its implementation would pull Ethiopia "out of economic backwardness and strengthen its economy and its position in international relations." A constant lack of funds, however, had slowed its implementation. This was particularly vexing considering that its most basic aim was to "accelerate development by a coordinated and actively pursued development policy in the immediate future," thereby laying "the foundation "for more intensive and overall development" in the future. The words employed in the introduction—acceleration, immediacy, coordination, intensity, and activity—betrayed the committee's, or, perhaps most correctly, Haile Selassie's, insistence on big change. Defying Point Four workers' attempts to end Ethiopia's underdevelopment through many small, grassroots projects, the IEG's plan called for a large-scale, centralized approach that attacked numerous development issues all at once. If implemented, the plan's authors promised, Ethiopia could potentially reach an annual increase in the national income of 3.7 percent, compared to current rates of 2 to 2.5 percent.[71]

Haile Selassie's Five Year Plan revolved around the construction of an "urban economy" as the most efficient means of ending peasant agriculture's stranglehold on the national market. He viewed Ethiopia's massive peasant class, representing about 90 percent of the population, as the premier impediment to modernization. "The great problem of future economic development," the IEG insisted, "is to find ways and means of transforming a subsistence economy into a monetary one. The development of industry, handicrafts, commerce and transport is a way of creating a monetary economy, of changing the social and economic structure, and of increasing income per head."[72] He wanted to turn a nation of farmers and pastoralists into a nation of merchants and industrialists. He wanted to move Ethiopia into the later stages of the Scottish Enlightenment's age of commerce, and he wanted to do it quickly.

He began with his largest resource: the people. All of those laborers in the field should be moved into factories. Investing most of the money allocated for the Five Year Plan into the transportation, communication, electrical, and manufacturing sectors, would, Haile Selassie believed, make that move a reality. According to the plan, these sectors would end up with 340.4 of the 534.6 million Ethiopian dollars budgeted for monetary investment by the government between 1957 and 1961. Meanwhile, agriculture, which employed the vast majority of the population, received only $40.3 million, and much of that was directed toward establishing large commercialized farms to produce crops such as coffee and cotton for export. The IEG insisted that industry would replace agriculture as the center of the economy, for as the factories were built, people would move from rural to urban areas. There consequently seemed little incentive to try to modernize individual farms and plans to create a national agricultural extension service had a budget of only $5 million for four years.[73] Haile Selassie did not want a nation of farmers; he wanted a nation of industrialists. That put him at odds with the United States, which wanted Ethiopia to be the breadbasket of the Middle East. Breadbaskets, however, as everyone involved well knew, cannot permanently sustain the massive economic growth required to earn a nation the adjective "wealthy." Haile Selassie was no one's fool and he did not intend to place any limitations on his nation's future progress, at least its future *economic* progress. Its *political* progress was another question entirely, but then, no one seemed particularly worried about that anyway.

Haile Selassie spoke the language of economic growth theory fluently. "The present high standard of development has been achieved through the accumulation of knowledge from time immemorial," he announced in a 1959 speech. "We would like Our people to realize that this is not something that has been accomplished at one stage nor by coincidence, nor has this stage been reached in one generation, but is the result of the toil, fortitude and sacrifice of succeeding generations." Although others are ahead of us now, he continued, we have "awakened" and are embarking down "the road to progress." Wanting will get us there. If all Ethiopians will "generate an unceasing desire for better and more things" and "eradicate idleness," then they "shall elevate their standard of living to that of the people inhabiting other parts of the world and be able to spare for others." Those nations that have "attained a high degree of progress" have done so by virtue of their "achievements," he insisted, "not because of the difference in their innate ability." We are behind only because we have not yet unfolded our potential. It starts with thrift, for although you must want unceasingly, you have to want something more than immediate pleasures. "Use your savings where it will pay you the most. The hoarding of money does not yield dividends!" Invest your money; turn cash into capital. If you do not have savings, then work to get some. If you farm, then plant commercial crops. If you have forests, then "make furniture and implements and exchange them for money."[74] His instructions revealed his familiarity with the intricacies of Anglo-American economics. Like the participants of the Scottish Enlightenment, Haile Selassie conceptualized progress as a movement through stages and described wanting to be the central engine of change. Like the early twentieth-century economists, he rejected nineteenth-century racial hierarchies of ability and embraced the principles of savings-unto-growth and entrepreneurship-unto-development. The emperor relied on the Western example of development for a great deal, but not for everything. Ethiopia's long history of achievement, he argued, warranted respect and some aspects of its glorious past had to be retained. The list included imperial authority.

Haile Selassie concluded his speech with specific instructions: "Henceforth, the next step for each Ethiopian, wherever he may be and whatever his endeavors are, is to follow Our directions and to devote himself assiduously to the execution of Our plan for the betterment of Our country."[75] The use of the royal "Our" emphasized the point that economic development demanded political obedience. The vast majority of the nation's development funds went into communication, transportation and industry, which were exactly the sectors best suited to increasing the IEG's influence. Haile Selassie had never been willing to separate modernization from centralization and integration and he was not about to start now.[76] Although he relied heavily on two-hundred years of conversations about the causes and consequences of economic growth, he forged his own path down "the road of progress."

The emperor desperately desired the economic development of his nation, but his motivations were complex. On the one hand, he simply wanted to improve the daily lot of his people, which was currently pretty dismal. He wanted them to have the same kinds of opportunities as the people he visited with on his trips abroad. At the same time, however, he rejected out of hand the idea of moving power away from the throne, renouncing the authority of the people that defined modern political development. It is worth remembering once again that he titled his autobiography, *My Life and Ethiopia's Progress*. For him, the two things could not be separated. He firmly believed that he had the *right* to rule, and he could justify God's choice to the outside world by making his nation strong.

Even in modernization, Haile Selassie followed in the footsteps of former emperors, using new tools to pursue old dreams of imperial consolidation. He wanted what his predecessors had wanted, and he was better situated to get it.[77] The Ethiopian philosopher Messay Kebede wrote of the emperor, "Modernization was for him nothing else but the use of modern means to assert his complete power over the nobility." Because he was ultimately more concerned with security than with development, Messay insisted, it was little wonder his development programs proved to have limited economic significance for Ethiopia: "Because modern means were used for a purpose which was not modern, they were unable to inaugurate any sustained and consistent process of modernization."[78] Haile Selassie shied away from meaningful reforms while enacting numerous development "programs." This proved particularly the case with the entrenched feudalesque system and the government's stubborn resistance to substantial land reform throughout the 1950s, which effectively kept provincial authority in crown-loyal hands and allowed peasant dependence to continue. The first Point Four technicians to Ethiopia had argued that reforming peasant agriculture had to serve as the foundation of any meaningful development program, but Haile Selassie consistently dedicated his limited development budget to infrastructural, industrial, and *commercial* agricultural projects. The IEG implemented over half of the infrastructural and industrial projects in Addis Ababa and put the rest in Asmara and Dire Dawa, which biased the north and the center. The same was true of the emphasis on coffee, which was predominately grown in the south on northern-owned estates. His Imperial Majesty wanted development-into-personal power along with development-into-wealth and he knew that technology was the key to securing both.[79]

Haile Selassie shared with Point Four administrators a common understanding of development as an economic process built on capital formation via technological progress. He differed from them in his effort to implement large-scale technological development from the top down as opposed to small-scale from the ground up. Some of the difference in methodology between the Point Four mission and the IEG's mission can be explained as a difference of funding and manpower, but a good deal of it can only be understood as a difference in politics. The U.S. Point Four Mission to Ethiopia was essentially a goodwill mission from one country, looking to maintain allies by providing a "valuable" service, to another, looking for funds and happy to have the service. From Washington's perspective, particularly by the mid-1950s when it seemed clear that creating "development" was trickier than originally thought, developing Ethiopia was viewed as more "useful" than "essential." Haile Selassie, however, believed it to be critical for the survival of both himself and his nation. That explains why he placed so much emphasis on military assistance and why he chose to create a highly publicized Five Year Development Plan. Although he did not believe that he should have to justify his continued rule, there were enough grumblings to convince him that it would be wise to do so. In addition, choosing the "five year" model followed the U.N.'s 1951 suggestion and certainly would not hurt relations with the Soviets (as, indeed, it did not, considering his fruitful 1959 visit). The emperor was no communist, but he was no republican either. He embraced the West's parliamentary system with its rule of law, but neutered it with constitutional guarantees of his own dictatorship. He greatly desired America's friendship and respect, but he was happy to accept Soviet money. He had bigger things to worry about than their cold war.

"Of the countries which We visited during Our recent trip, there are some whose economic and political systems are different from Ours. We believe that these are made to serve the particular needs of each country and are matters of domestic concern to each nation," Haile Selassie announced in his 1959 return speech. As such, they should not "stand as a hindrance to the understanding, collaboration and co-operation among nations on important matters that are of common concern."[80] Washington and Moscow fervently disagreed. Haile Selassie wanted to move his nation out of the "Third World" into the "First World," but he did not shun relations with the "Second World," because the stages for him were about wealth, not ideology. He embraced large-scale industrial development projects because the economic literature supported them as critical to growth, even though American technicians did not. Point Four tried to develop underdeveloped nations with relatively little money—particularly in comparison with the Marshall Plan—and its projects were correspondingly limited.

As the 1950s progressed and most underdeveloped nations did not, conversations about foreign aid became increasingly more complicated. Fears that the development model was not working were coupled with concern about how far aid dollars could be stretched as newly independent countries filed into the United Nations and onto the American aid payroll. Growing Soviet involvement kept Washington's pocketbook open, but had the troublesome effect of pushing military aid ahead of technical and economic assistance. Thinly spreading a limited foreign aid budget meant that no country got as much as it wanted, and, from the perspective of development, as much as it needed. From the beginning, the Truman administration sold Point Four as a program that would eventually make itself obsolete by pushing underdeveloped nations into the global market where the wonders of capitalism could work their economic magic. By the late 1950s, however, the reality was that nations such as Ethiopia—plagued by the ills of poverty, dictatorial government, and a national market dedicated almost entirely to one product—went looking for money anywhere they could get it because American programs were too limited in their vision and their funding.

In December 1958, Jahangir Amuzegar, of Occidental College in Los Angeles, and future Iranian finance minister, published an insightful analysis entitled "Point Four: Performance and Prospect." Though still popular with many people, the program had lost much of its initial support, following criticism on political, economic, and administrative grounds, most publicly in the congressional hearings. "Politically," Amuzegar reported, "the program has been accused of supporting undemocratic and nonprogressive governments. Economically, it has been criticized for hasty planning, poor selection of projects, and inadequate coordination amongst assistance activities. Administratively, it has been charged with inefficiency, waste and irregularities." These problems, Amuzegar insisted, were products of the program's "conflicting objectives" and its limited funding.

FIGURE 5.3 Douglas Baker, an ICA technician, discusses cattle inoculations with students at the Jimma Agricultural Technical School in May 1957. Lessons were often filmed so that they could be shown to people who were unable to attend the school. *Still Picture Records Section, National Archives, College Park, Maryland*

Point Four was initially designed to prevent communism from spreading, bolster the international market and "demonstrate" America's "philanthropic generosity," but "the realities of the mid-twentieth century politics, economics and ethics showed that these assumptions were largely aspirationally conditioned and somewhat unrealistic."[81] The United States essentially wanted Point Four to solve all of its problems in the underdeveloped world, but the program could not do so for a variety of reasons. Not only were the goals unrealistic, Amuzegar continued, but they were often in contention with the plans of the countries receiving Point Four assistance.

A belief in the value of jointly run programs, as seen in the wording of every technical agreement, remained at the center of the Point Four idea. Although this structure had been designed to foster greater unity between countries, it unfortunately also enhanced the problem of Point Four's "conflicting objectives," for the program had to absorb not only domestic differences of opinion, but international ones as well. Conflicts over what the program should be doing raged in Washington and in every country that had a U.S. technical assistance mission. Amuzegar believed that this situation created competing hierarchies, pitting U.S. strategic interests against the "social and economic interests" of the underdeveloped nation. The first hierarchy demanded that Point Four achieve two basic objectives: "(1) to serve as part of a *political* program designed to convince the people in the uncommitted areas that their interests lay in siding with the West; and (2) indirectly to assist a *military* program designed to strengthen the defense of the areas against the threat of Communist aggression or internal subversion." Meanwhile, the second "demanded that the program (1) pay greater heed to improving *social* and *economic* conditions, and (2) meet these objectives through the least possible interference with the existing political and social orders." As it was always difficult and often impossible simultaneously to satisfy both, "the Point Four program faced some serious and almost insoluble political, economic and administrative paradoxes."[82] In trying to be all things to all people, the program soon became overextended and failed to fulfill almost any of its objectives successfully.

Something, it seemed clear, needed to be done. Point Four's problems, Amuzegar insisted, should not lead to its destruction, but to its reform. Recent history has taught us, he argued, that Point Four should be "divorced from political and strategic programs" and moved out of the State Department into a separate, independent agency, responsible to Congress and dedicated to foreign assistance alone.[83] The idea was to turn Point Four back into the pure "instrument" of development that it had been imagined to be in

1949, before the Korean War broke out, changed the rules of the Cold War, and made technical assistance for development seem too small a project behind which to rally a fearful nation. An important part of its identity had gotten lost within the Mutual Security Act and needed to be recovered. People at the ICA agreed.

Dennis A. Fitzgerald, an agricultural economist from Harvard and director of the ICA from 1953 (when it was still the Foreign Operations Administration) to 1961, shared some of his former frustrations in a 1976 interview. "The State Department, and I think this is particularly true of Dulles, looked upon the AID agency—maybe this is unfair but certainly we felt this way—as just a convenient device by which you avoided the whole responsibility for anything that went wrong. But simultaneously you ordered it to do what the State Department wanted." Fitzgerald gave an example:

> Dulles went to Ethiopia once. He told Haile Selassie or somebody—(we had what was considered a highly important communications center somewhere in the country) that the U.S. would give him nine million dollars worth of aid as a quid pro quo. We didn't learn about it for a couple of months. We'd get communications from our embassy over there asking "Where's this nine million dollars we promised Haile Selassie?" We replied, "What nine million dollars?" It was a hell of a mess. Haile Selassie thought he was going to get a check the next day. I'm exaggerating, but not too much. We finally developed a program which had a price tag on it of the amount that Dulles had promised the Ethiopians, but it had no real underpinning and had a negligible effect on that country's development.[84]

The State Department viewed the ICA as a tool of foreign policy, whereas the ICA viewed itself as a tool of development. For the former, the satisfaction of the leaders of the client country was more important than the performance of the projects themselves, so there was pressure on the ICA to do whatever it could with its limited budget to secure loyalty. This caused a conflict of interest as ICA technicians wanted to work on grassroots agriculture, education, and public health projects, and foreign governments tended to want large-scale industrial projects, or, even better, checks for nine million dollars. "What they wanted and what they needed were very frequently entirely different," he recalled. "Instant modernization, I think was a kind of delusion. You just can't, there is no such thing as instant modernization."[85] Under Fitzgerald's direction, Point Four continued to favor the same types of programs throughout the Eisenhower administration that it had under the Truman administration. "Consideration must be given to just where the particular country is presently located on the long and unending road to development," he announced in a 1959 speech. "For instance, there is little point in giving high level advice on animal genetics to a country that has not yet accepted the idea that feed is good for livestock."[86] Progress comes one step at a time. His fellow economists tended to agree.

The debate in Washington over the purposes of foreign aid corresponded with discussions within the field of economics over economic growth, now central to the discipline, and developmental economics, a struggling outlier within the field. As always, the vast majority of economists concerned themselves with the issues facing the countries where most of them had been born and most of them worked. Booming growth in the United States and Western Europe during the 1950s made them optimistic for the first time in decades. Such confidence affected even those working on the "newly developing" nations, whose subjects did not perform nearly as well. Few fell into despair over aid's previous performance. It was simply a question of figuring out the proper formula. Policymakers at home, pleased by flourishing domestic economies, continued to turn to them for answers. Economists entered the second half of the twentieth century vastly more powerful than they had been during the first. They used their success to structure their discipline in ways that increasingly distanced it from the average person, thereby better insulating it from criticism and ensuring its mystique. *Economies* needed to be ruled by economists.

The man most responsible for the shift was a professor at the Massachusetts Institute of Technology (MIT) named Paul Samuelson who insisted in a 1947 work that economists start writing, once again, in mathematics. He directly attacked Alfred Marshall's efforts to use biological and mechanical analogies instead of mathematical formulas, which the older economist believed could not adequately express the complexities of economic behavior. Samuelson disagreed, insisting that the language of mathematics would take economics farther than prose ever could. His ideas became doctrine with the 1948 publication of *Economics: An Introductory Analysis*, which became the best-selling economic textbook of all time and the standard text of every undergraduate macroeconomics course. Unlike John Stuart Mill and Marshall, who "had dealt with essentially pure capitalism," Samuelson later recalled, "I had to grapple with the tradeoffs and opportunities inherent in the mixed economy." His was a decidedly post-Keynesian book that sold particular economic theories as truths and largely ignored voices of protest, most notably

Freidrich Hayek and Milton Friedman. Samuelson reflected the popular trend within the discipline that accepted the virtues of laissez-faire in terms of free trade, but favored heavy government involvement toward stabilization within the national economy. He called it "neoclassical" for its blending of Keynesian macroeconomics with the older marginal utility school's microeconomic emphasis on rational choice. The popularity of his work ensured that mainstream economics would, for the time being, be written in mathematics and theorized within the post-Keynesian paradigm. This trend within the discipline had ramifications throughout the political realm, of which Samuelson was well aware. "I don't care who writes a nation's laws—or crafts its advanced treaties," he later famously commented, "if I can write its economics textbooks."[87]

Samuelson's influence was most immediately apparent in what came to be called neoclassical growth theory—a 1950s spin on Harrod and Domar's 1940s model. As Harrod had "dynamized" Keynes, the new theory essentially "stabilized" the Harrod-Domar model, which revolved around a delicate, and therefore precarious, balance between the national savings rate (s), the product of the capital-output ratio (v), and the rate of growth of the labor force (n). The Harrod-Domar model argued that the savings rate had to equal the other two ($s = vn$ in the new language of choice) in order to secure steady growth. The problem with this, MIT economist Robert Solow wrote in a highly influential 1956 article, is that "were the magnitudes of the key parameters . . . to slip ever so slightly from dead center, the consequence would be either growing unemployment or prolonged inflation." In the optimistic atmosphere of the 1950s, Solow refused to accept this doctrine of "fixed proportions" and mathematically argued instead for a more flexible model that took technology into account. Technology could increase the productivity of capital, which would increase savings, which would increase investment and inspire long-term growth. The policy ramifications were that it "leaves a nation *some* leeway to choose whether it wants high employment with relatively high capital formation, low consumption, rapid growth; or the reverse; or some mixture." Solow's model did not challenge the idea of investment into growth; it just moved the previous model off "the knife-edge" by recognizing that exogenous technological change offered hope to nations worried about securing the perfect balance believed necessary for economic growth.[88]

Although Solow's model had clear implications for development, he was not a developmental economist and his work, like that of Harrod and Domar before him, reflected a preoccupation with securing growth in developed economies. His emphasis on technology transformed the field, but he himself admitted that his work was highly theoretical. In contrast, a number of economists working specifically with underdeveloped economies emphasized practice above theory, insisting that these economies were so different from developed ones that they demanded that economists reconsider what they "knew" about economic growth. Their work moved along different lines—including new ideas about the relationships among labor, capital, and investment; fresh analysis of national income statistics; and a revitalized appreciation for the value of economic history to economic doctrine. More democratic in their focus, developmental economists were also more democratic in their writing, preferring prose to mathematical formulas.

Developmental economists shared a focus on underdeveloped nations' potential for growth and a sense that economic growth defined development. They still looked at gross domestic product, and they still talked about balancing labor, capital, and investment, but they refused to stop there. In a 1953 lecture in Brazil, Princeton economist Jacob Viner argued that the realization of an underdeveloped nation's potential has to begin with investments in human capital. The "masses" need to be "literate, healthy, and sufficiently well fed to be strong and energetic" in order to enhance their productivity.[89] W. Arthur Lewis of the University of Manchester wrote that Keynesian arguments about growth based on a limited labor supply were completely unsuited to underdeveloped economies with large populations of workers employed in sustainable agriculture. "In the neoclassical model," he wrote in a famous 1954 article, "capital can only be created by withdrawing resources from producing consumer goods," but underdeveloped nations have surplus labor, which he described as labor involved in low-productive activities. The work of the classical economists, he insisted, was much more applicable in such situations than that of the Keynesians, because Smith and Malthus wrote about nations full of people engaged in subsistence agriculture. The discourse, Viner and Lewis insisted, needed to return to the question of agricultural productivity, which was no longer a concern of developed nations.[90]

Lewis's emphasis on a return to older economic ideas revealed developmental economists' tendency to place underdevelopment within an historical perspective. The idea that poorer nations simply had "younger" economies that would eventually grow into "older," wealthier ones was publically accepted. "What France, Britain, and America have accomplished through their own revolutions has to be attained in backward countries by a combined effort of popular forces, enlightened government, and unselfish foreign help," Stanford economist Paul Baran insisted, using words decidedly similar to those the Truman administration used to sell Point Four.[91] Simon Kuznets made the point more scientifically with his incredible compilations of international income statistics. The tables led him to a more complicated picture of economic growth. "The presently developed countries," he wrote in 1956, "were already in advance of the 'rest of the world' when modern industrialization began." In contrast, the currently underdeveloped nations "face the prospect of industrialization from a position of inferiority in that their per capita incomes lag substantially behind those of the advanced sector of the world's economy today," which makes their situation unique. "The intellectual, political, and geographic revolutions which occurred between the 13th and 16th centuries were important and indispensible antecedents to the economic expansion that followed," he argued. Today's underdeveloped nations "were outside the orbit of these revolutions and of the growth that preceded the economic and technological changes which began in the late 18th and continued through the following centuries." They were not underdeveloped because they had missed the Industrial Revolution; they were underdeveloped because they had missed the conditions that made that revolution possible. The politics came before the science that came before the technology that came before the economic growth.[92]

Kuznet's work stressed the historic particularities behind the West's progress and purposely complicated the applicability of the neoclassical growth model by insisting that growth was not simply a question of savings and investments, but of historical circumstances. The growth theorists had created their models for nations whose development was already established, so it was hardly their fault that the models did not work everywhere. For economists primarily interested in theory, questions of applicability were of little interest. For economists dedicated to manipulating economic change in the fight against poverty, applicability mattered a great deal. One such economist was Bert Hoselitz of the University of Chicago, who lamented that "the theoretical treatment of economic growth is either too strongly policy-oriented, or it is stated in an overly general form whose results are applicable only with difficulty, and often with grave reservations, to actual cases of economic growth." Critical of growth theory models that ignored historical and social conditions, Hoselitz insisted on bringing noneconomic variables into the discussion. There "is not a single, uniform theory of growth," he wrote in 1955, "but rather an array of typical situations conducive to growth."[93]

His ideas complemented those of a young economist at MIT. In 1952, W. W. Rostow wrote *The Process of Economic Growth*, "an historian's book about economic theory," in order to assist graduate students in his seminar on "the pattern of the evolution of the world economy since the mid-eighteenth century." It contained some charts and tables, but no formulas and was therefore open to anyone who was interested, as opposed to anyone who had undergone the proper professional training. Indeed, the book criticized the limitations of that training. Modern economic thought, Rostow wrote, developed "within Marshallian short-period assumptions; that is, the social and political framework of the economy, the state of the arts, and the levels of fixed capacity are assumed to be given and, usually, fixed." These work for most economists, who are trying to create theories, but "are intolerable assumptions for the historian" who "must take as unique events, in their full complexity, the situations he confronts." The historian cannot study events in isolation, as can the economist. The historian cannot embrace the concept of rational choice, because he knows that humans are far too complex to assume that they will act a certain way in a certain situation. Bridging the gap between economics, politics, and history, Rostow argued that "an appropriate scientific framework for the making of public policy... requires the development of improved tools for the handling of long-period factors and for relating social and political forces to the body of economics." In other words, economists needed to start thinking like historians, leaving behind the comfort of idealized theories of specific behavior in specific situations in order to study the unique realities of economies in action.[94]

"In entering this complex terrain, where variables long firmly nailed down are set in motion," Rostow wrote, "economists may take a certain comfort," for we are simply returning to our roots. Adam Smith "used history not simply to illustrate static relationships but to illuminate the processes by which the wealth of nations may increase or decrease." Smith looked at short-term fluctuations and long-term trends. "He was concerned not only with the relation of public policy to the rate of economic development, but also with what we would call social policy and social attitudes." He saw public education as a key determinant of national wealth. "It is not a distortion of *The Wealth of Nations*," Rostow asserted, "to regard it as a dynamic analysis of the forces determining change in long-period factors, placed in a setting of the social and political forces relevant to economic development." That way of thinking did not end with Smith, but continued on, notably with Malthus, Mill, and Marshall (although economists often ignore the latter's interest in long-period factors). Anyone truly interested in understanding economic growth, Rostow concluded, must combine the methods of the classical economists with the concepts of the professionalized social sciences. He or she must be willing "to bring to bear on this problem the accumulated knowledge and methods of the non-economic social scientists"—not simply because the quest for answers demands it, but because Marx already did it and hundreds of millions of people around the world are being taught his interpretation of economic growth. "I have," Rostow confessed, "by no means solved the problem of formulating an alternative to the Marxist system," but this is a beginning.[95]

Four years later, Rostow published a theory of economic growth based on the histories of world's many industrial revolutions. That history, he argued, reveals that the "sequence of economic development" can be broken down into three periods: "a long period (up to a century or, conceivably, more) when the preconditions for take-off are established; the take-off itself, defined within two or three decades; and a long period when growth becomes normal and relatively automatic." For the "take-off" to begin, he wrote, it is necessary "that the proportion of net investment to national income . . . rises from (say) 5% to over 10%, definitely outstripping the likely population pressure," but that, by itself, is not enough. A nation also needs "the development of one or more substantial manufacturing sectors with a high rate of growth" and "the existence or quick emergence of a political, social, and institutional framework which exploits the impulses to expansion in the modern sector and the potential external economy effects of the take-off." Growth, it seemed clear, depends upon a variety of conditions. It requires the movement of money from those who hoard to those who spend (as Adam Smith argued), "the existence and successful activity" of risk-taking entrepreneurs (as Schumpeter argued), and a complex economy with primary and secondary growth sectors to absorb investments (as Rosenstein-Rodan argued)—all of which depend upon a variety of historic political, social, and cultural factors. Man does not progress by savings and investments alone.[96]

In 1960, Rostow published *The Stages of the Economic Growth*, turning his 1956 article into "A Non-Communist Manifesto," and expanding his explanation of development. He now placed societies within five categories: "the traditional society, the preconditions for take-off, the take-off, the drive to maturity, and the age of high mass-consumption." The United States, Western Europe, and Japan were now in the "the age of high mass-consumption," he explained, and the rest of the world longed to catch up. Doing so required adopting the conditions necessary for "maturity": (1) a shift from a reliance on agriculture "to a predominance for industry, communications, trade and services"; (2) a shift from grassroots focus to one on a national and an international level; (3) a rejection of large family traditions; (4) a readjustment of capital out of the hands of landed aristocracy and into the hands of capitalists; (5) a willingness to value individuals not for who they are but for what they can do; (6) "and, above all, the concept must be spread that man need not regard his physical environment as virtually a factor given by nature and providence, but as an ordered world which, if rationally understood, can be manipulated in ways which yield productive change and, in one dimension at least, progress."[97] Development was no longer an economic exercise, but a social passage, and foreign aid for development was going to have to change.

In 1956, Senator John F. Kennedy told attendees of the Conference on Vietnam Luncheon that what "we must offer them is a revolution—a political, economic and social revolution far superior to anything the Communists can offer." It was a decidedly Rostowesque vision. "We must supply capital to replace that drained by the centuries of colonial exploitation; technicians to train those handicapped by deliberate policies of illiteracy; guidance to assist a nation taking those first feeble steps toward the complexities of a republican form of government," Kennedy continued. "All this and more we can offer Free Vietnam, as it passes through the present period of transition on its way to a new era—an era of pride and independence, and an era of democratic and economic growth—an era which, when contrasted with the long years of colonial oppression, will truly represent a political, social and economic revolution."[98] When he moved into the White House in January 1961, he brought Rostow with him.[99] The world waited to see how the ideas would play out in the policies.

Seven thousand miles away, in a marble palace eight-thousand feet above sea level, a diminutive Ethiopian in a military uniform watched the shift with apprehension. 1960 had been a very troublesome year. Britain withdrew from British Somaliland on June 26 and that territory united with Italian Somaliland, which had been under U.N. control, to create the independent Somali Republic. He had more than 350,000 ethnic Somalis living permanently within his borders and several hundred thousand more who annually migrated in and out with their cattle. Many of them believed that one-fourth of his empire belonged to Somalia. He would have to act forcefully to maintain control. It seemed likely that Nasser's United Arab Republic would try to exploit the tensions under the guise of Muslim friendship. Less certain was how the presence of a new, independent nation would affect the Horn of Africa's place in the Cold War divide. Luckily, the French continued to hold on to French Somaliland, so the railway from Addis Ababa to Djibouti remained secure for now.[100]

The other critical event of the year was almost too terrible to remember. Brigadier-General Mengestu Neway (commander of the bodyguard) and his brother Garmane (an employee of the Department of the Interior) had declared "The People's Government of Ethiopia" on December 14. It was clearly Garmane's doing. He took advantage of the state's generosity by attending Haile Selassie I Secondary School and then, under the sponsorship of the Crown Prince, earned a B.A. at the University of Wisconsin and an M.A. at Columbia. He returned full of ideas about modernization and applied for a post to work in the provinces. Possessed by an unnatural desire to make Ethiopia mimic the new policies of its African neighbors, he began giving government land away to peasants. He was promptly sent down to work with the Somalis in Jijiga, where it was believed he would be less trouble. Desirous of power, Garmane convinced his brother to use the military to force change at the top. The emperor's visit to South America determined the date. He had flown home immediately, concerned for his family and his throne, but need not have worried—most of the army and all of the air force had stood by him, though their loyalty had disappointingly followed a promise of the first salary increase in decades. The Americans, after a brief and rather unsettling hesitation, had publically declared their support as well. Mengestu was promptly captured, tried, and hanged, along with the other key traitors. Those university students who had demonstrated with bedsheet banners announcing a bloodless revolution and a belligerent manifesto about their "ever present ambition to develop *our* dear country, to civilize *our* country and to lead *our* dear country towards a prosperous future" were not punished but would be watched more closely in the future. Most said that they joined out of fear rather than hope. How could it be otherwise after all that he had done for them? The same was true of the Crown Prince. He claimed he gave that disgraceful radio broadcast admitting that the government "of the favored few" was manipulating the law "to deprive the common people of their rights and privileges in order to build up riches" under mortal threat. Perhaps he was lying. The prince must also be watched. Halie Selassie felt tired. It had been a difficult year and he worried about the new decade.[101]

6 THE DEVELOPMENT DECADE

On September 12, 1974, soldiers entered the palace on the hill in Addis Ababa, bundled up the old, partially senile emperor, and drove off with him, rather incongruously, in a Volkswagen beetle. Haile Selassie's reign was over. In the weeks immediately following, famed Polish journalist Ryszard Kapuściński traveled to Addis Ababa to interview members of the palace household and governmental staff. The city was dangerous—seething with conspiracies—and talking could get you killed. All of the interviews were conducted in secret; names were reduced to initials in order to protect the witnesses to the final years of Ethiopia's aristocracy. P.M. was one of these shadowy figures willing to speak with the outsider. The foreign journalist and the Ethiopian both had reason to fear lights and open windows. Throughout, while listening to each other, they each also listened to the angry city on the other side of the wall.

From the intensity of the interview's opening, it seems as if Kapuściński waited to turn on his tape recorder until he knew that P.M. was going to give him the "good stuff." Perhaps he sat in a darkened room through long explanations of ceremonial processes and the emperor's eating habits before he finally prodded P.M. into an emotional fervor by asking him how the emperor had lost his power. Or, perhaps P.M. had simply been waiting for someone to listen to thoughts that had been turning around in his head for years, and he started the conversation exactly where he had always wanted it to begin: with development.

"A kind of mania seized this mad and unpredictable world, my friend: a mania for development," P.M. opened. "Everybody wanted to develop himself! Everyone thought about developing himself, and not simply according to God's law that man is born, develops, and dies. No," they wanted something more. "Each one wanted to develop himself extraordinarily, dynamically, and powerfully, to develop himself so that everyone would admire, envy, talk, and nod his head. Where it came from no one knows. Like a herd of sheep, people went crazy with blind greed, and it sufficed that somewhere at the other end of the world someone developed himself. . . . Immediately they press, storm, urge that they be developed, too, be raised, that they catch up—and," he insisted, with the recent past fresh in his mind, " it's enough my friend to neglect these voices for you to get mutinies, shouts, rebellions, negativism, frustration, and refusal," all of which fractured Ethiopian history. "Our Empire," P.M. continued, "had existed for hundreds, even thousands of years without any noticeable development and all the while its leaders were respected, venerated, worshipped. . . . And who would ever have gotten it into his head to press his face to the floor in front of the Emperor and beg to be developed?" A good subject knows his place.[1]

Here, it seems certain that P.M.'s voice changed—got softer, less emphatic—as he shifted closer to his listener to make sure that he understood. "However, the world began to change. Our Emperor, innately infallible, noticed and generously agreed with this." His Highness, P.M. seemed to sigh, "had always had a weakness for all progress—indeed, he even liked progress—his most honorably benevolent desire for action manifested itself in the unconcealed desire to have a satiated and happy people cry for years after, with full approval, 'Hey! Did he ever develop us!'" And so, His Clement Highness built airports, bridges, and hospitals. He even wrapped all that progress up in a glittering new package:

> A map of the Empire's development hung in the Palace, on which little arrows, stars, and dots lit up, blinking and twinkling so that the dignitaries could gladden their eyes with the sight when His Venerable Majesty pressed a button, although some saw in all this the proof of the Emperor's growing eccentricity. But foreign delegations, whether African or from the wider world, obviously delighted in the map, and upon hearing the Emperor's explanation of the little lights, arrows, and dots, they too talked, asked questions, encouraged, and praised.

Human beings have a weakness for shiny objects.[2]

"And that is how it would have gone on for years, to the joy of His Supreme Highness and his dignitaries, had it not been for our grumbling students." The story and the voice shifted again. "Alas, my friend, it is a sad truth that, despite His Majesty's having led the Empire onto the path of development, the students reproached the Palace for demagoguery and hypocrisy. How, they said, can one talk of development in the midst of utter poverty?" It must have gotten louder as the speaker poured upon his listener the specifics of the complaints: misery, ignorance, illiteracy, desperation. "Finally the time came when they brought out their impudent whim of reforming. Development, they said, is impossible without reform." They insisted that "One should give the peasants land, abolish privileges, democratize society, liquidate feudalism, and free the country from dependence on foreigners. From what dependence? I ask," his voice ringing with indignation. "We were independent. We had been an independent country for three thousand years! That's thoughtlessness and running off at the mouth for you. Besides, I ask, how do you reform, how do you reform without everything falling apart?"[3]

The year 1960 should have changed everything for the emperor. It should have encouraged him to incorporate social and political changes into his development plans, but it did not. Haile Selassie most decidedly did not have "a weakness for all progress." He had a weakness for some progress—the type of progress that you can show off on a glittering map in a palace during the allotted "hour of development" between 4 and 5 p.m. Over the course of the 1960s, with the help of the United States, Addis Ababa became a little more modernized, with proper government buildings, a major university, and more paved roads. Coffee farms expanded along mountainsides in the provinces and the Imperial Ethiopian Government (IEG) built primary schools to combat rampant illiteracy. Throughout the so-called development decade, the emperor remained: growing older, becoming more set in his ways, and denying political change. It was a strange kind of "progress." The kind, some whispered at the time, bound to end in the fires of revolution. Others countered that the progress itself *was* the revolution. They found support in the United States.

In the spring of 1960, the Center for International Studies at Massachusetts Institute of Technology submitted a report to the Senate Committee on Foreign Relations titled "Economic, Social, and Political Change in the Underdeveloped Countries and its Implication for United States Policy." Its authors—who included Walt W. Rostow, Paul N. Rosenstein-Rodan, and Lucien Pye—warned that the "complex process of change shaping the lives of millions of people in the underdeveloped countries of the world" is "in a real sense" a type of "revolution." America's ability to influence this process is limited, they admitted, but the United States can "affect significantly the range of choice perceived by the governments and peoples of these nations as they confront the succession of inevitable problems that lie along the path to modernization." The United States, they continued, needs to adopt what we have labeled "the strategy of the third choice," where we use our influence to "minimize the likelihood of either of two undesirable outcomes": first, the repression of modernization by the conservative political elements and, second, the support of modernization via "dictatorial" means, "particularly of a Communist variety." The "third choice" offers another option: "an evolutionary path which can give constructive and progressive expression to modernizing impulses without removing by violence the obstacles which the traditional heritage may place in their path."[4] It was a bolder manifestation of promises Harry Truman had made ten years earlier.

Helping nations to find the "third choice" will take effort, the report's authors admitted. It will demand greater attention and greater assistance from American policymakers who must now recognize that each country's individual history, culture, political structure, and such, will shape its path to progress in important ways, and should consequently shape U.S. interventions. Foreign aid will remain central because "economic development does deeply though indirectly affect many other aspects of life in the modernizing societies."[5] Aid remained the primary tool through which the United States offered what Kennedy had promised Vietnam in 1956: "a revolution—a political, economic and social revolution far superior to anything the Communists can offer."[6] The progress would be the revolution: a bloodless version of the famously mild, yet no doubt transformative, American Revolution. This was the answer to P.M.'s question: "How do you reform without everything falling apart?" But it had already been proven false in Ethiopia by the time he asked it. There, the revolution cost the life of more than just an emperor and ushered in greater misery than Ethiopia had ever known. A decade of promised development ended in despair. The events of 1960 had hinted as much, but politicians in both Addis Ababa and Washington were confident that a new wave of progress would change the foreseeable future. The "third choice" would achieve what the Truman's fourth point had not: It would develop Ethiopia into a modern, democratic, capitalist society. Such were the dreams of 1960.

In his 1961 inaugural address, Kennedy told "those people in the huts and villages of half the globe struggling to break the bonds of mass misery" that the United States would pledge its "best efforts to help them help themselves" for however long necessary. We are going to do so, he explained, "not because the Communists may be doing it, not because we seek their votes, but because it is right."[7] Modernization gave U.S. foreign policy a moral purpose, and Kennedy loved it. He was confident that with a little reform, it could work miracles. The problems facing the development of the noncommunist world were "towering and unprecedented," he admitted in his State of the Union address ten days later, and they necessitated a response that was "towering and unprecedented as well." This time foreign aid reform required more than just a name change.

FIGURE 6.1 Hugh Rouk, the codirector of the Jimma Agricultural Technical School, discusses the cultivation of coffee trees with (left to right) the secretary to the district governor; Tesfa Bushan, the codirector of the Jimma Agricultural Technical School; and Tamarat Yigazu, the governor of Kaffa Province, in May 1957. The Imperial Ethiopian Government took experiments with coffee planting very seriously, in the hope that imported tools and techniques would expand production beyond areas where it was traditionally grown, making the nation more competitive in the global coffee market. *Still Picture Records Section, National Archives, College Park, Maryland*

The previous December his Task Force on Economic Policy had submitted a perceptive report detailing the limitations of current policies. "The present foreign economic aid program is not suited to the decade of the Sixties," it insisted. "It has been designed primarily as an instrument *against* Communism, rather than *for* constructive economic and social advancement. It is heavily *oriented* toward supporting military and short-run political objectives rather than toward the longer-run political problems of national development." It is too disorganized to be an effective tool and has become barely anything more than a ready source of cash for "those seeking to maintain the status quo," when we really need to be supporting "the leaders who are eager to modernize society." The stakes had gotten higher in the past ten years, because the Soviet Bloc had gotten good at foreign aid. Its efforts, the report's authors admitted, are "impressive." America's needed to be more so.[8] That January, Kennedy announced that he intended "to ask

Congress for authority to establish a new and more effective program for assisting the economic, educational and social development of other countries and continents."[9] The U.S. Agency for International Development (USAID) was born in Point Four's disappointments.

John Kenneth Galbraith and Walt Rostow—both of whom had served as consultants to the task force—spent the winter working on the specifics of reform. Galbraith sent a report to McGeorge Bundy, special assistant to the president, on February 1 titled "A Positive Approach to Economic Aid." Many nations, "including some heavily aided ones," have made no "appreciable advance" in the last twelve years, Galbraith wrote, primarily because "economic aid does not deal with decisive barriers to development—these being illiteracy, lack of an educated elite, inimical social institutions, no system of public administration, a lack of any sense of purpose." Economic aid is not enough, Galbraith concluded, and the Soviets know it, because their approach to development deals with those larger factors. We need to do so as well. "We *must* have a design for economic development which extends to *all* of the barriers to advance," and we "must have some objective test of progress." We cannot simply assume that aid will lead to progress. "If we are contributing to development, we need to know it and stick to our course. If we are on the wrong path, we also need to know it and change."[10] Foreign aid needed to be about more than economic growth—it needed to tackle the larger issues of social welfare and political structure.

In his capacity as the new deputy special assistant for national security affairs, Rostow sent Kennedy a memo later that month describing his own vision for aid. "We begin with a program that is almost wholly defensive in character and one which commands neither the resources, the administration, nor the criteria designed to move the underdeveloped countries towards sustained economic growth," he opened. The ICA is hindered by its "short-run perspective," its emphasis on specific projects instead of on entire nations, and its personnel of technical advisers instead of trained economists. "The goal is to help other countries learn how to grow," Rostow insisted, and this requires a "new look," instead of a "defensive effort to shore-up weak economies." We have to demand a program that will actually be able to move nations into self-sustained growth. Such a program had to be bigger—both in vision and in budget, Rostow wrote, with the latter increasing at an average rate of $1 billion a year more than the current $500 million. These funds had to be administered separately from military assistance. And the people administering them had to be "first-class development planners," which, for Rostow, clearly did not mean the "technical assistance types" now staffing the ICA. "We have stirred great hopes in Asia, the Middle East, Africa and Latin America," he warned, and "we must back our play or those hopes will fade."[11] Or, even worse, those hopes will drive them to Moscow.

That March, members of Kennedy's foreign policy staff met frequently to discuss the aid issue. Rostow had encouraged the president to convince the American people that aid remained in their best interest by making it the source of a major speech that "would give life to the new look, the turnaround process, and our whole stance towards the underdeveloped world."[12] The speech-writing team immediately began working on it. At a foreign aid meeting, staffers agreed that the speech would need to emphasize several points about the new program: "long-term rather than short; a country rather than a project approach; unified rather than diffuse legislation and responsibility; development rather than political or defensive objectives; scale adequate rather than inadequate to the problem; a coordinated international effort rather than discrete national efforts; a lending approach." We need to "try to cut down technical assistance and perhaps push it towards the UN," they concluded. It was too old-fashioned, too limited its ability to promote change to be included in the "new look."[13]

Two days later, after reading a preview of the upcoming speech, Rostow urged Ted Sorensen to make it bolder. "I think the message should dramatize that this is the crucial decade for foreign aid," he wrote. "The Kennedy Development Decade is the proper press release slogan, not the Kennedy plan," because this aid program will be truly transformative. Rostow predicted that "well over half of the peoples in underdeveloped areas should be living in societies which have attained self-sustained growth" by 1970 and the administration needed to be clear about how it was going to make that happen. "In general, I would go quite far in acknowledging the legitimacy of some of the complaints about the foreign aid program as it now stands. The President has an opportunity at this moment to put himself on the side of some of the critics of foreign aid by acknowledging that they are, in part, correct; and then meeting these criticisms in his program." Rostow hoped to sway the masses by convincing them that this time foreign aid would fulfill its promises.[14]

On March 22, Kennedy—taking Rostow's advice—told Congress, "no objective supporter of foreign aid can be satisfied with the existing program—actually a multiplicity of programs" whose administrative and procedural weaknesses "have begun to undermine confidence in our efforts both here and abroad." Foreign aid is disjointed and ineffective, Kennedy insisted. Our aid program "is based on a series of legislative measures and administrative procedures conceived at different times and for different purposes, many of them now obsolete, inconsistent and unduly rigid and thus unsuited to our present needs and purposes." Although U.S. foreign aid had helped recipient countries, he acknowledged, "it is a fact that many of the nations we are helping are not much nearer sustained economic growth than they were when our aid operations began." The world clearly required something new. "This Congress at this session must make possible a dramatic turning point in the troubled history of foreign aid to the under-developed world."[15] I need you to make a five-year commitment to a new aid program, the president asked his audience, one that will be separate from military assistance, because "our program of social and economic development must be seen on its own merits." He requested $2.4 billion for economic assistance to be distributed through this new organization the first year. It was, he noted, the "rock bottom minimum of funds necessary to do the job," and to do less would be "wasteful to the security interest of the free world." The new organization would contain within it the previous efforts of the ICA, the Development Loan Fund, the Food-for-Peace Program, parts of the Export-Import Bank, and the newly created Peace Corps. The greatest attention and funding would go to the Development Loan Fund, which would give money to finance specific large-scale projects, which Kennedy believed had a better chance of helping countries to achieve "self-sustained growth" than previous small-scale ones. "We are launching," he concluded, "a decade of development on which will depend, substantially, the kind of world in which we and our children shall live."[16]

The foreign aid–for–foreign policy rhetoric had a decidedly Trumanesque quality to it, but Kennedy's speech marked the end of Point Four and the beginning of the United States Agency for International Development. Reflecting many of Rostow's ideas, USAID emphasized funding a few large projects, instead of many little ones. It additionally argued that a nation's "economy" could not be separated from its "society," meaning the culture and the politics and everything else that governed people's existence. Kennedy insisted that "economic growth and political democracy can develop hand in hand," but the larger point was that they *should* develop hand in hand. We are no longer merely going "to react to the Communist threat," the new president announced. We are going to help underdeveloped countries "become self-reliant members of the community of nations."[17] A working paper on aid circulating around the White House that March read, "we need to replace our term insurance with an endowment policy."[18]

Senator J. William Fulbright, chairman of the Senate Foreign Relations Committee, introduced S. 1983, the Foreign Assistance Act, on behalf of the administration on May 31, 1961. The contrast of its length with that of the bill that introduced Point Four is striking and fit well with the tenor of top-down control that differentiated USAID from the TCA/FOA/ICA. "The Congress declares it to be a primary necessity, opportunity and responsibility of the United States," S. 1983 announced, "and consistent with its traditions and ideals, to renew the spirit which lay behind these past efforts, and to help make a historic demonstration that economic growth and political democracy can go hand in hand to the end that an enlarged community of free, stable, and self-reliant nations can reduce world tensions and insecurity." This new aid program promised to achieve its goals through "well-conceived plans" directed toward "the social as well as the economic aspects of economic development." It would "emphasize long-range development assistance as the primary instrument of such growth."[19] At the heart of the bill was a request to secure approval in 1961 to make large-scale loans through 1966. In the attached letter, Kennedy insisted that this was crucial, because "real progress in economic development cannot be achieved by annual, short-term dispensations of aid and uncertainty as to future intentions." This method represents "a departure from previous patterns in economic aid programs" that is "essential" to the effectiveness of our new approach, he wrote, because it allows for long-term planning and long-term commitments.[20] More cynical about foreign aid than their 1950 counterparts, the senators grilled the administration on its plans practically country by country, resulting in a record of the fifteen days of hearings that stretches over a thousand pages. Meanwhile, the House conducted hearings on the similar H.R. 7372.[21]

Congress approved the Foreign Assistance Act of 1961, "A Program for the Decade of Development," on September 4, directing the president to emphasize assistance to "long-range plans and programs" and to take into account "the extent to which the country is showing a responsiveness to the vital economic, political and social concerns of its people, and demonstrating a clear determination to take effective self-help measures."[22] The optimism of the spring faded into the realities of the fall as the administration worked to turn the policies into practice. This new approach "represents a major advance in our aid thinking and holds out the promise of more prudent and effective use of our aid funds," insisted an October report by the Policy Planning Council. We must put constant pressure on recipient governments to enact "progressive economic and social reforms" that will fight "the most deep-seeded obstacles to economic growth." We should also, the report continued, put our money into the projects that will have the biggest impact.

"Our assistance gives us only so much leverage in aid recipient countries within each group," they admitted, so we need to make the most of it.[23]

More countries needed aid and the United States wanted to do more with its aid, but there was only so much that Congress was willing to allocate. If the "new look" demanded more money and manpower to push a nation into self-sufficiency, then not everyone was going to make the cut. The Kennedy administration tried to relieve some of the pressure by arguing for a wider global aid effort at the first ministerial meeting of the Organization for Economic Co-operation and Development that November. Even though Canada and the eighteen European nations present promised to do more, the United States remained the largest distributer of bilateral aid and the administration knew that it would have to answer to Congress for that aid's effectiveness.[24]

Secretary of State Dean Rusk made the point explicitly in a November 1 memorandum to the Chairman of the Policy Planning Council commenting on the October report. There are two questions that must be considered, Rusk wrote. "First, will an investment of American aid yield a satisfactory return in results?" A "temporary amiability on the part of a government receiving aid" did not qualify, Rusk insisted, as an "adequate" return on an investment of "critically scarce resources." Second, "under what conditions are we justified in digging into our own taxpayers' pockets and postponing some of the great social needs of our own society in order to render assistance to another country?" Developing other countries is in our interest, Rusk conceded, but "we must not let this fact trap us into a responsibility for their standards of living or development."[25] The United States has created a global environment where many nations expect aid and will not cooperate without it and that puts us in a dangerous position. Leaving U.S. ambassadors dependent on foreign aid for securing support within the recipient nation made them weak and ineffective, he argued, and the United States should be careful not to view such aid as a permanent, necessary part of its foreign policy. "Surely our objective is to work toward an absence of need for American assistance; this means to me that there ought to be a number of countries in which we do not even start down the trail of providing assistance." Point Four initially went to 35 countries, but now the list of potential clients had grown much longer. "If we plan to continue to keep going to the Congress for aid programs for 70–80 countries, the Congress and the American public will rebel—and in my judgment that would be right," Rusk insisted. "We ourselves must establish some priorities and work toward some division of labor among the industrialized countries so that every underdeveloped country in the world is not an aid client of the United States." Limits need to be created now, at the beginning of the new program, and implemented strictly throughout. The government should create some kind of "citation or decoration," Rusk wryly added, for an ambassador who "gets his particular country off our aid list."[26]

Rusk feared foreign aid because it had few boundaries. Most of the world's countries could qualify for it and, once they began receiving it, could go on doing so for years. The administration must be careful not to make aid for aid's sake, he implied, so it did not betray the American people funding it. He was right to be worried. The same day he sent his message, Fowler Hamilton, the head of USAID stated at a meeting, "The motif of the new program is economic development. Whatever other purposes are expected to be served are supposed to be served as by-products of the process of aid-dispensing and the economic development that takes place."[27] On November 3, long before the differences between Rusk's and Hamilton's visions of aid's purpose could be decided, USAID became an active agency. The Kennedy administration was dedicated to the proposition that aid was a useful tool, but they were divided over what exactly they wanted to build with it.

These struggles reflected an important shift in 1950s academic thought that merged conversations about economic growth with conversations about social development and adopted the name "modernization theory" to differentiate itself from "economic development." Most visibly evident in Rostow's highly influential works on economic history, the shift was born in the sociologist Talcott Parsons's innovative work at Harvard's Department of Social Relations, which insisted that economic growth alone could not bring progress.[28] Economists had done an excellent job creating the framework of postwar European recovery, but they had failed to achieve the same results in the underdeveloped world. Modernization theory argued that they could never hope to do so alone, but needed to turn to anthropologists, sociologists, and psychologists "for a stipulation of the context of development."[29] Economic growth could solve economic problems in modern nations, but it needed social and cultural help in "traditional" ones. In his history of modernization theory, Michael Latham explained that it rested on four core concepts:

> (1) "traditional and "modern" societies are separated by a sharp dichotomy; (2) economic, political, and social changes are integrated and interdependent; (3) development tends to proceed toward the modern state along a common, linear path; and (4) the progress of developing societies can be dramatically accelerated through contact with developing ones.[30]

It was primarily (though certainly not entirely), an American ideology, based in large part on Americans' assumptions about their own superiority and their ability to influence the world for the better. In the hands of some of its academic adherents, including Rostow, Gabriel Almond, and Lucien Pye, modernization theory was viewed as an intellectual weapon against the Soviets, whereas others, including James Coleman and Gunnar Myrdal (notably not an American), preferred to see it as something outside of the Cold War struggle.[31] The academic divide mirrored conflicts within the Kennedy administration, as some focused on what aid could *do* and some on what aid could *get*.

Flowing out of a domestic environment where people believed that the government was responsible to the people for their welfare, modernization theory—manifested in USAID—sent abroad American confidence in the power of the state to use increased "knowledge" about society, along with technology, for the "greater good."[32] Kennedy insisted that he wanted to put aid on the offensive, transforming societies instead of just holding off communism. Although this sounded good to the Americans who contributed the funding, it had an ominous ring to recipient nations. Although the Truman administration had hoped that Point Four would inspire dramatic changes abroad, it had not forced them. The same could not be said of USAID, which based itself on the principle that small-scale technology and small-scale influxes of capital could not develop a nation. The USAID program relied on anthropologists, sociologists, and political scientists, along with economists and technicians, and, unlike Point Four, it refused to act quietly. Kennedy's program gave more and demanded more, which both delighted and worried foreign leaders such as Haile Selassie. Kennedy had proclaimed that what "we must offer them is a revolution."[33] Haile Selassie wanted nothing of the sort, but he did want foreign aid. He needed it to *prevent* a revolution.

In October 1961, Allan Loren, the director of ICA in Ethiopia, sent Fowler Hamilton a long letter detailing the situation on the ground. Ethiopia, he informed the new director of the not-yet running USAID, "is just beginning to emerge from feudalism into the modern world." The emperor had pursued progress from the beginning, but the Italian invasion wiped out his early efforts and he had to start anew in the 1940s. "Accordingly, Ethiopia still has most of the characteristics of a traditional society. Democratic institutions, including Parliament, are little more than a façade." Loren knew the lingo—using Rostow's "traditional society"—and he knew that the new aid bureaucracy cared a great deal about the political and social situation. "The abortive coup d'état last December destroyed the myth of the Emperor's infallibility," Loren continued. Mid-level civil servants and military officers are now engaging in open criticism on the regime, talking about the need for social progress. "It is this group also that has been responsive to the new AID concepts." The emperor has responded to this pressure by appointing a number of committees to study "constitutional reform, land reform, judicial reform, education, government organization and local administration." We should be prepared to help. It is a delicate matter, for while "we should continue to press for action and make known our support to the elements in the government sponsoring change, we must maintain sufficiently good relations with the Emperor" to ensure that our communication facilities at Kagnew, "regarded as vital by the Department of Defense," are not jeopardized.[34]

"Transition to the new aid criteria will require the phasing out of a number of smaller projects," Loren explained, but we have several existing projects that meet the new high priority standards and can continue to receive funding. The Public Health College in Gondar, which had been started with Point Four funds in 1953, was still training workers that were manning thirty-one rural health centers around the country, with more on the way. These centers, Loren explained, were the first organized effort to provide health care to countryside and rural communities wanted more. The College of Agriculture and Mechanical Arts, which had been established with assistance from Oklahoma A&M, had also proven to be a good Point Four investment. It is "now supplying trained manpower in the area which offers Ethiopia's greatest potential for increased production and income." We are additionally encouraged by the possibilities of the new Haile Selassie I University which we are hoping will "provide badly needed leadership in the whole development of an educational system in the Empire." There is a work-relief program in Eritrea that we would also like to continue supporting, Loren continued. It is operated out of Public Law 480, so we provide the grain that supplements their government income. He noted that the ICA was also in the midst of conversations with the IEG about selling surplus U.S. cotton under PL-480, which would help both countries. Additional projects that could potentially make "major contributions" included work on community water supplies, malaria eradication, and continued support for the Mapping and Geography Institute. We also, Loren announced with evident enthusiasm, "hope to accelerate the completion of 'one-time' projects," the largest being the Blue Nile River Basin survey.[35]

As Loren was positive about projects that should continue, so too was he negative about those that should not. "The Cooperative Services have outlived their usefulness and are to be abolished," he bluntly told Hamilton. They do not work, often because of our own failure to produce needed supplies in a timely manner. He was also pessimistic about getting an IEG commitment to developing its agricultural resources. With the exception of the university, "projects in agriculture . . . administered directly through the Ministry, are anything but promising." Despite the country's "great potential in agriculture, there has not been a Minister of Agriculture for several years." This is a serious problem, because agriculture is one of the few areas where the nation can absorb aid funding. Of the $100 million in credits that Haile Selassie received from the Soviet Bloc in 1959, Loren noted, the IEG has only spent $2 million. There are limitations to what can be done here. Keeping that in mind, U.S. objectives should be: "(1) to assist in building the pre-conditions for a more vigorous development effort through participation in a limited number of feasible projects, mainly in the area of human resources; and (2) to reinforce and exploit IEG initiatives in major areas of social or economic reform." Such objectives should enable us to both keep the regime pro-Western in its outlook and convince "the elements sponsoring change (who may soon be the country's leaders) of United States' support for social and economic progress."[36] This was to be a country program solidly built on modernization principles. Haile Selassie had good reason to be concerned.

William Witman II, the director of the Office of North African Affairs, stressed the probability of such concern the following month in a memo addressing a suggested aid cut for fiscal year (FY) 1962. The IEG will not be happy, he wrote. He quoted a letter from Ambassador Richards that stressed that "a major reversal of US aid policies in Ethiopia might so change the climate of US-Ethiopian relations as to endanger US base rights." We have both long-term and short-term priorities in Ethiopia, Richards insisted, and we need to emphasize our strategic military needs and our "posture toward the process of political change now accelerating in Ethiopia." Witman stressed the point that although Ethiopia did not meet the new USAID standards that prioritized aid to nations where it had the biggest bang for the buck, the United States could not afford to alienate the IEG. He warned of dire consequences because the Ethiopians, he insisted, "rarely, if ever, react in a logical manner."[37] He cited 1959 as an example, but, had he asked, Haile Selassie could have told him that turning to the Soviet Bloc for aid had been highly logical. Neutrality only seemed illogical to the people running the war.

Haile Selassie did not like all of the modernization theory principles behind the new USAID agenda, but he needed money. In 1962, he introduced the Second Five-Year Development Plan, which fit with the USAID desire to have national development strategies. Its first chapter, "Objectives of Planning for Economic and Social Development," explained that Ethiopia's modern development began in the late 1940s "when new institutions and economic activities were started. However, because economic and social development originated from a traditional basis, it could not achieve self-sustained economic growth. Conceived as an integrated part of a long-term development, recent economic and social progress is a sound and promising beginning to a better future."[38] Someone in the IEG had been reading Rostow and paying attention to the language used by the Kennedy administration when introducing USAID. The plan listed seven objectives, including, most importantly, increasing the economy's productive capacity in order to "secure an abundant and diversified production of goods and services" and "to accelerate the rate of economic growth by a better utilization of available resources." In addition, the IEG wanted to introduce modern machinery; "raise the skill and productivity of labour"; increase the annual savings rate so that Ethiopians can invest in the growing economy; "raise the standard of living"; provide "better social services"; enable citizens "equal opportunity" to participate in national life; and ensure better national security via a solid economic foundation. Our gross domestic product has grown at an average rate of 4.6% since 1949, the IEG explained, and we will push to perform even better. We are going to turn a "family type of economy and society" into a "modern one."[39]

The IEG undoubtedly wrote the plan with two specific audiences in mind. Most important was the world at large, particularly the United States and its partners at the World Bank and the United Nations, who controlled the aid funds that Ethiopia needed. In addition, however, the IEG must have been sensitive to the whispers for change that had grown louder in Addis Ababa since the failed coup of 1960. Mid-level bureaucrats and university students wanted social and political improvements. The IEG published a plan that addressed social change in a way that the previous plan had not and described new services that the government would provide for the people's welfare. The promises, however, were tempered by warnings. "The availability of the services concerned is closely associated with the level of economic development the country has attained," the IEG announced.[40] Such warnings allowed the IEG to defend its primary emphasis on expanding Ethiopia's industrial capabilities. Although the United States had long encouraged Haile Selassie to focus on agricultural production, the IEG wanted industry—giant factories of steel and tin whose overpowering noises announced "developed" to all in their vicinity. New fields did not pack the same punch. Ethiopia needed mines, roads, planes, and, above all, factories. As for political change, that was not even on the table. In a November 1962 speech following the publication of the new plan, the emperor proclaimed, "We believe in a progress that builds on a sound foundation and not on shifting sands. We believe in the adaptation of modern economic and social theories to local conditions and customs rather than in the imposition on Ethiopia's social and economic structure of systems which are largely alien to it and which [it] is not equipped to absorb or cope with."[41] There was a limit to His Imperial Majesty's enthusiasm for modernization and reducing his own power was it.

The Second Five Year Development Plan was immediately published in English so that USAID could see the extent of the IEG's vision. It was followed by memos to Washington that pointed out the plan's "highlights" and stressed the need for foreign assistance to the tune of 461 million Ethiopian dollars. The State Department estimated such appeals to be worth between $50 and $70 million, in addition to a request for $60 million worth of military aid that had been scaled down to $20 million by the fall of 1963. In a September memo to the White House, the State Department dismissed the idea of extending a new line of credit to Addis Ababa, but expressed a willingness to consider funding a series of specific aid projects. These included $15 to $30 million for a dam on the Finchaa River, $1.2 million for 154 Bailey bridges (prefabricated), $5 to $10 million for a meat processing plant, $10 million for grain storage facilities, $8 million to assist in the development of iron ore and gold mines, and $12.7 million for public health projects, including malaria eradication.[42] American interest in such projects stemmed from both the humanitarian concerns of aid and the practical realities of politics. The American ambassador to Ethiopia sent a message to Dean Rusk that summer warning Washington that it needed to start "delivering goods" to Addis Ababa to keep the emperor convinced of its commitment to the relationship. His prodding gained additional support from a July speech by Khrushchev where the premier promised that "the Soviet Union will continue to peacefully develop mutually beneficial economic cooperation with the African states."[43] Ethiopia needed to be wooed. The perfect opportunity came that fall, with the emperor's second trip to the United States.

Haile Selassie arrived in Washington, D.C., on October 1, 1963, on a train from Philadelphia. President and Mrs. Kennedy met him at Union Station in a grand ceremony of red carpets, trumpets, seventeen ambassadors from other African nations, and an estimated 200,000 onlookers. He and Mrs. Kennedy conversed in French about the recent loss of her baby son; this was the first time she had participated in a state function since August. Haile Selassie had lost his wife the year before and was no stranger to grief.

FIGURE 6.2 John F. Kennedy and Haile Selassie ride from Union Station to Blair House in 1963. The Lion of Judah had let it be known after his 1954 visit that he had been upset that Eisenhower had waited for him at the White House instead of meeting him upon his arrival in Washington. Almost a decade later, Kennedy gave the emperor the pageantry that he loved. *John F. Kennedy Presidential Library, Boston, Massachusetts*

Afterward, the emperor and the president headed to the White House for the first of two lengthy conversations, the *Washington Post* reported, about the "'Red Sea Complex,' that host of inter-related problems surrounded the strategic juncture between Africa and the Middle East, where Selassie is the principal pillar of rationality."[44]

The trick for Kennedy was to balance the need for Ethiopia's friendship with the desire for real political change. It was a delicate operation. Prior to the visit, the State Department sent Kennedy a briefing paper with thoughts on the situation. "The present highly personalized, virtually one-man rule of Emperor Haile Selassie is generally favorable to the short-term achievement of major United States policy objectives in Ethiopia," given his "pro-West orientation," it admitted, but his unwillingness to share power "enhances" resentment among the "constantly expanding educated elite" and "inhibits economic and political development." The threat of a repeat of 1960 lies "just below the surface" and the United States needs to encourage movement toward real political change. The difficulty, however, is that "direct reference to the need for reform in Ethiopia is likely to be counterproductive with the Emperor" and must be "conveyed obliquely." You need only publically celebrate his bold move in creating a Parliament in the 1955 constitution, the paper suggested, because Haile Selassie is "too astute to miss the hint that we are anxious to see more forward motion on the path to development of Ethiopian governmental institutions." Praising his accomplishments will remind him that we are looking for him to do more. His own nature will help us in this effort for "he is probably also anxious to be dealt with by future history books as the architect of modern Ethiopia, not as the last of the feudal autocrats." We have long used his rationality to benefit our strategic agenda for the region, the paper implied, and it seems hopeful that we can also rely on it to promote our dreams of democracy in Ethiopia, albeit via minute steps.[45]

At his luncheon meeting with Kennedy, Haile Selassie proposed a toast to the friendship between the two nations, "to the future development, in harmony and cooperation, of our two peoples; to the assurance of peace and liberty to all men of good will; and, Mr. President, to your health, welfare and prosperity."[46] In hindsight, it was a bittersweet moment, for Kennedy was assassinated the following month and the friendship between the two nations grew momentarily shakier, not stronger. In FY 1964, the United States provided Ethiopia with only $9.2 million in economic assistance, compared with $14.7 in FY 1963.[47] That December, Congress waged a fierce battle with Johnson over the foreign aid budget that ended in a Christmas Eve compromise of $3 billion.[48] The struggle highlighted the nation's conflicted feelings about foreign aid and placed USAID under heightened scrutiny to fulfill its promises. For Ethiopia, this meant a strict review of its policies and programs. American aid was going to be sent where it could be put to most useful use and Ethiopia was not at the top of the list.

The problem, as the State Department reported in a December policy paper, was that the United States still did not know what it wanted to accomplish with regards to Ethiopia. "Our immediate and short-term goals do not seem at first glance entirely consistent with our longer-term objectives," the report's authors admitted. "Some are essentially positive and progressive in character, looking forward to considerable change, while others appear negative, preclusive, or in support of the status quo." The United States wants to see real reforms, they continued, but "the risk is always present that the pursuit of longer-term policies relating to reform could unleash forces which could jeopardize immediate US interests."[49]

In April 1964, the American embassy in Ethiopia responded to the policy paper with a defense of the nation's strategic importance, which seemingly outweighed any concerns about whether or not the aid was producing reform. Since January, the embassy staff reported, there has been "the growing, vigorous push of the Soviets into the affairs of the Horn." Arms deliveries to the Somalis and "Khrushchev's polite but increasingly firm wrist-slapping of the Emperor" were slowly turning the Ethio-Somali issue into a Cold War one. Africa is changing, they warned, and the probable permanent location of the Organization of African Unity in Addis Ababa will make Ethiopia "the de facto capital of the continent." In addition, with the Wheelus air force base and the Moroccan naval communications facility "seemingly on the way out," Kagnew may soon be our only military base on the continent. "In this light, we should be absolutely clear in our minds concerning the importance of Kagnew, today and future, and how our interests in Kagnew promote or, detract from our other interests in the area." The larger point, however, the report concluded, is that "in African eyes there is no country more firmly linked to the United States than is Ethiopia" and "if we cannot see Ethiopia successfully through its current trials, the lesson will not be lost on other Africans."[50] From the embassy's perspective, the central point was not whether American aid was producing democracy in Ethiopia, but whether it was holding back the tide of Soviet influence across the entire continent. Ethiopia's role was larger than itself. The debate echoed one concurrently waging in Washington as the Johnson administration struggled to figure out the purpose and the costs of its aid agenda.

In a telephone conversation that May, Johnson warned Under Secretary of State George Ball that economic assistance was not popular with either party and that the Republicans were going to try to "add a couple hundred million to the military and take 500 million off the economics." He told advisers to "get reengaged" with foreign aid and organized the first of several task forces on foreign economic policy.[51] It was only the opening salvo. Between 1964 and 1968, the administration waged a fierce struggle with Congress to garner continued support for its development efforts while also funding the expanding war in Vietnam and the programs behind the Great Society. It was an uphill battle.

In 1965, Johnson created two committees to review America's foreign aid. The first, dubbed the "Cabinet Committee," consisted of the secretaries of state, defense, treasury, and agriculture; the under secretary of state for economic affairs; the AID administrator; and the deputy AID administrator, with the president's special assistant for national security affairs as executive secretary. Headed by Dean Rusk, the committee tackled the issues of USAID's general framework, military assistance to MAP countries, and the objectives and utility of foreign aid as a whole. The outside review committee, dubbed the "Clifford Committee," included Clark Clifford, Eugene Black (former president of the World Bank), Douglass Dillon (former treasury secretary), David Rockefeller, and Dean Acheson.[52]

Both committees struggled to bridge the existing gap between the White House and Congress on foreign aid, which was broken down in the 1966 Cabinet Committee report. Johnson, it explained, was "a long-time advocate of strengthening LDC's [least developed country]," but he "knew that the bulk of development job must be done by countries themselves, and that it is incompatible with simultaneous political and military adventures." He was also "concerned that we have not always used aid boldly enough as a negotiating tool to get our clients to make the hard choices essential to economic growth" and that "we have not sufficiently dove-tailed various forms of U.S. aid—food, capital, and technical assistance—so as to maximize development effect and negotiating leverage." Johnson was determined that American foreign aid should be structured in the most efficient manner possible. The Eighty-Ninth Congress, the committee reported, "continued, on the whole, to support theory and objectives of foreign aid, but raised questions about criteria determining country eligibility and program composition."[53] To make the point, the House Committee on Foreign Relations initiated its own review of foreign aid in the fall of 1965, which concluded that the main problem was the USAID focus on solving long-term problems, which leaves "taxpayers and their representatives" unable to relate foreign assistance "directly to solving the current assortment of crises and problems which are uppermost ... in their own minds." If foreign aid is first and foremost a tool of foreign policy, the congressional committee wrote, then it should be focused first and foremost on on securing cooperation, not creating development. This is particularly true, it continued, because we do not even know how to accelerate development and are putting billions of dollars into long-term "treatments" that are not certain to yield results.[54]

Kennedy had secured congressional support for his aid initiatives in a moment of widespread enthusiasm, flush with confidence that USAID would overcome many of the problems that had plagued the aid programs of the 1950s. Johnson shared his predecessor's commitment to aid, but, five years in, the White House continued to struggle to convince congress and the American people that USAID could fulfill its promises. The Cabinet Committee tackled the House report head-on in its report that January. Dean Rusk told Johnson that the group's study had "reinforced our belief in the basic proposition that a properly directed foreign assistance program is a vital instrument of United States foreign policy. Economic and military assistance remain far and away the most powerful means at our command to influence the massive forces at work in the less developed nations. They are our primary source of influence on the economic and military evolution of most of the countries of the non-communist world." We do not need to fundamentally change aid's structure, the committee concluded, but we do need to place new emphasis upon several principles:

1. *We must make better bargains for the use of aid resources.* . . . Aid must be used as a carrot, and the possibility of withholding it as a stick. We must not allow our zeal to help the needy to obscure the fact that their long-term interests and ours require maximum lasting return for every aid dollar.
2. *We must make it crystal clear that the basic principle of foreign aid is cooperation.*
3. *We must make a concerted attack on the roots of world poverty—hunger, ignorance, and disease.* . . . The overwhelming lesson of our experience in the developing world is that no amount of capital or technical training will result in sustained economic growth unless some progress is made against the basic conditions which dull the desire, sap the will, and destroy the capacity of most of the world's people to better their lives.
4. *We must stand ready to increase our support of multilateral lending agencies as soon as other donors will join us.* . . . But we should not delude ourselves that it is to our advantage to get completely out of the bilateral aid business. In the major theatres of action there is no refuge in all-out multilateralism.

The list continued to make a total of nine points, but the first four were the most significant. The United States has, Rusk reported, "been doing much that is right," but convincing congress and the American public to continue supporting its aid efforts means that the White House needed to make some critical adjustments.[55] The Clifford Committee largely agreed, noting that "in our opinion, the AID budget as a whole is as important to the national interest of the United States as the Defense budget itself," so use it wisely.[56]

The principles made sense, but they did not represent a revolutionary shift in the discussion about aid that had been ongoing since the Truman administration. As the Secretary of State, Rusk, like Dulles and Acheson before him, was temperamentally inclined to value aid specifically as a tool of foreign policy, not as a humanitarian mission. The difficulty with that position in the 1960s, however, was that the reigning ideology of aid (modernization theory) insisted that development required large amounts of money and effort distributed over long periods of time. The committee's third principle emphasized the importance of tackling the roots of poverty, but doing that effectively made it practically impossible to structure an aid program around simply securing cooperation—as Congress and, indeed, much of the American public wanted. From Washington's perspective, promoting the development of the underdeveloped world continued to be in everyone but the Soviet's long-term interest. As it gradually became clear that the influxes of aid money distributed through the new arrangements of USAID under the new prescriptions of modernization theory were being plagued by the old problems, the opening years of the development decade's enthusiasm gave way to frustration.

Following his 1968 decision not to run for the presidency, Johnson asked all departments and agencies to prepare histories of their activities and accomplishments under his administration. The highly thoughtful USAID history noted that "despite many important development successes, we have experienced a steady decline in the political and public support of the foreign aid program." Congress committed less money— $3.9 billion in '62, $3.8 billion in '63, $3 billion in '64, $3.3 billion in '65, $3.9 billion in '66, $2.9 billion in '67, $2.2 billion in '68—and demanded more results. Johnson pushed for more funding to initiatives on food, education, population, and family planning, but these were necessarily of a long-term centered outlook that went against congressional pressure for instant results. "No one was prepared to conceive of the effort as one of decades," it admitted. Even though Johnson cut funding from a number of nations (under congressional pressure) in order to focus on only a few (as Rusk had recommended to Kennedy years earlier), there was not enough time to see many of the hoped-for results. USAID claimed successes in Korea, Greece, Iran, Israel, Brazil, India, Turkey, Pakistan, and Taiwan during the development decade, but the gap between the poorest of the poor and the West did not shrink. Africa was the hardest hit region. Although Africa received the highest per capita assistance of any region—around $6 per person throughout the 1960s—USAID funding for the continent amounted to less than 10% of total grants and loans. Loans were limited to those nations who showed the most promise for development, with the exception of Ethiopia and Liberia, which were "in a 'special relationship' category."[57] Haile Selassie had worked very hard throughout the 1960s to make sure that that remained the case. Ethiopia got USAID assistance not because it showed the most promise, but because it promised the greatest allegiance.

In addition to creating the two committees to review foreign aid in 1965, Johnson also asked Edward Korry, the U.S. ambassador to Ethiopia, to write a report on the ways in which American assistance to Africa could be improved. The request was inspired by existing concerns about escalating conditions in the Horn of Africa in particular. In a July 1964 memorandum to Robert McNamara, the Joint Chiefs of Staff insisted that "Sino-Soviet progress in efforts to influence and subvert East Africa countries," as well as "the importance of Ethiopia to US politico/military interests" justified "a substantial and prompt increase in US political, economic, and military assistance to Ethiopia."[58] Ethiopia was already the largest recipient of U.S. military aid in Africa, but the Joint Chiefs were insistent that it needed more of all types of aid. And such aid, it seemed clear, was not to be of a "treatment," but of a "cooperative" nature. While working on his report, which eventually consisted of forty-two recommendations, including "support for arms limitation and control in Africa," Korry continued pressuring the White House for more assistance to Ethiopia.[59] At a 1965 meeting, Korry and McNamara discussed the utility of supplying Haile Selassie with napalm and antitank guns, before dismissing them as too much too soon.[60] The emperor did not get his desired weapons, but he received more than $60 million in military aid and $46.2 million in economic aid in FY 1966.

What Korry believed to be best for Africa as a whole did not necessarily apply to Ethiopia itself, which was, as the USAID report noted, "in a 'special relationship' category." Ethiopia, Korry reminded Ambassador at Large Averell Harriman that May, "is the only country in East Africa (with the exception of Malawi) which has not recognized Communist China." It has rebuffed North Korean and North Vietnamese attempts to establish embassies; it is encouraging African nations to adopt a gradualist, evolutionary course through its influence in the Organization of African Unity it continues to allow the Americans access to Kagnew Station "in the face of growing criticism by other African states"; and it continues to maintain a small contingent in Korea. Haile Selassie is the only African head of state to have attended Kennedy's funeral, he added, and he has recently renamed the university library in the former president's honor, which further opens to door to allegations by his neighbors of over-affection for the United States. The IEG, Korry argued, was risking its regional influence by working so openly with the Americans and it deserved substantial rewards for doing so.[61]

Ethiopia's strategic value momentarily secured it additional military and economic aid, but U.S. policymakers remained concerned about its domestic situation. In February 1966, the president's deputy special assistant for national security affairs, Robert Komer, sent a letter to the assistant secretary of state for African affairs asking, "Would there be any merit in a quiet US campaign to convince the Emperor of the need for some quick domestic reforms designed to eliminate the most threatening complaints?" He noted that they had been able to convince the shah and King Hassan "that they ought to be modern reformist monarchs" and wondered if the same would be possible with Haile Selassie, who seemed oblivious to the possibility of another coup. The assistant secretary was not hopeful. "There are similarities with the Shah and King Hassan," but "the Emperor belongs to a much older generation and has the underlying feel that domestic reforms, instead of strengthening his own position, would strike at the heart of his personal power, as indeed they probably would." It is, he concluded with more than a touch of evident exasperation, "becoming increasingly difficult to believe that anything or anyone can persuade the Emperor at this late stage of his career to do anything against his 'better' judgment." Komer wrote back that that State Department needed to come up with something that would work, because "if the present pattern continues in Ethiopia, our stake there will be in serious jeopardy." The emperor was currently relying on American military aid to secure his throne from domestic threats, instead of killing them with positive reforms; such a situation made the United States, which had long argued the moral validity of foreign aid, look very bad indeed.[62]

The Johnson administration's concern with the situation in Ethiopia came to a head in the winter of 1967. Haile Selassie had been asking for an audience for months and was finally granted one that February. In preparation for the visit, Rostow sent Johnson a memo that warned what the emperor would want and described what the United States could promise. "Your advisers are agreed that we should *not* agree to any major increase in military aid to Ethiopia. The Emperor's real security problems are internal," Rostow wrote. We have prepared a $2 million dollar counterinsurgency package that "will save him the embarrassment of returning empty-handed," but that is all the additional money that can be offered. "The important thing is to give the Emperor a sense that our interest in the future of Ethiopia—and your personal interest in HIM—remains strong," Rostow told Johnson. "He is extremely proud of his stature as a world leader and a spokesman for Africa. Butter, strategically applied, can make up for many tons of undelivered guns."[63] The State Department seconded Rostow's point in a message to Johnson a few days later. "We do not believe that the Emperor would oust us from Kagnew Station completely or affect our operations significantly, given the leverage on us this base gives him," a memo explained, but Kagnew Station is an "essential military communications installation (with important intercept functions, a fact not to be mentioned to the Emperor)" and "there is no alternative site presently available for many of these facilities." It was therefore important that a special effort be made to assure Haile Selassie of America's continued interest."[64]

The growing federal deficit—the unfortunate outcome of Johnson's efforts to wage wars at home and abroad—made that effort difficult. Haile Selassie got his desired meeting with the president and his $2 million package from the Department of Defense, but American economic aid to Ethiopia dropped to $19 million in FY 1967 and $9.3 million in FY 1968.[65] Those were still much larger totals than those seen in the 1950s, but they were devastating blows to the emperor. He realized that he needed to boost his development image in order to have both a "special relationship" with the U.S. Department of Defense and high priority on the USAID development loan list.

Haile Selassie worked quickly to put his nation back into favor, publishing a new five-year plan that addressed some of the aid bureaucracy's frustrations with Ethiopia. The Third Five Year Development Plan differed significantly from the first two by emphasizing agriculture, education, and public health over industrialization. "The modernization and expansion of agriculture, the mainstay of the Ethiopian economic and the livelihood of Our people, has always been at the forefront of Our government's preoccupations," His Imperial Majesty insisted in the speech introducing the new plan, but he admitted that the IEG had now placed agriculture in the center of its development agenda.[66] The move responded to USAID frustration with the IEG's previous attempts to ignore agriculture in favor of industrial development, in direct violation of modernization theory's stadial principles. The USAID appreciated large-scale projects, but those projects had to be tailored to fit into the current stage of a nation's development, and the preconditions for take-off had to come before take-off. The IEG had allocated only 2% of its budget for agriculture in 1967. Meanwhile, the nation's per capita income was estimated at just over $72.5 U.S. dollars and the vast majority of the population remained engaged in subsistence agriculture.⁶⁷ Clearly, something had to change.

Ethiopia needed to modernize its farming before it could properly industrialize its cities. Instead of focusing on its millions of peasant farmers, however, the IEG devoted most of the new agricultural funding to "develop modern commercial agriculture."⁶⁸ Large-scale farming promised faster, more visible rewards and had the advantage of more closely allying its wealthy administrators to the state that controlled their funding. Despite pushing for larger farms, the IEG also promised, somewhat incongruously, to address the wide gap between the landholding few and the landless many, who remained illiterate and isolated from the developments changing the face of Addis Ababa. A peasant uprising in Gojjam that year demonstrated the seriousness of the situation. Ethiopia needed change and the IEG renewed its promise that it would get it . . . eventually. The top-down modernization predicted trickle-down benefits for the poorest of the nation's poor, but it was clear that they would be a long time coming.

The U.S. government remained skeptical that vague promises of future prosperity could quell local unrest. In 1968, Deputy Secretary of Defense Paul Nitze sent a letter to the Under Secretary of State Nicholas Katzenbach addressing the feasibility of "relocating our current activities from Kagnew Station in Ethiopia." Kagnew, he explained, currently hosts United States Strategic Command and Navy communication facilities, along with "a small atomic explosion detection site" and duplicating is facilities will cost around $116 million. The Joint Chiefs of Staff think it unwise to relocate at this time, Nizte continued, though all remain concerned about "the uncertain political situation in Ethiopia." Katzenbach responded with a proposal to undertake no new constructions at Kagnew and to gradually move less-essential functions to more-stable facilities. "Meanwhile," he concluded, "we should continue refining our planning for an eventual withdrawal so that we can soon have in hand a scenario that will permit us to carry out an orderly phase-down, if necessary, well before our present agreement expires in 1978."⁶⁹ It seemed increasingly unsafe to maintain such an important facility in such an unstable place.

Haile Selassie's 1968 campaign to make Ethiopia a viable candidate for modernization resulted in $20.8 million in economic aid from the United States for FY 1969, which was a significant improvement over the previous year's $9.3 million. The U.S. government seemed ready once again to forgive the IEG for policies not enacted and fund policies now promised. Haile Selassie won the battle, however, he was losing the war, as the Nitze letter makes clear. The emperor's resistance to meaningful reform had created so serious a security situation that the U.S. government began working to relocate a facility on which the emperor depended for continued aid. The Central Intelligence Agency had noted in 1966 that "the death of Haile Selassie will probably be followed by a period of confusion, with traditional and modernized elements and factions of the armed forces contending for power. In these circumstances, the Ethiopian social and political order as now constituted is likely to be shaken, and even the territorial integrity of the Empire itself may be challenged."[70] Things had only gotten worse over the past two years, as neither the social nor the political order in Ethiopia experienced any meaningful movement toward change. Haile Selassie remained as determined as ever to continue his absolute rule. Hopes for reform born in the aftermath of the 1960 coup were slowly killed by the emperor's unceasing resistance. There would be no "third choice" in Ethiopia. While the United States secretly plotted retreat, dissenters around Addis Ababa secretly plotted rebellion.

Ethiopia was not alone in its struggles to reconcile monarchy with modernization. A similar story was playing out in Morocco, Iran, Libya, Afghanistan, Saudi Arabia, Cambodia, Nepal, Kuwait, and Thailand. The Harvard political scientist Samuel P. Huntington argued in 1968 that the royalty in these countries found themselves in a dilemma of success versus survival. "On the one hand, centralization of power in the monarchy was necessary to promote social, cultural, and economic reform. On the other hand, this centralization made difficult or impossible the expansion of the power of the traditional polity and the assimilation into it of the new groups produced by modernization." The king is left wondering: "Must he be the victim of his own achievements?"[71] Progress in one area of modernization, Huntington insisted, did not necessarily translate into progress in another. Huntington's book, *Political Order in Changing Societies*, revolutionized the academic and political discussion about modernization by questioning the idea that economic growth and enhanced social equality brought stable democracy. There "is a lag," he insisted, "in the development of political institutions behind social and economic change." Economic growth actually widened the political gap between stable and unstable nations while trying to bridge the economic one. The argument threatened one of the foundational doctrines of U.S. foreign aid: that a stronger, more efficient economy made for a stronger, more efficient government.

Huntington believed that the misconception lay in America's fortunate past. "In its development the United States was blessed with more than its fair share of economic plenty, social well-being, and political stability." That "happy history" led Americans to "assume that all good things go together and that the achievement of one desirable social goal aids in the achievement of others." The United States built its aid policy on a causal chain: "economic assistance promotes economic development, economic development promotes political stability," but "economic development and political stability are two independent goals."[72] Huntington backed up his claim with a great deal of statistical evidence showing that underdeveloped nations tended to become less politically stable as they became more economically viable. Violence increased in nations with a per capita gross national product (GNP) between $100 and $200. Ethiopia, which could only boast of a GNP of $72.5 in 1967, was on its way. "A purely traditional society would be ignorant, poor, and stable," he explained, but by this point, "all traditional societies [are] also transitional or modernizing societies" and incidents of violence around the world have risen accordingly. "The more man wages war against 'his ancient enemies: poverty, disease, ignorance' the more he wages war against himself."[73] For Huntington, Rostow's "traditional societies" were idealized relics of the past that said a great deal more about the West's economic history than they did about the world's political present. The United States needed to be more realistic about what it hoped to accomplish through foreign aid. The American experiment did not translate well, and the United States should stop pretending that it did.

Political Order in Changing Societies challenged the lines of causation that modernization theorists had drawn between the economy, the society, and the government, and called on America's aid bureaucracy to rethink its development policies. You are going to have to accept, he told them, that your programs for economic development are not necessarily going to bring peaceful democratic reform. Revolution is more likely than elections. The world's monarchs have known this for a while, he continued, and have tried to engage in modernization policies that centered on economic change alone. "Nineteenth-century monarchs modernized to thwart imperialism; twentieth-century monarchs modernize to thwart revolution." The United States needs to be cognizant that their success in this endeavor remains uncertain. "In a country like Ethiopia . . . the best that could be hoped for," he concluded with resignation, was a coup d'état that turned the ruling monarchy into an oligarchic monarchy, but a coup d'état that disposed of both the monarch and the monarchy while failing to produce any new "institutions of legitimacy" seemed more likely.[74] The Unites States had good reason to fear for Ethiopia's future stability, particularly if Haile Selassie somehow managed to raise the GNP. Such was the irony of economic growth: "How do you reform without everything falling apart?"[75]

Haile Selassie returned to Washington in July 1969, this time meeting with a U.S. president who had actually been to Ethiopia two times. During a conversation at the White House, Richard Nixon asked the emperor if he thought that the Soviets, the Chinese, or the Egyptians posed the greatest threat to Ethiopia. Haile Selassie pointed to the Soviets, noting that "their influence is strong in both Somalia and the Sudan, as well as in important parts of the Arabian peninsula. Their vessels have penetrated the Red Sea. Working through the UAR as a client state, he feared that they wished to make that body of water a Soviet-Egyptian lake." The Soviets have offered us military and economic assistance, he continued, but we have accepted very little from them, wishing, instead, to rely on "tried and traditional friends." Lest Nixon get too comfortable, he added: "At the same time, the government is under tremendous pressures from the Ethiopian people who yearn for security and for a hastened pace of development. They will not be able to understand if the government is not able to show progress in both fields."[76] Nothing either said was surprising.

In preparation for the emperor's visit, Nixon's assistant for national security affairs, Henry Kissinger, had provided him with a detailed memo explaining, "Ethiopia is our closest friend in Africa" and the purpose of this visit is to show Haile Selassie that this administration does not want that friendship to waiver, but this has to be done delicately. "The Emperor has an appetite for U.S. arms which we can neither satisfy under present military aid limitations nor justify in terms of our own estimate of his position. Moreover, military concerns divert the Emperor from economic development—where we can help and where prompt action is crucial to Ethiopia's stability and thus to our interests in the country." Since the early fifties, Kissinger continued, "we have been the heaviest contributor to their economic development, a primary market for their important coffee exports, and the ultimate quartermaster for the Ethiopian army and air force." We currently provide around $20 million per year in economic aid and $12 million per year in military aid. "In return," we get Kagnew, which "gives the Ethiopians the usual host-country leverage in extracting military aid for base rights." The special relationship remains strong, but our friendship with the seventy-six-year-old monarch potentially threatens the long-term stability of Ethiopia. "At home the Emperor is caught, like most modernizing monarchs, in a dilemma of his own making," Kissinger explained with words that echoed Huntington. "He has built a modern state from feudal fragments, surrendered some prerogatives to a constitution, and educated an urban elite—all in the interests of a stronger nationhood against the external danger. Now he is finding, inevitably, that these steps have only created greater political momentum—particularly among the young—toward a surrender of autocratic powers which he is determined to preserve." The IEG cannot reform while the emperor is alive, Kissinger acknowledged, "but a serious effort to spur economic development could provide an escape valve for the volatile energies and frustrations in Ethiopia." Haile Selassie has made some new efforts in this direction, including granting some key economic cabinet jobs to "younger progressives," who just might be the key determinates to Ethiopia's survival. "Modernization may make royal rule impossible but failure to modernize may produce an explosion."[77]

Uncertain how to prevent what it feared might be inevitable, the Nixon administration continued encouraging Haile Selassie to reach out to those in his nation who demanded reform, and the United States provided the funds to enable him to do it. Between 1969 and 1974, U.S. economic assistance to Ethiopia averaged $24.1 million a year. Military assistance averaged $14.2 million.[78] Meanwhile, U.S. aid to the neighboring Republic of Somalia dropped to zero, following the new Somali leader Siad Barré's declaration that his was an officially pro-Soviet state. Ethiopia remained America's "closest friend in Africa," but the emperor grew older and more isolated from his people, and the political momentum against him grew stronger.

The long-feared explosion began in January 1974 and continued burning throughout the year. First, soldiers stationed in the southern frontier mutinied in response to limited rations and delayed salary payments. Dissent quickly spread throughout the military, gathering momentum from a growing list of wrongs that needed to be righted. On February 18, Ethiopia's teachers went on strike in protest of a new government reform program that they believed discriminated against poor students. The same day, taxi drivers in the capital also went on strike to demand that they be able to increase their fares in response to the dramatic rise in the price of oil. Students joined in, and the strikes turned into riots. More kept coming each day with new grievances, and the protests quickly spread into the provinces. Public pressure forced the cabinet to resign, and Haile Selassie instructed the new one to promise to change, but the people yelled back, "changing the stove does not make the stew any better." It was too little, too late. Although the IEG spent the spring and summer trying to reinstate order, Ethiopia was a nation on fire.[79]

On the evening of September 11, a group of military officers calling themselves the "Derg" (loosely translatable as "committee") offered a public screening of a film by Jonathan Dimbleby on the horrendous famine of 1973, which had claimed 20 percent of the human population and 90 percent of the animal population in Wollo province. The film juxtaposed Haile Selassie feeding his dogs off crystal plates with citizens starving to death. It was a brilliant political move in preparation for the following day's events. Haile Selassie, now 82 and partially senile, had remained largely ambivalent about the year's events—hiding in his palace while his government fell apart. He would have sanctuary no more. On September 12, members of the Derg entered in the palace, announced his deposition, and drove him off to the headquarters of the Fourth Division in the back of a blue Volkswagen beetle. That November, the Derg executed sixty members of the IEG, including the emperor's grandson and two former prime ministers. Haile Selassie was imprisoned in a room in his former palace. Some members of the royal family fled abroad; others stayed. In March 1975, the Derg proclaimed the end of private land ownership, successfully destroying what was left of the aristocracy's power.[80] On the morning of August 27, a radio broadcast announced that a servant had found the former emperor dead in his bed, likely from complications from prostate surgery two months earlier. It was a quiet end to a long career.

"The prestige and power of Haile Selassie, waxing over more than half a century, made of him a personage larger than life," read the *New York Times*'s report on his passing. "With a splendid sense of theater, he lived up to, and even surpassed, the role in which he was cast."[81] Celebrated abroad, at home he was buried immediately with little ceremony. There was no room for living monarchs in the new Ethiopia.

The following month, Kissinger, now the secretary of state, met with Ethiopian Foreign Minister Kifle Wodajo in New York. The latter wanted assurances of continued friendship. The former was happy to provide them. "We consider the changes in Ethiopia essentially a matter of Ethiopian domestic affairs which do not affect our foreign policy," Kissinger reassured. "If you think there is disapproval in the United States of Ethiopia's domestic evolution, you are wrong. We are basically sympathetic to the modernization of Ethiopia. The internal changes do not affect conduct of our foreign policy." America's sentiments remained unaltered. "We want to see Ethiopia develop," Kissinger congenially insisted. "We will look sympathetically at military assistance and development programs that will be helpful to you."[82] The secretary was, above all, a practical man. With the Soviets and the Cubans heavily involved in Somalia, it really did not matter who was running Ethiopia, provided that they could maintain control and were open to remaining friendly with the United States. The following December, one of the Derg's leaders, Mengistu Haile Mariam, secretly traveled to Moscow to sign a new military aid agreement. The United States desired stability and continuity in the Horn of Africa; it was about to get a war and a reversal of strategic alliances. Haile Selassie never looked so good alive as he did dead.

At a 1968 meeting of the Society for International Development, William S. Gaud, the director of USAID, told the audience about the amazing strides being made to achieve food security in Pakistan, India, Turkey, and the Philippines. "These and other developments in the field of agriculture contain the makings of a new revolution," he gleefully announced. "It is not a violent Red Revolution like that of the Soviets, nor is it a White Revolution like that of the Shah of Iran. I call it the Green Revolution. This new revolution can be as significant and as beneficial to mankind as the industrial revolution of a century and a half ago. To accelerate it, to spread it, and to make it permanent, we need to understand how it started and what forces are driving it forward." Some of it can be attributed to simple good luck, he admitted. "But hard work, good management, and sound agricultural policies in the developing countries and foreign aid were also very much involved."[83] Gaud's speech provided a name for a process that had begun twenty-five years earlier with the Rockefeller Foundation's support to banish wheat rush from Mexico.

A young plant pathologist, Norman Borlaug, in the Office of Special Studies was asked to go down and see what he could do. He went, beginning a quest to end hunger around the world that did not end until his death in 2009. From Mexico, he moved on to India and Pakistan, and his miracle seeds moved on to Turkey, Afghanistan, Tunisia, Morocco, Lebanon, and Iraq. Meanwhile, the Rockefeller and Ford foundations opened a laboratory in the Philippines in 1960 to try to make similar improvements to rice as Borlaug had made to wheat. The results were astonishing. Millions who had been hungry now had food. It was arguably the most important revolution of the twentieth century. It was certainly the most beneficial to the greatest number of people. Borlaug wanted to make it even more so by bringing the Green Revolution to Africa. "If you desire peace, cultivate justice," he acknowledged in his 1970 Nobel Prize Lecture, "but at the same time cultivate the fields to produce more bread; otherwise, there will be no peace." People do not live by bread alone, but they cannot live without it.[84]

Borlaug's revolution began with science and food, but his was not the only one discussed in connection with the Third World during this period. In 1956, Senator John F. Kennedy told attendees of the Conference on Vietnam Luncheon that what "we must offer them is a revolution—a political, economic and social revolution far superior to anything the Communists can offer. We must supply capital to replace that drained by centuries of colonial exploitation; technicians to train those handicapped by deliberate policies of illiteracy; guidance to assist a nation taking those first feeble steps toward the complexities of a republican form of government."[85] He was talking specifically about South Vietnam, but his confidence in America's ability to promote democratic and economic revolutions abroad was not limited to Southeast Asia. And he was not alone. In 1952, Truman told attendees at the National Conference on International Economic and Social Development, "We want to help them find out and apply the secret of our success, the secret of our American revolution—the secret that the vitality of our science, our industry, our culture, is embedded in our political life."[86] When the Kennedy administration opened the Development Decade promising "a third choice"—"an evolutionary path which can give constructive and progressive expression to modernizing impulses without removing by violence the obstacles which the traditional heritage may place in their path"—it was trying to offer revolution without *a* revolution.[87]

Lyndon Johnson supported Borlaug's efforts with USAID funding, as is evident in William Gaud's 1968 speech, but his administration, like those before and after it, was not comfortable pinning its development hopes on revolutions of a scientific nature alone. As Truman had said, the key was that the science had to be connected to American-style politics and culture. Borlaug was a scientist, not a politician. His development was for development's sake; theirs was not. The Truman, Kennedy, Johnson, and Nixon administrations understood foreign aid to be a tool of foreign policy. They always had larger purposes in mind when they discussed sending tractors and technicians into cities whose names they could not pronounce, funding million dollar dams across rivers they could not locate on a map, or simply putting cash in the hands of leaders whose domestic offenses they willfully ignored. They were trying to direct modernization along the path that they believed was the most favorable to America's global security. They used a mixture of economic aid, military aid, diplomatic pressure, and sometimes even military intervention to do so. Aid was the carrot to the stick.

The weaknesses of this policy became evident in Ethiopia in 1974 (as they had become evident in Vietnam a few years earlier). The U.S. government attempted to give Ethiopia "a third choice" in the 1960s, but it did not prevent the revolution that distanced Addis Ababa from Washington and pushed it closer to Moscow. Samuel Huntington had insisted in 1968 that "The more man wages war against 'his ancient enemies: poverty, disease, ignorance' the more he wages war against himself," but Green Revolution successes around the world in the 1960s posed the question that perhaps it was not the war itself, but the chosen method of fighting it that was the mistake.[88] Ethiopia badly needed an agricultural revolution, but neither the United States nor Haile Selassie were willing to dedicate the resources necessary to making that happen.[89] Ethiopia got a political revolution instead. The terrible repercussions of that tragedy became evident in the early 1980s, when the Ethiopian people, once famous for their independence became famous for their starvation. Their fall from grace testified to the limitations of a foreign aid agenda that put international politics before international development.

7 RETHINKING THE "AMERICAN ANSWER"

On the evening of October 23, 1984, millions of Americans watching *NBC Nightly News* were horrified by a six-minute British Broadcasting Corporation report by Michael Buerk with footage gathered by Mohammed Amin at a feeding center in Ethiopia. "Dawn," Buerk explained, as the camera panned the ghastly scene, "and as the sun breaks through the piercing chill of night on the plain outside Korem, it lights up a Biblical famine, now, in the twentieth century. This place, say workers here, is the closest thing to hell on earth. Thousands of wasted people are coming here for help. Many find only death." In desperation, forty thousand people had congregated at the Korem food center. *Medecins sans Frontieres* and Save the Children were tirelessly working to alleviate some of the suffering, but there was little food and little medicine, and the prospects were grim. "The tragedy, bigger than anybody seems to realize," Buerk reported, "is getting worse every day."[1] The next edition of *Newsweek* reported that in "the 36 hours after the film first aired, more than 10,000 people called Save the Children to offer their help." "No one anticipated the public response," the article continued, and that was only the beginning.[2] All the rest of the fall and into the winter, Ethiopia dominated American news cycles. The story seemed clear, as *Time* reported that November: "The cause of Ethiopia's agony has been a series of disastrous harvests caused by the prolonged drought."[3] The reality was much more complicated, but it was also obvious to anyone familiar with the past fifty years of Ethiopian history.

Three years earlier, the economist Amartya Sen published *Poverty and Famines*, a groundbreaking explanation of famine as a political, not a natural phenomenon. "Starvation," Sen insisted, "is the characteristic of some people not having enough food to eat. It is not the characteristic of there being not enough food to eat." Starvation is almost always limited to the poorest members of society, and that poverty is a sociopolitical condition often maintained by unjust governmental practices. Sen argued that history provides no clear evidence that there has ever been a famine in which all groups within a country struggled with starvation, "since different groups do typically have very different commanding powers over food, and an over-all shortage brings out the contrasting powers in stark clarity."[4] Modern mass starvation occurs in only those countries whose political structure allows it to happen by maintaining economic inequalities that benefit the government's agenda. Although crop shortages usually begin with a drought, they become a famine only when the government decides not to distribute available food throughout the region.

In the specific case of Ethiopia, the 1982 harvest was the largest ever recorded and the main harvest of 1983 was the third largest on record, though both were still far below the nation's potential. Yet more than 1.5 million people starved to death in the provinces of Wollo, Tigray, and Eritrea between 1983 and 1985.[5] The vulnerability of Ethiopia's peasants stemmed from decades of missed agricultural development opportunities. Their actual deaths were the result of a deliberate government policy to use their vulnerability to its advantage. Most of the victims came from areas that resisted the Derg's tyrannical control.[6] At the height of the famine, Mengistu Haile Mariam was spending 46 percent of the national budget on armaments and used international food aid to fill bellies in his 3-million-man army—the largest in Africa. Ethiopia's main partner, the Soviet Union, did not reduce military assistance, and the United States sent a staggering $87.4 million worth of food aid through PL-480 in 1985 alone. That year, Ethiopia received 1.25 million tons of food relief, only 90,000 tons of which was distributed in the non-government-controlled regions of Tigray and Eritrea. *Medecins sans Frontieres* actually withdrew from the relief effort in protest of these polices, but the aid kept coming.[7]

The U.S. House of Representatives Subcommittee on Africa had held a hearing titled "Food Crisis in Africa" in November 1983 to confront the now-constant problem of widespread hunger across the continent. Throughout the hearing, politicians and experts gave statements that described famine as a sociopolitical as well as a natural disaster. "Africans are hungry because they are poor," the Representative from North Dakota insisted. "And of course, hunger feeds poverty itself by debilitating workers, sapping energy, and engendering disease."[8] Much of the blame was laid on governments that had expanded industry at the expense of the agricultural sectors of their economies, thereby inhibiting food production across the continent. Many of the policies that had emphasized agriculture, such as those undertaken in Tanzania, Ethiopia, and Mozambique, had, one expert explained, "run at odds with the outlook and life situation of most peasants" and ended up doing a great deal more harm than good. In addition, rampant violence threatened food security in numerous countries, including Ethiopia, where the government faced a resistant populace. "Where civic order rests on military rule," the same expert continued, "chronic food deficits have developed."[9] The roots of hunger went deep. "I think those of us who are searching for lasting solutions to the food security problem in sub-Saharan Africa are faced with an enormous challenge," admitted a U.S. Agency for International Development (USAID) official. "That challenge is to bring home to the American people the fact that those images of starving African mothers and children cannot be eradicated by food and feeding alone."[10] He was correct. Eradication demanded serious changes in the international community—changes that asked developed nations to rethink both their foreign and their domestic policies.

Between 1974 and 1977, the United States supplied Ethiopia with $79.8 million in economic assistance and $71.1 million in open military assistance—and, according to a former charge d'affaires at the American embassy in Addis Ababa, more than $100 million in arms—in an effort to keep the Derg from getting too friendly with the Soviet Union.[11] Despite the large amounts of requested military and economic funding, in December 1976, Mengistu signed a military aid agreement with Moscow that included a clause demanding Ethiopia sever its ties with the United States. His motivations remain unknown, though they were certainly influenced both by the Soviet Union's tendency to be more generous with its military assistance and its history of inclusivity, which undoubtedly meant something important to a man reported to have experienced American racism firsthand while training in Alabama in the early 1960s. In addition, although Mengistu possessed little familiarity with Marxist-Leninist doctrine, he recognized that it celebrated the weak over the strong, which likely proved appealing to the son of a former slave of a Shawan landowner. He also knew that it appealed to the masses of students who had rallied around the revolution. They had cheered the Derg's April declaration of the National Democratic Revolution Programme to fight feudalism, imperialism, and capitalism.[12] Continued friendship with the United States threatened that agenda and, as long as the Soviet Union was willing to provide the funding necessary to keep the government in power, it could be sacrificed on the altar of revolution.

The next year witnessed a shocking sequence of events in the Horn of Africa. In April 1977, citing rampant human rights violations, the United States announced that it would not renew its lease on Kagnew Station and stopped all military aid to Ethiopia. Mengistu promptly terminated the 1953 Mutual Defense Assistance Agreement, expelled three-quarters of the U.S.

personnel in the nation, and flew off to Moscow to announce that the Ethiopian revolution aimed to lay "a firm foundation for transition to Socialism."[13] Sensing that his position as Moscow's favored child in the Horn was about to end, Somalia's Siad Barré began sending signals to Washington that he might be ready to change teams.[14] By the end of the year, Somalia had renounced its ties to the Soviet Union in hopes of securing American aid. Although the Carter administration maintained previous refusals to send weapons, it increased economic aid to Somalia from $.8 million for 1977 to $19 million for 1978. The lack of military assistance forced an end to the conflict the following spring, as Washington had intended.

The Ogaden remained in Ethiopia, but although Barré lost the war, he won U.S. support. In 1980, the United States sent Somalia $62.3 million worth of economic aid and $20 million worth of military aid. Meanwhile, Ethiopia received only $15 million worth of PL-480 assistance, with no USAID funding. Even the food aid dwindled in coming years, amounting to only $2.8 million in 1983. That year, Somalia received $48.7 and $30.6 million, respectively, in economic and military assistance.[15] The money poured in from both sides—averaging around $150 million a year to Ethiopia from the Soviet Union—and the Horn remained a violent, poverty-ridden corner of the world that had the power to influence larger events. "SALT [Strategic Arms Limitation Talks]," National Security Advisor Zbigniew Brzezinski lamented, "lies buried in the sands of the Ogaden."[16] Hopes that foreign aid would transform the region lay next to it. From the perspective of the United States, Ethiopia's development seemed to have halted with its 1976 declaration of the National Democratic Revolution Programme. The 1984/85 famine provided the ultimate proof. Even though the United States blamed Ethiopia's devastation on its Soviet-style policies, the reality was that it was just one of dozens of nations that remained mired in poverty despite another decade's worth of foreign aid. Something had to change.

Attention focused on Africa. By the opening of the 1980s, the continent had received more than $36 billion (in historical dollars) in foreign assistance, yet remained staggeringly far "behind" the West. Although World Bank and USAID funding had emphasized ending rural poverty during the 1970s, the leaders of the underdeveloped nations themselves had spent the decade borrowing money to pay for grand development schemes and to fill up Swiss bank accounts. The system fell apart on August 12, 1982, when Mexico announced that it could not make payments on its loans. Other nations quickly followed suit, threatening the entire global financial system.[17] Convinced it was foolish to talk about alleviating poverty in countries that did not have functioning economies, the leading donor countries decided to focus on market reform. They got the idea from a 1981 World Bank report primarily drafted by Elliot Berg, a professor of economics at the University of Michigan, titled *Accelerated Development in Sub-Saharan Africa*. The report argued that Africa's recent "disappointing economic performance" stemmed from "'structural' factors that evolved from historical circumstance or from the physical environment." The World Bank decided to attack the political rather than the physical "structural factors." Even though Berg argued that Africa needed an agricultural revolution, it got a political one.[18]

In its most visible form, the new doctrine went into developing countries as International Monetary Fund structural adjustment packages, which called for privatization, the removal of artificial price distortions, trade liberalization, and decreased government expenditures. The packages marked a recommitment to neoclassical economics with their emphasis on free markets and private-led growth and with their demands to limit government intervention in the economy. Such efforts, dubbed the Washington Consensus, earned the 1980s the unwelcome title of "the lost development decade." Poverty reduction took a back seat to economic and political reform.[19] Meanwhile, a massive nongovernmental aid industry emerged to do what governments were not. The Ethiopian famine energized a new generation of aid enthusiasts. In 1984, there were less than twenty nongovernmental organizations in Ethiopia; in 1986, there were sixty. In the process, the idea that foreign aid was inherently beneficial became more deeply entrenched within policy and public circles and it became sacrilegious to question it.[20] How could helping people be bad?

In 1989, the journalist Graham Hancock answered the question with a scathing critique titled *Lords of Poverty: The Power, Prestige, and Corruption of the International Aid Business*. "Despite the fads, fancies," and "endless 'policy rethinks'" that "have characterized the development business," and despite hundreds of billions of dollars, there is "little evidence to prove that the poor in the Third World have actually *benefited*," he wrote in disgust.[21] There was, however, plenty of evidence that the development business had flourished. As the British economist Peter Bauer observed earlier in the decade, "Once aid got under way, it soon became clear that it served the political and financial interests of many people who accordingly joined in its support and administration. . . . As so often happens, people who set out to do good do well."[22] Noting innumerable instances where foreign aid actually proved *harmful* to the people receiving it, Hancock exposed the reality that government-funded aid organizations had virtually no accountability for their actions, or their inactions. As a result, they spent vast amounts of money running their institutions, buying dramatically overpriced "humanitarian goods" that were often inappropriate to their receivers' actual needs (though they were supposed to be grateful anyway), running ill-conceived and unwanted projects (even after locals asked them to stop), and assisting corrupt regimes to maintain power (albeit sometimes unintentionally). For Hancock, the problem of foreign aid's ineffectiveness lay squarely on the shoulders of the donors, in part because they lacked the incentive truly to develop countries, which would have put them out of their jobs.[23]

An increasing public flood of statistics and well-publicized humanitarian crises in the 1980s made it impossible to maintain the façade that aid was working. "Throughout history and pre-history all countries got by perfectly well without any aid at all," Hancock insisted, and they got by with less in the 1950s than they did in the 1970s, with no difference in living standards. "Now, suddenly, at the tail end of almost fifty years of development assistance, we are told that large numbers of these same countries have lost the ability to survive a moment longer unless they continue to receive ever-larger amounts of aid. If this is indeed the case—and if the only measurable impact of all these decades of development has been to turn tenacious survivors into helpless dependents—then it seems to me to be beyond dispute that *aid does not work*." If foreign aid can promote development, Hancock wryly concluded, "then aid's job should by now be nearly over and it ought to be possible to begin a gradual withdrawal without hurting anyone."[24] Aid had promised to make itself unnecessary, yet it had become more institutionalized as the years passed. Needless to say, at the end of the "lost development decade," the people running foreign aid decided not to take Hancock's advice and end their efforts. They had too much at stake to stop now.

By the early 1990s, when it seemed clear that the economic changes of the Washington Consensus were not yielding the desired results, emphasis shifted to reforming developing countries' political structures. The dream was democracy unto growth. The reality proved the opposite.[25] While the major aid organizations celebrated the wonder-working powers of democracy, which seemingly proved its superior ability to create change by winning the Cold War in 1991, a number of voices pointed out that many developing nations spent more each year servicing their debts than they received in foreign aid. In addition, American and European trade policies cost them billions and made it almost impossible to create internationally competitive industries. Frustrated, many Asian nations fought back against the international community by ignoring piracy laws and stealing industry secrets—the same type of activities that Americans used against the British in the early nineteenth century.[26] While these Asian Tigers—none of which was particularly democratic—began experiencing economic growth, most sub-Saharan African nations did not. South Africa, Botswana, and Mauritius became notable exceptions of a continental trend of increasing poverty, despite increasing democracy. The point was not that Africans wanted to be subjects instead of citizens, but that they wanted abundant food, clean water, and access to education too.

In Ethiopia, such hopes inspired a new revolution. In the spring of 1991, after suffering under the weight of the Derg's oppression for almost sixteen years, the Ethiopian People's Revolutionary Democratic Front, led by Meles Zenawi, and the Eritrean Popular Liberation Front, led by Isaias Afewerki, forced Mengistu into exile in Zimbabwe. Crowds poured into the streets of Addis Ababa and tore down the statue of Lenin, while the new acting government freed political prisoners and talked about reform. As promised to the United States, guerrilla forces sat outside until asked to move into the city and did not instantly seize power, but they arranged a July conference that would include representatives of all rebel groups and the former government to agree on a new government.[27] The United States watched the move toward democracy with delight and a reopened pocketbook. In 1991, Ethiopia received $52.2 million in economic aid from the United States. The following year, assistance jumped to $185.4 million.[28] Four years later, Eritrea was an independent nation, and Ethiopia had transformed itself into a federal republic of nine ethnically based states and two self-governing administrations. The Ethiopian people voted for the first time in their long national history. They asked their new government for the development long denied them.

That government took the call very seriously. Upon securing the presidency of the transitional government in Addis Ababa, Meles Zenawi enrolled at the Open University in Britain. Four years later, he had a master's degree in business administration. Now prime minister, he decided to continue his education, earning a master's degree in economics at Erasmus University in Rotterdam in 2004. His thesis, "African Development: Dead Ends and new Beginnings," rejected the neoliberal emphasis on free markets and defended government ownership of land. China, he insisted, has proven that state-directed development works. He made some excellent points—particularly with his attacks on the limitations of structural adjustments, but the analogy did not always work. China did not depend on aid for a large portion of its national budget. Ethiopia had many disadvantages, but it also had a leader determined to change its condition—one who, notably, was humble enough to realize that he did not have all of the answers and was actively

FIGURE 7.1 George W. Bush greets Kenyan president Daniel Arap Moi and Ethiopian prime minister Meles Zenawi at the White House in December 2002. *Photo by Eric Draper, courtesy George W. Bush Presidential Library, Lewisville, Texas*

furthering his education. Hope remained that this time things would change for Ethiopia. It was a new century, after all.[29]

Politically united by a shared sense of community and global responsibility, the world entered the twenty-first century firmly divided along economic lines, with African nations dominating the lowest end of the spectrum. The news was grim. At roughly one U.S. dollar per day, real per capita income on the continent was lower than it had been in 1970. Over the past twenty years, the number of Africans living in poverty had nearly doubled.[30] Why that was the case proved one of the most intellectually vibrant questions of the century's opening decade. Explaining the wealth and poverty of nations had been a fascinating intellectual question in the eighteenth century. In the twenty-first, it had become a pressing policy issue that occupied governments, nongovernmental organizations, and an increasing number of development entrepreneurs, including Bill Gates, George Soros, and Oprah Winfrey. Academics and policymakers spoke sometimes to each other and sometimes past each other, but they spoke a lot. The debate began where it had with Adam Smith two hundred years earlier: with markets, laws, and trade policies.

In 2000, the Peruvian economist Hernando de Soto published *The Mystery of Capital: Why Capitalism Triumphs in the West and Fails Everywhere Else*, in which he insisted that capital is the key to development. Capital exists everywhere, he pointed out, but the "poor" all over Africa, Asia, the Middle East, and Latin America are unable to use their capital as collateral for bank loans or further investment, due to the simple fact that they cannot prove ownership. Institutions are everything, de Soto wrote, most critically the institutions that define and defend private property, which is the key to wealth. Aid cannot bring development, because development has to come from inside. If the United States "were to hike its foreign-aid budget to the level recommended by the United Nations—0.7 percent of national income— it would take the richest country on earth more than 150 years to transfer to the world's poor resources equal to those that they already possess," he insisted.[31] Truly sharing the wealth cannot come from cash infusions, but requires sharing the systems that make possible the accumulation of wealth.

Western nations existed in a "one formal representational system" during the nineteenth century, de Soto explained, making it easy for people to use their property as capital for loans in order to create even more capital through production.[32] The end of underdevelopment, then, lay in giving people the capacity to join the international market system by giving them the ability to represent what they already own through legal titles and deeds. "In this case," de Soto concluded, "the poor are not the problem but the solution," implying that international development efforts would be best spent assisting countries to implement the legal framework necessary for allowing the poor to change the fortunes of their nations.[33] De Soto's argument garnered attention and adulation—particularly from political conservatives—for its de-emphasis of foreign aid in favor of legal reform and its celebration of the value of private property.[34] The World Bank took the point, admitting in its 2002 World Development Report that effective property law systems would help developing nations by lowering transaction costs.[35]

In the fall of 2000, Hans Binswanger and Ernst Lutz of the World Bank seconded de Soto's argument that foreign aid cannot bring development, but they came at the issue from a different direction. While de Soto discussed the value of reforming developing nations' laws, Binswanger and Lutz argued in a paper presented at the International Association of Agricultural Economists that the real key to development was reforming developed nations' trade policies. "Both developed and developing countries have erected massive barriers to agricultural trade over the course of this century," they wrote. "Their joint negative impact on agricultural growth rates in the developing world is a major reason for the slow progress of rural development and rural poverty reduction over the last half century." While developing nations have altered such policies, they continued, developed nations have not, creating a bizarre situation that puts their ostensible international development agenda completely at odds with their trade policies. Protectionism in the developed world costs the developing world more than it gets in foreign aid, they gloomily announced.[36] Accessing capital at home might be the first step out of underdevelopment, but it could only take a nation so far in a global marketplace that favored agricultural production in the richest countries at the expense of its growth in the poorest.

Washington was not deaf to the argument. In 2000, Congress passed the U.S. African Growth and Opportunity Act, which opened doors to some duty-free imports from African nations. The catch, however, was that those imports were dominated by petroleum, not the agricultural and manufactured commodities that most nations needed to sell in order to grow.[37] It could have been the start of real change, but it quickly stalled.

The international aid community and the leaders of developing nations were well aware of the problem. At the 2001 World Trade Organization Ministerial meeting in Doha, participants declared themselves "determined, particularly in the light of the global economic slowdown, to maintain the process of reform and liberalization of trade policies, thus ensuring that the system plays its full part in promoting recovery, growth and development." Participants agreed to a "reduction of, with a view to phasing out, all forms of export subsidies" and to "substantial reductions in trade-distorting domestic support."[38] It would, however, prove to be a great deal easier to make such pledges than to keep them. Trade reform was not nearly as popular as aid reform in most of the developed world at the opening of the twentieth century, and it did not become so as years passed. The problem was that aid was good international politics and ending protectionism was bad domestic politics, so politicians always chose aid.

In the 2002 *National Security Strategy of the United States of America*, the White House demonstrated that it had been listening to the growing frustration with its past development policies. "Decades of massive development assistance have failed to spur economic growth in the poorest countries," it admitted. "Worse, development aid has often served to prop up failed policies, relieving the pressure for reform and perpetuating misery."[39] The Bush administration promised that it was going to change the situation by changing its aid policies. That same year, it announced the creation of the Millennium Challenge Corporation, which dramatically increased development assistance to countries that met the agency's requirements of "good government, economic freedom, and investments in their citizens." Learning lessons from the past, the MCC adopted a grassroots approach that promoted country-led solutions and country-led implementations. As of September 2010, the MCC had signed five-year poverty reduction compacts with twenty-two nations and provided project-specific threshold program grants to another twenty, for a total of $7.9 billion.[40] The MCC was an effort to push foreign aid beyond the dictates of foreign policy. Its country-led approach was particularly laudable. Its possibilities, however, were severely hampered by the demands of a domestic constituency: American farmers.

The same year that Bush introduced the MCC, he signed into law a farm bill that negated much of the good that could come out of the MCC's work. Bulging with pork, the bill promised to "provide a safety net for American farmers." What it actually did was provide billions in subsidies to the wealthiest farmers in the United States, ensuring their prosperity at the sake of their counterparts in developing nations around the world. A 2006 investigation of the 2002 bill discovered that almost 50 percent of commodity subsidies went to just 5 percent of eligible farmers, or, more specifically, landowners (many of whom were absentee). In Georgia, 4 percent of eligible farmers averaged $200,900 in subsidies in 2005, while the other 96 percent averaged $8,300. In the United States as a whole in 2005, at least 195 farming operations each collected more than $1 million in subsidies. Between 2000 and 2006, the U.S. government paid $1.3 billion in subsidies to absentee landowners that did not engage in any farming at all.[41] This not only wasted taxpayer money, it flooded the international market and lowered international prices. In 2002, as they had been before and would be later, farm subsidies were sold to the American public as protection for farmers, but they were actually the strongest barrier to the development of the developing world, and the United States was not the only guilty party.

At the 2002 World Summit on Sustainable Development in Johannesburg, European Union delegates walked out in protest after representatives of developing nations wanted to submit a declaration calling for the elimination of farm subsidies. Japan refused to reconsider its incredibly high subsidies to rice producers. The year before, the United Nations had released a report explaining that although the thirty members of the Organization for Economic Co-operation and Development (OECD) gave $52 billion in development aid, they negated the benefit of that money with the $311 billion in farm subsidies that they gave to their own farmers, which cost poor nations about $50 billion in exports. To add insult to injury, the International Monetary Fund and the World Bank told those nations that they could not give their farmers subsidies, because it went against the principles of free trade. The irony was obvious, and tragic.[42]

In 2002, President Bush told listeners at the International Conference on Financing for Development that "when nations close their markets and opportunity is hoarded by a privileged few, no amount—no amount—of development aid is ever enough." In *The National Security Strategy*, the White House emphasized its insistence on "free trade and free markets" as the key to lifting people "out of poverty"—doing what the MCC could not, on its own, do.[43] The United States was willing to increase its foreign aid, but it insisted that such aid go to nations that had "freer" markets than, in actuality, did the United States. Its own market distortions were not discussed. The point was that the Bush administration recognized that America's foreign aid had not been an effective tool of *development* and it wanted to change that, but its desire for reform was limited by its recognition that foreign aid had been an at least somewhat effective tool of *diplomacy*. The U.S. government, it insisted, will use its "foreign aid to promote freedom and support those who struggle non-violently for it, ensuring that nations move toward democracy and are rewarded for the steps they take."[44] As this book has shown, it was not the first administration to value aid for its usefulness in securing a great many things besides development. From a political perspective, aid's failure "to spur economic growth in the poorest countries" did not necessarily mean it was not working.[45]

Although the developed world seemed to have forgotten trade promises made at Doha, the developing world had not. They forced a commitment to eliminate agricultural export subsidies at the World Trade Organization General Counsel Decision in August 2004, but, once again, promises were easier to secure than policy changes.[46] The OECD members still preferred to showcase their aid policies than to rethink their trade ones. In July 2005, Tony Blair put the problem of Africa's poverty at the top of the G8 summit's agenda. The "mood and the money are both on an upswing," the *Economist* reported, noting that in 2004 the aid budgets of the big OECD donors increased to more than $78 billion, which was the highest ever and quite a leap from an annual average in the early 1950s of $1.8 billion.[47] The money kept flowing, but the donors refused to meaningfully address the point that foreign aid's ability to promote real development was severely limited in an international system stacked against its poorest members.[48] Nobel Prize–winning economist Joseph Stiglitz urged change, explaining, "When subsidies lead to increased production with little increase in consumption, as is typical with agricultural commodities, higher output translates directly into higher exports. Higher exports translate directly into lower prices for producers ... and more poverty among poor farmers in the Third World."[49] But it was far more popular in diplomatic circles to talk about expanding aid, rather than about reforming trade.

In 2005, Jeffrey Sachs, Columbia University economist and special advisor to U.N. Secretary-General Kofi Annan, published *The End of Poverty: Economic Possibilities for Our Time*. In it, Sachs both delineated the shape of poverty in the contemporary world and laid out the formula for a poverty-reduction strategy based upon a "'global compact' between the rich and poor countries."[50] Visualizing economic development as a ladder "with higher rungs representing steps up the path to economic well-being," Sachs used World Bank data to conclude that "one sixth of humanity" is too destitute even to get its foot on the first rung.[51] The rich world had to keep helping. "The end of extreme poverty is at hand—within our generation, but only if we grasp the historic opportunity in front of us" by forcing governments to spend 0.7 percent of their gross national production on a grand-scale development program run by the United Nations.[52] Sachs explained that foreign aid had not worked in the past because there was never enough of it and it was rarely well directed. Dismissing as racist the common complaint, often from Africans themselves, that one of the main reasons that so many African countries have gotten little results from decades of aid is that their corrupt governments have essentially plundered the wealth, Sachs ascribed the failure of aid programs to their lack of funds and inability to take a holistic approach.[53]

William Easterly, a former World Bank economist, for one, was skeptical, writing in a review of the book: "'Success in ending the poverty trap,' Sachs writes, 'will be much easier than it appears.' Really? If it's so easy, why haven't five decades of effort gotten the job done? Sachs should redirect some of his outrage at the question of why the previous $2.3 trillion [in today's dollars] didn't reach the poor so that the next $2.3 trillion does." Ending poverty, he penned in frustration, "is not easy at all." During the past fifty years of foreign aid, "poverty researchers have learned a great deal about the complexity of toxic politics, bad history (including exploitative or inept colonialism), ethnic and regional conflicts, elites' manipulation of politics and institutions, official corruption, dysfunctional public services, malevolent police forces and armies, the difficulty of honoring contracts and property rights, unaccountable and excessively bureaucratic donors and many other issues." Yet, Sachs dismisses all of these factors, according to Easterly. "Indeed, he seems deaf to the babble and bungling of the U.N. agencies he calls upon to run the Big Plan, not to mention other unaccountable and ineffectual aid agencies."[54]

Easterly funneled his frustrations with Sachs's ideas into a 2006 book, *The White Man's Burden*, in which he lambasted the contemporary return to old ideas about foreign aid. "The legend that inspired foreign aid in the 1950s is the same legend that inspires foreign aid today," he wrote, reminding readers of the long history of failed promises from the United States government. We can help individuals at the grass-roots level, Easterly argued, with small-scale aid, but anything larger is folly. "Remember, aid cannot achieve the end of poverty. Only homegrown development based on the dynamism of individuals and firms in free markets can do that." He held up South Korea, China, Taiwan, Singapore, Thailand, and India as prime examples of countries that prospered because of national policies, not international aid.[55] Sachs responded with his 2008 book, *Common Wealth*, further stressing foreign aid's vital importance to helping nations escape the "Poverty Trap." Although Sachs triumphed in political circles, as will be discussed later in this chapter, Easterly gained ground among academics.[56]

In his 2007 book, *How Rich Countries Got Rich . . . and Why Poor Countries Stay Poor*, Eric S. Reinert, of *The Other Cannon* foundation in Norway, argued that the central point is not aid, which is simply a palliative, but trade. "The main difference between rich and poor countries is that rich countries have all moved through a stage *without* free trade," Reinert argued, "which—when successful—subsequently made free trade desirable." Rich countries became rich, he continued, by "moving away from raw materials and diminishing returns activities into manufacturing, where the opposite laws tend to operate" and free trade becomes desirable.[57] Specifically addressing the damage caused by international attempts to force free trade on poor nations in the name of progress, Reinert's book stressed that "the gap" lies between nations that specialize in "man-made comparative advantages" and those that specialize in "nature-made comparative advantages."[58] The former can always adjust to changes in demand with new technology, but the latter cannot. Ending global poverty thus means allowing nations to protect themselves long enough to develop viable, competitive industries. Fellow economist Ha-Joon Chang seconded Reinert's argument, using South Korea as a prime example of the importance of enabling nations to pursue both growth via trade and growth via technology at their own pace—as the rich countries have done before them. He also stressed the value of protectionist policies in developing economies. True foreign aid, he insisted, meant changing the international system so that it is less prejudiced against poor economies.[59]

Easterly, Reinert, and Chang shared their disillusionment with the Zambian economist Dambisa Moyo, but, like each of them, she offered her own solution. In her 2009 book, *Dead Aid*, Moyo argued that decades of foreign aid had crippled Africa by encouraging corruption and dependency and discouraging innovation and self-sufficiency. In Ethiopia today, she reported, 97 percent of the government budget comes from foreign aid, which proves beyond question that aid has failed to promote development in that nation.⁶⁰ Moyo drew on fellow economist Paul Collier's arguments about the various traps that African nations faced, which stemmed from conflicts, natural resource dependence, geography, and bad governance, and Moyo acknowledged that the problem of underdevelopment did not invite easy answers.⁶¹ "Africa's failure to generate any meaningful or sustainable long-run growth must, ostensibly, be a confluence of factors: geographical, historical, cultural, tribal and institutional," she wrote. Aid, in fact, hindered growth, she insisted and then cited the statistic that over the past thirty years, "the most aid-dependent countries have exhibited growth rates averaging minus 0.2 per cent per annum" to prove her point.⁶²

Although Moyo wanted the West to end aid, she by no means wanted it to give up on Africa. The focus just needed to shift to capital investments through government-issued bonds and foreign direct investment, both of which have been sadly lacking in countries that have grown almost totally dependent on aid. Nations needed to work for their money, Moyo argued, by reforming themselves into desirable investment clients. China has been leading the way in recent years ($100 billion worth of foreign direct investment in Africa in 2007) and the West should encourage its involvement, which makes a big difference in nations such as Ethiopia.⁶³ Even though Moyo emphasized investment (a reflection of her eight years of employment at Goldman Sachs), she also shared Reinert's concerns about the global trade imbalances that benefit the wealthy at the expense of the poor. "Africa's share of global trade remains around 1 per cent," she reported, and rich world subsidies keep it so tragically low. The continent, she gloomily continued, loses around $500 billion a year to restrictive trade embargoes, primarily in the form of European and American farm subsidies. Every cow in the European Union, Moyo wrote, gets around $2.50 a day in subsidies, which is greater than the per-day income of over a billion human beings. Meanwhile, one year's worth of subsidies to American cotton farmers has totaled more than the entire gross domestic product of Burkina Faso. "Trade is not the panacea of Africa's woes," Moyo admitted, but "it is bound to put a dent in them," if it can expand. China is opening its doors, but Europe and the United States continue to hesitate.⁶⁴

Beyond freeing trade, Moyo argued the benefits of microfinancing, remittances, and savings—endorsing Mohammad Yunus's revolutionary Grameen Bank. In 2006, Yunus and the Grameen Bank shared the Nobel Peace Prize. In his Nobel Lecture, Yunus described the vision that drove his efforts: "I believe that we can create a poverty-free world because poverty is not created by poor people. It has been created and sustained by the economic and social system that we have designed for ourselves; the institutions and concepts that make up that system; the policies that we pursue." If we can change our practices, he concluded, we can change the world.[65] Moyo agrees, and she too believes that the change needs to begin with ending bilateral foreign aid, which is more often used for diplomatic, rather than developmental purposes. Aid keeps bad governments in power, and she insists that the West needs to shut off the tap. Ugandan journalist Andrew Mwenda shares her concern. At the 2007 Technology, Education and Design Global Conference, Mwenda explained that "charity" to Africa had "distorted the incentive structure" and empowered corrupt governments. Do you know anyone who ever grew wealthy from charity, he asked the audience? Mwenda called for supporting entrepreneurship, instead of financing aid, which he labeled a "bad instrument" of development.[66]

De Soto, Easterly, Reinert, Chang, Moyo, Yunus, and Mwenda all argue persuasively for a global commitment to new paths to growth. Although their various paths do not follow the same route, each begins with local capital and local ingenuity and highlights the importance of local institution building. Several ask the world's wealthiest nations to give up something besides foreign aid—they ask them to give up a bit of their dominion. They also ask them to destabilize long-held beliefs by rethinking the best ways of producing economic growth. There is support for their ideas, but there is also resistance from those who have the most to lose—at home and abroad.

In a 2008 "Hearing to Review Efforts to Deliver International Food Aid and to Provide Foreign Agricultural Development Assistance" before a subcommittee of the House Committee on Agriculture, Chairman Mike McIntyre noted that fellow members were "uniquely aware" of the importance of "supply chains," functioning markets, and "the well developed system of land-grant institutions" in the story of America's economic success. "Underlying all of this," he continued, "our legal, judicial and regulatory systems help protect private property rights and other rights that we know are enshrined in our Constitution and by law. All of these elements are critical to our highly developed agricultural economy. Rarely are all of them present in the economies of developing countries that are experiencing food shortages, which is why we have to look at the broader picture."[67] It was a very modern understanding of America's past that drew from ideas that the development discourse had made popular. Development is about a great deal more than transfers of money. As de Soto had pointed out, sharing the wealth requires sharing the systems that make possible its accumulation. Development is an institutional problem. The only thing missing from the account was an acknowledgment that subsidies are one of those institutions. McIntyre urged fellow representatives "to look at the broader picture" to get a useful perspective on aid. The view should have included American trade policies, but it did not. In 2008, Congress passed a new farm bill, this one over a presidential veto in protest of its $104.2 billion budget for subsidies.

If the world's wealthiest nations cooperate by working toward a world connected by real free trade and open to the obvious benefits of modern science (including genetically engineered crops), they can transform lives.[68] Thomas H. Staal, the USAID Mission Director for Ethiopia, made this clear at the Sasakawa Africa Association Borlaug Symposium 2010 in Addis Ababa. "Africa must act now, and act decisively, to create its own Green Revolution," he insisted, "one that addresses the continent's unique circumstances and employs the power of both new technology and the market economy to maximize efficiency and increase access to food." Doing so, Staal continued, means securing new policies from the rich world, not more money. "TRADE, not AID, is the watchword—whether local, regional, or international—if any technology or other improvement is to be sustainable. Africa's Green Revolution must be a GRASSROOTS GREEN REVOLUTION,

FIGURE 7.2 Two workers in a USAID warehouse in Houston ready bags of flour for transport to the Horn of Africa in August 2008. The United States sent nearly 24,000 metric tons of food aid to the region that year. *United States Agency for International Development, Washington, D.C.*

which nurtures the entrepreneurial spirit of the smallholder farmer and connects her or him to the market," preferably a market unburdened by unfair manipulations.[69] Such a Green Revolution will still need outside assistance in terms of research and development, but the most important assistance will come through changes in subsidy policies in Europe and the United States. Sadly, neither seems ready to adopt this solution. Supporting research is easier in a nation where agribusiness lobbying tops $90 million a year and agribusiness campaign contributions top $40 million.[70]

In 2009, the U.S. government created Feed the Future, a program based on the Rome Principles outlined at the 2009 G8 Summit in L'Aquila, Italy, which promised to invest in country-owned plans and ensure a comprehensive approach to economic growth. It involved an initial American commitment of $3.5 billion and is jointly coordinated by USAID and the U.S. Department of Agriculture.[71] In 2010, it established the Norman Borlaug Commemorative Research Initiative, which will "leverage one of the world's largest public research systems, spanning the U.S. Department of Agriculture's research agencies, increasing its relevance and impact on problems and opportunities faced by smallholder farm families in Africa, Asia and Latin America."[72] The emphasis on agriculture is a significant change. As Ambassador William J. Garvelink, the deputy coordinator for development at Feed the Future, recently explained, "We know agricultural development is a springboard for broader economic development," yet, as recently as 2007, agricultural programs accounted for only 3.5 percent of American foreign aid efforts.[73]

For its part, Ethiopia is preparing itself to make the most of the coming Green Revolution by creating a sound domestic market structure. In the aftermath of the 2003 famine, Ethiopian economist Eleni Gabre-Madhin labored to create an Addis Ababa version of Chicago's Board of Trade, which was created in 1848 to stabilize the market in the flourishing commodities of the Midwest.[74] Ethiopia's farmers needed something similar to be able to move beyond their local trade networks. Markets, Eleni argued, do not just happen; they are created, and she proceeded to create one. The Ethiopia Commodity Exchange (ECX) opened in April 2008 with a fancy trading pit connected to warehouses around the country. It was the first of its kind in Africa.[75] As explained on the ECX website, previously "agricultural markets in Ethiopia had been characterized by high costs and high risks of transacting, forcing much of Ethiopia into global isolation. With only one third of output reaching the market, commodity buyers and sellers tended to trade only with those they knew, to avoid the risk of being cheated or default." This left most farmers "at the mercy of merchants in the nearest and only market they know, unable to negotiate better prices or reduce their market risk." They remained subsistence farmers because they could not sell their crops, even when they could grow them.[76]

The ECX is changing that by offering a safer, freer market system. Its mission is "to connect all buyers and sellers in an efficient, reliable, and transparent market by harnessing innovation and technology and based on continuous learning, fairness, and commitment to excellence."[77] Additional efforts are also being made to ensure that local farmers around the country are able to participate in the ECX, including a renewed commitment to small-farmer cooperatives that not only help members market their products, but also promote HIV/AIDS awareness and are involved in literacy training. Changes are happening all over the economy. The Ethiopian government is privatizing more public enterprises and working with the World Bank to develop a capital market. The service sector is booming, and in 2010 it actually overtook agriculture to claim the largest segment of gross domestic product. Ethiopia is still primarily an agricultural nation, as 85 percent of the population still farms the land, but the rise of the service sector supports the point that growth in one segment of the economy can also help growth in another. Most of Ethiopia's citizens remain desperately poor, but there is reason to hope that the promises that Haile Selassie made decades ago might indeed come true. "Once a commercial trading hub in antiquity linking markets of East and West," ECX's website boasts, Ethiopia "can again claim a place in the global market arena." The nation's economic future looks brighter than it has in decades.[78]

Recent developments in Ethiopia support arguments made by de Soto, Reinert, Chang, and Moyo about the importance of building up domestic capital and local capabilities. The nation is struggling to make positive steps toward better governance and a stronger economy. Concern, however, remains. Can such innovation make the nation a significant player in an international market burdened with inequalities? Ethiopia's future economic growth—the only viable path away from its current dependence on foreign aid—depends on its ability to be a competitive participant of the global market system. As already noted, people within USAID are aware that "TRADE, not AID, is the watchword" of sustainable development.[79] Their ability to influence the general public and their representatives in Congress, however, is another matter entirely. The agribusiness lobby is very strong, providing a great deal of money to a great many members of Congress. In addition, aid is a tangible item that can be given from one nation to another, initiating a reciprocal relationship, which is a useful diplomatic situation. Trade reform would be a more effective form of aid, but a less effective form of foreign policy. For the moment then, aid, not trade, is still viewed as the key to promoting economic growth—and the key to securing the U.S. government's global security vision.

In May 2010, Josh Rogin of the *Cable* published a leaked copy of a White House review titled "A New Way Forward on Global Development," also known as "Presidential Study Directive on Global Development" (PSD-7). The National Security Council document announced that the administration "recognizes that the successful pursuit of development is essential to our security, prosperity and values," because "countries that are able to achieve sustained development gains make more capable partners, can engage in and contribute to a growing global economy, and provide their citizens with the opportunity and freedom to improve their condition." History has proven that securing sustainable development is a difficult task, the report admitted, but it is clear that "progress depends primarily on the choices of political leaders in developing countries." (The negative impact of choices of political leaders in *developed* countries is not mentioned). We need to be more deliberate about our development policies, the report continued, to be sure that they are compatible with our goals. The United States "will always have multiple objectives for its development policy—supporting real-time national security challenges, responding to basic human needs, and creating the conditions for economic growth and more effective governance." The order is reminiscent of similar lists of foreign aid objectives from the Truman administration. So too is the report's reminder that "today's foreign policy challenges, especially those in complex security environments, demand an effective integration of all the tools of American power."[80] U.S. policymakers viewed foreign aid as tool of foreign policy in the 1950s, and they view it as a tool of foreign policy today. The U.S. government is determined not get rid of foreign aid. It is far too useful.

Washington's continued commitment to aid has inspired a renewed interest in making it an even more effective tool of foreign policy and of development. In July 2009, the Senate Foreign Relations Committee held hearings titled "The Case for Reform: Foreign Aid and Development in a New Era." No one discussed the virtue of reforming trade policies instead of aid, and it was Jeffrey Sachs, not Moyo or Reinert, who was invited to speak at the hearing. In fact, when Senator Bob Corker mentioned to Sachs that he had read an interesting article by Moyo in the *Wall Street Journal* about the damages that aid inflicts on recipient countries, Sachs brushed it aside as "a confusion," insisting that "nobody wants long-term aid," before continuing his argument that development cannot happen without it.[81] The "biggest problem" with aid in the past, Sachs insisted, "has been the lack of scale and the lack of clear goals and the lack of ambition." The United States needs to be bold, he continued, and it needs to put a great deal more money into its foreign aid budget. The point, it is important to note, is not that Sachs does not believe that trade reform has value, but that he believes that it is not the central issue—aid is the central issue. It is, Sachs told the senators, "absolutely vital to successful foreign policy." It was a message they were eager to hear, for, as Senator John Kerry pointed out in his opening statements, "Senators Lugar, Menendez, and Corker, and I have been developing initial reform legislation that we believe goes a long way toward improving our short-term capacity to deliver foreign aid in a more accountable, thoughtful, and strategic manner."[82]

The House had beaten the Senate to the punch that spring with H.R. 2139, the "Initiating Foreign Assistance Reform Act of 2009." Opening with a declaration that "poverty reduction" was in the nation's best interest because it "improves United States security by mitigating the underlying causes of violence and extremism, addresses threats like climate change and disease that know no borders, expands economic opportunities for United States producers and consumers, shows the best face of the United States to the world, and represents the values, kindness, and generosity of the American people," the bill's authors insisted that the current aid structure was out of date, still tied to policy relics of the 1961 Foreign Assistance Act, and in need of serious reform. The first step forward, H.R. 2139 insisted, is for the president to create a "comprehensive national strategy to further the United States foreign policy objective of reducing poverty and contributing to broad-based economic growth in developing countries."[83]

While the bill went to committee, the White House went into action, charging the State Department to create a review of foreign assistance in preparation for making it part of a new "comprehensive national strategy." In July 2009, the State Department announced that it was working on the *Quadrennial Diplomacy and Development Review* (*QDDR*), which would provide a "blueprint for our diplomatic and development efforts." Insisting that "no one set of tools is sufficient for solving or managing" the "complex, varied, and numerous foreign policy challenges" facing the United States, the State Department explained that the *QDDR* envisioned State and USAID "working side-by-side with a strong military. By using all the tools of American power," it explained, "we can pave the way for shared peace, progress and prosperity."[84] Aid is more popular than ever in an administration that is trying to rebrand the nation's foreign policy.

In his speech before the U.N. General Assembly in September 2009, President Obama "put forward four pillars" that he argued are "fundamental to the future that we want for our children." The list read, "non-proliferation and disarmament; the promotion of peace and security; the preservation of our planet; and a global economy that advances opportunity for all people." As Truman had before him, Obama dedicated his fourth point, or pillar, to development. He vowed that the United States would spend a great deal more money on the pursuit of the "eradication of extreme poverty in our time." But his talk was not all about aid. Obama insisted that "wealthy nations must open their markets to more goods and extend a hand to those with less, while reforming international institutions to give more nations a greater voice." In turn, "developing nations must root out the corruption that is an obstacle to progress."[85] Clearly the White House has been listening to the voices of discontent within the development discourse. The question remains of whether or not it will be able to turn those ideas into more effective policies.

In September 2010, Obama released a Presidential Policy Directive on Development, the first of its kind in American history, calling for a renewed emphasis on the particular areas of global health, food security, and global climate change. Aid investments in these areas, the White House explained, "can encourage broad-based economic growth and democratic governance, facilitate the stabilization of countries emerging from crisis or conflict, alleviate poverty, and advance global commitments to the basic welfare and dignity of all humankind." It will be "impossible," the press release continued, to meet such challenges without "sustained development."[86] Secretary of State Hillary Rodham Clinton seconded the point in an article in the November/December 2010 issue of *Foreign Affairs*, explaining that the world's many problems "cannot be solved unless a nation is willing to accept the responsibility of mobilizing action. The United States is that nation." And it is calling on its civilian instead of its military power. Clinton stressed the critical importance of the State Department and USAID in the new struggle. "Diplomacy and development often overlap and must work in tandem," she wrote.[87]

The article, titled "Leading Through Civilian Power," provided the foreign policy community with an introduction to the *2010 Quadrennial Diplomacy and Development Review* (also titled *Leading Through Civilian Power*), which Clinton introduced in a Town Hall Meeting at the State Department on December 15, 2010. The review stressed the vital connections between State and USAID, linking them in a way not unlike the branches of the United States Armed Services. As the title of both the article and the review suggests, the emphasis is on the utility of nonmilitary force to initiate vital changes abroad. "Civilian power," the *QDDR* explained, "is the combined force of women and men across the U.S. government who are practicing diplomacy, implementing development projects, strengthening alliances and partnerships, preventing and responding to crises and conflict, and advancing America's core interests." These interests were noted to be "security, prosperity, universal values—especially democracy and human rights—and a just international order."[88] The State Department promised to make this civilian power more efficient and more effective, turning it into "the partner" that the military "needs and deserves." The *QDDR* called for changes in the structure of State and USAID, in the staffing at both agencies, and in relationships with contracting organizations, to name a few. Most importantly for present purposes, it also called for a "modernization" of development "to deliver results" by focusing time and money on investments where the United States has "a comparative advantage: food security, global health, climate change, sustainable economic growth, democracy and governance, and humanitarian assistance—with an emphasis on the rights of women and girls throughout."[89] These are all laudable goals, but, with the exception of the focus on women and girls, not significantly different from those espoused by previous administrations, who struggled—often in vain—to achieve them. The *QDDR* promises real changes in the structure of American foreign aid, but aid's history of limited success makes it difficult to agree that those changes are the best way to promote development in the world's poorest nations.

Although it remains firmly committed to the idea that bilateral foreign aid from the United States is necessary to global development, the White House's new development agenda does make some concessions to the concerns of the development economists discussed earlier in this chapter. Clinton insists that "assistance must be coordinated with trade, finance, investment credits, and other economic policies to bolster emerging markets and to foster widespread and sustainable economic growth." The qualification acknowledges Moyo's point that developing nations need to become desirable investment clients and Easterly's point that "aid cannot achieve the end of poverty. Only homegrown development based on dynamism of individuals and firms in free markets can do that."[90] The *QDDR* demonstrates that people in Washington have been listening. The U.S. Agency for International Development has created a new Development Innovation Ventures program, which gives small, targeted awards to entrepreneurs. "Borrowing from the private venture capital model," the *QDDR* explains, "DIV seeks ideas from inside and outside USAID to invest resources in promising high-risk, high-return projects."[91] The program is part of a larger effort to refocus USAID on "smaller and more focused awards." We have tried to do too much with too little for too many years, the *QDDR* laments. These targeted efforts are described as a way to escape the limitations of the past, particularly by focusing on women, who have proven, on the whole, to be more reliable development partners.[92]

The State Department and USAID are well aware that long-term economic growth comes from within. "We know that economies grow faster when countries encourage entrepreneurship, invest in infrastructure and education, and expand trade," the *QDDR* explains. The United States promises to help by "promoting entrepreneurship, growing both the hard and soft infrastructure needed for increased trade, developing broad-based agricultural economies, educating their peoples, formalizing vast numbers of small- and medium-sized businesses, strengthening broad-based agricultural economies, and investing in clean energy technologies to reduce greenhouse gas emissions."[93] These are worthwhile goals that demonstrate an awareness of the types of changes that have preceded the movement of many countries out of poverty in recent decades. Its efforts, USAID notes, since 2004 to open business climates in several nations have made it easier for entrepreneurs to enter the marketplaces of goods and services. Such reforms are certainly beneficial and can make vital changes within the national economy, but they will have a difficult time affecting an individual's ability to act effectively within the global market without substantive international action to address current trade inequalities. The *QDDR* does not discuss the value of trade reform at home to encourage economic growth abroad. In all fairness, the issue is out of the State Department's and USAID's jurisdictions, but the review would have been an excellent forum with which to address the developmental *and* diplomatic problems that stem from domestic farm subsidies. Clinton rightly insists that the United States must "rethink, reform, and recalibrate" its foreign policy, but there appears to be walls around that intellectual enterprise. Some options are open for discussion. Some are not.

In January 1949, Harry Truman announced that the United States "must embark upon a bold new program for making the benefits of our scientific advances and industrial progress available for the improvement and growth of underdeveloped areas." We will, he explained, share our technology and our knowledge. "Our aim should be to help the free peoples of the world, through their own efforts, to produce more food, more clothing, more materials for housing, and more mechanical power to lighten their burdens." The United States would contribute the tools; the people themselves would do the work. At that moment, it was a modest program dedicated to a grand vision.

"We hope," he concluded, "to help create the conditions that will lead eventually to personal freedom and happiness for all mankind."[94] In the aftermath of Truman's speech, Jacob Javits boasted, "Our belief is that, if we make it better for the other fellow, we will make it better for ourselves.... I think fundamentally this is the American answer. It is the first basically new idea that has come along in our foreign policy."[95] It *was* a new idea, and it was an incredibly powerful one. Foreign aid transformed international relations. Sadly, it did not transform the lives of the world's poorest peoples. It is time to embrace a new "American answer." Such change has been a long time coming.

In the early 1960s, the political theorist Hans Morgenthau wrote, "Of the seeming and real innovations which the modern age has introduced into the practice of foreign policy, none has proven more baffling to both understanding and action than foreign aid."[96] Such confusion reached even the highest levels of the aid bureaucracy. In a 1976 interview for the Eisenhower Library, Dennis Fitzgerald, the former head of the International Cooperation Administration, admitted, "A program of this kind is never definitive. It has to be based on a great variety of assumptions and conclusions, many of which turn out to subsequently have changed. I'm not sure even today—in fact I'm perhaps more unsure today than I was twenty years ago—what is the logical, sound, constructive basis for 'foreign economic assistance.' There are very, very grave questions about its effectiveness in many circumstances."[97] Fitzgerald agreed to head the International Cooperation Administration because he believed in the moral, economic, and political purposes of foreign aid. He was confident that it could transform people's lives and, in turn, the world. At some point during the next twenty years, he lost that faith. It was clear that foreign aid was a useful tool of diplomacy, but its record on development was another matter entirely, which, in turn, begged the question of whether or not the government was forsaking its long-term diplomatic goals for short-term ones. If, as numerous administrations have argued, the United States will be economically and strategically better off in a world unburdened by underdevelopment, then it should adopt policies that will close the gap.[98]

The past thirty years of world history have, overall, been decades of improvement. Literacy rates and food production rates keep going up and more people live under governments that are accountable to them. The number living in "extreme poverty" dropped from around 800 million in 1980 to under 300 million.[99] If African nations are taken out of the equation, those statistics become even more impressive, and that reveals the most important weakness of post–Cold War international assistance. The masses of people moving out of poverty are doing so in nations that give, not receive, foreign aid. China, Taiwan, Singapore, Thailand, South Korea, and (to a lesser extent) India used policies, not aid, to transform their economic status. And such policies were often authoritarian, which leads to questions about the utility of the United States promoting development and democracy at the same time. Such questions cannot be answered in the capacity of this chapter, but they lurk below the surface of any discussion on development. Clearly, *development* is a much more complicated idea than the U.S. government has been willing to admit.

Disillusionment with bilateral foreign aid, however, is not the same as disillusionment with all international development efforts. Everyone is better off in a world free of smallpox and rinderpest. International campaigns against polio, malaria, and schistosomiasis are saving lives every day. These global public health initiatives are manifestly good things and they should continue. The United States should keep on supporting them, but it can disconnect such aid from its diplomatic efforts. Development does not have to come after diplomacy, as it does in the *QDDR*. It can come before it. There are even self-interested reasons for doing so, because it will promote America's long-term over its short-term interests.

If the world's wealthiest nations truly wanted to help the world's poorest nations, they would curb domestic agricultural subsidies, support global disease eradication efforts, and cut off most of their government-to-government assistance. Economic growth has to come from within. Under such a framework, there would still be room for grassroots-focused aid institutions to provide medical assistance, microfinancing, and education programs. The point is not to keep help from reaching the people who desperately need it, but to force vital changes in government policies that will help those people achieve better lives through their own initiatives. As Amartya Sen has perceptively argued, the end of development is *"the capability to choose a life one has reason to value."* Development cannot come from foreign aid, because development is fundamentally about the power of autonomy. "There is cogency in thinking not just about sustaining the fulfillment of our needs, but more broadly about sustaining—or extending—our freedom (including the freedom to meet our needs)."[100] Keeping bad governments in power through foreign aid is not the path to freedom. Neither is keeping poor farmers poor through subsidies to wealthy conglomerates. Change will not be easy, but it is certainly not impossible.

"We can be remembered," Obama told the U.N. General Assembly in 2009, "as a generation that chose to drag the arguments of the 20th century into the 21st; that put off hard choices, refused to look ahead, failed to keep pace.... Or we can be a generation that chooses to see the shoreline beyond the rough waters ahead; that comes together to serve the common interests of human beings...."[101] Bilateral foreign aid was a twentieth-century solution to the problem of underdevelopment. The world is ready for some twenty-first-century ones. In 1784, Immanuel Kant insisted, "to make a period of time fruitless in the progress of mankind toward improvement, thus working to the disadvantage of posterity—that is absolutely forbidden." A man can "postpone enlightenment in what he ought to know, but to renounce it for himself, and even more to renounce it for posterity, is to injure and trample on the rights of mankind."[102] Progress *is* possible, both on the ground and in our policies. We can reenlighten our quest to spread the freedoms and the comforts of expanded prosperity. We can improve.

NOTES

INTRODUCTION

1. Harry S. Truman, Address at the National Conference on International Economic and Social Development (April 8, 1952), Document 104 in *Documentary History of the Truman Presidency*, ed. Dennis Merrill, v. 27, 816.
2. Truman, "Inaugural Address," *New York Times,* January 21, 1949, 4.
3. Hearings Before the Committee on Foreign Affairs on H.R. 5615, International Technical Cooperation Act of 1949, House of Representatives, 81st Congress, Fall 1949 (Washington, D.C.: U.S. Government Printing Office, 1950), 29.
4. Ibid., 1–2.
5. Ibid., 34.
6. Ibid.
7. Adam Smith, *The Theory of Moral Sentiments*, ed. Ryan Patrick Hanley (New York: Penguin, 2009), 270.

CHAPTER 1

1. Richard Pankhurst, *An Introduction to the Economic History of Ethiopia* (Addis Ababa: Lalibela House, 1961).
2. Robert P. Skinner, *Abyssinia of Today: An Account of the First Mission Sent by the American Government to the Court of the King of Kings, 1903–04* (New York: Longmans, Green & Co., 1906), 91.
3. William Appleman Williams, *The Tragedy of American Diplomacy*, 50th anniversary ed. (New York: W. W. Norton, 2009), 34.
4. Eric T. L. Love, *Race Over Empire* (Chapel Hill: University of North Carolina Press, 2004), 196–200.
5. Theodore Roosevelt, "Second Annual Message," December 2, 1902.
6. Robert P. Skinner to Francis B. Loomis, May 13, 1903; Consular Letters from Marseilles; T 220; record group 59; National Archives and Records Administration.
7. Skinner, *Abyssinia*, 86–87.
8. Ibid., viii.
9. John Maynard Keynes, *The General Theory of Employment, Interest, and Money* (San Diego: Harcourt, Brace & World, Inc., 1964), 383.

10. Contemporary historians caution us not to claim nineteenth-century lifestyles for eighteenth-century British characters as the living conditions of the poor majority showed little substantive improvement, but it is undeniable that many people of the time believed themselves to be citizens of a new age along with a new political entity. See: Gregory Clark, *A Farewell to Alms* (Princeton, NJ: Princeton University Press, 2007); Emily Cockayne, *Hubbub* (New Haven, CT: Yale University Press, 2007); Tim Blanning, *The Pursuit of Glory* (New York: Penguin Books, 2007), 3–191; Joel Mokyr, "Editor's Introduction: The New Economic History of the Industrial Revolution," in *The British Industrial Revolution*, ed. Joel Mokyr (Boulder: Westview Press, 1999), 113–127.
11. "Progress, n.," *The Oxford English Dictionary*, online edition (viewed on December 15, 2008).
12. Daniel Defoe, *A Tour through the Whole Island of Great Britain*, abridged and edited by Pat Rogers (London: Penguin Books, 1971), 43.
13. Ibid., 79, 181–182.
14. Ibid., 327; Ronald Findlay and Kevin O'Rourke, *Power and Plenty* (Princeton, NJ: Princeton University Press, 2007), 259–260.
15. Daniel Defoe, *The Complete English Tradesmen* (London: BiblioBazaar, 2006), 111.
16. Liah Greenfeld, *The Spirit of Capitalism* (Cambridge, MA: Harvard University Press, 2001), 21–58.
17. Blanning, *The Pursuit of Glory*, 95–111.
18. Defoe, *Tradesmen*, 272.
19. Peter Lindert, "English Population, Wages, and Prices: 1541–1913," *Journal of Interdisciplinary History* 15:4 (Spring 1985): 609–634.
20. Jan de Vries, "The Industrial Revolution and the Industrious Revolution," *The Journal of Economic History* 54:2 (June 1994): 254–256.
21. Daniel Defoe, *Robinson Crusoe* (New York: Barnes and Noble Classics, 2003); Italo Calvino, *Why Read the Classics*, trans. Martin McLaughlin (New York: Vintage Books, 2000), 97–101.
22. Stephen Greenblatt, *Marvelous Possessions* (Chicago: University of Chicago Press, 1991); David Abulafia, *The Discovery of Mankind* (New Haven, CT: Yale University Press, 2008); Kim F. Hall, *Things of Darkness* (Ithaca, NY: Cornell University Press, 1995).
23. Samuel Johnson, *A Voyage to Abyssinia*, ed. Joel J. Gold (New Haven, CT: Yale University Press, 1985), 3–4; Richard Pankhurst, *An Introduction to the Economic History of Ethiopia* (Addis Ababa: Lalibela House, 1961), 97–99; W. B. Carnochan, *Golden Legends* (Stanford, CA: Stanford University Press, 2008), 3–4.
24. For information on Johnson's Ethiopian writings, see: Paul Goring, "Introduction" in Samuel Johnson, *The History of Rasselas, Prince of Abyssinia* (London: Penguin Books, 2007), xiii–xxxi; Ellen Douglas Leyburn, "'No Romantick Absurdities or Incredible Fictions': The Relation of Johnson's Rasselas to Lobo's Voyage to Abyssinia,"

PMLA 70:5 (December 1955): 1059–1067; Donald M. Lockhart, "'The Fourth Son of the Mighty Emperor': The Ethiopian Background of Johnson's Rasselas," *PMLA* 78:5 (December 1963): 516–528.
25. Samuel Johnson, *The History of Rasselas, Prince of Abyssinia*, ed. Paul Goring (London: Penguin Books, 2007).
26. Ibid., 30–32, 70.
27. James Bruce, *Travels and Adventures in Abyssinia and Nubia, 1768–1773, to Discover the Source of the Nile*, ed. J. Morison Clingan, 2nd ed. (Edinburgh: Adam and Charles Black, 1873), xiii–19; J. M. Reid, *Traveler Extraordinary* (New York: W. W. Norton, 1968), 28–71.
28. Richard Pankhurst, *Travelers in Ethiopia* (London: Oxford University Press, 1965), 47–50, 72–74; Alan Morehead, *The Blue Nile* (New York: Perennial, 1962), 17–32.
29. Bruce, *Travels and Adventures*, 212. W. B. Carnochan analyzes the romantic aspects of Bruce's account in *Golden Legends*, 16–52.
30. Bruce, *Travels and Adventures*, 90–91.
31. Bruce quoted in Morehead, *The Blue Nile*, 26.
32. Alexander Broadie, *The Scottish Enlightenment* (Edinburgh: Birlinn, 2001), 1–42; Christopher J. Berry, *The Social Theory of the Scottish Enlightenment* (Edinburgh: Edinburgh University Press, 1997), 1–20; Roger Emerson, "The contexts of the Scottish Enlightenment," in *The Cambridge Companion to the Scottish Enlightenment*, ed. Alexander Broadie (Cambridge: Cambridge University Press, 2003), 9–25.
33. Defoe, *A Tour through the Whole Island of Great Britain*, 560; Spiro Peterson, "Defoe in Edinburgh, 1707," *Huntington Library Quarterly* 38:1 (November 1974): 21–33.
34. John Clive and Bernard Bailyn, "England's Cultural Provinces: Scotland and America," *William and Mary Quarterly* 11:2 (April 1954): 200–213; James Buchan, *Crowded with Genius* (New York: Perennial, 2003), 208–240; Arthur Herman, *How the Scots Invented the Modern World* (New York: Three Rivers Press, 2001).
35. Quoted in Richard B. Sher, *The Enlightenment and the Book* (Chicago: University of Chicago Press, 2006), 115.
36. Buchan, *Crowded with Genius*, 24–84; Herman, *How the Scots Invented the Modern World*, 1–12; Blanning, *The Pursuit of Glory*, 11; Wendy Moore, *The Knife Man* (New York: Broadway Books, 2005), 13–24.
37. Quoted in the front of Broadie, *The Scottish Enlightenment*.
38. T. D. Campbell, "Francis Hutcheson: 'Father' of the Scottish Enlightenment," in *The Origins and Nature of the Scottish Enlightenment*, ed. R. H. Campbell and Andrew S. Skinner (Edinburgh: John Donald Publishers: 1982), 167–182; Roy Porter, *The Creation of the Modern World* (New York: W. W. Norton, 2000), 168–171.

39. David Hume, *A Treatise of Human Nature*, ed. David Fate Norton and Mary J. Norton (Oxford: Oxford University Press, 2000), 307–313.
40. Ibid., 314–322.
41. David Hume, *Essays, Moral, Political, and Literary*, ed. Eugene F. Millar, rev. ed. (Indianapolis: Liberty Fund, 1987), 271.
42. Nicholas Phillipson, *Adam Smith: An Enlightened Life* (New Haven, CT: Yale University Press, 2010), 65.
43. Ibid., 120–137; Buchan, *Crowded with Genius*, 122–130; Ian Simpson Ross, *The Life of Adam Smith* (Oxford: Clarendon Press, 1995), 1–127.
44. Jonathan Israel, *Enlightenment Contested* (Oxford: Oxford University Press, 2006), 287.
45. Montesquieu, *The Spirit of the Laws*, trans. and ed. Anne Cohler, Basia Miller, and Harold Stone (Cambridge: Cambridge University Press, 1989), 310.
46. Israel, *Enlightenment Contested*, 356–371.
47. Berry, *Social Theory of the Scottish Enlightenment*, 74–88; Murray G. H. Pittock, "Historiography," in *The Cambridge Companion to the Scottish Enlightenment*, ed. Alexander Broadie (Cambridge: Cambridge University Press, 2003), 258–276.
48. Adam Smith, *The Theory of Moral Sentiments* (New York: Penguin, 2009), 13–25.
49. Ibid., 103–106, 125–126, 133–136.
50. Quoted in Adam Smith, *Lectures on Jurisprudence*, ed. R. L. Meek, D. D. Raphael, and P. G. Stein (Indianapolis: Liberty Fund, 1978), 3.
51. Ibid., 14–16.
52. David Hume, *An Enquiry Concerning Human Understanding*, ed. Eric Steinberg, 2nd ed. (Indianapolis: Hackett, 1993), 55.
53. Broadie, *The Scottish Enlightenment*, 67, 69.
54. H. M. Hopfl, "From Savage to Scotsman: Conjectural History in the Scottish Enlightenment," *The Journal of British Studies* 17:2 (Spring 1978): 19–20, 37–38.
55. Broadie, *The Scottish Enlightenment*, 76–77.
56. Hume, *Essays, Moral, Political, and Literary*, 377–386.
57. Smith, *Lectures on Jurisprudence*, 14–16, 107, 208, 490.
58. Smith, *An Inquiry into the Nature and Causes of the Wealth of Nations*, ed. R. H. Campbell and A. S. Skinner (Indianapolis: Liberty Fund, 1981), 17.
59. Hume, *Essays, Moral, Political, and Literary*, 262–264, 277.
60. W. W. Rostow, *Theorists of Economic Growth from David Hume to Present* (New York: Oxford University Press, 1990), 35.
61. Smith, *An Inquiry into the Nature and Causes of the Wealth of Nations*, 345.
62. Ibid., 453.
63. Ibid., 366, 456.
64. Joel Mokyr, *The Lever of Riches* (New York: Oxford University Press, 1990), 13. The idea of labeling the Industrial Revolution as process or a movement comes from T. S. Ashton, *The Industrial Revolution* (New York: Oxford University Press, 1964).

65. Smith, *An Inquiry into the Nature and Causes of the Wealth of Nations*, 20.
66. Ibid., 111–112.
67. Ibid., 425.
68. Ibid., 448.
69. Ibid., 782–788.
70. Ibid., 96.
71. Istvan Hont and Michael Ignatieff, "Needs and Justice in The Wealth of Nations: An Introductory Essay," in *Wealth and Virtue: The Shaping of Political Economy in the Scottish Enlightenment,* ed. Istvan Hont and Michael Ignatieff (Cambridge: Cambridge University Press, 1983), 1–44. For a critical view of Smith's system, see Robert L. Heilbroner, "The Paradox of Progress: Decline and Decay in The Wealth of Nations," *Journal of the History of Ideas* 34:2 (April–June 1973): 243–262.
72. Thomas Malthus, *An Essay on the Principle of Population* (Oxford: Oxford University Press, 2008), 124.
73. Emma Rothschild, *Economic Sentiments* (Cambridge, MA: Harvard University Press, 2001), 112.
74. Smith, *An Inquiry into the Nature and Causes of the Wealth of Nations*, 341.
75. For information on how women did come up in conversation, see Pat Maloney, "Savages in the Scottish Enlightenment's History of Desire," *Journal of the History of Sexuality* 14:3 (July 2005): 237–265.
76. Hume, *Essays, Moral, Political, and Literary,* 208.
77. Israel, *Enlightenment Contested*, 545–614.
78. Lord Kames, *Sketches of the History of Man*, vol. 1, ed. James A. Harris (Indianapolis: Liberty Fund, 2007): 23–24.
79. Ibid. 48–51.
80. Malthus, *An Essay on the Principle of Population,* 9.
81. Ibid., 13.
82. Clark, *A Farewell to Alms,* 5.
83. Ashton, *The Industrial Revolution*, 4–7.
84. Rothschild, *Economic Sentiments*, 156.
85. Michael Adas, *Machines as the Measure of Men* (Ithaca, NY: Cornell University Press, 1989), 144.
86. François Guizot, *The History of Civilization in Europe*, trans. William Hazlitt, ed. Larry Siedentop (London: Penguin, 1997), 16.
87. Major W. Cornwallis Harris, *The Highlands of Ethiopia* (New York: J. Winchester, New World Press, n.d.), 2.
88. Ibid., 124–125.
89. Ibid., 232, 282.
90. Ibid., 338.
91. David Stack, *Queen Victoria's Skull* (London: Hambledon Continuum, 2008), xi–xvii, 19–26; Paul A. Erickson, "Phrenology and Physical Anthropology:

The George Combe Collection," *Current Anthropology* 18:1 (March 1977): 92–93.
92. Adrian Desmond and James Moore, *Darwin's Sacred Cause* (Boston: Houghton Mifflin Harcourt, 2009), 36–37.
93. Quoted in Stack, *Queen Victoria's Skull*, 218.
94. Quoted in Reginald Horsman, *Race and Manifest Destiny* (Cambridge: Harvard University Press, 1981), 58–59.
95. Quoted in Horsman, *Race and Manifest Destiny*, 127; Stephen Jay Gould, *The Mismeasure of Man* (New York: W. W. Norton & Company, 1996), 82–101; see also: A. Cameron Grant, "George Combe and American Slavery," *The Journal of Negro History* 45:4 (October 1960): 259–269.
96. Barry Werth, *Banquet at Delmonico's* (New York: Random House, 2009), 37, 135–137.
97. Stocking, George W., Jr. *Victorian Anthropology* (New York: The Free Press, 1987), 67; John S. Haller, Jr., "The Species Problem: Nineteenth-Century Concepts of Racial Inferiority in the Origin of Man Controversy," *American Anthropology* 72:6 (December 1970): 1319–1329.
98. Desmond and Moore, *Darwin's Sacred Cause*, 138.
99. Charles Darwin, *On the Origin of the Species*, A Facsimile of the First Edition (Cambridge: Harvard University Press, 1964), 490.
100. Charles Darwin, *Descent of Man*. (New York: D. Appleton, 1871), 154.
101. Ibid., 170.
102. Carl N. Degler, *In Search of Human Nature* (New York: Oxford University Press, 1991), 6–7; Louis Menand, *The Metaphysical Club* (New York: Farrar, Straus and Giroux, 2001), 123.
103. Edward J. Larson, *Evolution* (New York: The Modern Library, 2006), 38–41.
104. Richard Hofstadter, *Social Darwinism in American Thought* (Boston: Beacon Press, 1992), 31–39.
105. Ibid., 39; Stocking, *Victorian Anthropology*, 216–228.
106. Herbert Spencer, *The Man Versus the State* (Indianapolis: Liberty Fund, 1982), 228.
107. Ibid., 108.
108. Werth, *Banquet at Delmonico's*, 125–126.
109. William Graham Sumner, *On Liberty, Society, and Politics* (Indianapolis: Liberty Fund, 1992), 164–166, 172.
110. Henry Steele Commager, *The American Mind* (New Haven, CT: Yale University Press, 1950), 90; Robert H. Wiebe, *The Search for Order* (New York: Hill and Wang, 1967), 164–165.
111. "Through the Looking Glass," *Chicago Daily Tribune,* November 1, 1893, 9; Robert W. Rydell, *All the World's a Fair* (Chicago: University of Chicago Press, 1984).
112. John M. Jordan, *Machine-Age Ideology* (Chapel Hill: University of North Carolina Press, 1994), 20–21; Michael Adas, *Dominance by Design* (Cambridge, MA: The Belknap Press, 2006): 141–143; Adas, *Machines as the Measure of Men*, 142.

113. Merle Curti, *Human Nature in American Thought* (Madison: University of Wisconsin Press, 1980), 217–246; Thomas L. Haskell, *The Emergence of Professional Social Science* (Baltimore: The Johns Hopkins University Press, 2000): 14; Menand, *The Metaphysical Club*, 371–372.
114. Menand, *The Metaphysical Club*, 337–364; Hofstadter, *Social Darwinism in American Thought*, 67–71.
115. Haskell, *The Emergence of Professional Social Science*, 1–23; Wiebe, *The Search for Order*, 133–163; James Q. Dealey, Edward Alsworth Ross, Franklin H. Giddings, Ulysses G. Weatherly, Charles A. Ellwood, George Elliot Howard, Frank W. Blackmar, and Albion W. Small, "Lester Frank Ward," *The American Journal of Sociology* 19:1 (July 1913): 61–78.
116. Hofstadter, *Social Darwinism in American Thought*, 75; Commager, *The American Mind*, 211.
117. Lester Frank Ward, *The Psychic Factors of Civilization*, 2nd ed. (Boston: Ginn & Company, 1906): 135.
118. Commager, *The American Mind*, 211.
119. Ward, *The Psychic Factors of Civilization*, 286.
120. Hofstadter, *Social Darwinism in American Thought*, 83; Curti, *Human Nature in American Thought*, 248–253; James E. Fleming, "The Role of Government in a Free Society: The Conception of Lester Frank Ward," *Social Forces* 24:3 (March 1946): 257–266.
121. Skinner, *Abyssinia of Today*, 141.
122. Harold G. Marcus, *The Life and Times of Menelik II* (Oxford: Clarendon Press, 1975), 6–134; Richard Pankhurst, *The Ethiopians* (Oxford: Blackwell Publishers, 1998): 176–188; Chris Prouty, *Empress Taytu and Menilek II* (Trenton, NJ: The Red Sea Press, 1986), 1–25.
123. Paulos Milikias, "The Battle of Adwa: The Historic Victory of Ethiopia Over European Colonialism," in *The Battle of Adwa*, ed. Paulos Milikias and Getachew Metaferia (New York: Algora Publishing, 2005), 43–46.
124. Ibid., 48.
125. Dejasmach Zewde Gabre-Selassie, "Continuity and Discontinuity in Menelik's Foreign Policy," in *The Battle of Adwa*, 110.
126. Richard Pankhurst, "British Reactions to the Battle of Adwa as Illustrated by the Times of London for 1896," in *The Battle of Adwa*, 218, 224.
127. Theodore Roosevelt, *Letters and Speeches* (New York: The Library of America, 1951), 184–186.
128. Getachew Metaferia, "Ethiopia: A Bulwark Against European Colonialism and Its Role in the Pan-African Movement," in *The Battle of Adwa*, 183–185.
129. Quoted in Ibid., 188.
130. Degler, *In Search of Human Nature*, 61–83; Stephen Pinker, *The Blank Slate* (New York: Penguin Books, 2002), 22–23; Marshall Hyatt, *Franz Boas Social Activist* (New York: Greenwood Press, 1990); George W. Stocking, Jr., "Franz Boas and the Culture Concept in Historical Perspective," *American Anthropologist* 68:4

(August 1966): 867–882; Clarence C. Gravlee, H. Russell Bernard, and William R. Leonard, "Heredity, Environment, and Cranial Form: A Reanalysis of Boas's Immigrant Data," *American Anthropologist* 105:1 (March 2003): 125–138.

CHAPTER 2

1. Gordon MacCreagh, *The Last of Free Africa*, 2nd ed. (New York: D. Appleton-Century Company, 1935), 3.
2. Ibid., 180.
3. Ibid., 349, 360.
4. Ibid., xxi.
5. Alfred Marshall, *Principles of Economics* (New York: Prometheus Books, 1997), 1.
6. Ibid., 25–26.
7. Ibid., 4.
8. Ibid., 3, 7–8.
9. Ibid, 25.
10. Timothy Mitchell, *Rule of Experts* (Berkeley: University of California Press, 2002), 94.
11. W. W. Rostow, *Theorists of Economic Growth from David Hume to the Present* (New York: Oxford University Press, 1990), 154–159; Mark Blaug, *Economic Theory in Retrospect*, 4th ed. (Cambridge: Cambridge University Press, 1985), 294–325; John E. Elliot, "Introduction to the Transaction Edition," in Joseph A. Schumpeter, *The Theory of Economic Development,* trans. Redvers Opie (New Brunswick, NJ: Transaction Publishers, 2008), x–xv.
12. Marshall, *Principles of Economics*, 93.
13. Ibid., xii.
14. Robert L. Heilbroner, *The Worldly Philosophers,* 7th ed. (New York: Simon & Schuster, 1999), 205–212; Rostow, *Theorists of Economic Growth*, 170–173.
15. Markus C. Becker and Thorbjørn Knudsen, "Schumpeter 1911: Farsighted Visions on Economic Development," *American Journal of Economics and Sociology* 61:2 (April 2002): 392.
16. Schumpeter, *The Theory of Economic Development*, 64.
17. Ibid., 66–68.
18. Eric D. Beinhocker, *The Origin of Wealth* (Boston: Harvard Business School Press, 2006), 17.
19. H. W. Arndt, *The Rise and Fall of Economic Growth* (Chicago: University of Chicago Press, 1978), 17.
20. Allyn A. Young, "Increasing Returns and Economic Progress," *The Economic Journal* 38:152 (December 1928): 527–530.
21. Ibid., 533.
22. Ibid., 535–540.
23. Mitchell, *Rule of Experts*, 4, 81–84.

24. Allyn A. Young, "The Trend of Economics," *Quarterly Journal of Economics* 39:2 (February 1925): 167.
25. Young, "Increasing Returns and Economic Progress," 534.
26. V. I. Lenin quoted in Kendalle E. Bailes, "The American Connection: Ideology and the Transfer of American Technology to the Soviet Union, 1917–1941," *Comparative Studies in Society and History* 23:3 (July 1981): 426.
27. Lenin even invited capital investment into Russia under his New Economic Policy and by 1925, U.S.-Soviet trade reached $95 million, even though the U.S. government had not officially acknowledged the Soviet Union's existence (Walter LaFeber, *The American Age: U.S. Foreign Policy at Home and Abroad*, 2nd ed., vol. 2 [New York: W. W. Norton, 1994], 348); Bailes, "The American Connection," 429; Thomson P. Hughes, *American Genesis* (New York: Viking, 1989), 250–284.
28. Stalin quoted in David Engerman, *Modernization from the Other Shore: American Intellectuals and the Romance of Russian Development* (Cambridge, MA: Harvard University Press, 2003), 153–154.
29. Ibid., 155–159.
30. Karl Polanyi, *The Great Transformation*, 2nd ed. (Boston: Beacon, 2001), 3, 31.
31. Ibid., 263.
32. F. A. Hayek, *The Road to Serfdom* (Chicago: University of Chicago Press, 1994): 143.
33. Ibid., 147.
34. Blaug, *Economic Theory in Retrospect*, 655.
35. John Maynard Keynes, *Essays in Persuasion* (London: Macmillan, 1933), 312, 319–321.
36. John Maynard Keynes, *The General Theory of Employment, Interest, and Money* (San Diego: Harcourt, Inc., 1964), 27.
37. Heilbroner, *The Worldly Philosophers*, 270–275; Blaug, *Economic Theory in Retrospect*, 654–655.
38. Keynes, *Essays in Persuasion*, 380.
39. Joan Hoff Wilson, *Herbert Hoover: Forgotten Progressive* (Prospect Heights, IL: Waveland Press, Inc., 1975), 138; William J. Barber, *From New Era to New Deal* (Cambridge: Cambridge University Press, 1985), 4–5, 15.
40. Barber, 4, 15.
41. "The curious task of economics," Hayek wrote, "is to demonstrate to men how little they really know about what they imagine they can design" (*The Fatal Conceit, The Collected Works of F. A. Hayek*, vol. 1, ed. W. W. Bartley III [Chicago: University of Chicago Press, 1988], 76).
42. Metcalf, Evan B. "Secretary Hoover and the Emergence of Macroeconomic Management," *The Business History Review* 49:1 (Spring 1975): 61.
43. Alan Brinkley, *The End of Reform* (New York: Alfred A. Knopf, 1995): 7.
44. Ibid., 173, 229–235, 266–267.
45. Kenneth Hoover, *Economics as Ideology* (Lanham, MD: Rowman & Littlefield, 2003), 88.

46. Charles Frederick Roos, *Dynamic Economics* (Bloomington, IN: Principia Press, 1934), 5–7.
47. Ibid., 7.
48. Simon S. Kuznets, *Secular Movements in Production and Prices* (New York: Augustus M. Kelley, 1967), 3–4.
49. Serge Latouche, "Standard of Living," in *The Development Dictionary*, Wolfgang Sachs, ed. (London: Zed Books, 2003), 252.
50. Kuznets, *Secular Movements in Production and Prices*, 324–325.
51. Rostow, *Theorists of Economic Growth from David Hume to the Present*, 244.
52. Kuznets, *Secular Movements in Production and Prices*, 328.
53. Ibid., 329.
54. Colin Clark, *The Conditions of Economic Progress* (London: Macmillan, 1940), 4
55. H. W. Arndt, *Economic Development* (Chicago: University of Chicago Press, 1987), 35.
56. Clark, *The Conditions of Economic Progress*, 53.
57. Ibid., 39–41.
58. Colin Clark, *National Income and Outlay* (New York: Augustus M. Kelley, 1965), 1.
59. A. C. Pigou, *The Economics of Welfare*, 4th ed. (London: Macmillan, 1932), 12.
60. Clark, *National Income and Outlay*, 3–4.
61. Eugene Staley, *World Economy in Transition* (Port Washington, NY: Kennikat Press, 1971), 61.
62. Ibid., 96.
63. Ibid., 59.
64. Ibid., 128.
65. Ibid., 332.
66. Arndt, *Economic Development*, 47.
67. P. N. Rosenstein-Rodan, "Problems of Industrialization of Eastern and South-Eastern Europe," *Economic Journal* 53:210–211 (June–September 1943): 202.
68. Ibid., 203.
69. Young, "Increasing Returns and Economic Progress," 539; Yuan-Li Wu, "A Note on the Post-War Industrialization of 'Backward' Countries and Centralist Planning," *Economica* 12:47 (August 1945): 173.
70. Rosenstein-Rodan, "Problems of Industrialization," 208.
71. P. N. Rosenstein-Rodan, "The International Development of Economically Backward Areas," *International Affairs* 20:2 (April 1944): 158.
72. Ibid., 159.
73. Ibid., 161.
74. R. F. Harrod, "An Essay in Dynamic Theory," *Economic Journal* 49:193 (March 1939): 14.
75. Harrod maintained that the warranted rate of growth, that is, the rate which "will leave all parties satisfied that they have produced neither more nor less than the

right amount," is equal to the fraction of income saved by individuals and companies, divided by the value of the capital goods necessary for the "production of a unit increment of output" (Ibid., 16–17, 31).

76. Evsey D. Domar, "Capital Expansion, Rate of Growth, and Employment," *Econometrica* 14:2 (April 1946): 139.
77. Marshall, *Principles of Economics*, 4; Domar, "Capital Expansion, Rate of Growth, and Employment," 147.
78. Robert A. Pollard, *Economic Security and the Origins of the Cold War, 1945–1950* (New York: Columbia University Press, 1985), 9.
79. Dean Acheson, *Present at the Creation* (New York: W.W. Norton, 1969): 133.
80. John Maynard Keynes, *The Collected Writings of John Maynard Keynes*, vol. 26, ed. Donald Moggridge (London: Macmillan, 1980), 104.
81. Amy Staples, *The Birth of Development* (Kent, OH: Kent State University Press, 2006), 8–21; Acheson, *Present at the Creation*, 81–86.
82. Keynes, *The Collected Writings of John Maynard Keynes*, 211.
83. Ibid., 217–218.
84. Staples, *The Birth of Development*, 20–24.
85. Public Law 304, 79th Congress, 2nd Session; Bertram M. Gross and John P. Lewis, "The President's Economic Staff during the Truman Administration," *American Political Science Review* 48:1 (March 1954): 120–124; Hoover, *Economics as Ideology*, 145–146.
86. Roger B. Porter, "Presidents and Economists: The Council of Economic Advisers," in "Papers and Proceedings of the Hundred and Fourth Annual Meeting of the American Economic Association," edited by J. David Baldwin and Ronald L. Oaxaca. Program arranged by Arnold C. Harberer, special issue, *American Economic Review* 87:2 (May 1997): 104.
87. For a good example of his general disciplinary focus, see: E.G. Nourse, "Some Economic and Social Accompaniments of the Mechanization of Agriculture," *American Economic Review* 20:1 (March 1930): 114–132.
88. Oral history interview, Leon H. Keyserling, May 3–19, 1971, 1–24, 41–42, Truman Library; Oral history interview, Walter S. Salant, March 30, 1970, 1–30, Truman Library; Harry S. Truman, *Memoirs by Harry S. Truman: Years of Trial and Hope*, vol. 1 (Garden City, NY: Doubleday, 1955), 493–494; Leon H. Keyserling, "Leon H. Keyserling," in *The Truman White House*, ed. Francis H. Heller (Lawrence: Regents Press of Kansas, 1980), 180.
89. Michael A. Bernstein, *A Perilous Progress* (Princeton. NJ: Princeton University Press, 2001), 111–112.
90. Alonzo L. Hamby, *Beyond the New Deal: Harry S. Truman and American Liberalism* (New York: Columbia University Press, 1973), 295; Oral history interview, Keyserling, 56.
91. Walter S. Salant, "Some Intellectual Contributions of the Truman Council of Economic Advisers to Policy-Making," *History of Political Economy* 5 (1973): 37, 42.

92. Oral history interview, Salant, 61–62; W. Robert Brazelton, "Retrospectives: The Economics of Leon Hirsch Keyserling," *Journal of Economic Progress* 11:4 (Autumn 1997): 191; Harrod, "An Essay in Dynamic Theory," 16–17.
93. Oral history interview, Salant, 13–24.
94. Keyserling, in Heller, *The Truman White* House, 181.
95. Leon Keyserling, "Can We Achieve Lasting Prosperity?," December 5, 1948, Articles, Keyserling Papers, Truman Library; Monthly Report to the President, October 1949, quoted in Arndt, *The Rise and Fall of Economic Growth*, 35. Keyserling maintained these views for decades, writing in 1967: "I believe that the top priority for the foreseeable future is to restore and maintain a full-employment environment" (Keyserling, "Employment and the 'New Economies,'" *Annals of the American Academy of Political and Social Science* 373 [September 1967]: 103).
96. Acheson, *Present at the Creation*, 4.
97. Joseph Stalin, "New Five-Year Plan for Russia," (February 9, 1946), *Vital Speeches of the Day* 12 (March 1, 1946): 300–303.
98. Engerman, *Modernization from the Other Shore*; Alexander Gerschenkron, "The Rate of Growth in Russia: The Rate of Industrial Growth in Russia since 1885," *Journal of Economic History* 7 (1947): 144–174.

CHAPTER 3

1. *Lij* means "child" and was reserved for children of high-ranking nobility; *Ras* is roughly equivalent to a duke and literally means "head"; *Dejazmach* means "commander of the gate" and was roughly equivalent to a count; *Woizero* means "lady" (Harold G. Marcus, *A History of Ethiopia*, updated ed. [Berkeley: University of California Press, 2002], 279–284).
2. Harold G. Marcus, *Haile Selassie* I (Berkeley: University of California Press, 1987), 1–21; Indrias Getachew, *Beyond the Throne,* ed. Richard Pankhurst (Addis Ababa: Shama Books, 2001), 33–35.
3. John Sorenson, *Imagining Ethiopia* (New Brunswick, NJ: Rutgers University Press, 1993); Paulos Milkias and Getachew Metaferia, ed. *The Battle of Adwa* (New York: Algora Publishing, 2005); Donald N. Levine, *Greater Ethiopia*, 2nd ed. (Chicago: University of Chicago Press, 2000); Michela Wrong, *I Didn't Do It for You* (Hammersmith, UK: Fourth Estate, 2005; New York: Harper Perennial, 2006): 100–115.
4. Marcus, *Haile Selassie* I, 1–38; Indrias Getachew, *Beyond the Throne,* 36–50; Bahru Zewde, *A History of Modern Ethiopia*, 1855–1991 2nd ed. (Oxford: James Currey, 2001; Athens: Ohio University Press, 2001; Addis Ababa: Addis Ababa University Press, 2001), 114–130.
5. Bahru Zewde, *A History of Modern Ethiopia*, 98–99; Marcus, *Haile Selassie* I, 40–50; Richard Pankhurst, *The Ethiopians* (Oxford: Blackwell, 1998), 215–218.
6. Marcus, *Haile Selassie* I, 53–58.

7. Richard Pankhurst, *Economic History of Ethiopia* (Addis Ababa: Haile Selllassie I University Press, 1968): 27.
8. Margery Perham, *The Government of Ethiopia* (New York: Oxford University Press, 1948), 407–416; Bahru Zewde, *A History of Modern Ethiopia*, 137–148; Marcus, *Haile Selassie I*, 116–118; Marcus, *A History of Ethiopia*, 130–139; John Markakis, *Ethiopia: Anatomy of a Traditional Polity* (Addis Ababa: Shama Books, 2006): 95–130.
9. Marcus, *Haile Selassie I*, 127–139.
10. Negussay Ayele, *Ethiopia and the United States* (Santa Clara, CA: ocopy.com, 2003), PDF e-book, 96–100.
11. Haile Selassie, *Selected Speeches of His Imperial Majesty Haile Selassie First* (Addis Ababa: Imperial Ethiopian Ministry of Information, 1967), 314.
12. Haile Selassie, *My Life and Ethiopia's Progress*, vol. 2, trans. Ezekiel Gebissa, ed. Harold Marcus (East Lansing: Michigan State University Press, 1994), 22–23.
13. E. A. Speiser, "Oriental Studies and Society," *Journal of the American Oriental Society* 66:3 (July–September 1946): 193.
14. Douglas Little, *American Orientalism*, (Chapel Hill: University of North Carolina Press, 2002): 9–14; Michael B. Oren, *Power, Faith, and Fantasy* (New York: W. W. Norton, 2007), 17–321.
15. Alfred Thayer Mahan, "The Persian Gulf and International Relations," *National Review* (September 1902): 30.
16. Ibid., 34.
17. Ibid., 39.
18. Roger Adelson, *London and the Invention of the Middle East* (New Haven, CT: Yale University Press, 1995), 24–26. Valentine Chirol's 1903 collection was titled, *The Middle East Question or Some Political Problems of Indian Defence* (London: J. Murray, 1903).
19. Adelson, 24–26; John Keay, *Sowing the Wind* (New York: W. W. Norton, 2003), 24.
20. "In equal ships oil gave a large excess of speed over coal. It enabled that speed to be attained with far greater rapidity. It gave forty per cent greater radius of action for the same weight of coal. It enabled a fleet to refuel at sea with great facility" (Winston Churchill quoted in Rashid Khalidi, *Resurrecting Empire* [Boston: Beacon, 2004], 84).
21. Daniel Yergin, *The Prize* (New York: Free Press, 1991), 153–160.
22. Yergin, *The Prize*, 189; Niall Ferguson, *Empire* (New York: Basic Books, 2002), 256–261; Margaret MacMillan, *Paris 1919* (New York: Random House, 2003), 375, 396; Philip Marshall Brown, "From Sevres to Lausanne," *The American Journal of International Law* 18:1 (January 1924): 113–116.
23. Little, *American Orientalism*, 44–45, 48; Keay, *Sowing the Wind*, 25; Yergin, *The Prize*, 110.

24. C. G. Smith, "The Emergence of the Middle East," *Journal of Contemporary History* 3:3 (July 1968): 6–7.
25. Nathan Godfried, "Economic Development and Regionalism: United States Foreign Relations in the Middle East, 1942–5," *Journal of Contemporary History* 22:3 (July 1987): 482–483; W. B. Fisher, "Unity and Diversity in the Middle East," *Geographical Review* 37:3 (July 1947): 415.
26. The American Minister Resident in Saudi Arabia (Moose) to the Saudi Arabian Acting Minister for Foreign Affairs (Yusuf Yassin), July 29, 1944, in *FRUS*, 1944, vol. 5 (Washington, D.C.: U.S. Government Printing Office, 1965): 661–662; John A. DeNovo, "The Culbertson Economic Mission and Anglo-American Tensions in the Middle East, 1944–1945," *The Journal of American History* 63:4 (March 1977): 913–923; J. M. Landis, "Anglo-American Cooperation in the Middle East," *Annals of the American Academy of Political and Social Science* 240 (July 1945): 64–72; H. A. R. Gibb, "Middle East Perplexities," *International Affairs* 20:4 (October 1944): 458–460; Godfried, "Economic Development and Regionalism," 484–485.
27. President Roosevelt to the American Director of Economic Operations in the Middle East (Landis), March 6, 1944, in *FRUS*, 1944, vol. 5, 1.
28. Peter L. Hahn, *The United States, Great Britain, and Egypt, 1945–1956* (Chapel Hill: University of North Carolina Press, 1991): 19–20.
29. "Mr. Eden's Statement," Appendix C in Ibid., 417; Memorandum by the Liaison Officer with the War and Navy Department (Wilson), May 18, 1943, in *FRUS*, 1943, vol. 4 (Washington, D.C.: U.S. Government Printing Office, 1964), 96–97.
30. Haile Selassie, *My Life and Ethiopia's Progress,* 145, 167–176; Harold Marcus, *The Politics of Empire* (Lawrenceville, NJ: The Red Sea Press, 1995), 8–21; Bahru Zewde, *A History of Modern Ethiopia*, 178–180; Wrong, *I Didn't Do It for You*, 139–147; "Britain, Ethiopia Sign 2-Year Pact," *New York Times*, February 4, 1942, 7; "British Recognize Claim of Selassie," *New York Times*, February 5, 1941, 2.
31. Marcus, *The Politics of Empire*, 14.
32. Little, *American Orientalism*, 119–120.
33. E. Talbot Smith to Cordell Hull, February 18, 1943, record group 59; box 5790, 250/34/13/1; National Archives at College Park.
34. Report of Statement made by his Imperial Majesty, Haile Selassie, on the afternoon of February 11, 1943, to General Maxwell, Colonel Edwin N. Clark and E. Talbot Smith, attachment to E. Talbot Smith to Cordell Hull, February 18, 1943, record group 59; box 5790, 250/34/13/1; National Archives at College Park.
35. "War Blame Is Laid on Italian Nation," *New York Times*, June 20, 1943, 30.
36. The Ethiopian Vice Minister of Finance (Yilma Deressa) to President Roosevelt, (undated) in *FRUS*, 1943, vol. 4, 103–106; The Secretary of State to President Roosevelt, August 2, 1943, in *FRUS*, 1943, vol. 4, 106–108; Marcus, *The Politics of Empire*, 17–21.

37. The Chief of the Division of Near Eastern Affairs (Alling) to the First Secretary of the British Embassy (Hayter), December 31, 1943, in *FRUS*, 1943, vol. 4, 122–123; "Agreement between the United States and Ethiopia Respecting a Mutual Aid Settlement," May 31, 1949, in *FRUS*, 1949, vol. 6, 1798; "Lend-Lease Pact with Ethiopia," *New York Times*, August 10, 1943, 10; "British Privileges Curbed in Ethiopia," *New York Times*, December 20, 1944, 11.
38. Marcus, *The Politics of Empire*, 49–52; Negussay Ayele, *Ethiopia and the United States*, 172–175.
39. Markakis, *Ethiopia*, 391; Marcus, *A History of Ethiopia*, 153–163.
40. Quoted in Markakis, *Ethiopia*, 243–244.
41. Ibid., 245–246, 348–352; Perham, *The Government of Ethiopia*, 343–366.
42. A discussion of the contentious debate over the use of "feudal" in the Ethiopian case can be found in Messay Kebede, *Survival and Modernization, Ethiopia's Enigmatic Present* (Lawrenceville, NJ: The Red Sea Press, 1999), 125–178.
43. Bahru Zewde, *A History of Modern Ethiopia*, 191–193; Perham, *The Government of Ethiopia*, 277–292.
44. Report of Statement made by his Imperial Majesty, Haile Selassie, on the afternoon of February 11, 1943, to General Maxwell, Colonel Edwin N. Clark and E. Talbot Smith, attachment to E. Talbot Smith to Cordell Hull, February 18, 1943, record group 59; box 5790, 250/34/13/1; National Archives at College Park.
45. Quoted in Marcus, *The Politics of Empire*, 51–52.
46. John H. Spencer, *Ethiopia, The Horn of Africa, and U.S. Policy* (Cambridge, MA: Institute for Foreign Policy Analysis, Inc., 1977): 17–22; Semere Haile, "The Origins and Demise of the Ethiopia-Eritrea Federation," *Issue: A Journal of Opinion* 15 (1987): 10; F. E. Stafford, "The Ex-Italian Colonies," *International Affairs* 25:1 (January 1949): 47–55.
47. State Department, "Specific Current Questions," undated, in *FRUS*, 1947, vol. 5, 544.
48. Ibid., 533–534.
49. Ibid., 555; Statement by the United States and the United Kingdom Groups, "Anglo American Interest in Ethiopia," undated, in *FRUS*, 1947, vol. 5, 597.
50. Elizabeth Monroe, *Britain's Moment in the Middle East, 1914–1956* (Baltimore: The Johns Hopkins Press, 1963), 159.
51. State Department, Memorandum, undated, in *FRUS*, 1947, vol. 5, 511–513; Colin Clark, *The Conditions of Economic Progress* (London: Macmillan, 1940), 53–55.
52. Monroe, *Britain's Moment in the Middle East*, 148.
53. Advisory Committee on Technical Assistance, "Point Four Program in Relation to Dependent Areas," July 27, 1949, Student Research File: The Point Four Program, Truman Library; Vernon McKay, "Needs and Opportunities in Africa," *Annals of the American Academy of Political and Social Science* 268 (March 1950): 79–81.
54. State Department, Memorandum, undated, in *FRUS*, 1947, vol. 5, 513–521.

55. State Department, "Specific Current Questions," undated, in *FRUS*, 1947, vol. 5, 521–568.
56. Ibid., 551.
57. Ibid., 521–529.
58. Ibid., 545.
59. Ibid., 548–551.
60. Hahn, *The United States, Great Britain, & Egypt, 1945–1956*, 49–51.
61. Gordon P. Merriam, memo, June 13, 1949, in *FRUS*, 1949, vol. 6 (Washington, DC: U.S. Government Printing Office, 1977), 32. For another example of the growing importance of Middle East in Washington, see: Robertson to McGhee, U.S. Strategic Position in the Eastern Mediterranean and Middle East, November 14, 1949, in *FRUS*, 1949, vol. 6, 57.
62. Gordon P. Merriam, memo, June 13, 1949, in *FRUS*, 1949, vol. 6, 31–33.
63. NSC 5/2, 1948, quoted in Ibid., 39.
64. NSC 19/3, 1948, quoted in Gordon P. Merriam, memo, June 13, 1949, in *FRUS*, 1949, vol. 6, 40–41.
65. Gordon P. Merriam, memo, June 13, 1949, in *FRUS*, 1949, vol. 6, 33.
66. State Department, "A Report to the National Security Council on Coordination of Current Economic Warfare Operations," July 21, 1949, SMOF: National Security Council File, Truman Papers, Truman Library.
67. Marcus, *The Politics of Empire*, 73–75.
68. Bahru Zewde, *A Modern History of Ethiopia*, 183; Wrong, *I Didn't Do It For You*, 151–176; Pankhurst, *The Ethiopians*, 260–261.
69. Marcus, *The Politics of Empire*, 58.
70. Ibid., 64–67.

CHAPTER 4

1. "Text of Truman Message on Point-4 Plan," *New York Times*, June 25, 1949, 6.
2. Ibid.
3. David Hume, *Essays, Moral, Political, and Literary*, ed. Eugene F. Millar, rev. ed. (Indianapolis: Liberty Fund, 1987), 308–331.
4. Ibid.
5. Truman and Ethel Noland quoted in David McCullough, *Truman* (New York: Simon & Schuster, 1992), 43, 58, 141.
6. Ibid., 558.
7. Truman quoted in Walter Isaacson and Evan Thomas, *The Wise Men* (New York: Simon & Schuster, 1986), 257. For more on Truman's understanding of history, see Harry S. Truman, *Memoirs by Harry S. Truman: Years of Trial and Hope*, vol. 1 (Garden City, NY: Doubleday, 1955), 112–141. For an unflattering portrait of the president, see Arnold Offner, *Another Such Victory: President Truman and the Cold War, 1945–1953* (Stanford, CA: Stanford University Press, 2002).

8. For more on hunger and international politics, see Nick Cullather, *The Hungry World: America's Cold War Battle against Poverty in Asia* (Cambridge, MA: Harvard University Press, 2010), 11–42; and "The Foreign Policy of the Calorie," *The American Historical Review* 112:2 (April 2007): 337–364.
9. Harry Truman, *Memoirs by Harry S. Truman*, vol. 2 (Garden City, NY: Doubleday, 1956), 110.
10. Joint Statement by Agriculture, Commerce, and State, "Report on and Recommendations to Meet World Food Crisis," February 1, 1946, Wartime, box 1; Papers of Dennis A. Fitzgerald, 1945–1969; Eisenhower Presidential Library.
11. Address by the Hon. Herbert Hoover to the Famine Emergency Committee, May 17, 1946, Famine Emergency Committee—box 1; Papers of Dennis A. Fitzgerald, 1945–1969; Eisenhower Presidential Library; Harry Truman, *Memoirs by Harry S. Truman*, vol. 1, 474–480.
12. Address by Truman on the President's Citizens Food Committee Program, October 5, 1947, Cabinet Food Committee—box 1; Papers of Dennis A. Fitzgerald, 1945–1969; Eisenhower Presidential Library.
13. Clay quoted in Greg Behrman, *The Most Noble Adventure* (New York: Free Press, 2007), 29.
14. Robert A. Pollard, *Economic Security and the Origins of the Cold War, 1945–1950* (New York: Columbia University Press, 1985), 59–73.
15. Truman, *Memoirs*, vol. 1, 506.
16. Truman, *Memoirs*, vol. 2, 112–113.
17. Ibid., 174–175, 112–119; Pollard, *Economic Security*, 79–81, 136–140; Behrman, *The Most Noble Adventure*; Thomas W. Zeiler, *Free Trade, Free World* (Chapel Hill: University of North Carolina Press, 1999); Nicolaus Mills, *Winning the Peace* (Hoboken, NJ: John Wiley, 2008); Michael H. Hunt, *The American Ascendancy* (Chapel Hill: University of North Carolina Press, 2007), 162–165; Michael J. Hogan, "American Marshall Planners and the Search for a European Neocapitalism," *The American Historical Review* 90:1 (February 1985): 44–72; William L. Clayton, "GATT, The Marshall Plan, and OECD," *Political Science Quarterly* 78:4 (December 1963): 493–503.
18. Truman, *Memoirs*, vol. 2, 230.
19. Ibid., 231. For more on the connection between the Marshall Plan and Point Four, see Thomas G. Paterson, *Meeting the Communist Threat: Truman to Reagan* (New York: Oxford University Press, 1988), 18–53, 147–158.
20. Truman, *Memoirs*, vol. 2, 231.
21. Charles A. and Mary R. Beard, *The Rise of American Civilization*, one-volume ed. (New York: Macmillan, 1930), 737–738.
22. Wendell Wilkie, "One World," in Louis M. Hacker, *The Shaping of the American Tradition* (New York: Columbia University Press, 1947), 1235–1240.
23. For more on the Roosevelt-era origins of Point Four, see David Ekbladh "'Mr. TVA': Grass-Roots Development, David Lilienthal, and the Rise and Fall of the

Tennessee Valley Authority as a Symbol for U.S. Overseas Development, 1933–1973," *Diplomatic History* 26:3 (2002): 335–374; and *The Great American Mission: Modernization and the Construction of an American World Order* (Princeton, NJ: Princeton University Press, 2010).

24. Benjamin H. Hardy to Jonathan Daniels, November 19, 1950, Point IV file; Hardy papers; Truman Library; Benjamin Hardy to Mr. Russell, memo, November 23, 1948, Point IV file; Hardy papers; Truman Library.

25. Oral History Interview, Clark M. Clifford, March 1971–February 1973, 352–356, Truman Library.

26. Oral History Interview, Walter Salant, March 30, 1970, 37–40, Truman Library; Sergei Y. Shenin, *The United States and the Third World* (Huntington, NY: Nova Science Publishers, 2000): 12.

27. Margaret Truman, *Harry S. Truman* (New York: Pocket Books, 1973), 438–439.

28. Anthony Leviero, "Truman Sworn in, the 32nd President," *New York Times,* January 21, 1949, 1–2; McCullough, *Truman,* 723–725; Truman, *Memoirs,* vol. 2, 225–226; Margaret Truman, *Harry S. Truman,* 436–437.

29. Truman, "Inaugural Address," *New York Times,* January 21, 1949, 4.

30. James Reston, "Speech Seen As Aid to Western World," *New York Times,* January 21, 1949, 1.

31. Anthony Leviero, "Truman Sworn in, the 32nd President," *New York Times,* January 21, 1949, 2.

32. C. F. Trussell, "Praise in Congress," *New York Times,* January 21, 1949, 1, 5.

33. Shenin, *The United States and the Third World,* 23.

34. Donahue, in Dennis Merrill, ed., *Documentary History of the Truman Presidency,* vol. 27 (Frederick, MD: University Publications of America, 1999), 34–39; State Department, "Point Four," in ibid., 27–28.

35. Oral History Interview, Clifford, 364; Oral History Interview, Salant, 42.

36. Dean Acheson to Truman, March 14, 1949, document 13, in Merrill, *Documentary History of the Truman Presidency,* vol. 27, 63–64.

37. Ibid., 69.

38. State Department, "Building the Peace," *Foreign Affairs Outlines* 21 (Spring 1949): 1; Near Eastern and African Staff subject files 1951–1953; Technical Cooperation Administration; General Records of the Agency for International Development and its Predecessor Agencies, record group 469; National Archives at College Park.

39. Ibid., 1–2.

40. Ibid., 6.

41. State Department, OIR Report No. 4998, "Soviet Internal Situation," July 1, 1949, SRF: Ideological Foundations of the Cold War; Truman Library; Vojtech Mastny, *The Cold War and Soviet Insecurity* (New York: Oxford University Press, 1996), 58.

42. Truman, *Memoirs,* vol. 2, 171.

43. Clark Clifford, report, October 31, 1947, document 36, in Dennis Merrill, ed., *Documentary History of the Truman Presidency*, vol. 13 (Frederick, MD: University Publications of America, 1996), 434.
44. Truman, *Memoirs*, vol. 2, 247–251; Geir Lundestad, "Empire by Invitation? The United States and Western Europe, 1945–1952," *Journal of Peace Research* 23:3 (1986), 269–272; Melvyn P. Leffler, *A Preponderance of Power: National Security, the Truman Administration, and the Cold War* (Stanford: Stanford University Press, 1992), 361–397; Offner, *Another Such Victory*, 424–455.
45. Benjamin Hardy to Mr. Russell, "Significance of the Soviet-sponsored 'ECMA,'" January 27, 1949, Point IV file; Hardy papers; Truman Library.
46. Mr. Gross to James E. Webb, June 1, 1949, document 17, in Merrill, *Documentary History of the Truman Presidency*, vol. 27, 102.
47. Truman, Address at the Dedication of the World War Memorial Park, in Merrill, *Documentary History of the Truman Presidency*, vol. 27, 104–106.
48. Truman, "Text of Truman Message on Point-4 Plan," *New York Times*, June 25, 1949, 6.
49. Committee on Foreign Affairs, *Point Four: Background and Program* (Washington, D.C.: U.S. Government Printing Office, 1949); *Hearings before the Committee on Foreign Affairs House of Representatives, Eighty-First Congress, First Session on H.R. 5615, International Technical Cooperation Act of 1949*, House of Representatives, 81st Congress, Fall 1949 (Washington, D.C.: U.S. Government Printing Office, 1950), 1–3.
50. David Lloyd to Walter Salant, July 22, 1949, document 23, in Merrill, *Documentary History of the Truman Presidency*, vol. 27, 136.
51. David Lloyd to Joseph L. Rauh, September 28, 1949, document 33, in Merrill, *Documentary History of the Truman Presidency*, vol. 27, 186.
52. Ibid., 187.
53. See: Department of State, "Point Four" Booklet, January 1950, document 42, in Merrill, *Documentary History of the Truman Presidency*, vol. 27, 243–257; "Editorial," *Wall Street Journal*, September 29, 1949, in Walter M. Daniels, ed., *The Point Four Program* (New York: H. W. Wilson, 1951), 66–68; Isador Lubin, United States Representative, United Nations Economic and Employment Commission, *Social Action* 15 (October 15, 1949): 9–20, in Daniels, *The Point Four Program*, 129–138.
54. *Hearings before the Committee on Foreign Affairs on H.R. 5615, International Technical Cooperation Act of 1949*, House of Representatives, 81st Congress, Fall 1949 (Washington, D.C.: U.S. Government Printing Office, 1950), 6.
55. Ibid., 10–11, 20–22.
56. Ibid., 174–180.
57. Paul G. Hoffman, "Trade Restrictions: And Peace," *Proceedings of the Academy of Political Science* 23:4 (January 1950): 115–122; George Kennan, "Foreign Aid in the Framework of National Policy," *Proceedings of the Academy of Political Science* 23:4 (January 1950): 104–114.

58. Walter S. Salant, "The Domestic Effects of Capital Export under the Point Four Program," in "Papers and Proceedings of the Sixty-Second Annual Meeting of the American Economic Association," edited by James Washington Bell, *American Economic Review* 40:2 (May 1950): 495–500.

59. Ibid., 506; Evsey D. Domar, "Capital Expansion, Rate of Growth, and Employment," *Econometrica* 14:2 (April 1946): 139.

60. Allyn A. Young, "Increasing Returns and Economic Progress," *Economic Journal* 38:152 (December 1928): 539; Paul Rosenstein-Rodan, "Problems of Industrialization of Eastern and South-Eastern Europe," *Economic Journal* 53:210–211 (June–September 1943): 202–203.

61. Salant, "The Domestic Effects of Capital Export," 503.

62. H. W. Singer, "The Distribution of Gains between Investing and Borrowing Countries," in "Papers and Proceedings of the Sixty-Second Annual Meeting of the American Economic Association," edited by James Washington Bell, *American Economic Review* 40:2 (May 1950): 473–485.

63. Louis M. Hacker, "Capitalism and Economic Progress," in "Papers and Proceedings of the Sixty-Second Annual Meeting of the American Economic Association," edited by James Washington Bell, *American Economic Review* 40:2 (May 1950): 105–106.

64. Thomas Malthus, *An Essay on the Principle of Population* (Oxford: Oxford University Press, 2008), 124.

65. Department of State, memo, July 12, 1950, document 51, in Merrill, *Documentary History of the Truman Presidency*, vol. 27, 422–423.

66. *Hearings before the Committee on Foreign Relations on An Act for International Development*, United States Senate, 81st Congress, March and April 1950 (Washington, D.C.: U.S. Government Printing Office, 1950), 1–16.

67. Department of State, memo, July 12, 1950, document 51, in Merrill, *Documentary History of the Truman Presidency*, vol. 27, 425. For a detailed history of the legislative debate, see: *FRUS*, 1949, vol. 1 (Washington, D.C.: U.S. Government Printing Office, 1976), 757–788; and Shenin, *The United States and the Third World*, 23–73.

68. Public Law 535, 81st Congress, 2nd Session, in Daniels, *The Point Four Program*, 17.

69. Hume, *Essays, Moral, Political, and Literary*, 111–123.

70. J. K. Galbraith, "How to Make 'Point 4' Work," *Commentary* 10 (September 1950): 229–233, in Daniels, *The Point Four Program*, 47.

71. David Lloyd to Truman, memo, November 14, 1950, document 56, in Merrill, *Documentary History of the Truman Presidency*, vol. 27, 432; Truman, *Memoirs*, vol. 2, 233–234; Haldore Hanson, "United States Organization for Point Four," *Annals of the American Academy of Political and Social Science* 268 (March 1950): 36–39.

72. Advisory Committee on Technical Assistance, "Point Four Program in Relation to Dependent Areas," July 27, 1949, 10, SRF: The Point Four Program; Truman Library.

73. David Lloyd to Walter Salant, June 22, 1949, Point IV file; Salant papers; Truman Library.
74. Truman, Message to Congress, June 24, 1949, document 19, in Merrill, *Documentary History of the Truman Presidency*, vol. 27, 108–109; Walter Salant, The United States Economic Interest in Point IV, July 28, 1949, document 33, in ibid., 186–190; State Department, "Point Four," January 1950, Document 42, in ibid., 240–257.
75. Eugene Staley, *World Economy in Transition* (Port Washington, NY: Kennikat Press, 1971), 283. For more on Staley, see Ekbladh, *The Great American Mission*, 63–76, 111–113.
76. Ibid., 285–286.
77. Ibid., 322–326.
78. George McGhee to Acheson, memo, June 7, 1950, in *FRUS*, 1950, vol. 5 (Washington, D.C.: U.S. Government Printing Office, 1978), 169–170.
79. Not all foreign impressions of Point Four were positive. Jon Alterman notes that leftist Egyptian writer Ahmed Baha'al-Din published a scathing critique of the program in his book, *The New American Colonialism, or the Point Four Program*, right before it was implemented in Egypt. The program, al-Din wisely noted, was largely self-serving, arguing, "there is nothing new under the sun, except for honeyed words and tempting propaganda connected with this new colonialism." His view was not, however, the norm (Jon B. Alterman, *Egypt and American Foreign Assistance, 1952–1956* [New York: Palgrave Macmillan, 2002], 12–13).
80. Margaret Truman, *Harry S. Truman*, 438.
81. Memorandum of conversation between Stuart D. Nelson and Samuel P. Hays, undated, in *FRUS*, 1950, vol. 5, 279.
82. Ato Akilou Abte Wold, Aide-Mémoire of the Audience Held on March 15th, 1950 at the Imperial Palace, Addis Ababa, March 15, 1950, in *FRUS*, 1950, vol. 5, 1693–1695.
83. "United Nations: Charter of the United Nations," *American Journal of International Law* 39:3 (July 1945): 190.
84. Memorandum for William J. Hopkins, Letter addressed by the President to King Ibn Saud on May 23, 1949, February 23, 1950, WHCF-CF; State Department Correspondence, 1950; Truman papers; Truman Library; Summary of conversation between Assistant Secretary of State George C. McGhee and His Majesty King Ibn Saud of Saudi Arabia, April 10, 1950, WHCF-CF; State Department correspondence, 1950; Truman Papers; Truman Library.
85. Draft of First Annual Report on the Act for International Development, January 29, 1952, 4, SRF: The Point Four Program; Truman Library.
86. The American Embassy, "Point Four in Iran," March 15, 1952; Near Eastern and African subject files 1951–1953; Technical Cooperation Administration; General records of the Agency for International Development and Predecessor Agencies, 1948–1961; National Archives at College Park.

87. The exception was Syria, which did not sign an official Point Four agreement, but received Point Four aid throughout 1951 via the Near East Foundation (Clark to Department of State, May 28, 1951, in *FRUS*, 1951, vol. 5, 1076–1078).
88. "Point Four General Agreement for Technical Cooperation between the United States of America and Saudi Arabia," January 17, 1951; Near Eastern and African subject files 1951–1953; Technical Cooperation Administration; General records of the Agency for International Development and Predecessor Agencies, 1948–1961; National Archives at College Park; "Jordan: FY 1952 Program, Technical Cooperation and Economic Assistance," undated; Near Eastern and African subject files 1951–1953; Technical Cooperation Administration; General records of the Agency for International Development and Predecessor Agencies, 1948–1961; National Archives at College Park; "U.S.-Iraq Technical Cooperation Basic Agreements," undated; Near Eastern and African subject files 1951–1953; Technical Cooperation Administration; General records of the Agency for International Development and Predecessor Agencies, 1948–1961; National Archives at College Park; "Promulgation of the General Agreement between Egypt and the United States of America on Technical Cooperation in Accordance with the Program of Point IV, Signed in Cairo on May 5, 1951," January 15, 1953, Point IV Agreements; Mission to Egypt subject files; General records of the Agency for International Development and Predecessor Agencies, 1948–1961, record group 469; National Archives at College Park.
89. "Survey Shows How Point Four Program Tackles Basic Problems in Under-developed East," *New York Times*, January 12, 1953, 10–11; The United States Department of State, *The Point Four Program: Progress Report, no. 6*, Publication 4203, Economic Cooperation Series 26 (May 1951), in Daniels, 95.
90. U.S.A. Operations Mission to Ethiopia, "Point Four Agreements between the Imperial Ethiopian Government and the Government of the United States," August 31, 1953, Publications 1952–1953; Mission to Ethiopia subject files, 1951–1954; General records of the Agency for International Development and Predecessor Agencies, 1948–1961, record group 469; National Archives at College Park.
91. "Promulgation of the General Agreement between Egypt and the United States of America on Technical Cooperation in accordance with the program of Point IV, signed in Cairo on May 5, 1951," January 15, 1953, Point IV Agreements; Mission to Egypt subject files; General records of the Agency for International Development and Predecessor Agencies, 1948–1961, record group 469; National Archives at College Park.
92. See all of the previously cited Point Four general agreements from the general records of the Agency for International Development and Predecessor Agencies, 1948–1961, record group 469; National Archives at College Park.
93. "U.S.-Iraq Technical Cooperation Basic Agreements," undated; Near Eastern and African subject files 1951–1953; Technical Cooperation Administration; General records of the Agency for International Development and Predecessor Agencies, 1948–1961; National Archives at College Park.

94. The American Embassy, "Point Four in Iran," March 15, 1952; Near Eastern and African subject files 1951–1953; Technical Cooperation Administration; General records of the Agency for International Development and Predecessor Agencies, 1948–1961; National Archives at College Park.
95. The breakdown of Point Four funds in 1952 went as follows: Egypt—$103,000; Iran—$1,460,000; Iraq—$23,400; Israel—$96,300; Jordan—$132,700; Lebanon—$113,700; Libya—$157,400; Saudi Arabia—$97,300; Syria—$88,100; Ethiopia—$1,000,000 (Harry N. Howard, *The Development of United States Policy in the Near East, 1945–1951,* Department of State Publication 4446 [Washington, D.C.: U.S. Government Printing Office, 1952], 816). It is also important to note that although Israel and Saudi Arabia did not receive huge amounts of Point Four aid in 1951, the two countries had received $135 million and $44 million, respectively, from the Import-Export Bank over the previous two years (Ibid., 815).
96. Odd Arne Westad, *The Global Cold War: Third World Interventions and the Making of Our Time* (New York: Cambridge University Press, 2007), 8–38.
97. Acheson quoted in Walter LaFeber, *The American Age: U.S. Foreign Policy at Home and Abroad,* 2nd ed., vol. 2 (New York: W. W. Norton, 1994), 511–512.
98. Walter Salant to Charles Murphy, Memo, December 20, 1950, document 62, in Merrill, *Documentary History of the Truman Presidency*, vol. 27, 444–446.
99. Truman, State of the Union address, January 8, 1951, document 63, in Merrill, *Documentary History of the Truman Presidency*, vol. 27, 456.
100. Evsey D. Domar, Naum Jasny, Edward Ames, and Harry Schwartz, "Discussion," *American Economic Review* 41:2 (May 1951): 494.
101. Leon Keyserling to Truman, November 2, 1951, Correspondence with Truman 1947–1972; Keyserling papers; Truman Library.
102. Gordon Gray, *Report to the President on Foreign Economic Policy*, November 10, 1950, in Daniels, *The Point Four Program,* 76; Walter Salant, "Proposed Recommendations for Gray Report," August 4, 1950, International Relations 1950, Salant papers, Truman Library; Truman to Gray, March 31, 1950, WHCF:OF 426; Truman papers; Truman Library.
103. Shenin, *The United States and the Third World,* 84.
104. Truman, Statement, October 10, 1951, document 85, in Merrill, *Documentary History of the Truman Presidency,* vol. 27, 656.
105. Public Law 165, 82nd Congress, 1st Session.
106. Public Law 400, 82nd Congress, 2nd Session.
107. State Department, memo, November 24, 1951, document 89, in Merrill, *Documentary History of the Truman Presidency,* vol. 27, 686.
108. Ibid.
109. State Department, memo, in Merrill, *Documentary History of the Truman Presidency,* vol. 27, 692.
110. James E. Webb to Avery Johnston, August 21, 1951, document 83, in Merrill, *Documentary History of the Truman Presidency,* vol. 27, 636.

246 • Notes to Pages 116–123

111. The Secretary of State to the Consulate General at Tripoli, June 15, 1951, in *FRUS*, 1951, vol. 5,: 1330–1331; Steering Group on Preparations for Talks between the President and Prime Minister Churchill, Negotiating Paper, December 31, 1951, Churchill-Truman Meeting, PSF-GF, 1945–1953; Truman papers; Truman Library.
112. Donald Dawson to Joseph Short, November 13, 1951, document 88, in Merrill, *Documentary History of the Truman Presidency*, vol. 27, 671; newspaper clippings, Mission to the Near East, November 1951–April 1951, Papers of Edwin A. Locke, Jr.; Truman Library.
113. The Secretary of State to the Consulate General at Tripoli, June 15, 1951, in *FRUS*, 1951, vol. 5, 1331.
114. "International Trade Organization (Proposed)," *International Organization* 2:1 (February 1948): 134.
115. "Third Report to Congress on the Mutual Security Program," December 31, 1952, x; Near Eastern and African subject files 1951–1953; Technical Cooperation Administration; General Records of the Agency for International Development and Predecessor Agencies, 1948–1961; National Archives at College Park.
116. Ibid.
117. Ibid., xi–xii.
118. Howard, *The Development of United States Policy in the Near East*, 816.
119. The American Embassy, "Point Four in Iran," March 15, 1952; Near Eastern and African subject files 1951–1953; Technical Cooperation Administration; General records of the Agency for International Development and Predecessor Agencies, 1948–1961; National Archives at College Park.
120. "Survey Shows How Point Four Program Tackles Basic Problems in Under-Developed East," *New York Times,* January 12, 1953, 10.
121. Rosenstein-Rodan, "Problems of Industrialization of Eastern and South-Eastern Europe," 202–204; Rosenstein-Rodan, "Increasing Returns and Economic Progress," 539.
122. United Nations, *Measures for the Economic Development of Under-Developed Countries* (New York: United Nations, 1951), 3–4; Arturo Escobar, *Encountering Development* (Princeton, NJ: Princeton University Press, 1995), 22–24.
123. United Nations, *Measures for the Economic Development of Under-Developed Countries*, 13–15.
124. Ibid., 28–29.
125. Ibid., 49–60.
126. Ibid., 23–24, 84.
127. Ibid., 63–64.
128. Alfred Sauvy, "Trois Mondes, Une Planète," *L'Observateur* (August 14, 1952): 5.

CHAPTER 5

1. Henry Garland Bennett, "Point Four: The Maturing of a Policy," *Annals of the American Academy of Political and Social Science* 278 (November 1951): 58–61.

2. Department of State, Ethiopia Policy Statement, March 1, 1951, in *FRUS*, 1951, vol. 5 (Washington, D.C.: U.S. Government Printing Office, 1982), 1239–1245.
3. Ibid., 1242–1248.
4. Ato Aklilou Abte Wold, Aide-Mémoire of the Audience Held on March 15th, 1950 at the Imperial Palace, Addis Ababa, March 15, 1950, in *FRUS*, 1950, vol. 5 (Washington, D.C.: U.S. Government Printing Office, 1978), 1693–1694.
5. Ibid., 1694–1696.
6. Perry A. Fellows, Imperial Ethiopian Government Proposed Point Four Program, December 21, 1950, 1–7, Information—USIS 1952; Mission to Ethiopia subject files, 1951–1954; General records of the Agency for International Development and Predecessor Agencies, 1948–1961, record group 469; National Archives at College Park. Hereafter listed as RG 469 250/80/31/01.
7. Ibid., 11.
8. Ibid., 12–40.
9. Ibid. 17–24; United Nations, *Measures for the Economic Development of Under-Developed Countries* (New York: United Nations, 1951), 13–15.
10. Department of State, Ethiopia Policy Statement, March 1, 1951, in *FRUS*, 1951, vol. 5, 1242.
11. The Technical Cooperation Program in Ethiopia, February 8, 1952, Program—1952; RG 469 250/80/31/01.
12. Marcus G. Gordon to Perry Fellows, December 21, 1954, Program Planning—1954; RG 469 250/80/31/01.
13. Information for Evaluation TCA Program at Country Level, undated, Program—1952; RG 469 250/80/31/01; Marcus G. Gordon to Perry Fellows, December 21, 1954, Program Planning—1954; RG 469 250/80/31/01.
14. Information for Evaluation TCA Program at Country Level, undated, Program—1952; RG 469 250/80/31/01.
15. The Technical Cooperation Program in Ethiopia, February 8, 1952, Program—1952; RG 469 250/80/31/01.
16. U.S. Operations Mission to Ethiopia, The Point Four Program in Ethiopia, September 1954, Reports; RG 469 250/80/31/01; Oklahoma State University, "Operational Plan: Contract for Technical Assistance to Ethiopia," Contract no. 14554; collection #7005, box 49/folders 2–5; Special Collections; Oklahoma State University Library.
17. The Technical Cooperation Program in Ethiopia, February 8, 1952, Program—1952; RG 469 250/80/31/01.
18. U.S. Operations Mission to Ethiopia, The Point Four Program in Ethiopia, September 1954, Reports; RG 469 250/80/31/01.
19. Ibid.
20. "Point Four Promotes Better Life in 35 Nations, Survey Finds," *New York Times*, January 12, 1953, 1.

21. Eisenhower quoted in Sergei Y. Shenin, *The United States and the Third World* (Huntington, NY: Nova Science Publishers, 2000), 106.
22. Eric Johnston, "Memorandum for the President," May 13, 1953; OF 116-B-1, box 574; Central File; Official Files; Eisenhower Presidential Library.
23. D. A. Fitzgerald, *Foreign Assistance Programs*, Yearbook Separate No. 3321, reprinted from the *1964 Yearbook of Agriculture*; Miscellaneous (1), box 42; Papers of D. A. Fitzgerald; Eisenhower Presidential Library; Edward L. Schapsmeier and Frederick H. Schapsmeier, "Eisenhower and Agricultural Reform: Ike's Farm Policy Legacy Appraised," *American Journal of Economics and Sociology* 51:2 (April 1992): 147–159; James M. Hagen and Vernon W. Ruttan, "Development Policy under Eisenhower and Kennedy," *Journal of Developing Areas* 23:1 (October 1988): 1–30. For a critical analysis of PL-480, see, Richard Vengroff, "Food and Dependency: P.L. 480 Aid to Black Africa," *Journal of Modern African Studies* 20:1 (March 1982): 27–43. For more on the origins of PL-480, see Kristin L. Ahlberg, *Transplanting the Great Society: Lyndon Johnson and Food for Peace* (Columbia: University of Missouri Press, 2008), 11–41.
24. TCA Country Program for FY 1954: Ethiopia, undated, Program—1952; RG 469 250/80/31/01.
25. Marcus Gordon, Summary of Point 4 Operations in Ethiopia for Mr. Black, March 16, 1953, Administration—1953; RG 469 250/80/31/01.
26. Investment Climate, April 20, 1954, Industry-Investment—1954; RG 469 250/80/31/01.
27. P. N. Rosenstein-Rodan, "Problems of Industrialization of Eastern and South-Eastern Europe," *Economic Journal* 53:210–211 (June–September 1943): 203.
28. Marcus G. Gordon to Perry Fellows, December 21, 1954, Program Planning—1954; RG 469 250/80/31/01.
29. Ibid.
30. U.S. Operations Mission to Ethiopia, The Point Four Program in Ethiopia, September 1954, Reports; RG 469 250/80/31/01.
31. "Ethiopian Emperor Pays Visit to A&M," Reprinted from *Oklahoma A&M College Magazine*, July 1954, Emperor's Visit—1954; RG 469 250/80/31/01.
32. "Text of Haile Selassie's Address to U.S. Congress," *New York Times*, May 29, 1954, 14. For more on the emperor's visit, see Theodore M. Vestal, *The Lion of Judah in the New World* (Santa Barbara: Praeger, 2011), 48–94.
33. Letter from Counselor of the Embassy in Ethiopia (Taylor) to the Director of the Office of African Affairs, December 9, 1955, in *FRUS*, 1955–1957, vol. 18 (Washington, D.C.: U.S. Government Printing Office, 1989), 326.
34. Harold G. Marcus, *The Politics of Empire* (Lawrenceville, NJ: Red Sea Press, 1995), 92.
35. Memorandum to the President from His Imperial Majesty, May 28, 1954; Ethiopia (4); Whitman file; Dwight D. Eisenhower Papers as President; Eisenhower Presidential Library.

36. State Department, "Specific Current Questions," undated, in *FRUS*, 1947, vol. 5, 544.
37. Utilization of Defense Installations Within Empire of Ethiopia, Agreement between the United States of America and Ethiopia, signed May 22, 1953, reproduced July 31, 1961, U.S.-Ethiopia, 1955–1959; record group 59; 250/63/18/3–4; National Archives at College Park; Peter J. Schraeder, *United States Foreign Policy Toward Africa: Incrementalism, Crisis and Change* (Cambridge: Cambridge University Press, 1994), 118–119; John H. Spencer, *Ethiopia, The Horn of Africa, and U.S. Policy* (Cambridge, MA: Institute for Foreign Policy Analysis, 1977), 22–23; Edmund Keller, *Revolutionary Ethiopia* (Bloomington: Indiana University Press, 1988), 80.
38. "Text of Haile Selassie's Address to U.S. Congress," *New York Times*, May 29, 1961, 14.
39. Haggai Erlich, *Ethiopia and the Middle East* (Boulder: Lynne Rienner, 1994), 130–132.
40. Christopher Clapham, "Controlling Space in Ethiopia," in *Remapping Ethiopia*, ed. Wendy James, Donald L. Donham, Eisei Kurimoto, and Alessandro Triulzi (Oxford: James Currey, 2002), 12–13.
41. Gordon Waterfield, "The Horn of Africa," *African Affairs* 57:226 (January 1958): 11–19; Gordon Waterfield, "Trouble in the Horn of Africa?: The British Somali Case," *International Affairs* 32:1 (January 1956): 52–60; Bahru Zewde, *A History of Modern Ethiopia, 1855–1991*, 2nd ed. (Oxford: James Currey, 2001; Athens: Ohio University Press, 2001; Addis Ababa: Addis Ababa University Press, 2001), 180–182.
42. Thomas Borstelman, *Apartheid's Reluctant Uncle* (New York: Oxford University Press, 1993), 196.
43. Imperial Ethiopian Government, *Five Year Development Plan, 1957–1961* (Addis Ababa: Berhanena Selam Printing Press, n.d.), 2.
44. *Selected Speeches of His Imperial Majesty Haile Selassie First* (Addis Ababa: Imperial Ethiopian Ministry of Education, 1967): 396–408.
45. Bahru Zewde, *A History of Modern Ethiopia*, 206–207.
46. National Intelligence Estimate: The Outlook for US Interests in the Middle East, June 21, 1955, in *FRUS*, 1955–1957, vol. 12 (Washington, D.C.: U.S. Government Printing Office, 1991), 77–87; National Intelligence Estimate: The Outlook for US Interests in the Middle East, November 8, 1955, in *FRUS*, 1955–1957, vol. 12, 182–197; Ray Takeyh, *The Origins of the Eisenhower Doctrine* (New York: St. Martin's, 2000): 26–47; William L. Cleveland, *A History of the Modern Middle East* (Boulder: Westview, 2000), 300–301; Peter L. Hahn, *The United States, Great Britain, & Egypt, 1945–1956* (Chapel Hill: University of North Carolina Press, 1991), 181–184.
47. Cary Fraser, "Race and Realpolitik," in *Window on Freedom*, ed. Brenda Gayle Plummer (Chapel Hill: University of North Carolina Press, 2003), 118; Jason

Parker, "Cold War II: The Eisenhower Administration, the Bandung Conference, and the Reperiodization of the Postwar Era," *Diplomatic History* 30:5 (November 2006): 867–892.

48. National Intelligence Estimate: The Outlook for US Interests in the Middle East, November 8, 1955, in *FRUS*, 1955–1957, vol. 12, 185, 193.

49. Agriculture, Land & Water Resources; Mission to Egypt subject files; General records of the Agency for International Development and Predecessor Agencies, 1948–1961, record group 469; National Archives at College Park.

50. Herbert Hoover Jr. to Eisenhower, Attachment: An Outline of Short-Term and Long-Term United States Plans in the Middle East, November 21, 1956, in *FRUS*, 1955–1957, vol. 12, 347.

51. Haggai Erlich, *Ethiopia and the Middle East* (Boulder: Lynne Rienner, 1994), 133–138.

52. S. Everett Gleason, Memorandum of Discussion at the 304th Meeting of the National Security Council, November 15, 1956, in *FRUS*, 1955–1957, vol. 18, 332.

53. National Security Council Report, "U.S. Policy Towards Ethiopia," November 19, 1956, in *FRUS*, 1955–1957, vol. 18, 335.

54. Operations Coordinating Board, Analysis of Internal Security Situation, December 12, 1956; OCB 091, Ethiopia (File #1) (4) October 1956–March 1957; OCB Central File Series; Staff papers, 1948–1961; National Security Council; White House Office; Eisenhower Presidential Library.

55. Telegram from the Department of State to the Embassy in Ethiopia, April 11, 1957, in *FRUS*, 1955–1957, vol. 18, 350; International Cooperation Administration, Evaluation of Ethiopia Program, August 1, 1957; Records Africa, Near East, and South Asia Branch, subfile 1956–72, box 13; Records of the Operations Division; RG 286, 250/66/05/07; National Archives at College Park.

56. Operations Coordinating Board, Progress Report on Ethiopia, June 4, 1957; OCB 091, Ethiopia (File #1) (4) October 1956–March 1957; OCB Central File Series; Staff papers, 1948–1961; National Security Council; White House Office; Eisenhower Presidential Library.

57. "Text of the Address by Eisenhower to Congress Outlining New Program for Mideast," *New York Times,* January 6, 1957, 34; "Text of the Resolution Voted by House," *New York Times,* January 31, 1957, 8.

58. NSC-5719/1-US Policy Towards Africa (1), August 23, 1957; Policy Paper subseries, NSC series; Office for the Special Assistant for National Security Affairs: Records 1952–1961; White House Office; Eisenhower Presidential Library.

59. Ambassador Richards's Mission to the Middle East, Ethiopia, February 5, 1957; box 4/F14; record group 59; 250/63/18/3–4.

60. Paul Gordon Lauren, "The International Perspective," in Plummer, *Window on Freedom*, 32.

61. George B. N. Ayittey, *Africa Unchained* (New York: Palgrave Macmillan, 2005): 59–60.

62. Program of African Studies, Northwestern University, *Africa: A Study Prepared at the Request of the Committee on Foreign Relations, United States Senate* (Washington, D.C.: U.S. Government Printing Office, 1959), 9–12.
63. Richard Nixon, Report to the President on the Vice President's Visit to Africa, February 28–March 21, 1957 (April 5, 1957); NSC 5719/1 U.S. Policy Towards Africa (2); Policy Paper subseries, NSC series; Office for the Special Assistant for National Security Affairs: Records 1952–1961; White House Office; Eisenhower Presidential Library.
64. Richard Nixon to Secretary of Defense Wilson, March 25, 1957, in *FRUS*, 1955–1957, vol. 18, 349.
65. Dwight D. Eisenhower, "Message from the President of the United States Relative to Our Mutual Security Program," in *Mutual Security Act of 1958, Hearings before the Committee on Foreign Relations, United States Senate,* 85th Congress, 2nd Session (Washington, D.C.: U.S. Government Printing Office, 1958), 1–6.
66. Statement of Stuart H. Van Dyke, in ibid., 389–398.
67. Ibid.
68. Ibid., 403–407.
69. Editorial Note, in *FRUS*, 1958–1960, vol. 14, ed. Harriet Dashiell Schwar and Stanley Shaloff (Washington, D.C.: U.S. Government Printing Office, 1992), 185; Operations Coordinating Board, July 9, 1959; Records of the Africa, Near East and South Asian Branch, Subject File 1956–72 (box 1); Records of the Operations Division; record group 286, 250/66/05/07; National Archives at College Park.
70. Ethiopia, October 16, 1961; box 6/F2; record group 59, 250/63/18/3–4; National Archives at College Park; Marcus, *The Politics of Empire*, 111–112; Preliminary Notes of a Meeting of the Operations Coordinating Board, January 20, 1960, in *FRUS*, 1958–1960, vol. 14, 186–187; Memorandum of a Conversation with President Eisenhower, September 27, 1960, in ibid., 195–196.
71. Imperial Ethiopian Government, *Five Year Development Plan, 1957–1961,* 28–31.
72. Ibid., 28.
73. Ibid., 34, 63.
74. *Selected Speeches of His Imperial Majesty Haile Selassie First,* 441–458.
75. Ibid.
76. John Markakis, *Ethiopia: Anatomy of a Traditional Polity* (Addis Ababa: Shama Books, 2006), 391.
77. René Lefort, *Ethiopia: A Heretical Revolution?* (London: Zed Press, 1983), 13–14.
78. Messay Kebede, *Survival and Modernization, Ethiopia's Enigmatic Present* (Lawrenceville, NJ: Red Sea Press, 1999), 301–302.
79. Ibid., 304–306; Keller, *Revolutionary Ethiopia,* 98–101, 123–128; Bahru Zewde, *A History of Modern Ethiopia,* 191–201.
80. *Selected Speeches of His Imperial Majesty Haile Selassie First,* 450.
81. Jahangir Amuzegar, "Point Four: Performance and Prospect," *Political Science Quarterly* 73:4 (December 1958): 530–531.

82. Ibid., 535.
83. Ibid., 540–545.
84. Thomas Soapes, Interview with Dennis Fitzgerald, May 26, 1976, 20–21; Eisenhower Presidential Library.
85. Ibid., 8, 11.
86. Remarks by D. A. Fitzgerald, Helping Other Countries Improve Their Agriculture, November 18, 1959; Speeches 1954–61 (1); Papers of Dennis A. Fitzgerald; Eisenhower Presidential Library.
87. Paul Samuelson, *Economics: An Introductory Analysis* (New York: McGraw-Hill, 1948); Sylvia Nassar, "A Hard Act to Follow," *New York Times,* March 14, 1995, D1; Mark Skousen, "The Perseverance of Paul Samuelson's Economics," *Journal of Economic Perspectives* 11:2 (Spring 1997): 137–152; Paul Sameulson et al., "Samuelson's 'Economics' at Fifty," *Journal of Economic Education* 30:4 (Autumn 1999): 352–363.
88. Robert Solow, "A Contribution to the Theory of Economic Growth," *Quarterly Journal of Economics* 70:1 (February 1956): 65–94; Ryuzo Sato, "The Harrod-Domar Model vs. the Neo-Classical Growth Model," *Economic Journal* 74:294 (June 1964): 380–387; W. W. Rostow, *Theorists of Economic Growth from David Hume to the Present* (New York: Oxford University Press, 1990), 329–351. See also: James Tobin, "A Dynamic Aggregative Model," *Journal of Political Economy* 63:2 (April 1955): 103–115.
89. Jacob Viner, "The Economics of Development," in *The Economics of Underdevelopment*, A. N. Agarwala and S. P. Singh, ed. (London: Oxford University Press, 1958), 9–31.
90. W. Arthur Lewis, "Economic Development with Unlimited Supplies of Labour," in ibid., 400–449.
91. Paul Baran, "On the Political Economy of Backwardness," in ibid., 91.
92. Simon Kuznets, "Underdeveloped Countries and the Pre-Industrial Phase in the Advanced Countries," in ibid., 135–153; Simon Kuznets, "Quantitative Aspects of the Economic Growth of Nations: I. Levels and Variability of Rates of Growth," *Economic Development and Cultural Change* 5:1 (October 1956): 1–94.
93. Bert F. Hoselitz, "Patterns of Economic Growth," *Canadian Journal of Economics and Political Science* 21:4 (November 1955): 416–417.
94. W. W. Rostow, *The Process of Economic Growth* (New York: W. W. Norton, 1952), 1–4.
95. Ibid., 4–10.
96. W. W. Rostow, "The Take-Off Into Sustained Growth," *Economic Journal* 66:261 (March 1956): 25–48.
97. W. W. Rostow, *The Stages of Economic Growth*, 3rd ed. (Cambridge: Cambridge University Press, 1990): 4, 18–19.
98. Remarks of Senator John F. Kennedy at the Conference on Vietnam Luncheon in the Hotel Willard, Washington, D.C., June 1, 1956, http://www.jfklibrary.org.

99. Kimber Charles Pierce, *Rostow, Kennedy, and the Rhetoric of Foreign Aid* (East Lansing: Michigan State University Press, 2001).
100. Statement of U.S. Policy on the Horn of Africa, December 30, 1960, in *FRUS, 1958–1960*, vol. 14, 199–209.
101. Marcus, *The Politics of Empire*, 116–169; Bahru Zewde, *A History of Modern Ethiopia*, 211–215.

CHAPTER 6

1. Ryszard Kapuściński, *The Emperor*, trans. William R. Brand and Katarzyna Mroczkowska-Brand (New York: Vintage, 1989), 85–86.
2. Ibid., 86–87.
3. Ibid., 87–88.
4. Center for International Studies, Massachusetts Institute of Technology, *Economic, Social, and Political Change in the Underdeveloped Countries and its Implications for United States Policy*, Report for the Senate Committee on Foreign Relations (March 30, 1960), (Washington, D.C.: U.S. Government Printing Office, 1960), 1–3.
5. Ibid., 4.
6. Remarks of Senator John F. Kennedy at the Conference on Vietnam Luncheon in the Hotel Willard, Washington, D.C., June 1, 1956, http://www.jfklibrary.org.
7. "Text of Kennedy's Inaugural Outlining Policies on World Peace and Freedom," *New York Times*, January 21, 1961, 8.
8. The Task Force on Foreign Economic Policy, "Report to the Honorable John F. Kennedy," December 31, 1960; Task Force Report 12/31/60; Foreign Economic Policy, box 297; National Security Files; Kennedy Presidential Library.
9. "Transcript of the President's First Report to Congress on the State of the Union," *New York Times*, January 31, 1961, 16.
10. John Kenneth Galbraith, "A Positive Approach to Economic Aid," February 1, 1961; Foreign Aid 12/60-2/61; box 297; National Security files; Kennedy Presidential Library.
11. W. W. Rostow to Kennedy, February 27, 1961; Foreign Aid 2/24/61–2/28/61; Staff Memoranda, Walt Rostow; box 324; National Security files; Kennedy Presidential Library.
12. Ibid.
13. W.W. Rostow—Memo, Some Points Covered at the Foreign Aid Meeting, February 14, 1961; Foreign Aid 2/13/61–2/20/61; Staff Memoranda—Walt Rostow, box 324; National Security files; Kennedy Presidential Library.
14. Walt Rostow to Ted Sorensen, March 16, 1961; Foreign Aid 1/16/61 to 3/18/61; Staff Memoranda—Walt Rostow, box 325; National Security files; Kennedy Presidential Library. For more on Rostow's role in the Kennedy administration, see

David Milne, *America's Rasputin: Walt Rostow and the Vietnam War* (New York: Hill and Wang, 2008).
15. "Text of Kennedy's Message to Congress Proposing a New Foreign Aid Program," *New York Times*, March 23, 1961, 14.
16. Ibid.
17. Ibid.
18. "Foreign Aid: Kennedy's New Approach," *New York Times*, March 26, 1961, E6.
19. *Hearings on S. 1983 before the Committee on Foreign Affairs, United States Senate, (May–June 1961)*, 87th Congress, 1st Session (Washington, D.C.: U.S. Government Printing Office, 1961), 1–25.
20. Ibid., 25–26.
21. H.R. 7372, a Bill to Promote the Foreign Policy, Security, and General Welfare of the U.S. by Assisting Peoples of the World in their Efforts Toward Economic and Social Development and Internal and External Security, and for other Purposes, House of Representatives, 87th Congress (June 8, 1961).
22. Memorandum from the Under Secretary of State to the Administrator of the Agency for International Development, October 7, 1961, in *FRUS, 1961–1963*, vol. 9, ed. David S. Patterson, Evan Duncan, and Carolyn B. Yee (Washington, D.C.: U.S. Government Printing Office, 1997), 265.
23. Policy Planning Council, The New Aid Criteria and U.S. Foreign Economic Programs, October 26, 1961, in *FRUS, 1961–1963*, vol. 9, 272–273.
24. Report of the President's Task Force on Foreign Economic Policy, 1964, in *FRUS, 1964–1968*, vol. 9, 42–61.
25. Dean Rusk to George McGhee, November 1, 1961, in *FRUS, 1961–1963*, vol. 9, 274.
26. Ibid., 275.
27. Summary Minutes of Meeting of the Interdepartmental Committee of Under Secretaries on Foreign Economic Policy, November 1, 1961, in *FRUS, 1961–1963*, vol. 9, 276.
28. Nils Gilman, *Mandarins of the Future: Modernization Theory in Cold War America* (Baltimore: Johns Hopkins University Press, 2003), 72–112.
29. James Smoot Coleman, *Nationalism and Development in Africa: Selected Essays*, ed. Richard L. Sklar (Berkeley: University of California Press, 1994): 162.
30. Michael E. Latham, *Modernization as Ideology* (Chapel Hill: University of North Carolina Press, 2000), 4.
31. Colin Leys, *The Rise and Fall of Development Theory* (Bloomington: Indiana University Press, 1996), 10–11.
32. Latham, *Modernization as Ideology*, 46–59; Benjamin M. Friedman, *The Moral Consequences of Economic Growth* (New York: Alfred A. Knopf, 2005), 180–197; James C. Scott, *Seeing Like a State* (New Haven, CT: Yale University Press, 1998), 90–102.
33. Remarks of Senator John F. Kennedy at the Conference on Vietnam Luncheon in the Hotel Willard, Washington, D.C., June 1, 1956, http://www.jfklibrary.org.

34. Allan Loren to Fowler Hamilton, October 24, 1961, U.S.-Ethiopia, 1955–1959; RG 59 250/63/18/3–4; National Archives at College Park.
35. Ibid.
36. Ibid.
37. William Witman to Governor Williams, November 21, 1961; U.S.-Ethiopia, 1955–1959; RG 59 250/63/18/3–4; National Archives at College Park.
38. Imperial Ethiopian Government, *Second Five Year Development Plan, 1963–1967* (Addis Ababa: Berhanenna Selam Press, 1962), 33.
39. Ibid., 36–37, 77.
40. Ibid., 295.
41. Ibid., 5.
42. State Department Position Paper: Emperor Haile Selassie Visit to Washington (September 24, 1963); Briefing Book; Ethiopia—Haile Selassie's Visit, box 69a; National Security files; Kennedy Presidential Library; IEG, Memorandum, October 1, 1963; Memorandum and related documents, 9/63–10/63; Selassie Visit Briefing; William Brubeck—Ethiopia, box 384; National Security files; Kennedy Presidential Library.
43. Telegram from Edward M. Korry to Dean Rusk, July 25, 1963; Ethiopia General 6/63–7/63, box 69; National Security files; Kennedy Presidential Library; "Khrushchev Hails Africans' Decisions," USSR International Affairs, July 25, 1963; Ethiopia General 6/63–7/63, box 69; National Security files; Kennedy Presidential Library.
44. "Kennedy Greets Selassie as the Man History Will Recall," *New York Times*, October 2, 1963, 1, 8; Sterling Seagrave, "President Greets Ethiopian Chief," *Washington Post*, October 2, 1963, A1.
45. State Department Position Paper: Emperor Haile Selassie Visit to Washington (September 24, 1963); Briefing Book; Ethiopia—Haile Selassie's Visit, box 69a; National Security files; Kennedy Presidential Library.
46. Exchange of Toasts between His Imperial Majesty Haile Selassie I and President John F. Kennedy at a Luncheon at the Woodmont Country Club, October 2, 1963; box 47; Presidential Office files; Kennedy Presidential Library.
47. The Greenbook, http://qesdb.usaid.gov/gbk/index.html.
48. "$3.6 Billion in Aid is Voted by House," *New York Times*, December 10, 1963, 1; "Conferees Agree on $3 Billion Aid," *New York Times*, December 21, 1963, 1; "Crisis on Aid," *New York Times*, December 22, 1963, E1; "Goldwater Says Johnson Indulged in Arm-Twisting," *New York Times*, December 27, 1963, 1.
49. National Policy Paper, December 19, 1963, in *FRUS*, 1961–1963, vol. 21 (Washington, D.C.: U.S. Government Printing Office, 1995), 486–487.
50. Airgram from the US Embassy in Addis Ababa to the Department of State, April 22, 1964; Vol. 1, 11/63–2/65; Country File Ethiopia, box 88; National Security files; Johnson Presidential Library.
51. Record of Telephone Conversation between President Johnson and the Under Secretary of State (Ball), in *FRUS*, 1964–1968, vol. 9, 21–22.

52. Memorandum for the President, January 31, 1966; Cabinet Committee on Foreign Aid 65–66 (1 of 2); Files of Edward K. Hamilton, box 4; National Security files; Johnson Presidential Library.
53. Ibid.
54. Committee on Foreign Affairs, "What is Wrong with Foreign Aid," November 1965; Cabinet Committee on Foreign Aid 65–66 (2 of 2); Files of Edward K. Hamilton, box 4; National Security files; Johnson Presidential Library.
55. Memorandum for the President, January 31, 1966; Cabinet Committee on Foreign Aid 65–66 (1 of 2); Files of Edward K. Hamilton, box 4; National Security files; Johnson Presidential Library.
56. Clifford Committee Report to the President, December 16, 1965; 1965 Task Force on Foreign Aid; Task Force reports, box 3; Johnson Presidential Library.
57. The Agency for International Development during the Administration of President Lyndon B. Johnson (November 1963–January 1969), vol. I; Administrative History—AID, box 1; Johnson Presidential Library.
58. Memorandum for the Joint Chiefs of Staff to Secretary of Defense McNamara, July 11, 1964, in *FRUS, 1964–1968*, v. 24, ed. Nina Davis Howland (Washington, D.C.: U.S. Government Printing Office, 1991), 513–514.
59. Memorandum for the President, December 17, 1966; "Korry Report on African Development Policy and Programs"; Files of Edward K. Hamilton, box 3; National Security Ffiles; Johnson Presidential Library.
60. Memorandum for the Files, March 25, 1965, in *FRUS, 1964–1968*, vol. 24, 524–526.
61. Memorandum from Korry to Harriman, May 26, 1965; Files of Edward K. Hamilton, box 2; National Security files; Johnson Presidential Library.
62. Memorandum from the President's Deputy Special Assistant for National Security Affairs (Komer) to the Assistant Secretary of State for African Affairs (Williams), February 8, 1966, and follow-up letters dated February 11 and February 18, in *FRUS, 1964–1968*, vol. 24, 533–536.
63. Memorandum from the President's Special Assistant (Rostow) to President Johnson, February 11, 1967, in *FRUS, 1964–1968*, vol. 24, 562–563.
64. Memorandum from the Department of State to the President, February 11, 1967; Files of Edward K. Hamilton, box 2; National Security files; Johnson Presidential Library.
65. The Greenbook, http://qesdb.usaid.gov/gbk/index.html.
66. Imperial Ethiopian Government, *Third Five Year Development Plan, 1968–1973* (Addis Ababa: Berhanena Salem Printing Press, 1968), 8–9.
67. Bahru Zewde, *A History of Modern Ethiopia, 1855–1991,* 2nd ed. (Oxford: James Currey, 2001; Athens: Ohio University Press, 2001; Addis Ababa: Addis Ababa University Press, 2001), 194, 200–201.
68. Imperial Ethiopian Government, *Third Five Year Development Plan, 1968–1973*, 190.
69. Letter from the Deputy Secretary of Defense (Nitze) to the Under Secretary of State (Katzenbach), September 6, 1968, and December 16 response, in *FRUS, 1964–1968*, vol. 24, 606–609.

70. Special Memorandum Prepared in the Central Intelligence Agency, March 31, 1966, in *FRUS*, 1964–1968, vol. 24, 537.
71. Samuel P. Huntington, *Political Order in Changing Societies* (New Haven, CT: Yale University Press, 2006), 177.
72. Ibid., 5–8.
73. Ibid. 41–42.
74. Ibid., 155, 191, 461.
75. Kapuściński, *The Emperor*, 88.
76. Memorandum of Conversation, July 8, 1969, document 275 in *FRUS*, 1969–1972, vol. E-5 (Washington, D.C.: U.S. Government Printing Office, 2005), http://history.state.gov/historicaldocuments/frus1969-76ve05p1/d275.
77. Memorandum from the President's Assistant for National Security Affairs (Kissinger) to President Nixon, July 6, 1969, document 273 in *FRUS*, 1969–1972, vol. E-5), http://history.state.gov/historicaldocuments/frus1969-76ve05p1/d273.
78. Peter J. Schraeder, *United States Foreign Policy Towards Africa: Incrementalism, Crisis and Change* (Cambridge: Cambridge University Press, 1994), 184–185.
79. Bahru Zewde, *A History of Modern Ethiopia*, 228–235; Edmond J. Keller, *Revolutionary Ethiopia* (Bloomington: Indiana University Press, 1988), 164–187; Harold G. Marcus, *A History of Ethiopia*, updated ed. (Berkeley: University of California Press, 2002), 181–191.
80. Bahru Zewde, *A History of Modern Ethiopia*, 236–243; Keller, *Revolutionary Ethiopia*, 164–187; Marcus, *A History of Ethiopia*, 192–201.
81. Alden Whitman, "Haile Selassie of Ethiopia dies at 83," *New York Times,* August 28, 1975, 1, 40.
82. Memorandum of Conversation, September 30, 1975, document 148 in *FRUS*, 1973–1976, vol. E-6 (Washington, D.C.: U.S. Government Printing Office, 2006), http://history.state.gov/historicaldocuments/frus1969-76ve06/d148.
83. William S. Gaud, "The Green Revolution: Accomplishments and Apprehensions," The Society for International Development, March 8, 1968, http://www.agbioworld.org/biotech-info/topics/borlaug/borlaug-green.html.
84. Norman Borlaug, "The Green Revolution, Peace and Humanity," December 11, 1970, http://nobelprize.org/nobel_prizes/peace/laureates/1970/borlaug-lecture.html; Roger Thurow and Scott Kilman, *Enough: Why the World's Poorest Starve in an Age of Plenty* (New York: Public Affairs, 2009), 3–15; Gregg Easterbrook, "Forgotten Benefactor of Humanity," *Atlantic* 279: 1 (January 1997): 72–85; Nick Cullather, *The Hungry World* (Cambridge, MA: Harvard University Press, 2010), 232–262.
85. Remarks of Senator John F. Kennedy at the Conference on Vietnam Luncheon in the Hotel Willard, Washington, D.C., June 1, 1956, http://www.jfklibrary.org/Historical+Resources/Archives/Reference+Desk/Speeches.
86. Truman, Address at the National Conference on International Economic and Social Development, April 8, 1952, document 104 in Dennis Merrill, ed., *Documentary History of the Truman Presidency*, vol. 27 (Frederick, MD: University Publications of America, 1999), 818.

87. Center for International Studies, Massachusetts Institute of Technology, *Economic, Social, and Political Change in the Underdeveloped Countries and its Implications for United States Policy*, Report for the Senate Committee on Foreign Relations (March 30, 1960) (Washington, D.C.: U.S. Government Printing Office, 1960), 1–3.
88. Huntington, *Political Order in Changing Societies*, 41.
89. Mesfin Bezuneh and Carl C. Mabbs-Zeno argue in contrast that Ethiopia did, in fact, have a Green Revolution in the 1970s ("The Contribution of the Green Revolution to Social Change in Ethiopia," *Northeast African Studies* 6:3 [1984]: 9–17).

CHAPTER 7

1. Michael Buerk, BBC broadcast, October 23, 1984, http://www.youtube.com/watch?v=mj2jf0US8zI.
2. "Saving the Children," *Newsweek*, November 5, 1984, 46.
3. Jamie Murphy, "Finally, Relief," *Time*, November 12, 1984, 66.
4. Amartya Sen, *Poverty and Famines* (Oxford: Clarendon Press, 1981), 1, 43.
5. Alex de Waal, *Famine Crimes* (Oxford: James Currey; Bloomington: Indiana University Press, 1997): 112.
6. Dawit Wolde Giorgis, *Red Tears* (Trenton: Red Sea Press, 1989); Jason W. Clay and Bonnie K. Holcomb, *Politics and the Ethiopian Famine, 1984–1985* (Cambridge, MA: Cultural Survival, 1986).
7. de Waal, *Famine Crimes*, 124–125; Steven L. Varnis, *Reluctant Aid or Aiding the Reluctant* (New Brunswick, NJ: Transaction, 1990), 52.
8. House Committee on Foreign Affairs, *Food Crisis in Africa: Hearings before the Subcommittee on Africa*, 98th Congress, 1st Session, November 1, 1983 (Washington, D.C.: U.S. Government Printing Office, 1985), 16.
9. Ibid., 61–62.
10. Ibid., 20.
11. Peter J. Schraeder, *United States Foreign Policy toward Africa: Incrementalism, Crisis and Change* (Cambridge: Cambridge University Press, 1994), 184–185; David A. Korn, *Ethiopia, the United States, and the Soviet Union* (Carbondale: Southern Illinois University Press, 1986), 21.
12. Korn, *Ethiopia, the United States, and the Soviet Union*, 110–112; Donna R. Jackson, *Jimmy Carter and the Horn of Africa* (Jefferson, NC: McFarland, 2007), 40; Bahru Zewde, *A Modern History of Ethiopia*, 2nd ed. (Oxford: James Currey, 2001), 243–248.
13. John Darnton, "Ethiopian Move Breaking Old Links with U.S.," *New York Times*, April 25, 1977, 3; David K. Shipler, "Ethiopian Chief Starts Soviet Visit," *New York Times*, May 5, 1977, A6; Korn, *Ethiopia, the United States, and the Soviet Union*, 27–29; Jackson, *Jimmy Carter and the Horn of Africa*, 45–47.

14. James Buxton, "Secession Wars Push Ethiopia to the Brink," *New York Times*, August 7, 1977, E5.
15. Schraeder, *United States Foreign Policy towards Africa*, 184–187.
16. Zbigniew Brzezinski, *Power and Principle: Memoirs of the National Security Adviser, 1977–1981* (London: Weidenfield & Nicolson, 1983), 189.
17. Dambisa Moyo, *Dead Aid* (New York: Farrar, Straus and Giroux, 2009), 17–19.
18. The World Bank, *Accelerated Development in Sub-Saharan Africa: An Agenda for Action* (Washington, D.C.: World Bank, 1981); Roger Thurow and Scott Kilman, *Enough: Why the World's Poorest Starve in an Age of Plenty* (New York: Public Affairs, 2009), 27.
19. Thorbecke, in Finn Tarp, ed., *Foreign Aid and Development* (London: Routledge, 2000), 37; Carol Lancaster, *Aid to Africa* (Chicago: University of Chicago Press, 1999), 46.
20. Peter Gill, *Famines and Foreigners: Ethiopia since Live Aid* (Oxford: Oxford University Press, 2010), 69–70.
21. Graham Hancock, *Lords of Poverty* (New York: Atlantic Monthly Press, 1989), introduction.
22. Peter Bauer, *Equality, the Third World and Economic Delusion* (Cambridge, MA: Harvard University Press, 1981), 144.
23. Hancock, *Lords of Poverty*, 74.
24. Ibid., 190. His emphasis.
25. Lancaster, *Aid to Africa*, 26–30.
26. Ha-Joon Chang, *Bad Samaritans* (New York: Bloomsbury Press, 2008); Douglas North, *The Economic Growth of the United States 1790–1860* (New York: W. W. Norton, 1966).
27. Gayle Smith, "Birth Pains of a New Ethiopia," *Nation*, July 1, 1991, 1–20; Clifford Kraus, "Ethiopians Rejoice as Rebels Close In," *New York Times*, May 24, 1991, A1.
28. Schraeder, *United States Foreign Policy towards Africa*, 184–185.
29. Gill, *Famines and Foreigners: Ethiopia since Live Aid*, 79–96.
30. Moyo, *Dead Aid*, 5.
31. Hernando de Soto, *The Mystery of Capital* (New York: Basic Books, 2000), 5.
32. Ibid., 52.
33. Ibid., 227.
34. Richard Ebeling, the Ludwig von Mises Professor of Economics at Hillsdale College, positively reviewed the book for The Future of Freedom Foundation ("Book Review of The Mystery of Growth," February 2001, The Future of Freedom Foundation; http://www.fff.org/freedom/0201f.asp). Robert Skidelsky, a professor of political economy at Warwick University in England, who has written a multivolume biography of John Maynard Keynes, reviewed the book less favorably for the *New York Times* ("The Wealth of [Some] Nations," *New York Times*, December 24, 2000; http://www.nytimes.com/books/00/12/24/reviews/001224.24skidelt.html). Such clear political divisions were evident in other reviews as well.

35. Matthew J. Rosenberg, "Review of Hernando de Soto's Mystery of Capital," Council on Foreign Relations (January 1, 2002); http://www.cfr.org/publication/4517/review_of_hernando_de_sotos_mystery_of_capital.html.
36. Hans Binswanger and Ernst Lutz, "Agricultural Trade Barriers, Trade Negotiations, and the Interests of Developing Countries," Paper presented at the International Association of Agricultural Economists Meeting in Berlin, August 2000; http://siteresources.worldbank.org/INTARD/825826-1111044795683/20424524/Agtradeanddevelopingcountries.pdf.
37. Moyo, *Dead Aid,* 118. The African Growth and Opportunity Act website reports that in 2008, "U.S. imports from the oil producing countries grew in every case with imports from Nigeria growing by 16.2 percent, from Angola by 51.2 percent, from the Republic of Congo by 65.2 percent, from Equatorial Guinea by 89.5 percent, from Chad by 55.4 percent, and from Gabon by 4.4 percent" (statistics from the 2009 International Trade Administration, http://www.agoa.gov/build/groups/public/@agoa_main/documents/webcontent/agoa_main_002890.pdf).
38. World Trade Organization Ministerial Meeting, Doha 2001, "Ministerial Declaration," November 14, 2001; http://www.wto.org/english/thewto_e/minist_e/min01_e/mindecl_e.htm.
39. *The National Security Strategy of the United States of America* (September 2002), 21; http://georgewbush-whitehouse.archives.gov/nsc/nss/2002/.
40. About MCC, http://www.mcc.gov/pages/about.
41. Daniel Imhoff, *Food Fight: The Citizen's Guide to a Food and Farm Bill* (Healdsburg, CA: Watershed Media, 2007), 59–64. For more on the history of American farm bills, see Nadine Lehrer, *U.S. Farm Bills and Policy Reforms: Ideological Conflicts over World Trade, Renewable Energy, and Sustainable Agriculture* (Amherst, NY: Cambria Press, 2010).
42. Thurow and Kilman, *Enough: Why the World's Poorest Starve in an Age of Plenty,* 53–70, 182–185.
43. *The National Security Strategy of the United States of America* (September 2002), 17; http://georgewbush-whitehouse.archives.gov/nsc/nss/2002/.
44. Ibid., 4.
45. Ibid., 21.
46. Ralf Peters, *Roadblock to Reform: The Persistence of Agricultural Export Subsidies,* Policy Issues in International Trade and Commodities Study Series No. 32 (New York: United Nations, 2006), 1.
47. "Special Report: Aid to Africa. The $25 billion question," *Economist,* July 2, 2005, 24; Hancock, *Lords of Poverty,* 187.
48. Peters, *Roadblock to Reform,* 1–2.
49. Stiglitz quoted in Imhoff, *Food Fight,* 74.
50. Jeffrey D. Sachs, *The End of Poverty* (New York: Penguin, 2005), 266.
51. The World Bank breaks poverty down into three categories: extreme/absolute, moderate, and relative, with the first being defined by an income of $1 per day per

person, measured at purchasing power parity. An income between $1 and $2 qualifies as moderate poverty and relative poverty means that a household income is at a level "below a given proportion of average national income" (Sachs, 20).
52. Ibid., 288.
53. Ibid., 207. In contrast to Sachs, the Ghanian economist George B. N. Ayittey, the Ugandan journalist Andrew Mwenda, and the Zambian economist Dambisa Moyo have all argued quite persuasively that many of Africa's current problems stem from corrupt politicians and policies.
54. William Easterly, "A Modest Proposal," *Washington Post*, Book World, March 13, 2005, 3.
55. William Easterly, *The White Man's Burden* (New York: Penguin, 2006), 346, 368.
56. Jeffrey D. Sachs, *Common Wealth* (New York: Penguin, 2008). For an interesting critic of both economists through the work of Esther Duflo, see Ian Parker, "The Poverty Lab," *New Yorker,* May 17, 2010, 79–89.
57. Eric S. Reinert, *How Rich Countries Got Rich . . . and Why Poor Countries Stay Poor* (New York: Carroll & Graf, 2007), xxviii, 6.
58. Ibid., 111.
59. Chang, *Bad Samaritans*.
60. Moyo, *Dead Aid*, 72.
61. Paul Collier, *The Bottom Billion* (Oxford: Oxford University Press, 2007).
62. Moyo, *Dead Aid*, 35, 46.
63. Ibid., 105.
64. Ibid., 115–124.
65. Mohammad Yunus, Nobel Lecture, December 10, 2006; http://nobelprize.org/nobel_prizes/peace/laureates/2006/yunus-lecture-en.html.
66. Jason Pontin, "What Does Africa Need Most: Technology or Aid?" *New York Times,* June 17, 2007, 3. A video of Mwenda's talk is available on www.TED.com.
67. Hearing before the Subcommittee on Specialty Crops, Rural Development and Foreign Agriculture, *Hearing to Review Efforts to Deliver International Food Aid and to Provide Foreign Agricultural Development Assistance,* July 16, 2008, 110th Congress, 2nd Session, Serial No. 110–41 (Washington, D.C.: U.S. Government Printing Office, 2009), 2.
68. On the importance of genetically engineered crops see Robert Paarlberg, *Starved for Science: How Biotechnology Is Being Kept out of Africa* (Cambridge, MA: Harvard University Press, 2008).
69. Thomas H. Staal, "Africa: The Donor View on Development," SAA Borlaug Symposium 2010 Addis Ababa, July 13, 2010; http://www.usaid.gov/press/speeches/2010/sp100713.html. Staal's emphasis.
70. "Agribusiness," Center for Responsive Politics; http://www.opensecrets.org/industries/indus.php?cycle=2010&;ind=A.
71. *Feed the Future E-Newsletter* 1, June 15, 2010; http://www.feedthefuture.gov/ftfnews/ftfnews_01_061510.pdf.

72. Feed the Future Fact Sheet, "The Norman Borlaug Commemorative Research Initiative: Leveraging U.S. Research to Reduce Hunger and Poverty"; http://www.feedthefuture.gov/research.html.
73. William J. Garvelink, "Remarks at 2010 International Food Aid and Development Conference," August 4, 2010; http://www.usaid.gov/press/speeches/2010/sp100804.html.
74. William Cronon, *Nature's Metropolis* (New York: W. W. Norton, 1991), 97–147.
75. Thurow and Kilman, *Enough: Why the World's Poorest Starve in an Age of Plenty*, 207–215.
76. The Ethiopia Commodity Exchange website, http://www.ecx.com.et/CompanyProfile.aspx#AU.
77. Ibid.
78. Bernard Tanguy, David J. Spielman, Alemayehu Seyoum Taffesse, and Eleni Z. Gabre-Madhin, *Cooperatives for Staple Crop Marketing: Evidence from Ethiopia*, Research Monograph 164 (Washington, D.C.: International Food Policy Research Institute, 2010); Access Capital, *The Ethiopia Macroeconomic Handbook 2010* (Addis Ababa: Access Capital, 2010).
79. Thomas H. Staal, "Africa: The Donor View on Development," SAA Borlaug Symposium 2010 Addis Ababa, July 13, 2010; http://www.usaid.gov/press/speeches/2010/sp100713.html.
80. "A New Way Forward on Global Development," published by Josh Rogin, "White House Proposed Taking Development Role Away from State," *Cable,* May 3, 2010; http://thecable.foreignpolicy.com/posts/2010/05/03/white_house_proposed_taking_development_role_away_from_state.
81. *The Case for Reform: Foreign Aid and Development in a New Era, Hearing before the Committee on Foreign Relations United States Senate,* 111th Congress, July 22, 2009 (Washington, D.C.: U.S. Government Printing Office, 2009), 24–26; Dambisa Moyo, "Why Foreign Aid is Hurting Africa," *Wall Street Journal,* March 21, 2009; http://online.wsj.com/article/SB123758895999200083.html.
82. *The Case for Reform: Foreign Aid and Development in a New Era,* 1–24.
83. H.R. 2139, "Initiating Foreign Assistance Reform Act of 2009," 111 Congress, Referred to House Committee on Foreign Affairs on April 28, 2009; http://thomas.loc.gov/cgi-bin/bdquery/z?d111:h_r_2139.
84. State Department Press Release, "The Department of State's Quadrennial Diplomacy and Development Review," July 10, 2009; http://www.state.gov/r/pa/prs/ps/2009/july/125956.htm.
85. "Obama's Speech to the United Nations General Assembly," *New York Times,* September 23, 2009; http://www.nytimes.com/2009/09/24/us/politics/24prexy.text.html?_r=1&sq=obama&st=cse&scp=1&%2339;s%20speech%20to%20the%20UN%20general%20assembly=&;pagewanted=all.
86. The White House, "Fact Sheet: U.S. Global Development Policy" (September 22, 2010); http://www.whitehouse.gov/the-press-office/2010/09/22/fact-sheet-us-global-development-policy.

87. Hillary Clinton, "Leading through Civilian Power," *Foreign Affairs* 89:6 (November/December 2010): 13–24.
88. The State Department, *Leading through Civilian Power: 2010 Quadrennial Diplomacy and Development Review:* ii; http://www.state.gov/s/dmr/qddr/.
89. The State Department, *The 2010 Quadrennial Diplomacy and Development Review Fact Sheet,* 2; http://www.state.gov/s/dmr/qddr/.
90. Moyo, *Dead Aid*, 118; Easterly, *The White Man's Burden*, 368.
91. The State Department, *Leading through Civilian Power: 2010 Quadrennial Diplomacy and Development Review,* 185.
92. Ibid., 87.
93. Ibid., 87–88.
94. Truman, "Inaugural Address," *New York Times,* January 21, 1949, 4.
95. *Hearings before the Committee on Foreign Affairs on H.R. 5615, International Technical Cooperation Act of 1949, House of Representatives,* 81st Congress, Fall 1949 (Washington, D.C.: U.S. Government Printing Office, 1950), 34.
96. Hans Morganthau, "A Political Theory of Foreign Aid," *American Political Science Review* 56:2 (June 1962): 301.
97. Thomas Soapes, Interview with Dennis Fitzgerald, May 26, 1976, 7; Eisenhower Presidential Library.
98. Nick Cullather has persuasively argued that foreign aid's inefficiencies have also been located in policymakers "conceptual limitations" and over-reliance upon technology (*The Hungry World* [Cambridge: Harvard University Press, 2010], 270-271). Ideas for new, better policy options can be found in Abhijit Banerjee and Esther Duflo, *Poor Economics: A Radical Rethinking of the Way to Fight Global Poverty* (New York: Public Affairs, 2011).
99. Timothy Ferris, *The Science of Liberty: Democracy, Reason, and the Laws of Nature* (New York: HarperCollins, 2010), 153–157.
100. Amartya Sen, *The Idea of Justice* (Cambridge, MA: Harvard University Press, 2009), 18, 251; Amartya Sen, *Development as Freedom* (New York: Anchor, 1999), 87.
101. "Obama's Speech to the United Nations General Assembly," *New York Times,* September 23, 2009; http://www.nytimes.com/2009/09/24/us/politics/24prexy.text.html?_r=1&sq=obama&st=cse&scp=1&%2339;s%20speech%20to%20the%20UN%20general%20assembly=&;pagewanted=all.
102. Immanuel Kant, "What is Enlightenment?" in *The Portable Enlightenment Reader,* ed. Isaac Kramnick (New York: Penguin, 1995), 5.

SELECTED BIBLIOGRAPHY

UNPUBLISHED SOURCES

Dwight D. Eisenhower Presidential Library, Abilene, KS
Harry S. Truman Presidential Library, Independence, MO
Institute for Ethiopian Studies, Addis Ababa, Ethiopia
John F. Kennedy Presidential Library, Boston, MA
Lyndon B. Johnson Presidential Library, Austin, TX
Massillon Museum, Massillon, OH
National Archives and Records Administration, College Park, MD
Oklahoma State University Special Collections, Stillwater, OK

PUBLISHED

Abulafia, David. *The Discovery of Mankind*. New Haven, CT: Yale University Press, 2008.
Access Capital. *The Ethiopia Macroeconomic Handbook 2010*. Addis Ababa: Access Capital, 2010.
Acheson, Dean. *Present at the Creation*. New York: W. W. Norton, 1969.
Adams, Henry. *The Education of Henry Adams*. New York: Modern Library, 1999.
Adas, Michael. *Dominance By Design*. Cambridge, MA: Belknap Press, 2006.
———. *Machines as the Measure of Men*. Ithaca, NY: Cornell University Press, 1989.
Adelson, Roger. *London and the Invention of the Middle East*. New Haven, CT: Yale University Press, 1995.
Agarwala, A. N., and S. P. Singh, eds. *The Economics of Underdevelopment*. London: Oxford University Press, 1958.
Ahlberg, Kristin L. *Transplanting the Great Society: Lyndon Johnson and Food for Peace*. Columbia: University of Missouri Press, 2008.
Albanese, Denise. *New Science, New World*. Durham, NC: Duke University Press, 1997.
Alterman, Jon B. *Egypt and American Foreign Assistance, 1952–1956*. New York: Palgrave Macmillan, 2002.
Amuzegar, Jahangir. "Point Four: Performance and Prospect." *Political Science Quarterly* 73:4 (December 1958): 530–546.
Anderson, Fred, and Andrew Cayton. *The Dominion of War*. New York: Penguin, 2005.
Arndt, H. W. *Economic Development*. Chicago: University of Chicago Press, 1987.

———. "Economic Development: A Semantic History." *Economic Development and Cultural Change* 29:3 (April 1981): 457–466.
———. *The Rise and Fall of Economic Growth*. Chicago: University of Chicago Press, 1978.
Arrow, Kenneth J. "The Economic Implications of Learning by Doing." *Review of Economic Studies* 29 (June 1962): 155–173.
Ashton, T. S. *The Industrial Revolution*. New York: Oxford University Press, 1964.
Ater, Renée. "Making History: Meta Warrick Fuller's 'Ethiopia.'" *American Art* 17:3 (Autumn 2003): 12–31.
Ayittey, George B. N. *Africa in Chaos*. New York: St. Martin's Griffin, 1998.
———. *Africa Unchained*. New York: Palgrave Macmillan, 2005.
Bahru Zewde. *A History of Modern Ethiopia, 1855–1991* 2nd ed. Oxford: James Currey, 2001; Athens: Ohio University Press, 2001; Addis Ababa: Addis Ababa University Press, 2001.
Bailes, Kendall E. "The American Connection: Ideology and the Transfer of American Technology to the Soviet Union, 1917–1941." *Comparative Studies in Society and History* 23:3 (July 1981): 421–448.
Banerjee, Abhijit, and Esther Duflo. *Poor Economics: A Radical Rethinking of the Way to Fight Global Poverty*. New York: Public Affairs, 2011.
Barber, William J. *From New Era to New Deal*. Cambridge: Cambridge University Press, 1985.
Bardhan, Paul. "Economics of Development and the Development of Economics." *Journal of Economic Perspectives* 7:2 (Spring 1993): 129–142.
Barnett, Thomas P. M. *The Pentagon's New Map*. New York: G. P. Putnam, 2004.
Bartlett, Ruhl J., ed. *The Record of American Diplomacy*. New York: Alfred A. Knopf, 1950.
Bauer, Peter. *Equality, the Third World and Economic Delusion*. Cambridge, MA: Harvard University Press, 1981.
Beard, Charles A., and Mary R. *The Rise of American Civilization*. New York: Macmillan, 1930.
Beard, William. "Technology and Political Boundaries." *American Political Science Review* 25:3 (August 1931): 557–572.
Becker, Markus C., and Thorbjørn Knudsen. "Schumpeter 1911: Farsighted Visions on Economic Development." *American Journal of Economics and Sociology* 61:2 (April 2002): 387–403.
Behrman, Greg. *The Most Noble Adventure*. New York: Free Press, 2007.
Beinhocker, Eric D. *The Origin of Wealth*. Boston: Harvard Business School Press, 2006.
Bennett, Henry Garland. "Point Four: The Maturing of a Policy." *Annals of the American Academy of Political and Social Science* 278 (November 1951): 56–61.
Bentwich, Norman. "Ethiopia Today." *International Affairs* 20:4 (October 1944): 509–518.
Bernstein, Michael A. *A Perilous Progress*. Princeton, NJ: Princeton University Press, 2001.

Berry, Christopher J. *The Social Theory of the Scottish Enlightenment.* Edinburgh: Edinburgh University Press, 1997.

Bhagwati, Jagdish. *In Defense of Globalization.* Oxford: Oxford University Press, 2004.

Binder, Leonard. "A Natural History of Development Theory." *Comparative Studies in Society and History* 28:1 (January 1986): 3–33.

Bingham, Jonathan B. *Shirt-Sleeve Diplomacy: Point 4 in Action.* New York: The John Day Company, 1953.

Binswanger, Hans, and Ernst Lutz, "Agricultural Trade Barriers, Trade Negotiations, and the Interests of Developing Countries." Paper presented at the International Association of Agricultural Economists Meeting in Berlin. August 2000.

Blanning, Tim. *The Pursuit of Glory.* New York: Penguin, 2007.

Blaug, Mark. *Economic Theory in Retrospect.* 4th ed. Cambridge: Cambridge University Press, 1985.

Blundell, Herbert Weld. "A Journey through Abyssinia to the Nile." *Geographical Journal* 15:2 (February 1900): 97–118.

Bobbitt, Philip. *The Shield of Achilles.* New York: Anchor, 2002.

Borstelman, Thomas. *Apartheid's Reluctant Uncle.* New York: Oxford University Press, 1993.

Braudel, Fernand. *A History of Civilizations.* Trans. Richard Mayne. New York: Penguin, 1993.

Brazelton, W. Robert. "Retrospectives: The Economics of Leon Hirsch Keyserling." *Journal of Economic Progress* 11:4 (Autumn 1997): 189–197.

Brinkley, Alan. *The End of Reform.* New York: Alfred A. Knopf, 1995.

Broadie, Alexander, ed. *The Cambridge Companion to the Scottish Enlightenment.* Cambridge: Cambridge University Press, 2003.

———. *The Scottish Enlightenment.* Edinburgh: Birlinn, 2001.

Brown, Henry Phelps. "Sir Roy Harrod: A Biographical Memoir." *Economic Journal* 90:357 (March 1980): 1–33.

Brown, Philip Marshall. "From Sevres to Lausanne." *American Journal of International Law* 18:1 (January 1924): 113–116.

Bruce, Dickson D., Jr. "Ancient Africa and the Early Black American Historians, 1883–1915." *American Quarterly* 36:5 (Winter 1984): 684–699.

Bruce, James. *Travels and Adventures in Abyssinia and Nubia, 1768–1773, to Discover the Source of the Nile.* Ed. J. Morison Clingan. 2nd ed. Edinburgh: Adam and Charles Black, 1873.

Brzezinski, Zbigniew. *Power and Principle: Memoirs of the National Security Adviser, 1977–1981.* London: Weidenfeld & Nicolson, 1983.

Buchan, James. *Crowded with Genius.* New York: Perennial, 2003.

Burns, William J. *Economic Aid and American Policy Toward Egypt, 1955–1981.* Albany: State University of New York Press, 1985.

Calvert, Susan, and Peter Calvert. *Politics and Society in the Third World.* London: Prentice Hall, 1996.

Calvino, Italo. *Why Read the Classics*. Trans. Martin McLaughlin. New York: Vintage, 2000.
Campbell, R. H., and Andrew S. Skinner, eds. *The Origins and Nature of the Scottish Enlightenment*. Edinburgh: John Donald Publishers, 1982.
Carnochan, W. B. *Golden Legends*. Stanford, CA: Stanford University Press, 2008.
Chang, Ha-Joon. *Bad Samaritans*. New York: Bloomsbury Press, 2008.
Chirol, Valentine. *The Middle East Question or Some Political Problems of Indian Defence*. London: J. Murray, 1903.
Clark, Colin. *The Conditions of Economic Progress*. London: Macmillan, 1940.
———. *National Income and Outlay*. New York: Augustus M. Kelley, 1965.
Clark, Henry C., ed. *Commerce, Culture, & Liberty*. Indianapolis: Liberty Fund, 2003.
Clark, Gregory. *A Farewell to Alms*. Princeton, NJ: Princeton University Press, 2007.
Clay, Jason W., and Bonnie K. Holcomb. *Politics and the Ethiopian Famine, 1984–1985*. Cambridge, MA: Cultural Survival, 1986.
Clayton, William L. "GATT, The Marshall Plan, and OECD." *Political Science Quarterly* 78:4 (December 1963): 493–503.
Cleveland, William L. *A History of the Modern Middle East*. Boulder: Westview, 2000.
Clinton, Hillary. "Leading through Civilian Power." *Foreign Affairs* 89:6 (November/December 2010): 13–24.
Clive, John, and Bernard Bailyn. "England's Cultural Provinces: Scotland and America." *William and Mary Quarterly* 11:2 (April 1954): 200–213.
Cockayne, Emily. *Hubbub*. New Haven, CT: Yale University Press, 2007.
Coleman, James Smoot. *Nationalism and Development in Africa: Selected Essays*. Ed. Richard L. Sklar. Berkeley: University of California Press, 1994.
Collier, Paul. *The Bottom Billion*. Oxford: Oxford University Press, 2007.
Commager, Henry Steele. *The American Mind*. New Haven, CT: Yale University Press, 1950.
Conger, Charles T. "Geography at the World's Columbian Exposition." *Geographical Journal* 3:2 (February 1894): 130–134.
Crapol, Edward. "Some Reflections on the Historiography of the Cold War." *History Teacher* 20:2 (February 1987): 251–262.
Cronon, William. *Nature's Metropolis*. New York: W. W. Norton, 1991.
Crozier, Andrew J. "The Establishment of the Mandates System 1919–25: Some Problems Created by the Paris Peace Conference." *Journal of Contemporary History* 14:3 (July 1979): 483–513.
Cullather, Nick. "Development: It's History." *Diplomatic History* 24:4 (Fall 2000): 641–653.
———. "The Foreign Policy of the Calorie." *American Historical Review* 112:2 (April 2007): 336–364.
———. *The Hungry World: America's Cold War Battle against Poverty in Asia*. Cambridge, MA: Harvard University Press, 2010.
———. "Miracles of Modernization: The Green Revolution and the Apotheosis of Technology." *Diplomatic History* 24:2 (April 2004): 227–254.

Curti, Merle. *Human Nature in American Thought*. Madison: University of Wisconsin Press, 1980.

Curti, Merle, and Kendall Bir. *Prelude to Point Four: American Technical Missions Overseas, 1838–1938*. Madison: University of Wisconsin Press, 1954.

Daniels, Walter M., ed. *The Point Four Program*. New York: H. W. Wilson, 1951.

Darwin, Charles. *Descent of Man*. New York: D. Appleton, 1871.

———. *On the Origin of the Species*. Facsimile of 1st ed. Cambridge, MA: Harvard University Press, 1964.

Dawit Wolde Giorgis. *Red Tears*. Trenton, NJ: Red Sea Press, 1989.

Dealey, James Q., Edward Alsworth Ross, Franklin H. Giddings, Ulysses G. Weatherly, Charles A. Ellwood, George Elliot Howard, Frank W. Blackmar, and Albion W. Small. "Lester Frank Ward." *American Journal of Sociology* 19:1 (July 1913): 61–78.

Defoe, Daniel. *The Complete English Tradesmen*. London: BiblioBazaar, 2006.

———. *Robinson Crusoe*. New York: Barnes and Noble Classics, 2003.

———. *A Tour through the Whole Island of Great Britain*. Abridged and edited by Pat Rogers. London: Penguin, 1971.

Degler, Carl N. *In Search of Human Nature*. New York: Oxford University Press, 1991.

DeNovo, John A. "The Culbertson Economic Mission and Anglo-American Tensions in the Middle East, 1944–1945." *Journal of American History* 63:4 (March 1977): 913–936.

De Soto, Henando *The Mystery of Capital*. New York: Basic Books, 2000.

Desmond, Adrian, and James Moore. *Darwin's Sacred Cause*. Boston: Houghton Mifflin Harcourt, 2009.

Desrosières, Alain. *The Politics of Large Numbers*. Cambridge, MA: Harvard University Press, 1998.

De Vries, Jan. "The Industrial Revolution and the Industrious Revolution," *Journal of Economic History* 54:2 (June 1994): 249–270.

Diamond, Jared. *Guns, Germs, and Steel*. New York: W. W. Norton, 1997.

Diggins, John Patrick. *The Proud Decades*. New York: W. W. Norton, 1994.

DiLorenzo, Thomas J. *How Capitalism Saved America*. New York: Crown Forum, 2004.

Doherr, A. "Enter Japan." *The Living Age* 348:4422 (March 1935): 10–14.

Domar, Evsey D. "Capital Expansion, Rate of Growth, and Employment." *Econometrica* 14:2 (April 1946): 137–147.

Domar, Evsey D., Naum Jasny, Edward Ames, and Harry Schwartz. "Discussion." *American Economic Review* 41:2 (May 1951): 483–494.

Du Bois, W. E.B. "Inter-Racial Implications: A Negro View." *Foreign Affairs* 14:1/4 (1935/1936): 82–92.

———. *The Souls of Black Folks*. Ed. David W. Blight. Boston: Bedford, 1997.

Duggan, Laurence. "Our Relations with the Other American Republics." *Annals of the American Academy of Political and Social Science* 198 (July 1938): 128–132.

Easterbrook, Gregg. "Forgotten Benefactor of Humanity," *Atlantic* 279:1 (January 1997): 72–85.

Easterly, William. *The Elusive Quest for Growth.* Cambridge, MA: MIT Press, 2001.
———. *The White Man's Burden.* New York: Penguin, 2006.
Ehret, Christopher. *The Civilizations of Africa: A History to 1800.* Charlottesville: University of Virginia Press, 2002.
Ekbladh, David. *The Great American Mission: Modernization and the Construction of an American World Order.* Princeton, NJ: Princeton University Press, 2010.
———. "'Mr. TVA': Grass-Roots Development, David Lilienthal, and the Rise and Fall of the Tennessee Valley Authority as a Symbol for U.S. Overseas Development, 1933–1973." *Diplomatic History* 26:3 (2002): 335–374.
Engerman, David C. *Modernization from the Other Shore: American Intellectuals and the Romance of Russian Development.* Cambridge, MA: Harvard University Press, 2003.
———. "The Romance of Economic Development and New Histories of the Cold War." *Diplomatic History* 28:1 (January 2004): 23–54.
———, ed. *Staging Growth.* Amherst: University of Massachusetts Press, 2003.
Erickson, Paul A. "Phrenology and Physical Anthropology: The George Combe Collection." *Current Anthropology* 18:1 (March 1977): 92–93.
Erlich, Haggai. *Ethiopia and the Middle East.* Boulder: Lynne Rienner, 1994.
Escobar, Arturo. *Encountering Development.* Princeton, NJ: Princeton University Press, 1995.
———. "Power and Visibility: Development and the Invention and Management of the Third World." *Cultural Anthropology* 3:4 (November 1988): 428–443.
Espy, Willard R. *Bold New Program.* New York: Harper & Brothers, 1950.
———. "Point Four and the Will to Reform." *Far Eastern Survey* 20:5 (March 7, 1951): 45–49.
Fairbank, John King. *The Great Chinese Revolution.* New York: Harper Perennial, 1987.
Ferguson, Niall. *Empire.* New York: Basic Books, 2002.
Ferris, Timothy. *The Science of Liberty: Democracy, Reason, and the Laws of Nature.* New York: HarperCollins, 2010.
Findlay, Ronald, and Kevin O'Rourke. *Power and Plenty.* Princeton, NJ: Princeton University Press, 2007.
Fisher, W. B. "Unity and Diversity in the Middle East." *Geographical Review* 37:3 (July 1947): 414–435.
Fitzgerald, Deborah. *Every Farm a Factory.* New Haven, CT: Yale University Press, 2003.
Fitzsimons, M. A. "Britain and the Middle East, 1944–1950." *Review of Politics* 13:1 (January 1951): 21–38.
Fleming, James E. "The Role of Government in a Free Society: The Conception of Lester Frank Ward." *Social Forces* 24:3 (March 1946): 257–266.
Fredrickson, George M. *Black Liberation.* New York: Oxford University Press, 1995.
Friedman, Benjamin M. *The Moral Consequences of Economic Growth.* New York: Alfred A. Knopf, 2005.

Fromkin, David. *A Peace to End All Peace.* New York: Henry Holt, 1989.
Gaddis, John Lewis. *The United States and the Origins of the Cold War.* New York: Columbia University Press, 1972.
Galbraith, John Kenneth. *The Affluent Society.* 40th anniversary ed. Boston: Houghton Mifflin, 1998.
Gelvin, James L. *The Modern Middle East.* New York: Oxford University Press, 2005.
Gerschenkron, Alexander. "The Rate of Growth in Russia: The Rate of Industrial Growth in Russia, Since 1885." *Journal of Economic History* 7 (1947): 144–174.
Gibb, H. A. R. "Middle Eastern Perplexities." *International Affairs* 20:4 (October 1944): 458–472.
Gill, Peter. *Famines and Foreigners: Ethiopia since Live Aid.* Oxford: Oxford University Press, 2010.
Gilman, Nils. *Mandarins of the Future: Modernization Theory in Cold War America.* Baltimore: Johns Hopkins University Press, 2003.
Godfried, Nathan. "Economic Development and Regionalism: United States Foreign Relations in the Middle East, 1942–5." *Journal of Contemporary History* 22:3 (July 1987): 481–500.
Godley, Michael R. "Socialism with Chinese Characteristics: Sun Yatsen and the International Development of China." *Australian Journal of Chinese Affairs* 18 (July 1987): 109–125.
Gould, Stephen Jay. *The Mismeasure of Man.* New York: W. W. Norton, 1996.
Grant, A. Cameron. "George Combe and American Slavery." *Journal of Negro History* 45:4 (October 1960): 259–269.
Gravlee, Clarence C., H. Russell Bernard, and William R. Leonard, "Heredity, Environment, and Cranial Form: A Reanalysis of Boas's Immigrant Data." *American Anthropologist* 105:1 (March 2003): 125–138.
Greenblatt, Stephen. *Marvelous Possessions.* Chicago: University of Chicago Press, 1991.
Greenfeld, Liah. *The Spirit of Capitalism.* Cambridge, MA: Harvard University Press, 2001.
Gross, Bertram M., and John P. Lewis, "The President's Economic Staff during the Truman Administration." *The American Political Science Review* 48:1 (March 1954): 114–130.
Gruesser, John Cullen. *Black on Black.* Lexington: University Press of Kentucky, 2000.
Guizot, François. *The History of Civilization in Europe.* Trans. William Hazlitt. Ed. Larry Siedentop. London: Penguin, 1997.
Gunning, Tom. "The World as Object Lesson: Cinema Audiences, Visual Culture and the St. Louis World's Fair, 1904." *Film History* 6:4 (Winter 1994): 422–444.
Habermas, Jürgen. *The Structural Transformation of the Public Sphere.* Trans. Thomas Burger. Cambridge, MA: MIT Press, 1991.
Hacker, Louis M. "Capitalism and Economic Progress." In "Papers and Proceedings of the Sixty-Second Annual Meeting of the American Economic Association." Ed. James Washington Bell. *American Economic Review* 40:2, (May 1950): 105–106.

———. *The Shaping of the American Tradition.* New York: Columbia University Press, 1947.

Hagen, James M., and Vernon W. Ruttan, "Development Policy under Eisenhower and Kennedy," *The Journal of Developing Areas* 23:1 (October 1988): 1–30.

Hahn, Peter L. *The United States, Great Britain, and Egypt, 1945–1956.* Chapel Hill: University of North Carolina Press, 1991.

Haile Selassie. *My Life and Ethiopia's Progress.* Vol. 2. Trans. Ezekiel Gebissa. Ed. Harold Marcus. East Lansing: Michigan State University Press, 1994.

———. *Selected Speeches of His Imperial Majesty Haile Selassie First.* Addis Ababa: Imperial Ethiopian Ministry of Information, 1967.

Hall, Kim F. *Things of Darkness.* Ithaca, NY: Cornell University Press, 1995.

Haller, John S., Jr. "The Species Problem: Nineteenth-Century Concepts of Racial Inferiority in the Origin of Man Controversy." *American Anthropology* 72:6 (December 1970): 1319–1329.

Hamby, Alonzo L. *Beyond the New Deal: Harry S. Truman and American Liberalism.* New York: Columbia University Press, 1973.

Hancock, Graham. *Lords of Poverty.* New York: Atlantic Monthly Press, 1989.

Hansberry, William Leo. "The Material Culture of Ancient Nigeria." *Journal of Negro History* 6:3 (July 1921): 261–295.

Hanson, Haldore. "United States Organization for Point Four." *Annals of the American Academy of Political and Social Science* 268 (March 1950): 36–44.

Harbutt, Fraser. "American Challenge, Soviet Response: The Beginning of the Cold War, February–May 1946." *Political Science Quarterly* 96:4(Winter 1981–1982): 623–639.

Harlen, Christine Margerum. "A Reappraisal of Classical Economic Nationalism and Economic Liberalism." *International Studies Quarterly* 43:4 (December 1999): 733–744.

Harris, Abram L. "Economic Evolution: Dialectical and Darwinian." *Journal of Political Economy* 42:1 (February 1934): 34–79.

Harris, Major W. Cornwallis. *The Highlands of Ethiopia.* New York: J. Winchester, New World Press, n.d.

Harris, Marla. "Not Black and/or White: Reading Racial Difference in Heliodorus's Ethiopica and Pauline Hopkins's of One Blood." *African American Review* 35:3 (Autumn 2001): 375–390.

Harrod, R. F. "An Essay in Dynamic Theory." *Economic Journal* 49:193 (March 1939): 14–33.

Haskell, Thomas L. *The Emergence of Professional Social Science.* Baltimore: Johns Hopkins University Press, 2000.

Hayek, Friedrich August. *The Fatal Conceit, The Collected Works of F. A. Hayek*, vol. 1, ed. W. W. Bartley III. Chicago: University of Chicago Press, 1988.

———. "The Pretense of Knowledge." *The American Economic Review* 79:6 (December 1989): 3–7.

———. *The Road to Serfdom.* Chicago: University of Chicago Press, 1994.

Hayford, J. E. Casely. *Ethiopia Unbound*. 2nd ed. Intro. F. Nnabuenyi Ugonna. London: Frank Cass, 1969.

Headrick, Daniel R. *The Tentacles of Progress*. New York: Oxford University Press, 1988.

———. *The Tools of Empire*. New York: Oxford University Press, 1981.

Hegel, George W. F. *The Philosophy of History*. Trans. J. Sibree. Amherst, NY: Prometheus Books, 1991.

Heilbroner, Robert L. "The Paradox of Progress: Decline and Decay in The Wealth of Nations." *Journal of the History of Ideas* 34:2 (April–June 1973): 243–262.

———. *The Worldly Philosophers*. 7th ed. New York: Simon and Schuster, 1999.

Heller, Francis H., ed. *The Truman White House*. Lawrence: Regents Press of Kansas, 1980.

Helpman, Elhanan. *The Mystery of Economic Growth*. Cambridge, MA: Belknap Press, 2004.

Herman, Arthur. *How the Scots Invented the Modern World*. New York: Three Rivers Press, 2001.

Herring, George C. *From Colony to Superpower*. Oxford: Oxford University Press, 2008.

Herskovits, Melville J. "Peoples and Cultures of Sub-Saharan Africa." *Annals of the American Academy of Political and Social Science* 298 (March 1955): 11–20.

Himmelfarb, Gertrude. *The Roads to Modernity*. New York: Vintage, 2004.

Hoffman, Paul G. "Trade Restrictions: And Peace." *Proceedings of the Academy of Political Science* 23:4 (January 1950): 115–122.

Hofstadter, Richard. *Social Darwinism in American Thought*. Boston: Beacon, 1992.

Hogan, Michael J. "American Marshall Planners and the Search for a European Neocapitalism." *American Historical Review* 90:1 (February 1985): 44–72.

Hogarth, D. G. *The Nearer East*. New York: D. Appleton and Company, 1902.

Hont, Istvan, and Michael Ignatieff, eds. *Wealth and Virtue: The Shaping of Political Economy in the Scottish Enlightenment*. Cambridge: Cambridge University Press, 1983.

Hoover, Kenneth. *Economics as Ideology*. Lanham, MD: Rowman & Littlefield Publishers, 2003.

Hopfl, H. M. "From Savage to Scotsman: Conjectural History in the Scottish Enlightenment." *The Journal of British Studies* 17:2 (Spring 1978): 19–46.

Hopkins, Pauline. *Of One Blood*. New York: Washington Square Press, 2004.

Horsman, Reginald. *Race and Manifest Destiny*. Cambridge, MA: Harvard University Press, 1981.

Hoselitz, Bert F. "Patterns of Economic Growth." *The Canadian Journal of Economics and Political Science* 21:4 (November 1955): 416–431.

Hoskins, Halford L. "Point Four with Reference to the Middle East." *Annals of the American Academy of Political and Social Science* 268 (March 1950): 85–95.

House Committee on Foreign Affairs. *Food Crisis in Africa: Hearings before the Subcommittee on Africa*, 98th Congress, 1st Session, 1 November 1983. Washington, D.C.: U.S. Government Printing Office, 1985.

Howard, Harry N. *The Development of United States Policy in the Near East, 1945–1951*. Department of State Publication 4446. Washington, D.C.: U.S. Government Printing Office, 1952.

Hughes, Thomas P. *American Genesis*. New York: Viking, 1989.

Hume, David. *An Enquiry Concerning Human Understanding*. Ed. Eric Steinberg. 2nd ed. Indianapolis: Hackett, 1993.

———. *Essays, Moral, Political, and Literary*. Ed. Eugene F. Millar. Rev. ed. Indianapolis: Liberty Fund, 1987.

———. *A Treatise on Human Nature*. Ed. David Fate Norton and Mary J. Norton. Oxford: Oxford University Press, 2000.

Hunt, Michael H. *The American Ascendancy*. Chapel Hill: University of North Carolina Press, 2007.

Huntington, Samuel P. *Political Order in Changing Societies*. New Haven, CT: Yale University Press, 2006.

Hurt, R. Douglas. *Agricultural Technology in the Twentieth Century*. Manhattan, KS: Sunflower University Press, 1991.

Hyatt, Marshall. *Franz Boas, Social Activist: The Dynamics of Ethnicity*. New York: Greenwood, 1990.

Imhoff, Daniel. *Food Fight: The Citizen's Guide to a Food and Farm Bill*. Healdsburg, CA: Watershed Media, 2007.

Imperial Ethiopian Government. *Five Year Development Plan, 1957–1961*. Addis Ababa: Berhanena Selam Printing Press, n.d.

———. *Second Five Year Development Plan, 1963–1967*. Addis Ababa: Berhanena Selam Printing Press, 1962.

———. *Third Five Year Development Plan, 1968–1973*. Addis Ababa: Berhanena Selam Printing Press, 1968.

Indrias Getachew. *Beyond the Throne*. Ed. Richard Pankhurst. Addis Ababa: Shama Books, 2001.

Inglehart, Ronald, and Christian Welzel. *Modernization, Cultural Change, and Democracy*. Cambridge: Cambridge University Press, 2005.

"International Trade Organization (Proposed)." *International Organization* 1:1 (February 1947): 139–140.

"International Trade Organization (Proposed)." *International Organization* 2:1 (February 1948): 133–136.

"Interview with Egypt's Prime Minister Lieut. Col. Gamal Abdel Nasser." *U.S. News & World Report* (September 3, 1954): 26–32.

Iriye, Akira. *Cultural Internationalism and World Order*. Baltimore: Johns Hopkins University Press, 1997.

Ironmonger, Duncan, J. O. N. Perkins, and Tran Van Hoa, eds. *National Income and Economic Progress*. New York: St. Martin's, 1988.

Isaacson, Walter, and Evan Thomas. *The Wise Men*. New York: Simon & Schuster, 1986.

Israel, Jonathan. *Enlightenment Contested*. Oxford: Oxford University Press, 2006.

Jackson, Donna R. *Jimmy Carter and the Horn of Africa*. Jefferson, NC: McFarland, 2007.
Jacob, Margaret C., and Larry Stewart. *Practical Matter*. Cambridge, MA: Harvard University Press, 2004.
Jacobson, Matthew Frye. *Barbarian Virtues*. New York: Hill and Wang, 2000.
James, Wendy, Donald L. Donham, Eisei Kurimoto, and Alessandro Triulzi, eds. *Remapping Ethiopia*. Oxford: James Currey, 2002.
Japtok, Martin. "Pauline Hopkins's 'Of One Blood,' Africa, and the 'Darwinist Trap.'" *African American Review* 36:3 (Autumn 2002): 403–415.
Johnson, Samuel. *The History of Rasselas, Prince of Abyssinia*. Ed. Paul Goring. London: Penguin, 2007.
———. *A Voyage to Abyssinia*. Ed. Joel J. Gold. New Haven, CT: Yale University Press, 1985.
Jordan, John M. *Machine-Age Ideology*. Chapel Hill: University of North Carolina Press, 1994.
Kames, Lord. *Sketches of the History of Man*. Vols. 1–3. Ed. James A. Harris. Indianapolis: Liberty Fund, 2007.
Kaplan, Robert D. *Surrender or Starve*. New York: Vintage, 2003.
Kapuściński, Ryszard. *The Emperor*. Trans. William R. Brand and Katarzyna Mroczkowska-Brand. New York: Vintage, 1989.
Kasson, John F. *Civilizing the Machine*. New York: Hill and Wang, 1999.
Kay, John. *Culture and Prosperity*. New York: Harper Business, 2004.
Keay, John. *Sowing the Wind*. New York: W. W. Norton, 2003.
Keller, Edmond. *Revolutionary Ethiopia*. Bloomington: Indiana University Press, 1988.
Kennan, George. "Foreign Aid in the Framework of National Policy." *Proceedings of the Academy of Political Science* 23:4 (January 1950): 104–114.
Kennedy, Paul. *The Rise and the Fall of Great Powers*. New York: Random House, 1987.
Keynes, John Maynard. *The Collected Writings of John Maynard Keynes*. Vol. 26. Ed. Donald Moggridge. London: Macmillan, 1980.
———. *Essays in Persuasion*. London: Macmillan, 1933.
———. *The General Theory of Employment, Interest, and Money*. San Diego: Harcourt, 1964.
Keyserling, Leon H. "Employment and the 'New Economics.'" *Annals of the American Academy of Political and Social Science* 37:3 (September 1967): 102–119.
Khalidi, Rashid. "The 'Middle East' as a Framework of Analysis: Re-mapping a Region in the Era of Globalization." *Comparative Studies of South Asia, Africa and the Middle East* 18:1 (1998): 74–80.
———. *Resurrecting Empire*. Boston: Beacon, 2004.
Korn, David A. *Ethiopia, the United States, and the Soviet Union*. Carbondale: Southern Illinois University Press, 1986.
Kramnick, Isaac, ed. *The Portable Enlightenment Reader*. New York: Penguin, 1995.
Kuhn, Thomas. *The Structure of Scientific Revolutions*. Chicago: University of Chicago Press, 1962.

Kuniholm, Bruce Robert. *The Origins of the Cold War in the Near East*. Princeton, NJ: Princeton University Press, 1980.

Kuznets, Simon S. "Quantitative Aspects of the Economic Growth of Nations: I. Levels and Variability of Rates of Growth." *Economic Development and Cultural Change* 5:1 (October 1956): 1–94.

———. *Secular Movements in Production and Prices*. New York: Augustus M. Kelley, 1967.

LaFeber, Walter. *The American Age: U.S. Foreign Policy at Home and Abroad*. 2nd ed. Vol. 2. New York: W. W. Norton, 1994.

———. "Technology and U.S. Foreign Relations." *Diplomatic History* 24:1 (Winter 2000): 1–19.

Lancaster, Carol. *Aid to Africa*. Chicago: University of Chicago Press, 1999.

Landes, David. *The Wealth and Poverty of Nations*. New York: W. W. Norton, 1998.

Landis, J. M. "Anglo-American Cooperation in the Middle East." *Annals of the American Academy of Political and Social Science* 240 (July 1945): 64–72.

Larson, Edward J. *Evolution*. New York: Modern Library, 2006.

Larson, John Lauritz. *Internal Improvement*. Chapel Hill: University of North Carolina Press, 2001.

Latham, Michael E. *Modernization as Ideology*. Chapel Hill: University of North Carolina Press, 2000.

———. *The Right Kind of Revolution: Modernization, Development, and U.S. Foreign Policy from the Cold War to the Present*. Ithaca, NY: Cornell University Press, 2011.

Lears, T. J. Jackson. "The Concept of Cultural Hegemony: Problems and Possibilities." *The American Historical Review* 90:3 (June 1985): 567–593.

Lees, G. M. "The Search for Oil." *Geographical Journal* 95:1 (January 1940): 1–16.

Leffler, Melvyn P. "The American Conception of National Security and the Beginnings of the Cold War, 1945–1948." *American Historical Review* 89:2 (April 1984): 346–381.

———. *A Preponderance of Power: National Security, the Truman Administration, and the Cold War*. Stanford, CA: Stanford University Press, 1992.

Lefort, René. *Ethiopia: A Heretical Revolution?* London: Zed Press, 1983.

Lehrer, Nadine. *U.S. Farm Bills and Policy Reforms: Ideological Conflicts over World Trade, Renewable Energy, and Sustainable Agriculture*. Amherst, NY: Cambria Press, 2010.

Lesch, David W. "Introduction," in *The Middle East and the United States*. Ed. David W. Lesch. Boulder: Westview, 1996.

Levine, Donald N. *Greater Ethiopia*. 2nd ed. Chicago: University of Chicago Press, 2000.

Lewis, W. Arthur. "The State of Development Theory." *American Economic Review* 74:1 (March 1984): 1–10.

Leyburn, Ellen Douglas. "'No Romantick Absurdities or Incredible Fictions': The Relation of Johnson's Rasselas to Lobo's Voyage to Abyssinia." *PMLA* 70:5 (December 1955): 1059–1067.

Leys, Colin. *The Rise and Fall of Development Theory*. Bloomington: Indiana University Press, 1996.

Lindert, Peter. "English Population, Wages, and Prices: 1541–1913." *Journal of Interdisciplinary History* 15:4 (Spring 1985): 609–634.

Little, Douglas. *American Orientalism*. Chapel Hill: University of North Carolina Press, 2002.

Locke, John. *An Essay Concerning Human Understanding*. Ed. Kenneth P. Winkler. Indianapolis: Hackett, 1996.

Lockhart, Donald M. "'The Fourth Son of the Mighty Emperor': The Ethiopian Background of Johnson's Rasselas." *PMLA* 78:5 (December 1963): 516–528.

Longrigg, Stephen H. "Disposal of Italian Africa." *International Affairs* 21:3 (July 1945): 363–369.

———. "The Future of Eritrea." *African Affairs* 45:180 (July 1946): 120–127.

Love, Eric T. L. *Race Over Empire*. Chapel Hill: University of North Carolina Press, 2004.

Lundberg, David, and Henry F. May. "The Enlightened Reader in America." *American Quarterly* 28:2 (Summer 1976): 262–293.

Lundestad, Geir. "Empire by Invitation? The United States and Western Europe, 1945–1952." *Journal of Peace Research* 23:3 (1986): 263–277.

MacCreagh, Gordon. *The Last of Free Africa*. 2nd ed. New York: Appleton-Century, 1935.

MacMillan, Margaret. *Paris 1919*. New York: Random House, 2001.

Mahan, Alfred Thayer. "The Persian Gulf and International Relations." *National Review* (September 1902): 27–45.

Maloney, Pat. "Savages in the Scottish Enlightenment's History of Desire." *Journal of the History of Sexuality* 14:3 (July 2005): 237–265.

Malthus, Thomas. *An Essay on the Principle of Population*. Oxford: Oxford University Press, 2008.

Marcus, Harold G. *Haile Selassie I*. Berkeley: University of California Press, 1987.

———. *A History of Ethiopia*. Updated ed. Berkeley: University of California Press, 2002.

———. *The Life and Times of Menelik II*. Oxford: Clarendon Press, 1975.

———. *The Politics of Empire*. Lawrenceville, NJ: Red Sea Press, 1995.

Maren, Michael. *The Road to Hell*. New York: Free Press, 1997.

Markakis, John. *Ethiopia: Anatomy of a Traditional Polity*. Addis Ababa: Shama Books, 2006.

Marshall, Alfred. *Principles of Economics*. New York: Prometheus, 1997.

Marx, Karl, and Friedrich Engels. *The Communist Manifesto*. Trans. Samuel Moore. London: Penguin, 1985.

Mastny, Vojtech. *The Cold War and Soviet Insecurity*. New York: Oxford University Press, 1996.

McCann, James C. *People of the Plow*. Madison: University of Wisconsin Press, 1995.

McCoy, Drew R. *The Elusive Republic.* Chapel Hill: University of North Carolina Press, 1980.
McCracken, John. "African History in British Universities: Past, Present and Future." *African Affairs* 92:367 (April 1993): 239–253.
McCullough, David. *Truman.* New York: Simon & Schuster, 1992.
McDougall, Walter A. *Promised Land, Crusader State.* Boston: Houghton Mifflin, 1997.
———. *The Heavens and the Earth.* Baltimore: Johns Hopkins University Press, 1985.
McGee, W. J. "Opportunities in Anthropology at the World's Fair." *Science* 20:5 (August 19, 1904): 253–254.
McKay, Vernon. "Needs and Opportunities in Africa." *Annals of the American Academy of Political and Social Science* 268 (March 1950): 75–84.
Menand, Louis. *The Metaphysical Club.* New York: Farrar, Straus, and Giroux, 2001.
Merrill, Dennis, ed. *Documentary History of the Truman Presidency.* Vol. 13. Frederick, MD: University Publications of America, 1996.
———. *Documentary History of the Truman Presidency.* Vol. 27. Frederick, MD: University Publications of America, 1999.
Mesfin Bezuneh and Carl C. Mabbs-Zeno. "The Contribution of the Green Revolution to Social Change in Ethiopia." *Northeast African Studies* 6:3 (1984): 9–17.
Messay Kebede. *Survival and Modernization, Ethiopia's Enigmatic Present.* Lawrenceville, NJ: Red Sea Press, 1999.
Metcalf, Evan B. "Secretary Hoover and the Emergence of Macroeconomic Management." *Business History Review* 49:1 (Spring 1975): 60–80.
Milikias, Paulos, and Getachew Metaferia, ed. *The Battle of Adwa.* New York: Algora Publishing, 2005.
Millar, John. *The Origin and Distinction of Ranks.* Ed. Aaron Garrett. Indianapolis: Liberty Fund, 2006.
Mills, Nicolaus. *Winning the Peace.* Hoboken, NJ: John Wiley, 2008.
Milne, David. *America's Rasputin: Walt Rostow and the Vietnam War.* New York: Hill and Wang, 2008.
Mitchell, Timothy. *Rule of Experts.* Berkeley: University of California Press, 2002.
Mokyr, Joel, ed. *The British Industrial Revolution.* Boulder: Westview, 1999.
———. "The Intellectual Origins of Modern Growth Theory." *Journal of Economic History* 65:2 (June 2005): 285–351.
———. *The Lever of Riches.* New York: Oxford University Press, 1990.
Monroe, Elizabeth. *Britain's Moment in the Middle East, 1914–1956.* Baltimore: Johns Hopkins Press, 1963.
Montesquieu. *The Spirit of the Laws.* Trans. and ed. Anne Cohler, Basia Miller, and Harold Stone. Cambridge: Cambridge University Press, 1989.
Moore, Wendy. *The Knife Man.* New York: Broadway Books, 2005.
Morehead, Alan. *The Blue Nile.* New York: Perennial, 1962.
Morgenthau, Hans. "A Political Theory of Foreign Aid." *American Political Science Review* 56:2 (June 1962): 301–309.

Morris, Ian. *Why the West Rules—For Now*. New York: Farrar, Straus, and Giroux, 2010.
Moses, Wilson Jeremiah. *The Golden Age of Black Nationalism, 1850–1925*. New York: Oxford University Press, 1978.
Moyo, Dambisa. *Dead Aid*. New York: Farrar, Straus, and Giroux, 2009.
Mudimbe, V. Y. *The Invention of Africa*. Bloomington: Indiana University Press, 1988.
Munro-Hay, Stuart. *Ethiopia: The Unknown Land*. London: I. B. Tauris, 2002.
Myrdal, Gunnar. *Asian Drama: An Inquiry into the Poverty of Nations*. Vol. 1. New York: Pantheon, 1968.
Negussay Ayele. *Ethiopia and the United States*. Santa Clara, CA: ocopy.com, 2003. PDF e-book.
Netschert, Bruce Carlton. "Point Four and Mineral Raw Materials," *Annals of the Association of American Geographers* 41:2 (June 1951): 133–145.
Ninkovich, Frank. "No Post-Mortems for Postmodernism, Please." *Diplomatic History* 22:3 (Summer 1998): 451–466.
———. *The Wilsonian Century*. Chicago: University of Chicago Press, 1999.
North, Douglas C. *The Economic Growth of the United States, 1790–1860*. New York: W. W. Norton, 1966.
Nourse, Edwin G. "Some Economic and Social Accompaniments of the Mechanization of Agriculture." *American Economic Review* 20:1 (March 1930): 114–132.
Nourse, Edwin G., and Bertram Gross, "The Role of the Council of Economic Advisers." *American Political Science Review* 42:2 (April 1948): 283–295.
O'Connor, Alice. *Poverty Knowledge*. Princeton, NJ: Princeton University Press, 2001.
Offner, Arnold A. *Another Such Victory: President Truman and the Cold War, 1945–1953*. Stanford, CA: Stanford University Press, 2002.
Oren, Michael B. *Power, Faith, and Fantasy*. New York: W. W. Norton, 2007.
Paarlberg, Robert. *Starved for Science: How Biotechnology Is Being Kept out of Africa*. Cambridge, MA: Harvard University Press, 2008.
Pankhurst, Richard. *Economic History of Ethiopia*. Addis Ababa: Haile Selllassie I University Press, 1968.
———. *The Ethiopians*. Oxford: Blackwell, 1998.
———. *An Introduction to the Economic History of Ethiopia*. Addis Ababa: Lalibela House, 1961.
———. *Travelers in Ethiopia*. London: Oxford University Press, 1965.
Parker, Jason. "Cold War II: The Eisenhower Administration, the Bandung Conference, and the Reperiodization of the Postwar Era." *Diplomatic History* 30:5 (November 2006): 867–892.
Paterson, Thomas G. *Meeting the Communist Threat: Truman to Reagan*. New York: Oxford University Press, 1988.
Perham, Margery. *The Government of Ethiopia*. New York: Oxford University Press, 1948.
Perkins, John. *Confessions of an Economic Hit Man*. New York: Plume, 2005.

Peters, Ralf. *Roadblock to Reform: The Persistence of Agricultural Export Subsidies.* Policy Issues in International Trade and Commodities Study Series Number 32. New York: United Nations, 2006.

Peterson, Spiro. "Defoe in Edinburgh, 1707." *Huntington Library Quarterly* 38:1 (November 1974): 21–33.

Phillipson, Nicholas. *Adam Smith: An Enlightened Life.* New Haven, CT: Yale University Press, 2010.

Pierce, Kimber Charles. *Rostow, Kennedy, and the Rhetoric of Foreign Aid.* East Lansing: Michigan State University Press, 2001.

Pierson, John H. G. "Point Four, Dollar Gap, and Full Employment." *Annals of the American Academy of Political and Social Science* 270 (July 1950): 8–15.

Pigou, A. C. *The Economics of Welfare.* 4th ed. London: Macmillan, 1932.

Pinker, Stephen. *The Blank Slate.* New York: Penguin, 2002.

Pletsch, Carl E. "The Three Worlds, or the Division of Social Science Labor, circa 1950–1975." *Comparative Studies in Society and History* 23:4 (October 1981): 565–590.

Plummer, Brenda Gayle, ed. *Window on Freedom.* Chapel Hill: University of North Carolina Press, 2003.

Polanyi, Karl. *The Great Transformation.* 2nd ed. Boston: Beacon, 2001.

Pollard, Robert A. *Economic Security and the Origins of the Cold War, 1945–1950.* New York: Columbia University Press, 1985.

Pollard, Sidney. *The Idea of Progress.* London: Penguin, 1971.

Pomeranz, Kenneth. *The Great Divergence.* Princeton, NJ: Princeton University Press, 2000.

Porter, Roger B. "Presidents and Economists: The Council of Economic Advisers." In "Papers and Proceedings of the Hundred and Fourth Annual Meeting of the American Economic Association." Ed. J. David Baldwin and Ronald L. Oaxaca. Program arranged by Arnold C. Harberer. Special issue, *American Economic Review* 87:2 (May 1997): 103–106.

Porter, Roy. *The Creation of the Modern World.* New York: W. W. Norton, 2000.

Porter, Theodore M. *The Rise of Statistical Thinking, 1820–1900.* Princeton, NJ: Princeton University Press, 1986.

Program of African Studies, Northwestern University. *Africa: A Study Prepared at the Request of the Committee on Foreign Relations, United States Senate.* Washington, D.C.: U.S. Government Printing Office, 1959.

Prouty, Chris. *Empress Taytu and Menilek II.* Trenton, NJ: Red Sea Press, 1986.

Reid, J. M. *Traveler Extraordinary.* New York: W. W. Norton, 1968.

Reinert, Eric S. *How Rich Countries Got Rich . . . and Why Poor Countries Stay Poor.* New York: Carroll & Graf, 2007.

Ricardo, David. *The Principles of Political Economy and Taxation.* London: J. M. Dent, 1911.

Ridley, Matt. *The Rational Optimist.* New York: HarperCollins, 2010.

Romer, Paul M. "Increasing Returns and Long-Run Growth." *Journal of Political Economy* 94:5 (October 1986): 1002–1037.
Roos, Charles Frederick. *Dynamic Economics*. Bloomington, IN: Principia Press, 1934.
Roosevelt, Theodore. *Letters and Speeches*. New York: Library of America, 1951.
Rosenberg, Emily S. *Spreading the American Dream*. New York: Hill and Wang, 1982.
Rosenberg, Nathan, and L. E. Birdzell. *How the West Grew Rich*. New York: Basic Books, 1986.
Rosenstein-Rodan, Paul. "The International Development of Economically Backward Areas." *International Affairs* 20:2 (April 1944): 157–165.
———. "Problems of Industrialization of Eastern and South-Eastern Europe." *Economic Journal* 53:210–211 (June–September 1943): 202–211.
Ross, Ian Simpson. *The Life of Adam Smith*. Oxford: Clarendon Press, 1995.
Rostow, W. W. *How It All Began*. New York: McGraw-Hill, 1975.
———. *The Process of Economic Growth*. New York: W. W. Norton, 1952.
———. *The Stages of Economic Growth*. 3rd ed. Cambridge: Cambridge University Press, 1990.
———. "The Take-Off Into Sustained Growth." *Economic Journal* 66:261 (March 1956): 25–48.
———. *Theorists of Economic Growth from David Hume to the Present*. New York: Oxford University Press, 1990.
Rothschild, Emma. *Economic Sentiments*. Cambridge, MA: Harvard University Press, 2001.
Rudwick, Elliot M., and August Meier, "Black Man in the 'White City': Negroes and the Columbian Exposition, 1893." *Phylon* 26:4 (4th Quarter, 1965): 354–361.
Rydell, Robert W. *All the World's a Fair*. Chicago: University of Chicago Press, 1984.
Rydell, Robert W., John E. Findling, and Kimberly D. Pelle. *Fair America*. Washington, D.C.: Smithsonian Books, 2000.
Rydell, Robert W., and Rob Kroes. *Buffalo Bill in Bologna*. Chicago: University of Chicago Press, 2005.
Sachs, Jeffrey D. *Common Wealth*. New York: Penguin, 2008.
———. *The End of Poverty*. New York: Penguin, 2005.
Sachs, Wolfgang, ed. *The Development Dictionary*. London: Zed Books, 2003.
Said, Edward W. *Culture and Imperialism*. New York: Vintage, 1993.
———. *Orientalism*. New York: Vintage, 1979.
Salant, Walter S. "The Domestic Effects of Capital Export under the Point Four Program." In "Papers and Proceedings of the Sixty-Second Annual Meeting of the American Economic Association." Ed. James Washington Bell. *American Economic Review* 40:2 (May 1950): 495–510.
———. "Some Intellectual Contributions of the Truman Council of Economic Advisers to Policy-Making." *History of Political Economy* 5 (1973): 36–49.
Samuelson, Paul. *Economics: An Introductory Analysis*. New York: McGraw-Hill, 1948.

Samuelson, Paul, Harold W. McGraw, Jr., William D. Nordhaus, Orley Ashenfelter, Robert M. Solow, and Stanley Fisher. "Samuelson's 'Economics' at Fifty." *Journal of Economic Education* 30:4 (Autumn 1999): 352–363.

Sanders, Edith R. "The Hamitic Hypothesis: Its Origin and Functions in Time Perspective." *Journal of African History* 10:4 (1969): 521–532.

Sato, Ryuzo. "The Harrod-Domar Model vs. the Neo-Classical Growth Model." *Economic Journal* 74:294 (June 1964): 380–387.

Sauvy, Alfred. "Trois Mondes, Une Planète." *L'Observateur* (August 14, 1952): 5.

Schapsmeier, Edward L., and Frederick H. Schapsmeier. "Eisenhower and Agricultural Reform: Ike's Farm Policy Legacy Appraised," *American Journal of Economics and Sociology* 51:2 (April 1992): 147–159.

Schraeder, Peter J. *United States Foreign Policy towards Africa: Incrementalism, Crisis and Change*. Cambridge: Cambridge University Press, 1994.

Schumpeter, Joseph A. *The Theory of Economic Development*. Trans. Redvers Opie. New Brunswick, NJ: Transaction Publishers, 2008.

Scott, James C. *Seeing Like a State*. New Haven, CT: Yale University Press, 1998.

Seers, Dudley. "The Meaning of Development." *International Development Review* 11 (December 1969): 2–6.

Semere Haile. "The Origins and Demise of the Ethiopian-Eritrea Federation." *Issue: A Journal of Opinion* 15 (1987): 9–17.

Sen, Amartya. *Development as Freedom*. New York: Anchor, 1999.

———. *The Idea of Justice*. Cambridge, MA: Harvard University Press, 2009.

———. *Poverty and Famines*. Oxford: Clarendon Press, 1981.

Shenin, Sergei Y. *The United States and the Third World*. Huntington, NY: Nova Science Publishers, 2000.

Sher, Richard B. *The Enlightenment and the Book*. Chicago: University of Chicago Press, 2006.

Singer, H. W. "The Distribution of Gains between Investing and Borrowing Countries." In "Papers and Proceedings of the Sixty-Second Annual Meeting of the American Economic Association." Ed. James Washington Bell. *American Economic Review* 40:2, (May 1950): 473–485.

Skinner, Robert P. *Abyssinia of Today: An Account of the First Mission Sent by the American Government to the Court of the King of Kings, 1903–04*. New York: Longmans, Green & Co., 1906.

Skousen, Mark. "The Perseverance of Paul Samuelson's Economics." *Journal of Economic Perspectives* 11:2 (Spring 1997): 137–152.

Slater, David. "The Geopolitical Imagination and the Enframing of Development Theory." *Transactions of the Institute of British Geographers* 18:4 (1993): 419–437.

Smith, Adam. *An Inquiry into the Nature and Causes of the Wealth of Nations*. Ed. R. H. Campbell and A. S. Skinner. Indianapolis: Liberty Fund, 1981.

———. *Lectures on Jurisprudence*. Ed. R. L. Meek, D. D. Raphael, and P. G. Stein. Indianapolis: Liberty Fund, 1978.

———. *The Theory of Moral Sentiments*. New York: Penguin, 2009.

Smith, C. G. "The Emergence of the Middle East." *Journal of Contemporary History* 3:3 (July 1968): 3–17.

Solow, Robert. "A Contribution to the Theory of Economic Growth." *Quarterly Journal of Economics* 70:1 (February 1956): 65–94.

Sorenson, John. *Imagining Ethiopia*. New Brunswick, NJ: Rutgers University Press, 1993.

Spencer, Herbert. *The Man versus the State*. Indianapolis: Liberty Fund, 1982.

Spencer, John H. *Ethiopia, The Horn of Africa, and U.S. Policy*. Cambridge, MA: Institute for Foreign Policy Analysis, 1977.

Spiegel, Henry William. "Theories of Economic Development: History and Classification." *Journal of the History of Ideas* 16:4 (October 1955): 518–539.

Speiser, E. A. "Oriental Studies and Society." *Journal of the American Oriental Society* 66:3 (July–September 1946): 193–197.

Staal, Thomas H. "Africa: The Donor View on Development." SAA Borlaug Symposium 2010 Addis Ababa. July 13, 2010. Available at http://www.partnership-africa.org/content/donor-view-development.

Stack, David. *Queen Victoria's Skull*. London: Hambledon Continuum, 2008.

Stafford, F. E. "The Ex-Italian Colonies," *International Affairs* 25:1 (January 1949): 47–55.

Staley, Eugene. *World Economy in Transition*. Port Washington, NY: Kennikat Press, 1971.

Stalin, Joseph. "New Five-Year Plan for Russia." *Vital Speeches of the Day* 12 (March 1, 1946): 300–304.

Standage, Tom. *An Edible History of Humanity*. New York: Walker, 2009.

Staples, Amy. *The Birth of Development*. Kent, OH: Kent State University Press, 2006.

State Department. "Building the Peace." *Foreign Affairs Outlines* 21 (Spring 1949): 1.

Stocking, George W., Jr. "Franz Boas and the Culture Concept in Historical Perspective." *American Anthropologist* 68:4 (August 1966): 867–882.

———. Victorian Anthropology. New York: The Free Press, 1987.

Sumner, William Graham. *On Liberty, Society, and Politics*. Indianapolis: Liberty Fund, 1992.

Takeyh, Ray. *The Origins of the Eisenhower Doctrine*. New York: St. Martin's, 2000.

Tanguy, Bernard, David J. Spielman, Alemayehu Seyoum Taffesse, and Eleni Z. Gabre-Madhin. *Cooperatives for Staple Crop Marketing: Evidence from Ethiopia*. Research Monograph 164. Washington, D.C.: International Food Policy Research Institute, 2010.

Tarp, Finn, ed. *Foreign Aid and Development*. London: Routledge, 2000.

Teshale Tibebu. "Ethiopia: The 'Anomaly' and 'Paradox' of Africa." *Journal of Black Studies* 26:4 (March 1996): 414–430.

———. *The Making of Modern Ethiopia, 1896–1974*. Lawrenceville, NJ: Red Sea Press, 1995.

Thomas, Alan. *Third World Atlas*. 2nd ed. Washington, D.C.: Taylor & Francis, 1994.

Thomas, Benjamin E. "'Middle Africa' and Other Regional Terms." *African Studies Bulletin* 3:3 (October 1960): 15.

Thurow, Roger, and Scott Kilman. *Enough: Why the World's Poorest Starve in an Age of Plenty*. New York: Public Affairs, 2009.

Tobin, James. "A Dynamic Aggregative Model." *Journal of Political Economy* 63:2 (April 1955): 103–115.

Truman, Harry S. *Memoirs by Harry S. Truman: Years of Trial and Hope*. Vols. 1 and 2. Garden City, NY: Doubleday, 1955, 1956.

Truman, Margaret. *Harry S. Truman*. New York: Pocket, 1973.

"United Nations: Charter of the United Nations." *American Journal of International Law* 39:3 (July 1945): 190–229.

United Nations. *Measures for the Economic Development of Under-Developed Countries*. New York: United Nations, 1951.

Varnis, Steven L. *Reluctant Aid or Aiding the Reluctant*. New Brunswick, NJ: Transaction, 1990.

Veblen, Thorstein. "On the Nature of Capital." *Quarterly Journal of Economics* 22:4 (August 1908): 517–542.

Vengroff, Richard. "Food and Dependency: P.L. 480 Aid to Black Africa." *Journal of Modern African Studies* 20:1 (March 1982): 27–43.

Vestal, Theodore M. *The Lion of Judah in the New World*. Santa Barbara: Praeger, 2011.

Waal, Alex de. *Famine Crimes*. Oxford: African Rights & the International African Institute in association with James Currey and Indiana University Press, 1997.

Wallace, Henry A. "The Way to Peace." *Vital Speeches of the Day* 12:24 (October 1, 1946): 738–741.

Wallis, Brian. "Black Bodies, White Science: Louis Agassiz's Slave Daguerreotypes." *American Art* 9:2 (Summer 1995): 39–61.

Ward, Lester Frank. *The Psychic Factors of Civilization*. 2nd ed. Boston: Ginn, 1906.

Waterfield, Gordon. "The Horn of Africa." *African Affairs* 57:226 (January 1958): 11–19.

———. "Trouble in the Horn of Africa?: The British Somali Case." *International Affairs* 32:1 (January 1956): 52–60.

Werth, Barry. *Banquet at Delmonico's*. New York: Random House, 2009.

Westad, Odd Arne. *The Global Cold War: Third World Interventions and the Making of Our Time*. New York: Cambridge University Press, 2007.

———. "The New International History of the Cold War: Three (Possible) Paradigms." *Diplomatic History* 24:4 (2000): 551–565.

Wheatcroft, S. G., R. W. Davies, and J. M. Cooper. "Soviet Industrialization Reconsidered: Some Preliminary Conclusions about Economic Development between 1926 and 1941." *Economic History Review* 39:2 (May 1986): 254–294.

Wiebe, Robert H. *The Search for Order*. New York: Hill and Wang, 1967.

Williams, George Washington. *History of the Negro Race in America from 1619 to 1880.* Vol. 2. New York: Putnam, 1883.

Williams, William Appleman. "The Frontier Thesis and American Foreign Policy." *Pacific Historical Review* 24:4 (November 1955): 379–395.

———. *The Tragedy of American Diplomacy.* 50th anniversary ed. New York: W. W. Norton, 2009.

Wilson, Joan Hoff. *Herbert Hoover: Forgotten Progressive.* Prospect Heights, IL: Waveland Press, 1975.

Woolbert, Robert Gale. "Feudal Ethiopia and Her Army." *Foreign Affairs* 14:1–4 (1935–1936): 71–81.

Woolf, Stuart. "Statistics and the Modern State." *Comparative Studies in Society and History* 31:3 (July 1989): 588–604.

World Bank, the. *Accelerated Development in Sub-Saharan Africa: An Agenda for Action.* Washington, D.C.: World Bank, 1981.

Worsley, Peter. *The Third World.* Chicago: University of Chicago Press, 1964.

Wright, David McCord. "Mr. Harrod and Growth Economics." *Review of Economics and Statistics* 31:4 (November 1949): 322–328.

Wrong, Michela. *I Didn't Do It for You.* Hammersmith, UK: Fourth Estate, 2005; New York: Harper Perennial, 2006.

Wu, Yuan-Li. "A Note on the Post-War Industrialization of 'Backward' Countries and Centralist Planning." *Economica* 12:47 (August 1945): 172–178.

Yapa, Lakshman. "Reply: Why Discourse Matters, Materially." *Annals of the Association of American Geographers* 87:4 (December 1997): 717–722.

———. "What Causes Poverty?: A Postmodern View." *Annals of the Association of American Geographers* 86:4 (December 1996): 707–728.

Yat-sen, Sun. *The International Development of China.* New York: Putnam, 1929.

Yergin, Daniel. *Shattered Peace: The Origins of the Cold War and the National Security State.* Boston: Houghton Mifflin, 1977.

———. *The Prize.* New York: Free Press, 1991.

Young, Allyn A. "Increasing Returns and Economic Progress." *Economic Journal* 38:152 (December 1928): 527–542.

———. "The Trend of Economics." *Quarterly Journal of Economics* 39:2 (February 1925): 155–183.

Zeiler, Thomas W. *Free Trade, Free World.* Chapel Hill: University of North Carolina Press, 1999.

INDEX

(page references to images are in bold)

1942 Anglo-Ethiopian Agreement, 71
Abyssinia. *See* Ethiopia
Acheson, Dean
   at Bretton Woods, 57
   on Clifford Committee, 180
   on Point Four, 94–95, 103, 107–108, 144, 182
   on postwar politics, 60, 87, 111
Act for International Development, 103, 112–113
Addis Ababa, 3, **35**, 66, 70, 73–74, 82, 122, 134–135, 138, 144, 159, 179, 197, 211
   and development, 148, 163–164, 176, 186, 212
   establishment, 36
   and Haile Selassie's rise to power, 63–65
   and revolution, 161, 175, 187, 193–194, 201
Advisory Committee on Technical Assistance, 105
Afghanistan, 79, 109, 187, 192
African and Asian Development Service, 113
African Growth and Opportunity Act, 204
Agribusiness lobby, 212–213
Agricultural development, 196, 210, 212–213
   in economic growth theory, 43, 57, 155, 158
   and the Green Revolution, 192–193
   in Ethiopia, 64, 76, 123–124, 126–129, 136, 143–146, 148, 152, 174, 180, 185–186, 196, 212–213
   in Point Four, 110–111, 118, 143
   Smith on, 17–18
Aklilu Habte Wolde, 141
Almond, Gabriel, 172
Amhara, 62–63, 76, 135
Amin, Mohammed, 195
Amuzegar, Jahangir, 150–152
Anglo-Ethiopian Treaty, 74
Annan, Kofi, 207
Arab League, 137
Asmara, **141**, 148
Asmara Barracks, 80, 134, 148

Bahrain, 79
Ball, George, 179
Baran, Paul, 155
Barré, Siad, 190, 198
Battle of Adwa, 36–37, 63
Bauer, Peter, 199
Beard, Charles and Mary, 89
Belgium, 50, 104, 145
Bennett, Henry Garland, 104, 121
Berg, Elliot, 199
Binswanger, Hans, 203–204
Black, Eugene, 180
Blair, Tony, 206
Blue Nile River Basin survey, 173
Boas, Franz, 37

288 • Index

Bolivia, 109
Borlaug, Norman, 192–193
   Norman Borlaug Commemorative Research Initiative, 212
   Sasakawa Africa Association Borlaug Symposium, 211
Botswana, 201
Brazil, 90, 109, 131–132, 155, 182
British Military Mission to Ethiopia, 71
Bretton Woods, 57–58, 86
Bruce, James, 10–12, 24
Brzezinski, Zbigniew, 198
Buerk, Michael, 195
Buffon, Comte de, 10–11
Burkina Faso, 209
Burma, 82, 109
Bush, George W., **202**, 204–206
Byrd, Harry F, 94

Cambodia, 187
Center for International Studies at MIT, 163
Central Powers, 63
Clark, John Davidson, 58–59
Combe, George, 28–29
Council of Economic Advisors to the President (CEA), 58–60
Center for International Studies at MIT, 163
Chang, Ha Joon, 208, 210, 213
Chile, 109
China, 8, 20, 58, 66, 104
   and the Cold War, 81, 103, 142, 183
   as a development model, 201, 208–209, 220
   and U.S. aid, 112
China Area Aid Act of 1950, 112
Chirol, Valentine, 67
Churchill, Winston, 68
Clark, Colin, 51–57, 78, 98, 117
Clifford, Clark, 91, 94, 111
   Clifford Committee, 180–182

Clinton, Hillary Rodham, 216–218
Coffee, and development, 130–132, 146, 163
Coleman, James, 172
Collier, Paul, 209
Colombia, 109
Cold War,
   and American fears, 57–58, 59–61, 69–70, 85–88, 95–96, 101, 103, 108–115, 140, 142, 151, 167
   and the American modernization paradigm, 158–159, 166, 172, 200
   and the establishment of foreign aid, 60–61, 69–70, 81–115
   and Ethiopia, 82, 144–145, 149, 159, 179, 189, 191–193, 197–198
   See also USSR
Congo, 145
Corker, Bob, 214–215
Costa Rica, 109
Cotton, 5, 50, 146, 173, 209
Cuba, 5, 109, 191
Czechoslovakia, 82, 137, 145

Darwin, Charles, 30–31. *See also* Social Darwinism
Derg,
   1974 revolution, 190–191
   National Democratic Revolution Programme, 197–198
   policies, 196–198, 201
Defoe, Daniel, 7–9, 12–13, 25
Desire as a source of economic growth
   in the eighteenth century, 8, 23
   in the nineteenth century, 32–34
   in the twentieth century, 41–42, 53, 83, 90, 96, 120, 146–147, 181
De Soto, Hernando, 202–203, 210, 213
Development, 1–3, 117–119
   contemporary discourse on, 199–221
   in Ethiopia, 6–7, 26–28, 38–39, 64–65, 74–77, 122–136, 140–149, 161–164, 172–194,

in the Middle East, 55, 78–82,
    106–110, 114–116, 137–139,
    167, 203
in nineteenth-century thought,
    28–34, 41
in Scottish Enlightenment theory,
    7, 10, 12–13, 16, 18–20, 23–26
in twentieth-century economic
    thought, 39–46, 50–55, 57, 131,
    153–159, 163–172, 187, 203, 208
and U.S. foreign aid, 82–85, 89–122,
    140–144, 149–152, 164–194,
    214–216, 218
See also Agricultural development
Development Loan Fund, 129, 168
Dewey, John, 33
Dillon, Douglass, 180
Dimbleby, Jonathan, 190–191
Dire Dawa, 148
Djibouti, 74, 159
Doha, 204, 206
Domar, Evsey, 56, 100, 112
    Harrod-Domar model, 56, 59, 154
Dominican Republic, 109
Dulles, Allen, 144
Dulles, John Foster, 152, 182

Easterly, William, 207–208, 210, 217
Economic Cooperation Act of 1948,
    103, 112
Ecuador, 109
Ethiopia Commodity Exchange (ECX),
    212–213
Economic Cooperation Act of 1948, 112
Economic growth, 1, 6, 37, 169, 201,
    204, 206
    Haile Selassie on, 145–150, 174–176
    Huntington on, 187–188
    Johnson administration on, 180–181
    Malthus on, 24–26
    in modernization theory, 171–172
    Rostow on, 156–159, 166–168
    Smith on, 18–22

in twentieth-century economics,
    39–60, 100–103, 153–159, 210–220
Economy, the,
    origins of the concept, 44–46, 48–57
Eden, Anthony, 71
Edinburgh, 12–15, 28
Egypt, 9–10, 29, 79–81, 135–138,
    145, 189
    and Great Britain, 58, 69–71, 77
    and U.S. aid, 106, 108–109, 128,
    137–139
    See also Nasser
Eisenhower, Dwight D
    doctrine, 139
    on foreign aid, 128–129
    relations with Ethiopia, **116**,
    128–143
Eisenhower, Mamie, **116**
Ejersa Goro, 62
Eleni Gabre-Madhin, 212
El Salvador, 109
Elsey, George, 91
Employment Act of 1946, 58–59
Eritrea,
    cession to the Italians, 35–36, 63–65
    famine, 195–197
    federation and annexation, 71–82,
    108, 121–122, 134–135. *See also*
    Asmara Barracks
    independence, 201
Eritrean Popular Liberation Front, 201
Ethiopia, 2–4
    and American aid, 121–153, 172–178,
    183–187, 197–198, 211–218
    and Great Britain, 9–12, 16, 24,
    26–28, 35–36, 66, 70–78, 135–136,
    159, 201
    and Italy, 27, 34–36, 62–66, 70–77, 80
    as part of the Middle East, 69–82
    relationship with the U.S. 5–7, 34,
    38–39, 58, 70–77, 82, 108, 122–152,
    159–160, 172–179, 183–202,
    208–213

Ethiopia (*continued*)
  relationship with the USSR, 70, 144–145, 149, 179, 189–198
  See also Five Year Plans
  See also Haile Selassie
Ethiopia Commodity Exchange (ECX), 212–213
Ethiopian Development Bank, 125
Ethiopian People's Revolutionary Democratic Front, 201
European Recovery Act. *See* Marshall Plan

Famine
  Darwin on, 29
  in Ethiopia in 1973, 190
  in Ethiopia in 1984–1985, 195–196, 198–199
  in Ethiopia in 2003, 212
  in Europe in 1946, 86
  Malthus on, 25
  Sen on, 195–196
  Smith on, 22
Far Eastern Economic Assistance Act of 1950, 112
Federation of Rhodesia, 143
Feed the Future, 212
Fellows, Perry A, 122–126, 131–136
  1944 mission, 69–70, 122
Fitzgerald, Dennis, 152, 219
Five Year Plans (Ethiopia)
  first plan, 145–147
  second plan, 174–176
  third plan, 185–187
Food-for-Peace Program. *See* PL-480
Foreign aid
  as a tool of diplomacy v. development, 3, 79, 109, 152–153, 164–165, 171, 180, 182, 193, 206, 214–215, 219
  See also ICA
  See also Point Four
  See also USAID

Foreign Assistance Act of 1961, 169, 215
Foreign Economic Assistance Act of 1950, 103
Foreign Operations Administration (FAO), 129, 152, 169
France, 2, 25, 35, 57, 84, 145
  colonial welfare program, 104
  in the Middle East, 68, 138
  revolution, 119, 155
Friedman, Milton, 154
Fulbright, J. William, 168

Galbraith, John Kenneth, 104, 166
Garmane Neway, 159–160
Garvelink, William J, 212
Gaud, William S, 192–193
General Agreement on Tariffs and Trade (GATT), 87
Germany, 35, 68, 79, 84–86, 145
Ghana, 140, 143
Gliddon, George, 28–29
Gojjam, 186
Graunt, John, 50
Gray, Gordon, 112
Great Britain, 2, 3, 41
  and the Colonial Development and Welfare Program, 78, 104–105
  and Ethiopia, 9–12, 16, 26–28, 35–36, 66, 70–78, 135–136, 159, 201
  in the eighteenth-century, 7–30
  in the Middle East, 67–71, 78–82, 137–138
  trade policies, 57–58, 86
Great Depression.
  shaping economic thought, 47, 50, 57
"Greater Ethiopia," 63, 74, 82
Greece, 69, 78–80, 87, 182
Green Revolution, 192–193, 211–212
Guatemala, 58, 82, 109
Guizot, François, 26
Gurage, 62

Hacker, Louis M, 90, 102–103
Haile Selassie, 2–3, **72**, **75**, **107**, **116**, **130**, 177
   1960 rebellion against, 159–160
   1974 revolution against,161–163, 190–191
   death, 191
   despotism, 64–65, 126–127, 136, 149, 163
   development, 65, 161–163. *See also* Five Year Plans
   at the League of Nations, 64–66
   rise to power, 62–66
   relationship with the U.S. 70–77, 108, 122–152, 159–160, 172–179, 183–193
   relationship with the USSR, 144–145, 179
Haiti, 109
Hamilton, Alexander, 57
Hamilton, Fowler, 171–173
Hancock, Graham, 199–200
Harar, 62–63, 127
Hardy, Benjamin, 90–96
Harriman, Averell, 183
Harris, Major W. Cornwallis, 26–28
Harrod, Roy, 56
   Harrod-Domar model, 56, 59, 154
Hayek, F.A, 46–47
Her Imperial Majesty's Handicraft School, 128
Herter, Christian, 99, 103
Hoffman, Paul. G, 100–101
Home, Henry (Lord Kames), 14, 23–24
Honduras, 58, 109
Hoover, Herbert, 48, 85–86
Hoselitz, Bert, 156
Hull, Cordell, 72–74
Hume, David
   influence in nineteenth-century economics, 40
   on trade, 83–84, 104
   role in the Scottish Enlightenment, 13–23
Huntington, Samuel, 187–189, 193
Hutchinson, Francis, 13, 15

International Cooperation Administration (ICA)
   conflicts with the State Department, 152–153
   establishment, 129
   programs in Ethiopia, 129–132, 142–145
   replaced by USAID, 167–169
   Rostow's critique of, 166–167
   See also Point Four
International Development Advisory Board, 128
Imperial Ethiopian Government (IEG), 190–191
   and Fellows's Proposal, 125–127
   and Point Four, 109, 123, 127–136, 139–148
   and USAID, 163, 173–174, 184
   See also Haile Selassie
   See also Five Year Plans (Ethiopia)
Imperial Ethiopia College of Agriculture and Mechanical Arts, 143, 173
Import-Export Bank, 125
India
   and Britain, 26–28, 67, 71
   and development, 109, 182, 192, 208, 220
Indonesia, 109, 137
Industrial Revolution, 20–32, 156–158, 192
Inter-American Development Service, 113
International Bank for Reconstruction and Development, 125
International Monetary Fund, 57, 60, 199, 205

International Technical Cooperation
    Act of 1949, 1, 97
Iraq, 137
    and Great Britain, 68–69, 79, 81
    and Norman Borlaug, 192
    and U.S. aid, 109–110
Iran, 109–110, 115, 137, 187, 192
Isaias Afewerki, 201
Israel
    and Egypt, 137–138
    and Ethiopia, 138
    and U.S. aid, 109, 115–116, 128, 182
Italy
    and Haile Selassie, 65–66, 70–77, 80
    and Menelik II, 27, 34–36, 62–63
Itegue Menen School of Nursing, 141
Iyassu, 63

James, William, 33
Javits, Jacob K, 2–4, 93–94, 219
Jevons, Stanley, 40
Jijiga, 160
Jimma Agricultural and Technical
    School, 127, 143, **130**, **150**, **165**
Johnson, Lyndon B
    relationship with Ethiopia, 183–187
    review of USAID, 178–183
    struggles with Congress, 178–180
    support of the Green Revolution, 192–193
Johnson, Samuel, 9–12
Johnston, Erik, 128–129
Jordan, 81–82, 109–110, 128

Kagnew Station. *See* Asmara Barracks
Kant, Immanuel, 221
Kapuściński, Ryszard, 161–163
Katzenbach, Nicholas, 186
Kee, John, 97–103
Kennan, George, 45, 100
Kennedy, Jacqueline, 176
Kennedy, John F
    meeting with Haile Selassie, 176–179
    on foreign aid, 159, 164–172, 180, 192–193
Kenya, 71, 143
Kerry, John, 215
Keynes, John Maynard, 46–49, 51
    at Bretton Woods, 57–58
    "dynamized" by Harrod, 56
    on the influence of economists, 7
    influence on Salant, 59–60
    Keynesian economics, 48
    "post-Keynesian" economics, 153–155
Keyserling, Leon H, 58–60, 112
Kifle Wodajo, 191
Kissinger, Henry, 189–191
Komer, Robert, 184
Korea, 182 *See also* Korean War
Korean War, 111–112, 152
    and Ethiopia's troops, 122, 127, 134, 138, 141, 183
Korem, 195
Korry, Edward, 183–184
Kuwait, 68, 79–80, 187
Kuznets, Simon S, 50–51, 156–157

laissez-faire, 19, 25, 31, 34, 154
    Keynes on, 47
Lake Tana, 124
Lamarck, chevalier de, 30–31
League of Nations, 52, 64, 66
Lebanon, 109–110, 128, 192
Lend-lease aid to Ethiopia, 69
Lenin, 45, 197, 201
Lewis, W, Arthur, 155
Liberia
    independence, 5, 38
    and U.S. foreign aid, 106, 109, 143, 183
Libya, 77, 79, 187
    and U.S. aid, 106, 109–110, 114, 143
Livestock, and development, 115–116, 125, 130, 143, 153
Lloyd, David, 91, 97, 105–106
Locke, John, 13

Lodge, Henry Cabot, 5
Loren, Allan, 172–174
Lugar, Dick, 215
Lutz, Ernst, 203–204

MacCreagh, Gordon, 38–39
McGhee, George C, 108–109, 114, 123
McNamara, Robert, 183
McIntyre, Mike, 210
Mahan, Alfred Thayer, 67
Makonnen Welde Michael, 62–63
Malthus, Thomas
    influence on Darwin and Spencer, 29–31
    on population, 24–26, 155, 157
    on Smith, 22, 102
Mapping and Geography Institute, 173
Marshall, Alfred, 39–44, 52, 56
    influence on later economists, 101, 153, 157
Marshall, George C, 87–88
Marshall Plan, 88–91, 96, 102
    comparison to Point Four, 88, 108, 117, 149
Marx, Karl, 40–41, 157–158, 197
Mauritius, 201
McKinley, William, 5
Measures for the Economic Development of Under-Developed Countries, 117–119, 124–125
Medecins sans Frontieres, 195–196
Meles Zenawi, 201–202, **202**
Menger, Karl, 40
Mengestu Neway, 159–160
Mengistu Haile Mariam, 191–198, 201
Menedez, Robert, 215
Menelik II, 34–37, **35**, 62–64, 76, 140
    fight against the Italians, 34–37, 62–63
    Skinner mission, 5–7, 34
Menen Asfaw, 63, 176
Merrell, George, 108
Messay Kebede, 148

Mexico, 58, 66, 109, 192, 198
Middle East, 59, 85
    and Cold War, 66, 70, 77–82, 112
    and development, 55, 106–110, 114–116, 167, 203
    and Ethiopia, 70–71, 79, 106, 126, 133–142, 146, 177
    origins of the term, 67–70
Middle East Supply Centre (MESC), 69, 78
Mill, John Stuart, 40–41, 153
Millar, John, 16
Millennium Challenge Corporation (MCC), 204–206
Millikin, Eugene, 103
Modernization, 193, 217
    in economic growth theory, 117, 119, 152
    and Haile Selassie, 65, 73–74, 125, 133, 136, 148, 160 *See also* Five Year Plans
    theory, 163–164, 171–174, 182, 185–191
Moi, Daniel arap, **202**
Montesquieu, Baron de, 13–16
Morgenthau, Hans, 219
Morgenthau, Henry, 57–58
Morocco, 143–144, 187, 192
Morton, Samuel George, 28
Moyo, Dambisa, 208–210, 213–214, 217
Mozambique, 196
Murphy, Charles, 111
Mussolini, Benito, 65–66
Mutual Defense Agreement of 1953, 197
Mutual Defense Assistance Act of 1949, 112
Mutual Security Act of 1951, 112–114
Mutual Security Program, 112–115, 139, 142
Mwenda, Andrew, 210
Myrdal, Gunnar, 172

294 • Index

Nasser, Gamal Abdel, 135–138, 159
National Democratic Revolution
    Programme, 197–198
National Economic Council,
    136, 145
Neoclassical economics
    origins, 39
    growth model, 154–156, 199
Nepal, 109, 187
New Deal, 34, 48–49, 59
New Zealand, 66
Nicaragua, 109
Nitze, Paul, 186
Nixon, Richard, 139–142, 189–193
Nkrumah, Kwame, 140
North Atlantic Treaty Organization, 82
Norway, 82, 208
Nott, Josiah, 28–29

Obama, Barack, 216–220,
Office of Inter-American Affairs, 90
Ogaden, 198
    and the British, 71, 74, 77, 82, 135
Oklahoma A&M
    development projects in Ethiopia, 127,
        143, 173
    Haile Selassie's visit, 132–133
    and Henry Garland Bennett, 104
Organization of African Unity, 179, 183
Organization for Economic
    Co-operation and Development
    (OECD), 170, 205–206
Oromo, 62–63

Pakistan, 82, 109, 137, 182, 192
Panama, 109
Paraguay, 109
Parson, Talcott, 33, 171
Peace Corps, 168
Peru, 109
Phrenology, 28–29
Pigou, Arthur C, 52–53

PL-480, 129, 168
    to Ethiopia, 173, 196, 198
Point Four, 1–4
    1950–51 general agreements, 109–110
    becomes FOA, then ICA, 129
    creation, 83–113
    contrast with USAID, 164, 168, 172,
        182, 193
    critique of, 149–159, 163–169
    in Ethiopia, 121–153, 173
    hearings, 96–99, 103
    in the Middle East, 108–111, 113–116,
        137–138
    and Mutual Security Act of 1951,
        113–114
Polanyi, Karl, 46
Policy Planning Council, 169–170
Population
    control, 182
    growth and progress, 18–19, 24–25,
        29–31, 40, 136, 155, 158
    statistics, 52
Portugal, 145
Poultry, and development, 115, 124,
    130
Presidential Policy Directive on
    Development, 216
Progress, 1–2, 117–119, 221
    See also Development
Public Health College, 173
Puerto Rico, 5
Pye, Lucien, 163, 172

Qatar, 79
*Quadrennial Diplomacy and
    Development Review* (QDDR),
    215–198, 220

Racism
    discredited as source of development,
        37, 52, 117
    Menelik's challenge to, 36–37

problem for U.S. foreign policy, 6, 37, 122, 140, 197
Reinert, Eric. S, 208, 210, 213–214
Ricardo, David, 40
Richards, James P, 139–140, 174
Robertson, William, 17
Rockefeller, David, 180
Rogin, Josh, 214
Roos, Charles Frederick, 49
Roosevelt, Eleanor, **107**
Roosevelt, Franklin D, 69–77
Roosevelt, Theodore, 5–6, 36, 76
Root, John, 144
Rosenstein-Rodan, Paul N, 53–56, 163
   influence on later economic thought, 101, 117, 131, 158
Rostow, Walt W
   on Haile Selassie, 184–185
   influence on Huntington, 188
   and modernization theory, 171–172, 175
   on economic growth, 156–159
   on reforming foreign aid, 163–164, 166–168
Rouk, Hugh, **166**
Rusk, Dean, 170–171, 180–182
Russia, 35, 54 *See also* Union of Soviet Socialist Republics

Sachs, Jeffrey, 207–208, 214–215
Sahle Selassie, **116**
Sáhela Seláscie, 27
Salant, Walter
   linking economic and military aid, 111–112
   marketing Point Four, 100–101, 105–106
   role on the CEA, 59–60
   role in the creation of Point Four, 91, 94, 97
Samuelson, Paul, 153–154
Saudi Arabia, 68–70, 79–80, 109, 128, 187

Sauvy, Alfred, 119–120
Say, Jean Baptiste, 41
Schumpeter, Joseph A, 42–44, 49–51, 118, 158
Scottish Enlightenment, 13–24, 89, 145, 147
Sebla Desta, **116**
Sen, Amartya, 195–196, 220
Shawa, 62–63, 76, 197
Sinclair Oil Company, 82, 123
Singapore, 208, 220
Singer, H. W, 101–102
Skinner, Robert P, 5–7, 34
Smith, Adam, 14–23
   influence on economic thought, 31, 39–40, 43–44, 47, 60, 157–158
   Lectures on Jurisprudence, 16–18
   on progress, 4, 7, 25, 102, 118
   Theory of Moral Sentiments, 15–16
   The Wealth of Nations, 18–23, 157
Smith, E. Talbot, 71–73
Social Darwinism, 31–33
Solow, Robert, 154–155
Somalia
   and Ethiopia, 159, 189–191, 198
   "Greater Somaliland," 135
   and U.S. aid, 143, 198
Sorensen, Ted, 167
South Africa, 82, 201
Southard, Addison, 65–66
South Korea, 208, 220
Speiser, E. A, 66
Spencer, Herbert, 30–31, 33
Staal, Thomas H, 211–212
Stadial Theory, 17–18
Stalin, Joseph, 45, 61, 85, 88
Staley, Eugene, 53, 106
State Department
   and the Cold War, 80, 87
   and Ethiopia, 73–74, 77–79, 121–122, 144, 152, 176–178, 184–185
   and the 1947 Pentagon Talks, 78–79

State Department (*continued*)
  and Point Four, 90–91, 94–96, 98, 100, 103–105, 113, 151–152
  and USAID, 215–218
Stewart, Dugald, 17
Stiglitz, Joseph, 206
Subsidies, as a barrier to development, 204–206, 209, 211, 218, 220
Sudan, 10, 77, 139, 189
Sumner, William Graham, 31–32
Syria, 69, 79, 110, 128

Tafari Makonnen. *See* Haile Selassie
Taft, Robert, 103
Taitu Betul, 63
Taiwan, 182, 208, 220
Tamarat Yigazu, **165**
Tanzania, 196
Task Force on Economic Policy, 165
Technical Cooperation Administration (TCA). *See* Point Four
Technology, its role development, 208, 211–213, 218
  for Adam Smith, 20
  and democracy, 89
  in economic growth theory, 25–27, 36–37, 40, 43–45, 49–51, 53–55
  in modernization theory, 154–156, 172
  and Point Four, 98–104, 111, 116–119, 124, 127–128, 143, 148
Tesfa Bushan, **165**
Thailand, 220
The "Third Choice," 163–164, 187, 193
The "Third World," 119–120, 192
Thorp, Willard, 98–99
Tigray, 62–63, 196
Treaty of Wuchalé, 35
Truman, Bess, 86
Truman, Harry S, 1–3, 164, 193, 216, 218–219

  1949 inaugural address, 91–95, **92**
  and the CEA, 58–60
  Cold War concerns, 60–61, 69–70, 81–115, 151
  Doctrine, 78, 87–88
  intellectual pursuits, 84–91
  and GATT, 87
  on post-war Europe, 85–88
  See also Marshall Plan
  See also Point Four
Truman, Margaret, 91, 108
Turkey, 70, 182, 192
  and the Baghdad Pact, 137
  and the Truman Doctrine, 78–80, 87
Tunesia, 143

Uganda, 143, 210
Underdevelopment, 145, 155, 203–204, 209, 219, 221
  and Point Four, 2, 96, 98, 115–116
Union of Soviet Socialist Republics (USSR)
  in the Horn of Africa, 70, 149, 179, 189–198
  industrialization, 45–47, 49
  as a perceived threat, 57–61, 85–88, 95–96, 101, 103, 108–115, 140
  policies toward the Third World, 61, 96, 142, 165, 167, 176
United Nations, 93–97, 149
  Committee of Trade, 115
  decision on Eritrea, 82, 134
  support for development, 84, 102, 103, 108, 115, 117–119, 125, 175, 203, 205, 207
United Nations Relief and Rehabilitation Administration (UNRRA), 57, 85
United States African Growth and Opportunities Act, 204
United States Agency for International Development (USAID)

creation of, 166–172
  in Ethiopia, 172–178, 183–187,
    197–198, 211–218
  and the Green Revolution, 192–193,
    211–212
  Johnson's review of, 178–183
United States Department of
  Agriculture, 85, 123, 212
United State Department of the Interior,
  124, 159
United States Office of Education,
  123–124
Uruguay, 109

Van Dyke, Stuart H, 142–144
Venezuela, 109
Vietnam, 159, 164, 179, 192–193
Viner, Jacob, 155
Vinson, Frederick Moore, 57–58

Wagner Act, 59
Walras, Leon, 40
Ward, Lester Frank,
  33–34, 39
Washington Consensus,
  199–200
Webb, James E, 98

White, Harry, 57
Wiley, Alexander, 103, 144
Witman, William II, 174
Wollo, 62–63, 76, 190, 196
World Bank, 60, 87, 102, 175,
  180, 203, 213
  Bretton Woods, 57
  Structural adjustment packages,
    198–199
World Health Organization, 143
World War I, 45–46, 68, 70
World War II, 53, 57
  aftermath in Europe, 85–87
  rise of term "Middle East" during,
    69–70, 78

Yemen, 79
Yeshimebet Ali, 62
Yilma Deressa, 70–74, 129
Yohannes, Emperor, 75
Young, Allyn A, 43–45, 49–54,
  101, 117
Yugoslavia, 145
Yunus, Mohammed, 209–210

Zawditu, 63–64
Zimbabwe, 201

www.ingramcontent.com/pod-product-compliance
Ingram Content Group UK Ltd.
Pitfield, Milton Keynes, MK11 3LW, UK
UKHW042005230426
12048UKWH00009B/576